Multicultural Perspectives in Music Education

Multicultural Perspectives in Music Education

2ND edition

Edited by William M. Anderson and Patricia Shehan Campbell

MENC MENC
MENC MENC

Music Educators
National Conference

The editors wish to dedicate this book to William P. Malm, musicology professor emeritus at the University of Michigan–Ann Arbor, whose early interest and strong encouragement for music education to embrace a broad spectrum of musical traditions had a profound impact on our profession. A former president of the Society for Ethnomusicology, Malm is widely recognized as a legendary teacher whose intellectual prowess, challenge, and wit have had an indelible impact on generations of students.

In addition, the authors would like to dedicate this book to the memory of Selwyn Ahyoung, who passed away during the writing of the first edition.

Cover: *Top photograph*, student playing the *kendang*, courtesy of Kent State University, Kent, Ohio;

second photograph, Hawaiian students displaying the *'uli'uli* (feathered gourd) and the *ipu* (hollowed gourd), courtesy of Robert Engle;

third photograph, student playing the *kenong*, courtesy of Kent State University, Kent, Ohio;

bottom photograph, student playing the sitar, courtesy of Kent State University, Kent, Ohio.

Copyright © 1996 by the Music Educators National Conference
1806 Robert Fulton Drive
Reston, Virginia 20191-4348

ISBN 1-56545-097-3

CONTENTS

CONTRIBUTORS

William M. Anderson, editor, is professor of music education, codirector of the Center for the Study of World Musics, and associate dean for academic affairs in the College and Graduate School of Education at Kent State University. He is the author of *Teaching Asian Musics in Elementary and Secondary Schools* and was the director of the 1990 national symposium on "Multicultural Approaches to Music Education."

Patricia Shehan Campbell, editor, is professor of music at the University of Washington. She is the author of *Lessons from the World* and coauthor of *Music in Childhood* and *Roots and Branches: A Legacy of Multicultural Music for Children.* She serves on the editorial boards of the *Journal of Research in Music Education* and the *College Music Symposium,* and she is the American board member of the International Society for Music Education.

Selwyn E. Ahyoung was a native of Trinidad who, at the time of his death in 1988, was completing his doctoral degree in music education/ethnomusicology at Florida State University. A promising young scholar, he was active in the Society for Ethnomusicology and was the first teacher of FSU's steel band.

Michael B. Bakan is assistant professor of ethnomusicology at Florida State University, where he directs the university's Balinese gamelan ensemble and the New Baru World Band. He is a contributor to a forthcoming book from the University of California Press on African American music in California. Bakan has done extensive research in Bali and other parts of Indonesia and has presented workshops on Balinese music throughout the United States.

J. Bryan Burton is associate professor of music education at West Chester University. He has written two books on Native American music and dance and has contributed songs and lessons to major classroom music textbook series. He is a frequent presenter at state, national, and international music education conferences on the topics of multicultural music, curriculum development, and instrumental literature and methods.

Robert Engle currently teaches choral music, music education, and ethnomusicology courses at the University of Hawaii at Hilo. For twenty years, his Maile Aloha Singers—featuring the choral music of Polynesia—have performed, recorded, presented a television show, and toured abroad. Engle speaks three Polynesian languages and is the editor of the *Pacific Island Choral Series* with Foxhall Publishing of North Carolina.

Han Kuo-Huang is professor of music in the School of Music at Northern Illinois University, where he teaches courses on the musics of China and Southeast Asia, world music, ethnomusicology, and the playing of Indonesian gamelan and Chinese instruments. His articles have appeared in many music journals, and he gives numerous demonstrations and workshops. He was a visiting professor at the National Institute of the Arts in Taiwan from 1992 to 1994.

Rita Klinger has taught music to students from preschool through college in both the United States and Israel. Her article, "Multiculturalism in Music Education: Authenticity versus Practicality," appears in *Musical Connections: Tradition and Change,* the Proceedings of the 21st ISME World Conference. Klinger currently teaches K–8 general and choral music at the Jewish Day School of Greater Seattle and is also adjunct faculty member at Seattle Pacific University.

Ellen McCullough-Brabson is professor of music education at the University of New Mexico. She has presented numerous teacher workshops on world music and is coauthor of *Roots and Branches: A*

Legacy of Multicultural Music for Children. Her research focuses on multicultural music for young children, Anglo-American music, and music of the Navajo. She is a Regents' Lecturer at her university, a title awarded for teaching excellence.

Elizabeth Oehrle is professor of music education at the University of Natal in Durban, South Africa, and president-elect of the International Society of Music Education's Commission on Community Music Activity. She is also coordinator of a network for promoting intercultural education through music in southern Africa. She is the author of *A New Direction for South African Music Education.*

Dale A. Olsen received his Ph.D. in ethnomusicology from the University of California at Los Angeles and is currently professor of ethnomusicology at Florida State University. He has conducted research in South America and was a Fulbright scholar in Peru. He performs on numerous musical instruments from the Andes and has produced many publications about Latin American music.

Milagros Agostini Quesada is assistant professor of music education at Kent State University, Tuscarawas Campus. She received a Ph.D. in music education with a concentration in ethnomusicology from Kent State University. She has presented numerous workshops on Hispanic-Caribbean music and has published articles related to this topic. A native of Puerto Rico, Quesada was a regional music superviser for the Puerto Rican Department of Education.

George Sawa, a native of Egypt, is currently the director of the Centre for Studies in Middle Eastern Music, a private institute devoted to teaching Arabic vocal and instrumental musics and researching medieval Arabic music history. He has taught at the University of Toronto, York University, and in the Toronto inner city schools and has given demonstration-lectures and concerts in North America, Europe, and the Middle East.

James A. Standifer is professor in the School of Music at the University of Michigan and director of the Oral History archive of the African American music collection. He was a Fellow for the Ford Foundation, the NEH, and the United States Information Agency. He has coauthored several books and has served as an adviser to educational television. He is currently producer and project director for a PBS documentary on the history of *Porgy and Bess.*

Tatsuko Takizawa is professor of music education and ethnomusicology at the Aichi University of Education in Japan. She is the video producer of *Shoga* (an oral learning system of Japanese traditional music) and *Sound World in Drama Making—Kabuki and Chinese Opera.* She was a Fulbright Senior Fellow and is currently a member of the advisory board of ISME's World Musics Project.

Ricardo D. Trimillos is professor in ethnomusicology and chair of Asian Studies at the University of Hawaii. He has developed curricular materials for world musics and music theory. His research focuses on traditional learning, transculturation, ethnic identity, and the geocultural areas of Japan, insular Southeast Asia, and Hawaii. A consultant on arts and public policy, he performs music for *goto, gagaku,* and *kabuki.*

Linda Miller Walker is associate professor of music education at Kent State University. She has conducted workshops on multicultural music, special learners, general music, and early childhood. Her articles have been published in several scholarly music education journals, and she is the coeditor (with Barbara Andress) of *Readings in Early Childhood Music.*

Kazadi wa Mukuna, a native of Zaire, is associate professor of ethnomusicology at Kent State University. As a scholar, he is best known for his contributions in the field of traditional African music on the continent and in the Diaspora, and in the field of urban music in Zaire and Brazil. He is the author of *Contribuicao Bantu na Musica Popular Brasileira* and *African Children's Songs for American Elementary Schools.*

PREFACE

The content of music programs in American schools has been historically associated with the art and traditional musics of Western Europe. Despite the presence of American Indians long before (as well as during) the formative years of the republic, the arrival of Africans beginning in the seventeenth century, and the waves of immigrants from Asia, Latin America, and Europe that have come to this country since the 1840s, the K–12 music curriculum has seldom reflected the ethnic diversity of American society. Rather, the schools have been a bastion for teaching European choral and instrumental music, and students of every color and creed have always been (and remain) more likely to learn music that is Germanic rather than Japanese, French rather than Filipino, and Irish rather than either Native American or Asian Indian.

Our colonial heritage was linked to Western civilization by the nature of those Europeans who first settled the eastern seaboard, and our pervading sociopolitical system is an extension of Anglo-Saxon and Germanic traditions, but American society has emerged as a unique blend of cultures from every part of the world. To believe that we can blindly continue to maintain a narrow focus on the customs and values of a single culture in the social sciences and the arts is to ignore the realities of our multicultural society. Moreover, in this international age, we must seek to understand the perspectives of people from every part of the globe. Cultures and countries are increasingly interdependent in economic and political matters. Our survival as a world community may depend on our ability to understand the similarities that bind and the differences that distinguish us as subsets of the human species.

The Music Educators National Conference maintains the slogan "Music for *every* child—every child *for* music" as the core of its professional philosophy. Embedded in this slogan is the knowledge that school music must be more broadly defined to encompass the ethnic diversity of American schools and society. Beginning with Karl W. Gherkens's recommendation in 1924 that music instruction be available to all children, a gradual awakening of interest in music of other cultures has been evident: at that time, music educators began to make isolated attempts to feature a variety of the world's musics in school programs and textbooks.

The Tanglewood Symposium paid tribute to the importance of musics of various ethnic and racial groups, triggering the first substantial movement of music educators in the direction of multicultural music education. By the 1970s, MENC had established a Minority Concerns Commission, followed by a Multicultural Awareness Commission, with the intention of raising the level of consciousness and promoting the use of traditional musics of many cultures in the curriculum. In the past two decades, the growing interest among music educators in world musics was evident in workshops at national conferences and in special issues of the *Music Educators Journal* (such as October 1972, May 1983, and May 1992). The 1990 Washington, D.C., Pre-Conference Symposium on Multicultural Approaches to Music Education, presented under the auspices of MENC's

Society for General Music, the Society for Ethnomusicology, and the Smithsonian Institution, was a seminal event in urging the development of broadly based multicultural curricula in music at all educational levels.

The Society for Ethnomusicology has continued to develop ways to infuse world musics into collegiate, secondary, and elementary school programs. Beginning with philosophical statements that provided a rationale for world musics, the society established an Education Committee to review appropriate curricular materials and to provide workshops for educators at their national conferences. These efforts lessened the gap between research in the field and the dissemination of world musics to the general public.

Teaching resources, however, were not developed fast enough for those who were philosophically convinced of the merits of multicultural teaching in music. Teachers were largely left to their own imaginative devices, to their own extended efforts to design lessons from Folkways recordings, and to summers spent reading scholarly writings on the music traditions of unfamiliar cultures. The commitment to providing students with global perspectives in music involved a considerable time expenditure for those few teachers who translated, interpreted, and finally applied the results of independent research to their classrooms.

In 1989, *Multicultural Perspectives in Music Education* was published as both a compendium of descriptions of the world's musical cultures and a collection of lessons for application in upper-elementary and secondary school general music classes. Seven years later, this second edition is intended to provide practical means, via lessons and lesson models, for the integration of world music traditions within the full expanse of the school curriculum. There are singing games for young children in the primary and intermediate grades, a sampling of unison and multipart songs for secondary school choral ensembles, and percussion (and other instrument ensemble) pieces of varying levels of complexity for students in every music educational context. Far beyond the first edition's focus on general music classes, the musical materials and instructional suggestions within this second edition are designed more broadly to provide experiences for students in diverse musical cultures at every level and in every setting.

The spectrum of musical cultures is expanded in this second edition, and new lessons have been added to every chapter. Particularly notable is the new chapter on the music of Oceania and the conversion of the first edition's "North America" chapter into three separate chapters: "African American Music," "Anglo-American Music," and "Native Peoples of North America." "Sub-Saharan African Music" has been substantially revised, the "Middle East" chapter is offered in two segments ("The Arab Middle East" and "Jewish Music in Israel"), "Latin America and the Caribbean" now includes lessons pertaining to Puerto Rican and Mexican music, and the chapter on "Music of Southeast Asia" is enriched by a segment on Balinese music. As before, the material will serve a dual purpose: to reinforce the knowledge of music elements through their use and interpretation in various musical styles, and to develop a greater understanding of people in other cultures. The contributions of music educators and ethnomusicologists come together in this volume, ensuring that music examples are both representative and realistic for use in teaching in the schools.

We would like to thank the principal contributors; Barbara Reeder Lundquist; and Cheryl Rudaitis, Jeanne Spaeth, and Peggy Senko of the MENC publications staff for their hard work.

FOREWORD

It is very exciting to witness the appearance of this greatly expanded second edition of *Multicultural Perspectives in Music Education*. Shortly after the publication of the first edition, the Music Educators National Conference (MENC), the Society for Ethnomusicology (SEM), and the Smithsonian Institution collaborated in presenting a symposium on multicultural approaches to music education. We hoped the synergy of expertise in classroom teaching provided by MENC, expertise in the study of many musical traditions in their cultural contexts provided by SEM, and experience in the presentation of a variety of musical traditions to the general public provided by the Smithsonian would contribute in concrete ways to the development of materials for classroom teachers. The success of the first edition and the need for this new edition have justified our hopes.

North America has been multicultural since the American Indians spread throughout its vast extent, speaking a variety of languages, creating a multitude of cultures, and exchanging objects and ideas with one another. The creation of the United States out of English colonies, French territories, Spanish settlements, and Native American nations resulted in a multilingual and multicultural nation that has been subsequently nourished by millions of immigrants. Today, even small towns may be ethnically and culturally diverse; large cities have long been so. Sometimes viewed negatively, sometimes positively, the cultural heterogeneity of the United States presents a challenge to its entire population that can best be met through education and experience from preschool onward.

Contemporary music is already multicultural; it is our music education that is predominantly Eurocentric. Whether one spins the radio dial, samples music videos, or examines the work of late twentieth-century American composers of concert music, one discovers a creative mixture of musical styles that draws on many different traditions and processes. Our students come from many different traditions, wear clothes made in many different countries, eat food from many different cuisines, and have families with roots in many different places. Just as spicy salsa has joined ketchup as a national condiment of choice, so have Caribbean-born reggae, Afro-pop, Indian film music, and hundreds of other genres found a place in the entertainment centers of American homes. As the authors of this volume argue, we must address this new reality in our classrooms, our ethnomusicological theory, and our exhibits.

Not every member of an ethnic or cultural group will prefer the music, cuisine, and culture of his or her ancestors. For example, some European Americans may choose to dine on Chinese food and dance to Caribbean music, while some immigrants from Asia and the Caribbean may prefer fast food from McDonald's and heavy metal music or French cuisine and nineteenth-century European classical music. The exposure to a variety of traditions is, however, a central part of education for the twenty-first century, a century certain to be filled with complex cultural choices and increasing international and intercultural interdependence.

This expanded second edition of *Multicultural Perspectives in Music Education* goes much further than its predecessor in providing materials to assist music teachers in modifying their classes and involving their students in new forms of music making and new understandings about sounds. The seven-year-old first edition has seen a number of updates and improvements, and the authors and MENC are to be congratulated on this new publication. I hope it will be read with care, used with imagination, and received by all with surprise, enthusiasm, and enjoyment.

Anthony Seeger
Curator, Smithsonian Institution
Former president of the Society for Ethnomusicology

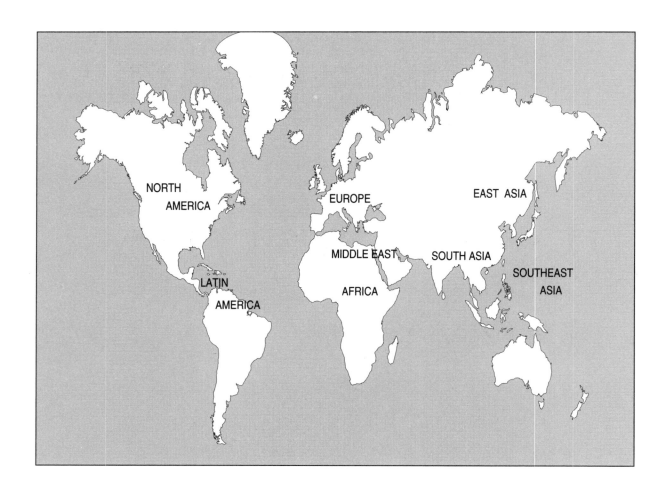

NORTH
AMERICA

EUROPE

EAST ASIA

MIDDLE EAST

SOUTH ASIA

LATIN

SOUTHEAST
ASIA

AMERICA

AFRICA

Map of the world, showing the geographic areas described in the text.

TEACHING MUSIC FROM A MULTICULTURAL PERSPECTIVE

by William M. Anderson and Patricia Shehan Campbell

A multicultural approach to learning centers around organizing educational experiences for students that develop sensitivity, understanding, and respect for peoples from a broad spectrum of ethnic-cultural backgrounds.[1] If students are to learn from a multicultural perspective, teachers must develop an educational philosophy that recognizes the many cultural contributions made by different peoples. That philosophy centers on developing an understanding that there are many different but equally valid forms of cultural expression and encourages students to develop a broad perspective based on understanding and tolerance for a variety of opinions and approaches.

Multicultural music education reflects the cultural diversity of the world in general and of the United States in particular by promoting a music curriculum that includes songs, choral works, instrumental selections, and listening experiences representative of a wide array of ethnic-cultures. It also encourages the interdisciplinary study of different cultural groups through not only music but also art, dance, drama, literature, and social studies. Performances by choral and instrumental ensembles, as well as stories told by storytellers, dramatic presentations, puppet shows, and folk dances, are some of the experiences that enliven classroom study based on a multicultural curriculum. The ultimate challenge in multicultural music education is to provide avenues of exploration so that students can gain a better understanding of the world and of their American heritage.

Rationale

A multicultural approach to music learning in American schools is important for many reasons. For one thing, the United States has an extremely diverse population. People from more than one hundred world cultures now reside in the United States, and many ethnic groups now number in the tens of thousands and some in the millions.

Major changes in the patterns of immigration to this country have occurred in the nearly four centuries since the founding of Jamestown, Virginia, in 1607, when American Indian nations were the only diverse cultural groups. The largest number of immigrants has come from European countries, first from northwestern Europe and then from southeastern Europe. Substantial numbers of peoples from the African continent also arrived during the eighteenth and nineteenth centuries. Today, approximately 15 percent of United States immigrants come from Europe, 37 percent from Asia, and 44 percent from Latin America and the Caribbean.[2] The 1990 census revealed a nation of fewer than 1 percent Native American peoples, 3 percent Asians, 9 percent Hispanics, 12 percent African Americans, and 75 percent of people of European or mixed ancestry.[3] By the year 2050, the population distribution of the United States is projected to be 10 percent Asian, 16 percent Black, 22 percent Latino, and 52 percent of European heritage.[4]

The United States currently has a population of approximately 258 million people, which includes 50 million Blacks, Hispanics, and Asians. Many geographical areas throughout the country now have large ethnic populations, some of which have been increasing at dramatic rates in recent years. Cleveland identifies itself as a "city of nations," and this description is surely appropriate for metropolitan regions such as New York, Washington, D.C., Houston, Chicago, Miami, and Los Angeles. Ethnic diversity has also spread beyond major metropolitan areas to now affect large numbers of smaller communities throughout the nation. Florida, for example, currently has 153 distinct cultural groups,[5] and demographers predict that by 2010, California will be the first state, with the exception of Hawaii, "to have a population whose majority is made up of minorities."[6]

At one time it was fashionable to speak of America's cultural diversity in terms of a "melting pot," but the acceptance of this myth is clearly waning. The civil rights movements of the 1950s and 1960s stimulated ethnic revitalization: Groups that had previously denied their cultures now proclaim their unique identities. Thus, the United States of today is best described as a country composed of a mosaic of various ethnic communities that contribute to the national culture as they maintain distinct identities.

The dynamics of cultural diversity are reflected at all levels in American schools. More than one hundred languages are now spoken in the New York, Chicago, Los Angeles, and Fairfax County, Virginia, school systems.[7] Some of America's major school systems, like those in Chicago, Los Angeles, and New York, now offer instruction in a dozen different languages. The superintendent of the Milwaukee Public Schools remarked that in a visit to one school, the pupils displayed a sign that said "welcome" in twenty-seven different languages, because those languages are represented at that one school.[8]

Ernest Boyer, president of the Carnegie Foundation for the Advancement of Teaching, stated that "what is coming toward the educational system is a group of children who will be...more ethnically and linguistically diverse" than ever before.[9] It has been predicted that by the year 2000, one out of three United States school children will be either Black or Hispanic and that in fifty-three major cities the majority of students will be nonwhite.[10]

As Americans become more aware of their nation's ethnic diversity, curricula in all subject areas are now being designed to encourage the broadest cultural perspectives. Educational administrators and school faculties have placed a major emphasis on designing study programs that help students develop an understanding of the cultural diversity of their world and their own country. The former is designed to help students develop international perspectives that will prepare them to live in a global environment; the latter focuses on the very nature of the United States itself, a country composed of a large variety of different cultures that must understand each other and work together for the common good of the nation.

In music, a multicultural approach to education is clearly in keeping with perhaps the most significant trend of the past half century: the growing understanding of music as a global phenomenon in which there are a number of highly sophisticated musical traditions based on different but equally logical principles. Many who have studied a variety of the world's musical cultures have come to realize that the often-used phrase "music, the international language" has little validity. In summary, our world contains many musical "languages," and we must learn the operative principles of these traditions in order to understand them.

In the past, as a result of emphasizing selected aspects of Western European and American classical and folk music, teachers have often led students to believe there was only one major musical system in the world, the Euro-American system. By stressing the importance and perhaps "superiority" of that system, educators have taught by implication the relative unimportance, if not the actual inferiority, of other musical systems. Today's scholars have clearly demonstrated that educational institutions at all levels need to ensure that music curricula contain balanced programs that are representative of the world and also of the multicultural nature of the United States itself.

Many teachers are now aware of the need to present a broad spectrum of music to their students. The Music Educators National Conference has given priority attention to the multicultural mandate in music education with numerous sessions on various musical traditions being presented at national, regional, and state conventions. The 1990 Washington Symposium on Multicultural Approaches to Music Education, cosponsored by MENC, the Society for Ethnomusicology, and the Smithsonian Institution, and attended by nearly three hundred music teachers from all educational levels throughout the United States, was a seminal event. The symposium resolution for future directions and actions clearly articulated the breadth of responsibility that music educators have in addressing the issue of multiculturalism in music education:

- Be it resolved that music teachers will seek to assist students in understanding that there are many different but equally valid forms of musical expression.

- Be it resolved that multicultural approaches to teaching music will be incorporated into musical experiences from the very earliest years of music education.

- Be it resolved that instruction in *multicultural approaches to teaching music* will incorporate both *intensive experiences in other music cultures* and *comparative experiences among music cultures*.

- Be it resolved that music instruction will include not only the *study of other musics*, but also the *relationship of those musics to their respective cultures*; be it resolved further that the *meaning of music within each culture* be sought for its own value.

- Be it resolved that we will seek to ensure that *multicultural approaches to teaching music* will be incorporated into every elementary and secondary school music curriculum. These should include experiences in singing, playing instruments, listening, and creative activity and movement or dance experiences with music.

- Be it resolved that *multicultural approaches to teaching music* will be incorporated into music curricula in all educational settings including general, instrumental, and choral music education. Such studies will involve both product and process.

- Be it resolved that *multicultural approaches to teaching music* will be incorporated into all phases of teacher education in music: music education methods classes and clinical experiences, music history and literature, theory, composition, and performance.[11]

A number of other national and international organizations, including the Society for Ethnomusicology, the National Association of Schools of Music, and the International Society for Music Education, have strongly endorsed the study of world musics at all levels of instruction.[12] The release of the National Standards for Arts Education in 1994 further stressed the importance of multicultural perspectives. These Standards, developed by a consortium of national arts education associations, state that students should:

- Sing from memory a *varied repertoire* of songs representing genres and styles *from diverse cultures*.
- Demonstrate perceptual skills by moving and by answering questions about and describing aural examples of music of *various styles representing diverse cultures*.
- Identify the sounds of a variety of instruments, including many orchestra and band instruments, and instruments from *various cultures*.
- Identify by genre or style aural examples of music from *various historical periods and cultures*.
- Describe in simple terms how musical elements are used in music examples from *various world cultures*.
- Identify and describe the roles of musicians in *various music settings and cultures*.
- Perform music representing *diverse genres and cultures*.
- Analyze the uses of musical elements in aural examples representing *diverse genres and cultures*.
- Describe distinguishing characteristics representative of music genres and styles for a *variety of cultures*.
- Compare, in *several cultures of the world*, functions music serves, roles of musicians, and conditions under which music is typically performed.[13]

To support the increasing interest in multicultural approaches to music education, domestic and international book, record, and film companies have produced numerous materials on world musics. Contemporary music series text books for elementary and secondary schools have now embraced a music curriculum based on examples from a wide variety of music cultures. Clearly, the concept of studying music from a multicultural perspective is becoming an integral part of music instruction at all educational levels.

Some musical benefits of multicultural music education

Although many people have encouraged an investigation of world musics as a way to promote intercultural and interracial understanding, multicultural music study can also provide a number of strictly musical benefits. First, students are introduced to a great variety of musical sounds from all over the world. Their palette of musical experiences is expanded as they come to realize the extraordinary variety of sonic events worldwide. An early exposure to a large array of musical sounds is important in helping students become receptive to all types of musical expression.

Second, students begin to understand that many areas of the world have music as sophisticated as their own. Until recently, peoples of both Western and non-Western cultures believed that Euro-American classical music was "superior" to other musics.[14] Today, composers, performers, and teachers are coming to realize that many equally sophisticated music cultures are found throughout the globe and that Western classical music is just one of the many varied styles.

Third, students can discover many different but equally valid ways to construct music. For many students, this may be one of the most important gains derived from a study of music in its multicultural manifestations. They discover that music from a given culture may have principles that differ significantly from those principles contained in the music of their own culture and that one should learn the distinctive, inherent logic of each type. What would be an unacceptable practice in Western music may be perfectly acceptable in music from another area of the world. Also, the terminology used to describe Western music often is not appropriate for describing another musical tradition, so more global-oriented nomenclature is needed.

Fourth, by studying a variety of world musics, students develop greater musical flexibility, termed by some as "polymusicality." They increase their ability to perform, listen intelligently, and appreciate many types of music. Some teachers find that when students gain a positive attitude toward one "foreign" music and are able to perform and listen intelligently to that music, they become more flexible in their attitudes toward other unfamiliar musics. Through their involvement with other musics, students develop a number of vocal and instrumental techniques. Their capacity for learning different musics grows, and they are able to study and perform new musics with increased understanding and ease. Furthermore, with this flexibility, they are much less prone to judge a new music (whether Western or non-Western) without first trying to understand it. In addition, by studying the function of such elements as melody, rhythm, texture, timbre, and form in producing various musics, students begin to reappraise Western music and often come to view it in a completely different manner. When students study a variety of musics, they become more aware of aspects of their own music that they have previously taken for granted.

Instructional approaches

Teaching from a multicultural or global perspective can be done in a variety of ways. Music specialists, working in conjunction with classroom teachers and subject specialists, can develop curricula for the study of a number of cultures, both from the world at large and from the United States. While there are a number of approaches, teachers may wish to consider organizing study units around cultural groups highlighted in the social studies curricula at each grade level. At the elementary level, the musical study for each of these units might include singing songs, making and playing instruments, improvisation, movement or dance, and focused listening. In conjunction with the art teacher, the students may study visual art examples from the culture currently under study. The physical education teacher may be solicited for assistance with dance and other movement exercises. Classroom teachers, and teachers of social studies and language arts, bring other dimensions to the study of a culture by having students read folktales, poetry, and other literature; produce dramatic productions; view films and videotapes; write reports; and design bulletin boards. These experiences help students learn not only the history and geography of another people but also the unique ways in which music and other art forms are expressive of that culture.

While young children are in the early stages of their musical development, upper elementary, middle school, and secondary school students are at a pivotal point in their development of skills, knowledge, and attitudes toward music. They possess the coordination and strength needed for performing vocally or on instruments. They can think in abstract, critical, and analytical ways. They are often intrigued by the new and unfamiliar and may be fascinated by a comparison of "new" to "known" phenomena. These students have the potential to examine musical cultures beyond their immediate surroundings. They do not easily change their preference for their own music, but they may explore with enthusiasm various musics through active participation.

In addition to gaining a more global perspective, students can learn that many musical styles of the world are represented in the United States. This nation of immigrants provides ample opportunities for discovering the music, literary and visual arts, cuisine, and various customs of different cultural groups. Students who experience a variety of what now constitute "American musics" will gain a new understanding of the cultural plurality of their country. The study of this plurality has become an important curricular theme in the upper elementary grades and in secondary schools nationwide.

The following are some of the approaches music teachers may wish to consider in broadening musical study for their students.

Music concepts. A music curriculum based on multicultural musical experiences can focus on the study of the fundamental concepts of music. A musical concepts chart can be made on the chalkboard, a poster board, or as a bulletin board, and as students learn a new music through performance experiences and directed listening, they are asked to "fill in" information on distinctive aspects of melody, rhythm, timbre, texture, dynamics, and form.

Organizing musical study in terms of a concepts chart provides an effective way of summarizing how distinctive treatments of melody, rhythm, timbre, texture, dynamics, and form identify a particular musical style. It also allows students to focus on contrasts among different musical styles, which lead to an understanding that there are many different but equally logical ways to construct musical sounds.

Performance. Multicultural music study should be approached through various performance experiences in singing, playing instruments, and moving to music. Through performance, students become actively involved in experientially discovering how musics of various cultures are constructed. The pedagogical principles of Europeans Emile Jacques-Dalcroze, Zoltan Kodály, and Carl Orff provide teachers with excellent models for designing multicultural musical experiences. In addition, the musical skills of teachers developed through many years of ear training, conducting, and applied lessons are invaluable in the engagement of students in music-making experiences.

From preschool and the primary years onward, children can learn to sing songs that represent numerous cultures. These songs should be taught as authentically as possible and often in the original languages. Children enjoy learning to pronounce new words, and they may best identify with the cultures and people by using a song's original languages. In secondary school choral ensembles, students are capable of performing multipart pieces with sensitivity to the nuances of both music and language. Their performances can be further enhanced by the addition of gestures and movement associated with the vocal tradition. Teachers should avoid using harmonic piano accompaniments when they do not resemble the practice of the original cultures; many traditional songs may be most accurately performed without accompaniment or with basic rhythmic patterns.

In addition to singing, students can also learn to play musical instruments from various cultures. Native instruments from many areas of the world are now available in the United States and can be used effectively in schools. For example, schools can purchase an African *mbira* (plucked idiophone), *shekere* (gourd rattles with a netted covering of beads), and *agogo* (iron bells). These instruments, or replicas of them, are effective in teaching students about musical heritages from sub-Saharan Africa. Likewise, xylophones are key when playing traditional music from Cambodia to Zimbabwe and can be easily played by both young and older students. Other percussion ensembles, including those from West African, Caribbean, Latin American, and even Chinese cultures, can be organized to perform important drum and gong traditional music that uses available classroom instruments.

In school systems that do not have access to authentic musical instruments from various cultures, teachers can frequently create instruments that simulate the sight and sounds of real instruments. By coordinating performance on handmade instruments with pictures (slides, color transparencies, posters, films, or videotapes) of the original instruments, teachers can provide effective and valid presentations of different musical cultures.

People from other areas of the world perform their own native musics in many areas of the United States. This is particularly true in urban areas and in college and university communities in which there are distinguished performers from many different cultures. Such persons provide an important resource for teachers and schools, and many are willing to instruct and perform.

Along with singing and playing instruments, students can experience various musical traditions by moving to music. Movement activities can center around developing an understanding of basic concepts such as rhythm and form. Students move to the beat, meter, rhythmic patterns, and tempo changes in music. They also learn to "feel" the form in a work by devising movement activities to illustrate different sections. Students can also experience different musics by learning the folk dances of these traditions. Because of the close relationship between motor activity and mental activity, movement is likely to facilitate and enhance conceptual learning. In music learning, the mind and body function together, and the sensory feedback from movement is connected to higher mental processes. Children create natural and spontaneous rhythms when they listen to music; these movements provide the impetus for expressive movement and patterned folk dance.

Guided listening. Along with experiencing the fundamental structural principles of other musics through performance, students are ready to listen perceptively to recorded performances of world musics. Listening to examples of many different musical cultures is an important component of any instructional program. A large number of recordings from most areas of the world are now available in the United States, and many excellent examples of world musics also appear on films and videotapes. In addition, a number of performing artists from other countries now live in the United States, and others come to visit this country each year. Thus, teachers can have actual performances in their classrooms. Such presentations are especially effective in helping children identify with the cultures from which the music is derived.

Integrated learning. Developing a cultural context of featured musical pieces or styles is an important part of a multicultural music program. Although students can explore other musics without investigating the cultures themselves, the most effective approach coordinates a study of the people and their music. Students enjoy learning about different peoples from both their own and other countries by studying unfamiliar customs, crafts, paintings, sculptures, architecture, literature, music, and dance. Through an interrelated study of many aspects of a culture, students develop new and important understandings of other peoples, and they begin to realize the inherent place of music and the arts in other cultures.

Concept and content

This book includes information and suggestions for teaching students their musical heritages. It is designed as a practical experience-oriented guide for helping students develop a broad understanding of musics in their world and an appreciation of their multicultural musical heritage in the United States. The lessons are intended to serve as launches to the adaption and development by teachers of one class period—or two or more classes—of students' knowledge of a musical culture. In this way, the book is a stimulus to the teacher's creative curriculum. It focuses on helping students discover some of the inherently different but equally valid ways in which various cultural groups organize musical events. Finally, this book is intended to help students learn to understand and appreciate their exciting world of music.

NOTES

1. While some people differentiate between multicultural and multiethnic, we refer here to ethnic-culture and leave other cultural considerations (such as age, gender, religious affiliation, and lifestyle) beyond the scope of this discussion. See James A. Banks, *Multiethnic Education: Theory and Practice*, 3d ed. (Boston: Allyn & Bacon, 1994).
2. *Time*, 2 December 1993, 14.
3. *Monthly News from the U. S. Bureau of the Census* (Census Bureau, September 1991) 26, no. 9.
4. *Time*, 2 December 1993, 14.
5. CBS's "Sunday Morning," 4 September 1994.
6. "Patterns in Our Social Fabric Are Changing," *Education Week* 5, no. 34, 14 May 1986, 16.
7. *Time*, 2 December 1993, 14.
8. "Patterns in Our Social Fabric Are Changing," 16.

9. ABC News, "To Save Our Schools, To Save Our Children," 4 September 1984.

10. ABC News, "To Save Our Schools, To Save Our Children," 4 September 1984.

11. Synopsis of "Symposium Resolution for Future Directions," in William M. Anderson, *Teaching Music with a Multicultural Approach* (Reston, Virginia: Music Educators National Conference, 1991), 89–91.

12. See ISME Policy on Music of the World's Cultures, adopted July 1994, in *International Journal of Music Education*, 1995.

13. *National Standards for Arts Education: What Every Young American Should Know and Be Able to Do in the Arts* (Reston, Virginia: Music Educators National Conference, 1994), 26–29, 42–45.

14. See Judith Becker, "Is Western Art Music Superior?" *Musical Quarterly*, 72 (1986): 341–59.

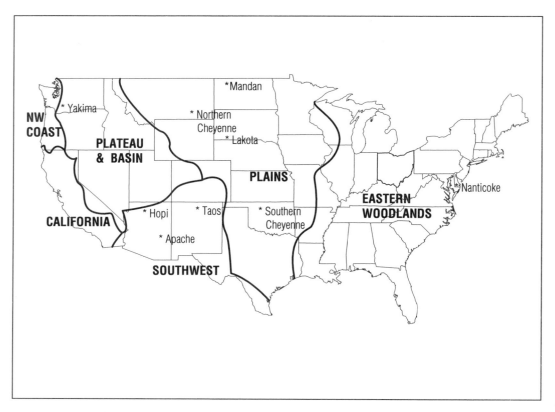

Figure 1. Regions of Native American music

NATIVE PEOPLES OF NORTH AMERICA

by J. Bryan Burton

L ong before the arrival of European explorers and settlers, a mosaic of cultures covered the North American continent. Hundreds of tribes, languages, religions, and life-styles developed among these diverse peoples. At the heart of Native American culture was music. Songs and dances were central to each facet of life from birth until death, including every occasion—sacred or secular, significant or insignificant—that occurred in the lives of these peoples. Songs and dances were integral parts of ceremonies (worship, healing, hunting, and agriculture), social events (dances and courtship), and entertainment. A vast repertoire of stories and songs was transmitted intergenerationally by an oral/aural process from the most distant past to the present-day descendants of the original peoples of the Americas. Despite five centuries of subjugation and assimilation during which much of the rich Native American culture—lands, languages, religions, and millions of lives—was lost, this vibrant music continues not only to exist, but to thrive, evolve, and enrich the lives of both the Native Americans and the new Americans.

To speak of Native American music as a single style ignores the richness and diversity

Regional Style Traits

REGION	REPRESENTATIVE TRIBES	STYLE TRAITS
Eastern Woodlands	*Micmac, Nanticoke, Seneca, Mohawk, Cherokee, Narragansett, Penobscot*	Relaxed voices in medium and high ranges; vocal shake/pulsing at ends of phrases; use of call and response form; agricultural themes of hunting and raising crops frequently used in lyrics; some use of song cycles; great variety of rhythmic accompaniment on drums, including instances of syncopation; instruments such as small hand drums, water drums, rattles made of turtle shell, cow horn, and bark
Plains	*Absarokee (Crow), Dakota, Lakota, Kiowa, Comanche, Cheyenne, Mandan*	Tense, tight, and strained vocal style; Northern tribes prefer a high vocal range; Southern tribes prefer a medium vocal range; melodies frequently begin high, drop dramatically over the course of the song, and end with repetitions of tonal center; rapid changes in pitch and volume; note pulsations frequently occur; "trills" produced by rapidly fluttering the tongue against the roof of the mouth; sing mostly in unison; one large drum played by several people accompanies the music; use flutes and whistles; bells, shells, and other attachments produce ambient musical sounds
Great Basin–Plateau	*Ute, Paiute, Washoe, Bannock, Yakima, Nez Perce, Shoshone*	Vocal style similar to Plains except lower in pitch; simple accompaniments; melodious, frequent use of melodic rise
California	*Diegueno, Mojave, Yurok, Pomo, Miwok, Yokut*	Vocal range usually low with a relaxed style; mostly solo singing with occasional examples of polyphony in northern regions; frequent use of rattles and rasps

Figure 2.

of musical expressions found among the Native Peoples. Native American music within the continental United States is divided into six general stylistic regions differentiated by such factors as preferred vocal style, song forms, types of instruments, song accompaniments, and type and form of ceremonial music and dance. These regions are Eastern Woodlands (sometimes divided into Northeastern and Southeastern styles), Plains (sometimes divided into Northern and Southern styles), Great Basin and Plateau, Northwest Coast, California, and Southwest (usually divided into Pueblo and Apachean styles). The accompanying map (figure 1) shows the location of these regions, and figure 2 identifies some of the general characteristics of each style.

Music is considered to be functional, serving to connect the natural and the supernatural through the spiritual power of the music and dance with specific roles assigned to

Regional Style Traits, continued

REGION	REPRESENTATIVE TRIBES	STYLE TRAITS
Northwest Coast	*Salish, Haida, Tlingit, Kwakiutl, Chinookans, Suquamish, Skagit, Snohomish*	Complex percussion rhythms; eloquently staged dramas feature song, dance, and carved masks with moving parts; drums include slit boxes and hollowed logs; some instances of polyphony; complex song forms and melodies may include chromatic intervals; some upward keys change as melodies progress
Southwest Pueblo	*Hopi, Zuni, Acoma, Santa Clara, Taos, Laguna, Tewa, Tigua*	Vocal style similar to Plains, with lower range and "growling" timbre; melodies lengthy and complex; frequent vocal tension and pulsation; drum sizes vary; each drum played by one person; most singing done in unison; most rituals directed toward agriculture and crop cycles
Southwest Apachean	*Navajo, Apache (including Chiricahua, Mescalero, White Mountain, San Carlos, Jicarilla)*	Light, nasal singing style; mixed vocal ranges; frequent use of natural overtone series in melodic structure (with microtonal variations); singing done mostly in unison, but some responsorial songs; occasional use of flutes and whistles; use of Apache violin (made from the agave plant), sole stringed instrument indigenous to North America; drums, water drums, rasps and bullroarers used as accompaniment; practice elaborate multiday ceremonials incorporating singing, chanting, and sandpainting guided by highly trained practitioners

instruments (the drum is used to communicate with the Creator, for example) or unique dance. The "Jingle Dress Dance," for example, is said to have been given through a vision as a cure for a plague devastating a tribe. Among the functions served by music in Native cultures are religious ceremonies; healing ceremonies; work songs; game songs; songs to bring success in hunting, war, or agriculture; honoring songs in recognition of worthy individuals; courting songs; storytelling; and social songs and dances. Although great latitude is allowed when performing social songs and game songs, ceremonial songs must be performed perfectly in order to ensure a successful outcome of the ceremony. Traditionally, many songs and dances were performed exclusively by a specific person or group within a tribe; there were songs and dances exclusively for men, exclusively for women, or for performance by both men and women. In contemporary Native American society, these once-strict distinctions are beginning to relax, and performances at tribal fairs and powwows are now given more and more frequently by mixed gender groups.

Song texts may be in a tribal language, vocables, or a combination of both. Vocables are not mere nonsense syllables, but have significance to the performer and initiated listener. These vocables tend to match the vowel structure of the tribal language and, in some cases, provide clues to the function of the song. Many theories have been advanced as to the origin of vocables. For example, they may be the remnants of an archaic language, or they may represent "meanings beyond words" on a spiritual level, or they may be the final result of several transmissions of songs learned from another tribe. One Lakota musician has stated that songs given by animal spirits or animals use vocables because "animals do not use human language."

Intertribal music and the modern powwow

During the mid-twentieth century, an intertribal style of song and dance based loosely on Northern Plains traditions developed among people of all Indian nations. Many tribes—particularly those on the East Coast—had lost cultural elements including language, religion, song, and dance during generations of assimilation and persecution. Performers from Plains tribes traveling with Wild West shows and circuses during the early years of the century passed on songs and dances to Native Peoples. From these small beginnings, traditions have been rebuilt around borrowed music and dance, as well as around materials from historical archives.

The intertribal powwow serves as a contemporary gathering place for all Native Peoples to celebrate their identity and to promote Native culture. These gatherings also provide forums for Natives to exchange information and to discuss Native rights and health and education concerns. Music and dance are the centerpiece of these occasions. Social and competitive dancing, such as the Grand Entry, Flag Song, Intertribal, Hoop Dance, Men's Fancy Dance, Women's Fancy Shawl Dance, and specialty dances unique to a particular tribal tradition, go on long into the night. The modern powwow tradition began near the end of World War I, although tribal and intertribal gatherings have been ongoing for centuries. Among the oldest continuously operating tribal gatherings is the Crow Fair, which began in 1918 under the guidance of famed Chief Plenty Coups. The Gallup Intertribal Ceremonial in New Mexico, the Nanticoke Powwow in Delaware, and the United Tribes Powwow in North Dakota are but a few of the hundreds of powwows open to the public each year.

Instruments of the Native Peoples

The most popular instruments used in Native American music are drums and rattles to accompany Native song and dance. Other percussion instruments include rasps, large sticks used to beat rhythms, and bells (frequently attached to clothing or tied around arms, legs, or wrists). Melodic instruments include flutes, whistles, and stringed instruments such as the Apache violin or the folk fiddles of the Yaqui (of southern Arizona) and Tarahumara (of northwestern Mexico).

Drums are made in many sizes and shapes and from such diverse materials as logs, pottery, baskets, animal skins, and metal. Many traditions equate the drumbeat with the heartbeat of Mother Earth or as a means of communication with supernatural powers. In contemporary pow-wows and tribal fairs, the term "drum" refers not only to the instrument, but also to the performers who play it and sing. Strict codes of behavior and conduct are followed by musicians gathered as part of the "drum."

Perhaps the most familiar drums from the Native culture are the Pueblo-style drums of the Southwest. These drums are constructed from sections of properly selected and cured cottonwood logs that have been carefully hollowed by master craftsmen. (Traditional drum makers from Cochiti Pueblo (of New Mexico) prefer to use materials from trees that have fallen due to natural causes such as windstorms or lightning strikes rather than cut down a living tree.) Skin heads are placed on each end of the drum and are laced together with rawhide lacing. The heads and bodies of the drums may be decorated with appropriate symbols or left plain according to the taste of the performer for whom the instrument is made. Beaters consist of a wool or cotton pad that has been covered by leather and tied to a trimmed stick (often a dowel) by a sinew thong.

Frame drums are found throughout the North American continent and vary in size, shape, and decoration. The frame may be simply a section of tree trunk cut to a desired thickness and hollowed out, with a hide stretched across one or both ends. Frames made of sections of wood may be square, hexagonal, or octagonal, according to tribal tradition or individual preference. The animal skins used for the drum head may be decorated with paintings of animals, persons, or symbols, or left plain. Some drums have a short handle, and others may be held by grasping strips of the hide that have been gathered and tied at the back of the drum. These smaller drums are played either with the hand or with a small beater, according to tribal tradition or individual taste.

Water drums are popular among many Native Peoples. Among the Eastern Woodland tribes, drums are made from tree sections or "recycled" from discarded kegs or casks. Most drums have a small plug for draining water, and the inside is frequently coated with pitch to prevent water leakage or warping and cracking of the drum's body. A varying amount of water is placed in the drum to determine pitch and resonance. The head is wetted and stretched until the desired pitch and tonal quality is achieved. The skin head is held in place by either a leather thong or a carved wooden hoop. Among the Apaches and Navajos of the Southwest, water drums may be made from ceramic or metal pots that sometimes serve double-duty as cooking vessels (or even cookie jars). Beaters for water drums range from the curved sticks of the southwest to elaborately carved drumsticks of the northeast.

The large drum used in most contemporary powwows may be as large as a coffee table and is placed on a special stand or suspended frame. (Some drums are actually discarded Scotch bass drums, once popular in school marching bands, which have been adapted and decorated.) A large number of drummers—usually a multiple of four—play these drums.

Slit log drums, large log drums, and other box drums are found among tribes of the northwest coast and Alaska. Frame drums among these peoples are often elaborately decorated with tribal symbols. These frame drums bear striking resemblances to those found in Siberia and northeastern Asia.

Rattles display the great inventiveness of Native Peoples in creating instruments from any possible material. Materials may include gourds, turtle shells, rawhide, animal horns, deer hooves, tobacco can lids, discarded metal cans, rattlesnake rattles, bird beaks, sea shells, cocoons—every type of material imaginable. Some are quite plain in appearance, while others are elaborately carved and decorated. Regarding the symbolism of turtle shell rattles favored by many east coast tribes, Nanticoke Assistant Chief Charles C. Clark IV says, "When you look at the shell of a turtle, you will see that the number of large segments is equal to the number of lunar months in a year and that the number of small segments around the top of the shell is often equal to the number of days in a lunar month. This honors the turtle for her part in the creation of Mother Earth."

Miscellaneous percussion instruments include rasps, split-stick clappers, scrapers, and bullroarers. Bells, bits of metal, and shells attached to clothing provide ambient musical accompaniment to dance movements. To enhance the sound projection of rasps, a common practice is to place one end of a rasp against an upturned dish or basket while the rasp is scraped. Sometimes the resonator is floated in a dish of water to further amplify the sound.

Flutes and whistles are found among most contemporary tribes although, historically, these instruments are most commonly associated with peoples from the Plains and Southwest traditions. Flutes may be made from a variety of materials, including wood, bamboo, ceramics, bone, and metal. Often associated with courtship and love songs, flutes from the Plains traditions are most often constructed from cedar and may have elaborately carved or painted decorations. In the Southwest, bamboo (cane) is the preferred material, with decorations including painted designs, feathers, and bits of precious stones. Ceramic flutes are found in Mexico and Central America, with only limited examples found within the United States.

Native American flutes are constructed from selected materials according to a common acoustical design. The tube (bamboo or wood) is hollowed into two chambers separated by a blockage near the tip of the instrument. The air stream is diverted over this blockage, outside the body of the instrument, and back into the lower chamber through an air channel carved into an external decoration referred to as the "bird." Pitches are changed by covering and uncovering tone holes (from three to six according to tribal tradition or personal preference). Pitches may be shaded by finger and breath manipulation to create an infinite variety of sounds and tonal effects.

Whistles may be made from any material, but bone and antler horn are the most popular. The large leg bone of the eagle is used in ceremonial music and dance. Smaller whistles may be carved from sections of antler or wood or from other bones.

The Apache violin is unique among Native instruments and is the only stringed instrument indigenous to North America. This instrument is made from a section of stalk from the century plant (a type of agave plant); tone holes are carved at appropriate points and one or two strings are placed lengthwise across the top of the instrument. The bow is constructed from a bent willow branch with horse hair attached. The body of the instrument may be decorated with geometric patterns or symbolic pictorial designs. Apache violins are used in a variety of circumstances including social dances, healing, and courtship. Famed Apache leader Geronimo, known among his people for his powers as a healer, prophet, and musician, was one of the craftsmen of this instrument. An example of his work is in the Peabody Museum at Harvard University.

Another stringed instrument tradition, dating back to the seventeenth century, exists among the Yaqui and Tarahumara of the southwest United States and northern Mexico. Native artisans originally copied European instruments—violins, harps, and vihuelas—brought by missionaries, but the designs, individual natures of the instruments, and musical usages have long since transformed these instruments into an authentic folk form of these Native Peoples.

Contemporary Native American music

Musical taste and style are as diverse among Native Americans as among the remainder of American society. In addition to preserving music from past generations, contemporary Native musicians such as the Porcupine Singers (Lakota) produce new songs in these traditional styles. New Age, jazz, country, and rock groups have been formed by musicians from all tribal backgrounds. Native composers and performers are also active in producing symphonic works, including ballets, chamber works, symphonies, and operas.

Although the styles and forms have changed, contemporary Native American music in many cases continues to serve the same social and ceremonial functions as in the past. No matter how removed this music has become from traditional styles, contemporary music deals with important social issues, provides entertainment, honors the "Indian way" (traditional lifestyles and beliefs), and incorporates elements of traditional musics, including the use of vocables, Native instruments, and Native languages.

Native musicians using popular genres have created syncretic styles that incorporate elements of Native American music and Western popular sounds. For example, instruments may include Native drums, rattles, and flutes in addition to the drum sets, guitars, pianos, and synthesizers of contemporary popular styles. Waila music (popularly known as "chicken scratch"), performed throughout southern Arizona by Tohono O'Odham, Pima, and Maricopa musicians, resembles a hybrid of Native American, Hispanic, and polka band music of the Midwest. Lyrics may be in a Native language or in English or any combination of English, a tribal language, and vocables. Tom Bee's "Nothing Could Be Finer Than a Forty-Niner" includes Native instruments, descriptions of popular Native dance styles, quotations from a traditional social dance song ("One-Eyed Ford"), and the vocables "be bop a lu la" from Gene Vincent's early 1960's rock tune. Sharon Burch creates haunting folk-rock style melodies with Navajo lyrics and themes concerning tribal issues and traditional ceremonies.

Some prominent Native American performers in these syncretic styles include Buddy Red Bow (country), Keith Secola (country), Tom Bee and XIT (rock), Red Thunder (rock), Jackalope (jazz-fusion, termed "synthacousticpunkarachinavajazz" by members of the group), A. Paul Ortega (country blues), and Joanne Shenandoah (folk rock). R. Carlos Nakai performs not only with Jackalope but also with other artists, including William Eaton and Peter Kater in a series of New Age recordings. Nakai has also recorded a number of traditional Native American flute albums.

John Rainer, Jr., a member of the Taos tribe, bridges the gap between traditional Native American and symphonic works with his album *Songs for the American Indian Flute, Volumes 1 and 2* (Red Willow Songs). Songs are presented in a strictly traditional style on one side of each album. On the other, contemporary accompaniments and orchestrations have been created for the songs through the use of synthesizer and studio orchestration techniques.

The collaborative efforts of R. Carlos Nakai and James DeMars have created a series of works featuring Native American flute and chamber orchestra. "Premonitions of Christopher Columbus," from *Spirit Horses* (Canyon Records CR 7014), uses Native American flute to represent the original settlers of the Western continents, the violoncello to represent European cultural influences, African percussion to represent African cultural influences, and the saxophone to represent the "new Americans" in a concerto grosso format. Mohican composer Brent Michael Davids composed "Mtukwekok Naxkomao" ("The Singing Woods") for the Kronos Quartet, incorporating an Apache

Native Americans

Time is Unimportant. Time is a very relative thing. Natives don't watch clocks—they do things when they need to be done. The family often gets up at sunrise and retires after sunset. "Indian time" means "when everyone gets there." A community meeting can be set for 1:00 p.m., and people will come as near that time as they wish. So, the meeting may actually begin an hour or more later—or earlier—and this bothers no one.

"Today" Concept. Native Peoples generally live each day as it comes. Plans for tomorrow are left until the future becomes the present.

Patience. To have much patience and to wait is considered to be a good quality.

Shame. Native American groups often shame an individual, but once this is over, no guilty feeling is held by the individual.

Extended Family. Aunts are often considered to be mothers; uncles may be called fathers; cousins are brothers and sisters of the immediate family. Clan members are considered relatives. Native cultures consider many more individuals to be family than do most non-Native Americans.

Age. Natives respect their elders and feel that experience brings knowledge. Therefore, the older one is, the more knowledgeable he or she is considered. No effort is made to conceal white hair or other signs of age.

Giving. The respected member of many Native Peoples is the one who shares and gives all his wealth to others.

Few Material Things. Members of the tribe are often suspicious of individuals who collect many material possessions. Some tribes hold celebrations and give away most of their possessions to others as "love gifts."

Humans Live in Balance with Nature. The Earth is here to enjoy. If humankind accepts this world as it is and lives with this world as they should, there will not be sickness or lack of food.

Euro-Americans

Time is Very Important. Time is of the utmost importance. When a person says he or she will be somewhere at 10:00 a.m., he or she must be there at 10:00 a.m. Otherwise, he or she is felt to be a person who "wastes" another person's time. More and more, non-Native Americans rush. Members of this culture want to use time to its fullest extent.

"Tomorrow" Concept. Non-Native Americans are constantly looking to tomorrow. Such items as insurance, savings for college, plans for vacation, and so on suggest to what extent non-Native Americans value this belief.

Action. Euro-Americans admire people who are quick to act. A person tries to finish a task quickly and moves on to the next thing. To sit "idly" and let one's competition pass ahead by acting more quickly is considered bad business.

Guilt. After a person commits an act he or she considers "wrong," the individual often feels guilty. This terrible feeling may make one ill physically or mentally.

Family. Immediate biological family is of the utmost importance, and relationships are usually limited to these groups.

Youth. Thousands of dollars are spent yearly for hair dyes, make-up, and other items that make older people look younger. Even whole towns have sprung up in the United States that advertise "youthful living" and that are designed for "senior citizens."

Saving. "Thrift" is considered an admirable value.

Many Material Things. Non-Native Americans have increasingly measured wealth in terms of material things. Many expensive possessions, or "status symbols," are considered highly desirable.

Humans Control Nature. This culture constantly searches for methods for controlling and mastering the elements. Members of this culture make artificial lakes, control natural waters, and generate and control electricity. Euro-Americans are proud of these accomplishments.

Figure 3. A comparison of cultural values

violin, specially constructed instruments, and fragments of Native American melodies in what may well be the first string quartet composed by an indigenous composer.[1] Louis Ballard (of the Cherokee-Quapaw) has composed many works in all symphonic genres. In addition, Ballard was the first Native American composer to conduct a major symphony orchestra.

Contemporary Native American musical life is extraordinarily diverse and encompasses every sound and style of music performed on the North American continent. Despite evolutions of style and use of contemporary sounds and techniques, Native American musicians keep "one foot planted firmly in tradition," placing an indelibly Native American stamp upon these modern musics.

Teaching Native American music

When preparing lessons that incorporate Native American music, teachers should keep in mind several important guidelines for maintaining respect and honor for this musical culture:

- Remember that Native American music is the only music indigenous to the American continents. Other American music, including jazz, was derived from combinations of African, European, and Native American musical styles and forms. (Some Asian influences have occurred in modern popular songs, jazz, and New Age musics.)
- Native American music is not static, but is a living, evolving art form. Teach music from this culture not as "museum pieces," but rather as part of a centuries-long tradition. In addition to traditional and historical Native selections, teach examples of contemporary Native American music ranging from expanded contemporary to rock, country, jazz, New Age, and symphonic.
- Treat the music with respect. Do not refer to "weird sounds," "funny voices," or "nonsense syllables." Approach Native American music, dance, and performance as culturally valid; it is different from Western-art music, but not inferior. Point out similarities and differences in styles and forms as one would when comparing Western works of different periods, styles, and genres.

In addition to teaching Native American music as part of a multicultural enrichment unit, use examples from this culture to illustrate musical concepts. Native American music has form, melody, rhythm, timbre, and so on. For example, many songs follow an A-B form, while others follow uniquely Native American forms.

Use Native-made instruments in the classroom rather than imitations. These materials are not prohibitively expensive and may be readily obtained through major general music supply companies and through Native American culture centers and retail dealers. Instruments are usually individually made by a Native artisan rather than mass produced. Each instrument is created as a work of art, not as a toy. Some major distributors of Native-made instruments include Canyon Records and Indian Arts, the Taos Drum Company, and Indian Pueblo Cultural Center.

Seek out Native American performers from the local community to use as resources and performers for music classes. Many publications list tribes, reservations, cultural centers, recreational areas, newspapers, public events, and so on for Native American interest groups in each state. Two major resources for identifying Native American centers are *Indian America* by Eagle Walking Turtle (Santa Fe, NM: John Muir Publications, 1991) and *Discovering Indian Reservations* by Veronica Tiller (Denver, CO: Council Publication, 1992).

Visit Native American events and observe music and dance performances firsthand to gain a deeper understanding of the role of music within the culture. Be respectful as a guest of such events: ask permission before photographing or recording, do not join in the singing or dancing unless invited, and refrain from making insensitive comments. Native Americans are proud of their heritage and will always assist the genuinely interested observer in gaining insight into their culture. Refer to figures 3 and 4 before beginning Lessons 1–6.

Unless otherwise noted in an individual lesson, transcriptions of lyrics and vocables follow the guide provided below.

Vowels:	Vowel	As in....	In song pronunciation line as...
	A	"father"	ah
	E	"met"	eh
	I	"hit"	ih
	O	"hope"	oh
	U	"boot"	oo

Consonants: Consonants are usually pronounced as they normally are in standard English with exceptions as noted in individual lessons.

"G" is usually hard, as in "go"

"H" is sometimes preceded by a slight aspiration

"HWE" is pronounced "whey" (as in "curds and whey")

"LWE" is pronounced like "hallway" ("hah-lway")

Figure 4. Pronunciation guide

L E S S O N   1

■ **Objectives**

1. Students will identify and describe a call-and-response form as used in "O Hal'Lwe."
2. Students will identify the use of the pentatonic scale in "O Hal'Lwe."
3. Male students will perform "O Hal'Lwe" in call-and-response style with drum accompaniment (one note per beat).
4. Female students will perform the dance, changing dance movements as cued aurally (in call-and-response sections).

■ **Materials**

1. Song "O Hal'Lwe"
2. Drums (Native American or classroom hand drums)
3. Map of the United States with Nanticoke lands (southern Delaware) clearly marked

■ **Procedures**

1. Provide a brief historical and cultural background of the Nanticoke people and locate southern Delaware on the map of the United States.

    The historical information you tell students might include the following: The Nanticoke people hail from the Eastern Woodlands. As early as the 1580s, English and Spanish explorers encountered the Nanticoke living along the Nanticoke River in the Chesapeake Bay region of present-day Delaware and Maryland. Following several failed treaties, most Nanticoke left their homes and moved to Pennsylvania and New York, where they were placed under the protection of the Cayuga Nation. A few families, however, remained on traditional lands enduring prejudice as "free colored" through the nineteenth and early twentieth centuries. In recent years, the Nanticoke have reasserted their cultural identity and have actively promoted their ancient heritage by hosting powwows, establishing a tribal museum, and obtaining state recognition as Native Peoples. On the weekend following Labor Day each year, the Nanticoke host one of the largest pow-wows in the eastern United States as a celebration of their cultural pride.

    The cultural information you tell students might include the following: The important role played by women in the Nanticoke culture contrasts sharply with the male-dominated society of early European settlers. As with numerous other Native Peoples, the women traditionally managed the affairs of the tribe, owned the property, and were honored as the true preservers of the tribe's cultural heritage. This women's dance is to honor the women of the Nanticoke as the force that both preserves and protects tribal culture. Although the specific meaning of the words to this song has been lost, the Nanticoke remember that "O Hal'Lwe" (see figure 5) refers to the mighty oak tree and compares the role of women in their culture to the oak tree that brings forth new life (acorns) and provides shelter and protection as each new generation grows to maturity, thereby guaranteeing the survival of the people and their culture. While the men accompany the dance with singing and drumming, women—often many generations of women from the same family—dance together as a demonstration of multigenerational bonding.

Figure 5. "O Hal'Lwe," a Nanticoke women's dance

2. Introduce "O Hal'Lwe."
3. Teach the song, identifying call-and-response sections. Solo male begins the song; the refrain is sung by all males. Assign a few students to play drum accompaniment using one note per beat.
4. Teach the dance this way:
   a. Females form a large, counterclockwise circle.
   b. During the call section, each female student moves forward (starting with the left foot), tapping her toe on the downbeat of each pulse and patting the ground with her flattened foot on the upbeat of each pulse, like this:

   tap   pat   tap   pat   etc.
   1   +   2   +

5. During the response section, each student rotates clockwise (in individual circles) using the tap-pat pattern of motion, resuming the forward counterclockwise movement when the call section is repeated.
6. Perform "O Hal'Lwe."
7. Following several performances, review the Nanticoke historical and cultural background, call-and-response form, and use of aural cues to change dance movements.

LESSON 2

■ Objectives

Students will:
1. Identify and describe stylistic elements drawn from Western popular music after listening to a recording of "Heartbeat."
2. Identify and describe stylistic elements drawn from traditional Native American music.
3. Demonstrate a basic understanding of the historical processes that led to the synthesis of the elements following a class discussion of cultural context.

> *Optional:* Students will play drums and rattles using appropriate rhythms to accompany a recording of "Heartbeat."

> *Optional:* Students will create their own rock songs, synthesizing elements of both Western popular music and traditional Native American music.

■ Materials

1. "Heartbeat," from *Makoce Wakan* (Eagle Thunder Records 3-7916-2-H1)

> *Optional:* A variety of Native American instruments, including rattles, hand drums, and flutes[2]

■ Procedures

1. Discuss contemporary intertribal musical styles; explain syncretic processes and historical processes. Tell students that the traditional sense of regional style does not apply to this song, as the writers and performers of "Heartbeat" represent several tribes, including Apache, Taos, and Lakota. "Heartbeat" represents a contemporary synthesis of traditional instruments and sounds with elements of Western popular music. From a cultural perspective, contemporary Native popular music blends elements of traditional Native styles with elements of country, rock, folk, jazz, and blues from the Euro-American tradition, though the exact synthesis of styles varies from performer to performer. Some of the factors influencing this development in Native music include the radio broadcasts reaching the reservations in the mid-twentieth century, exposure to white popular culture beyond the reservations (particularly during the relocation efforts of the 1950s, in which Native Peoples were moved from reservations to urban areas in an attempt to completely assimilate them into "American" culture), folk rock protest music and musicians popular among Indian rights activists, and live performances on or near reservations by popular entertainers. Each contemporary popular Native group retains strong ties to traditional music and culture through use of Native instruments, Native languages, topics drawn from Native literature, and topics drawn from Native rights issues. Whatever the degree of synthesis found in contemporary popular Native music, the performers always keep one foot firmly planted in traditions.
2. Play the recording of "Heartbeat," instructing students to listen for and list instruments and stylistic traits drawn from Western popular music and instruments and stylistic traits drawn from traditional Native American music.
3. Discuss "Heartbeat," inviting students to identify elements of Western popular music

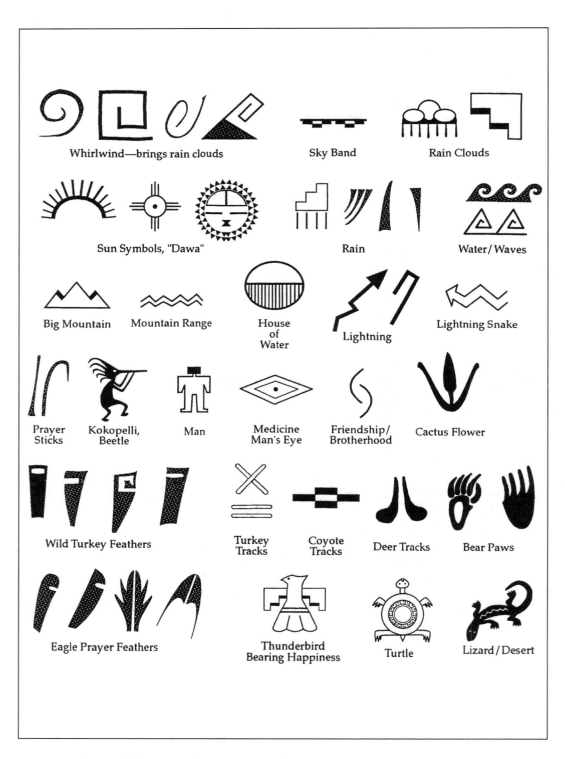

Figure 6. Indian symbols, copyright 1993 by K. Edwards. Used by permission.

(guitars, a synthesizer, English lyrics, rock improvisation for the solo, Western verse-refrain form) and Native American music (use of rattles, hand drums, the Native American flute, chanting, the theme of the song). Show Native instruments to the class (use photos, if necessary).

4. Discuss the meaning of the lyrics and their relevance to Native issues ("Heartbeat" of the Earth, "revolution" to win Native rights, call for return to traditional values and beliefs, and criticism of apathy).

5. Invite students to give opinions as to how or why the synthesis of styles occurred.
    Optional: Play "Heartbeat" again, assigning students to accompany the recording using appropriate rhythms.
    Optional: Have the class create its own rock song, synthesizing elements of Native American and Western popular music.

L E S S O N   3

■ Objectives

Students will:

1. Identify and describe the sounds of various Hopi rattles through experimental playing and listening to recordings of Hopi traditional and contemporary music after guided participation in a cooperative learning environment.

2. Suggest possible meanings of rattle decorations based on a chart of Indian symbols.

3. Share observations and conclusions with other students in a brief oral presentation.

4. Play rattles, using appropriate rhythms, to accompany recordings of Hopi traditional and contemporary music.

5. Identify and describe differences in style and instrumentation between traditional Hopi and contemporary songs while listening to selected recorded examples.

■ Materials

1. Recordings of "Water Maiden Dance," from *Hopi Social Dance Songs* (Canyon Records CR 6108) and "The Rain Song," from *Yazzie Girl* (Canyon Records CR 534)

2. Four to six assorted Hopi rattles

3. Listening stations with four headphones (optional)

4. Page of Indian symbols

5. Map of the United States with the location of the Hopi reservation clearly marked

■ Procedures

1. Locate the Hopi reservation on the map of the United States. Discuss their historical background and provide a cultural context for the use of rattles in Hopi music.

    Historically speaking, the Hopi have lived in some of the longest continually occupied villages in North America (Southwest region) and were first visited by European explorers in 1540. The Hopi call themselves "Hopitu"—"peaceful ones." Except for a few periods of confrontation during the Spanish exploration of the Southwest, the Hopi have been a people of peace and spirituality. Known for their Kachina dances, Kachina carvings, jewelry, baskets, and pottery, the contemporary Hopi continue to live on the lands they have occupied for at least a thousand years.

The present-day Hopi reservation is completely surrounded by the large Navajo reservation in northern Arizona.

Rattles are an important part of the Hopi culture. These rattles, made from dried gourds, are decorated with symbols (see figure 6) representing natural phenomena, spirits, or other beings from Hopi traditional stories, or abstract designs. These rattles are used in elaborate dance ceremonies as well as in social songs and dances. Specialized Kachina rattles are made in the likenesses of specific Kachina spirits and use stylized colors, geometric patterns, or stylized physical features. Contemporary musicians of many tribes use the high-quality Hopi-made rattle in their own songs and dances.

2. Organize the class into groups of four (explaining that the number four has special significance to Native Peoples); assign one of the following duties to each group member:

   Reader/Spokesperson: Reads the tasks and materials aloud to the group; speaks for the group as necessary

   Materials Coordinator: Gets the necessary materials for the group

   Secretary: Writes down the ideas and responses that group members agree upon

   Checker/Encourager: Checks to make sure that all group members understand the task, that all group members' ideas are heard, and that all group members agree and can explain why. This person also encourages the group with positive remarks.

3. Explain the criteria for success. The group should be prepared to share its results with the rest of the class after spending three or four minutes on Task 1, and group members should be able to hear and perform rattle-playing techniques for Task 2.[3] Group members should also exhibit knowledge of the social skills they have learned in this lesson (for example, sharing, taking turns, and showing respect for instruments).

   Task 1. Take turns playing the rattle. Listen to other groups' rattles and compare their sound to yours. Examine the rattle with your group and study your list of Indian symbols. Discuss and decide what the symbols on your rattle might mean.

   The Materials Coordinator gets the rattle and list of symbols for the group, the Reader/Spokesperson reads the instructions for Task 1, and the groups complete Task 1. The Reader/Spokesperson for each group shares the group's findings with the class and demonstrates the rattle's sound. This task should be completed within five minutes.

   Comment on the groups' insights and ideas. Explain that one cannot be completely sure of the rattle's meaning unless told by the maker of the rattle. Then provide feedback on the students' mastery of the social skills they were expected to exhibit during this task.

   Task 2. Listen to the way the rattle is played on the recordings; take turns playing along with the recordings.

   The Reader/Spokesperson for each group reads the instructions for Task 2, and each group member plays the rattle with one taped example. Groups listen to each example before joining in (the volume of the recordings must be relatively high to hear above the rattles).

4. Play the "Water Maiden Dance." Ask questions like: Was this music very easy to play along with, or was the rattle pattern tricky? (It's tricky.) Did this sound like traditional or nontraditional Hopi music? (traditional). Share the meaning of the music briefly before playing the next example. Explain that this dance is primarily a winter dance, as the water maidens cause cold weather. It is primarily a traditional social dance song, but, in a way, it is also a prayer. Part of the song translates: "We are going out into the field to get some yellow and blue flowers to put in our hair. We are dancing for the enjoyment and appreciation of the people watching. We are so happy that all the crops are good; that's why we are singing."

5. Play "The Rain Song" (performed by contemporary Navajo singer Sharon Burch) Ask questions like: Did this sound like traditional or contemporary Indian music? (Contemporary—uses guitar and employs other Western techniques). Discuss the similarity of "The Rain Song" and the "Water Maiden Dance." (They are prayers for and celebrations of rain to bring successful crops.) This task should be completed within ten minutes.

6. Ask the Materials Coordinator for each group to return all rattles and materials to proper storage space. Review the lesson, inviting student responses.

This lesson is based on materials provided by Kay Edwards, University of North Carolina–Greensboro.

L E S S O N   4

■ Objectives

Students will:
1. Identify repeated measures and measures that are similar (in rhythm and pitch) and describe differences between selected measures and phrases while listening to the "Dancing Song of the Skunk."
2. Sing "Dancing Song of the Skunk" in Mandan and English.
3. Accompany "Dancing Song of the Skunk" with specified drum and rattle rhythms.
4. Perform a dance to "Dancing Song of the Skunk."

■ Materials

1. "Dancing Song of the Skunk" story, song, and recording from *Maa-baa-hi Ma-hac (We're Going Singing): A Traditional Song Collection of the Mandan and Hidatsa Tribes* by Jane K. Booher (New Town, ND: Fort Berthold Community College, 1992)
2. Several drums (Native American or classroom hand drums) and rattles
3. Map of the United States with the location of the Fort Berthold reservation clearly marked

■ Procedures

1. Locate the reservation on the map of the United States and provide the students with a brief historical background of the Mandan tribe and the cultural context for this lesson.

Dancing Song of the Skunk

Transcribed by Frances Densmore
English by Jane Booher

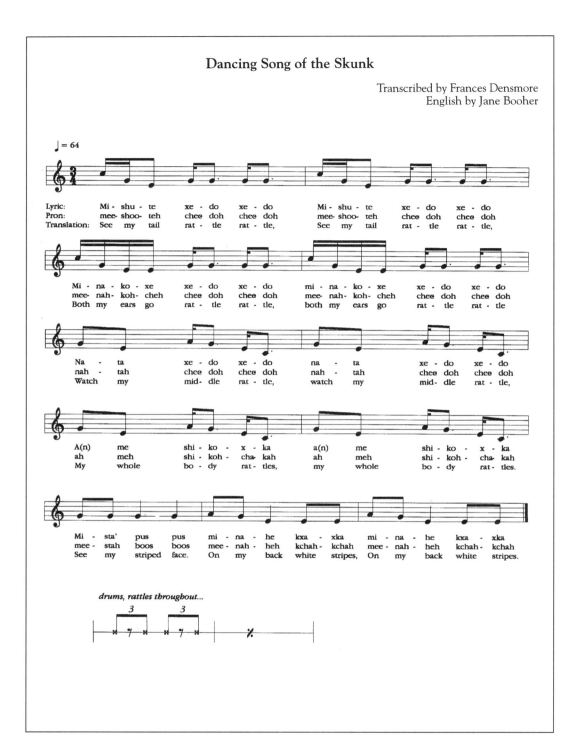

Figure 7. "Dancing Song of the Skunk," copyright 1992 by Fort Berthold Community College. Used by permission.

Mandan	Pronunciation	English Equivalent
mi-shu-te	*mee-shoo-teh*	my tail
xe-do, xe-do	*cheh-DOH, cheh-DOH*	rattles, rattles
mi-na-ko-xe	*mee-NAH-koh-cheh*	my ears
na-ta	*nah-tah*	middle of the body
a-me	*AH-meh*	all of the body
shi-ko-xka	*SHI-ko-cha-kah*	rattles
mi-sta-pus-pus	*MEE-stah BOOS boos*	my face is striped
mi-na-he	*mee-NAH-heh*	my back
kxa-kxa	*KCHAH-kchah*	painted

Figure 8. Mandan pronunciation guide

The historical background is as follows: The first recorded encounter between Euro-American explorers and the Mandan peoples of the northern Plains occurred in 1738. In 1804, Lewis and Clark visited the Mandan, who were living in several villages near the mouth of the Knife River in present-day North Dakota. Subsequent visits by Maximillian and Catlin made the Mandan widely familiar to nineteenth-century Americans. A smallpox outbreak in 1837 almost destroyed the tribe, forcing them into a closer affiliation with the Hidatsa. Today's Mandan live on the Fort Berthold reservation in North Dakota as part of the Three Affiliated Tribes—Mandan, Hidatsa, and Arikira. Fort Berthold Community College is owned and operated by the Three Affiliated Tribes.

The cultural context is as follows: "Dancing Song of the Skunk" is a story-song accompanying the Mandan traditional story "Coyote and the Skunk" (see figure 7). Coyote and Skunk were both very hungry and decided to trick prairie dogs into being their meal. According to the story, Coyote disguised Skunk and instructed him to perform a dance to arouse the curiosity of the prairie dogs. As Coyote sang, Skunk performed his dance and led the prairie dogs over a hill to where Coyote was waiting. Coyote and Skunk then captured and ate several of the prairie dogs. Educators on the Fort Berthold reservation have created a dance to accompany the story and song. Frances Densmore collected the story and song during her research among the tribes in the early twentieth century.

2. Introduce "Dancing Song of the Skunk" through a discussion of the cultural context and a reading of the story "Coyote and Skunk" (in *Maa-baa-hi Ma-hac*, p. 10).

3. Play the recording of "Dancing Song of the Skunk," instructing students to listen for measures in which pitches and rhythms are repeated. Students should also listen for measures that are similar (but not exactly the same) and be able to describe the similarities and differences between them.

4. Discuss "Dancing Song of the Skunk" with the class, asking student volunteers to

identify and describe repeated measures. (Pitches and rhythms are repeated this way: measure 1 = measure 2; measure 3 = measure 4; measure 5 = measure 6 = measure 7 = measure 8; measure 10 = measure 11. Only measure nine is not repeated. Words are repeated this way: measure 1 = measure 2; measure 3 = measure 4; measure 5 = measure 6; measure 7 = measure 8; measure 10 = measure 11. The words to measure nine are the only ones not repeated.) Invite students to describe the melody. For example, how many different pitches are contained in the song? Is the melodic pattern similar to other folk songs? (It's built around the C major chord with "A" added.)

5. Teach the song by phrase and then have students perform it, first in Mandan (following the pronunciation guide in figure 8) and then in English. Several students may be assigned to accompany the singing on drums and rattles.

6. Teach the dance this way:
    a. Students should form a line, holding on to the shoulder of the person in front of them.
    b. While singing "Dancing Song of the Skunk," students should move in a counterclockwise circle, taking one step to each beat.

7. Perform "Dancing Song of the Skunk," assigning students roles as dancers and drummers. Student assignments will rotate with repeated performances of the song.

8. Following several performances, review the historical and cultural background of the Mandan people, the repetition in the music, the comparison of languages, and the use of music in story telling.

    Optional: Create a play based on the story of "Coyote and the Skunk" using song and dance as an integral part of the drama.

    Optional: Have several students perform the melody of the song on recorders. The Mandan people have a strong tradition of playing the Native American flute—a follow-up lesson could feature Native American flute music.

This lesson is based on materials provided by Fort Berthold Community College, New Town, North Dakota.

L E S S O N   5

■ **Objectives**

Students will:

1. Listen to a recording of the "Owl Dance," and then identify and describe changes in the sound and style of the drum beats that accompany the singing.

2. Perform the "Owl Dance" and respond to changes in the sound and style of the drum beats that accompany the singing with specified changes in dance movement and style.

■ **Materials**

1. "Owl Dance" from the recording and booklet *Wapato Indian Club: Traditional Dances and Stories of the Yakima Indian Nation* by Lisa A. Parker

2. Map of the United States with the location of the Yakima reservation clearly marked

■ **Procedures**

1. Locate the reservation on a map of the United States and give the students a brief historical background and cultural context for the Yakima tribe.

   A brief history of the Yakima peoples is as follows: In 1805, Lewis and Clark identified the present-day Yakima under the name Cutsahnim after encountering these people on the lower course of the Yakima River in the Great Basin and Plateau regions. The Yakima called themselves "Waptailmin"—"people of the narrow river"—referring to the narrows of the Yakima River where their principal village was located. The Confederated Tribes and Bands of the Yakima Indian Nation reside on the eastern slopes of the Cascade Range in the Yakima Reservation, with tribal headquarters located in Toppenish, Washington.

   The cultural context is as follows: The "Owl Dance" is a social dance performed at dance ceremonies to encourage social interaction between the tribe's young men and women. It is a "ladies' choice" couples dance. The name comes from the timing of the owl dance in the dance sequence—late at night. The following quote can be found in the booklet: "It was said by one of our elders, 'Well, I guess it's time for the "Owl Dance"—the owls should be out by now.' "

2. Introduce the "Owl Dance" through a discussion of the cultural context of the dance and a description of the music to be heard during the lesson.

3. Play a recording of the "Owl Dance," instructing students to listen for and be able to identify and describe any changes in the drum beats that accompany the singing.

4. Lead the class in a discussion of the "Owl Dance," asking student volunteers to identify and describe the changes they hear in the drum accompaniment. (The drum begins with the drummer striking the drum head. For certain sections of the song, he also strikes the drum's rim. This change of styles alternates throughout the song and is an aural cue for changes in dance movement.)

   Optional: Have a student volunteer demonstrate differences in sound by playing on a classroom drum.

5. Teach the "Owl Dance" this way:

   a. Couples form a large circle. Partners face each other, with boys on the outside of the dance circle. Dancers will be in ballroom dance formation.

   b. As the drum begins, step forward, with the leading leg moving in a counter-clockwise circle; left/right knee (male/female) moves up, and then the other foot slides forward as the knee comes down. Extended hands "pump" in and out to the drum beat, with the hand "in" when the knee is "up."

   c. When the drummer begins playing on the rim, the couples travel around in their own small circles for eight beats. They resume the larger formation movement when the drummer returns to playing on the drum head.

      Optional: Assign several students as drummers to reinforce changes in drum sound.

   After the class has performed the "Owl Dance," review the cultural context of the dance, the changes in the drumming, and how this serves as an aural cue for changes in dance movement.

This lesson is based on materials provided by Sue Rigdon, director of the Wapato Indian Club.

LESSON 6

■ Objectives

Students will:
1. Identify repeated measures and phrases while listening to "Flying Around."
2. Sing "Flying Around" in Cheyenne language (male students may be selected to provide drum accompaniment).
3. Perform a simple hand game while singing "Flying Around."

■ Materials

1. "Flying Around," from the recording accompanying *Southern Cheyenne Women's Songs* by Virginia Giglio (Norman, OK: University of Oklahoma Press, 1994)
2. Two objects to be hidden (marked and unmarked beads or buttons)
3. Scoring sticks approximately twelve inches long (If a student guesses correctly, the stick is given to the guesser's team; if a student guesses incorrectly, the stick is given to the hider's team.)
4. Guessing stick (This is slightly longer than the scoring stick and is often decorated with a bell or feathers on one end.)
5. Hand drum (if the teacher elects to use drum accompaniment)
6. Map of the United States with the location of Cheyenne lands clearly marked

■ Procedures

1. Locate the Cheyenne lands on the map of the United States and provide a brief historical background of the tribe and cultural context for the lesson.

   The historical background is as follows: Cheyenne peoples originally lived a nomadic lifestyle as hunters in the North American Great Plains. Today, the tribe occupies two areas: the Northern Cheyenne live in Montana and the Southern Cheyenne live in western Oklahoma. These lands were assigned to them by the U.S. government in the nineteenth century. The Euro-American quest for gold and farmland caused conflicts among the Cheyenne, miners, and settlers. Tragedies ensued, such as the Sand Creek Massacre, in which nearly two hundred Cheyenne men, women, and children were killed and mutilated by the Colorado militia. Despite these demoralizing and decimating events, the Cheyenne endured. Today, their customs and ceremonies are in revival, and the young people have an increasing interest in upholding the values and beliefs of their elders. Modern Cheyenne enjoy traditional social dances, pow-wows, and games, in which the entire family participates in some way, from the oldest grandparent to the tiniest baby.

   This lesson's cultural context is as follows: Hand game is a centuries-old Plains tribal guessing game. Today, there are intertribal hand game tournaments, with money wagered on team skill and strategy. Among the Cheyenne people, hand game is also a nongambling recreational activity that is easy to play and requires few materials (two beads or buttons, one marked and the other plain; about sixteen scoring sticks, eight red and eight black; and two optional pointing sticks). To play, two teams (the "hiders" and the "guessers") sit in rows facing one another. The "hider" team

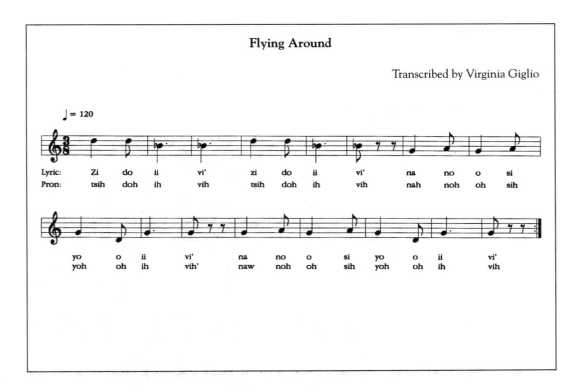

Flying Around

Transcribed by Virginia Giglio

♩ = 120

| Lyric: | Zi | do | ii | vi' | zi | do | ii | vi' | na | no | o | si |
| Pron: | tsih | doh | ih | vih | tsih | doh | ih | vih | nah | noh | oh | sih |

| | yo | o | ii | vi' | na | no | o | si | yo | o | ii | vi' |
| | yoh | oh | ih | vih' | naw | noh | oh | sih | yoh | oh | ih | vih |

Figure 9. "Flying Around," from *Southern Cheyenne Women's Songs* by Virginia Giglio. Copyright 1994 by the University of Oklahoma Press. Used by permission.

Cheyenne	Approximate Pronunciation	Translation
zi do	*tsih doh*	this one
ii vi'	**ih vih'*	flying around
na	*nah*	this thing (I'm hiding)
no o si yo	*noh oh sih yoh*	hand game

* The first syllable ("ii") is like the "i" in "pit" but is drawn out longer. The mark after "vi" (') indicates a glottal stop, equivalent to the stop one makes between the syllables of "uh-oh."

Figure 10. Cheyenne pronunciation guide

captain chooses someone to conceal a button in each hand, and the "guesser" team captain chooses one person to guess for the team. The whole group sings a song while the "hider" swings his or her hands in time to the music. When ready, the "guesser" points a stick (or his or her thumb) in the direction of the hand believed to hold the marked bead. The "hider" then shows the beads. If the guess is correct, the scorekeeper removes a stick from the "hiding" team's row of scoring sticks. The "hiders" then surrender their buttons to the other team, who become the new "hiders." If the guess is incorrect, the "hiders" keep the buttons until they are lost to a correct guess; each wrong guess means the loss of a "guesser" team's stick. All players sing continually during the game, and the men on the "hiding" team play hand-held drums. Women often put pebbles inside colorfully fringed and decorated soda cans and use them as shakers. A losing team might pay a forfeit, such as providing food for the next game meeting or performing a dance for everyone's enjoyment.

2. Play "Flying Around," instructing students to listen for repeated melodic phrases and lyrics (see figure 9). Tell students the functional translation of the song:

> This one's flying around,
> This one's flying around,
> This hand game thing, this hiding thing, is flying around!
> This hand game thing, this hiding thing, is flying around!

3. Discuss "Flying Around" with your students, inviting them to identify and describe repeated melodic phrases and lyrics (measures 1–3 = measures 4–6; measures 7–11 = measures 12–16).
4. Teach the song by phrases (see figure 10). If desired, have several male students accompany the song on hand drums.
5. Divide the class into two teams for the hand game. Distribute scoring sticks; teach the hand game.
6. Play the hand game while the song is being performed.
7. Following several repetitions of the song, review historical background, cultural context, repeated patterns, and hand game procedures.

This lesson is based on materials provided by Virginia Giglio of Wesleyan University.

NOTES

1. This recording is not yet available commercially but can be obtained from the composer at PO Box 333, Tempe, AZ 85280.
2. Some major distributors of Native-made instruments include Canyon Records and Indian Arts (4143 North 16th Street, Phoenix, AZ 85016), the Taos Drum Company (PO Box 1916, Taos, NM 87571), and Indian Pueblo Cultural Center (2401 12th Street NW, Albuquerque, NM 87102), All One Tribe (PO Drawer N, Taos, NM 87771), NA Enterprises (1706 Pamela Circle, Norman, OK 73071).
3. Hopi rattles are available from Canyon Records, 4143 North 16th Street, Phoenix, AZ 85016; Heard Museum Gift Shop, 22 East Monte Vista, Phoenix, AZ 85004; and the Hopi Cultural Center, PO Box 123, Kykotsumovi, AZ 86039.

BIBLIOGRAPHY

Ballard, Louis W. *American Indian Music for the Classroom.* 2d ed. Santa Fe, NM: New Southwest Music Publications, 1996. This is an updated version of Ballard's classic work previously published by Canyon Records and Indian Arts. It contains traditional songs with appropriate activities for classroom teaching. A recording is included.

Booher, Jane K. *Maa-baa-hi Ma-hac (We're Going Singing): A Traditional Collection of the Mandan and Hidatsa Tribes.* New Town, ND: Fort Berthold Community College, 1992. (This is available from Fort Berthold Community College, PO Box 490, New Town, ND 58767.) This book contains fifteen traditional Mandan and Hidatsa songs originally collected by Frances Densmore and adapted for use in elementary and middle school music classes by a teacher working on the Fort Berthold reservation. The accompanying recording features children from the tribal schools.

Burton, J. Bryan. *Moving within the Circle: Contemporary Native American Music and Dance.* Danbury, CT: World Music Press, 1993. These are twenty-four social songs and dances, flute songs, and guided listening experiences as well as instructions for making instruments. The book also includes background information on culture and several traditional stories. The accompanying recording features musicians from many tribes.

Burton, J. Bryan, Chesley Wilson, and Ruth Wilson. *When the Earth Was Like New: Western Apache Songs and Stories.* Danbury, CT: World Music Press, 1994. This book contains songs and selections for Apache flute and Apache violin from the repertoire of Chesley Goseyun Wilson, great-great grandson of Cochise and the latest in a line of distinguished instrument makers and singers. The accompanying recording features all music in text as performed by Chesley Wilson.

Curtis, Natalie. *The Indians' Book.* New York: Dover Publications, 1987. This book contains stories, songs, and artwork collected in the early twentieth century from the tribal elders of many tribes. Contributors include the noted leaders Short Bull and Geronimo.

DeCesare, Ruth. *Myth, Music, and Dance of the North American Indians.* Van Nuys, CA: Alfred Publishing Company, Inc., 1988. This is a collection of songs and lessons adapted for use in elementary music classrooms. It includes instrument-making instructions and a pronunciation guide. Student text and songbook are available separately, and recordings of all songs are available separately.

Densmore, Frances. *Chippewa Music, Volumes 1 and 2.* Washington, DC: Bureau of American Ethnology, 1910 and 1913. These volumes are known as Bulletins 45 and 53 of the Bureau of American Ethnology.

Densmore, Frances. *Teton Sioux Music and Culture.* Lincoln, NE: University of Nebraska Press, 1992. This publication was originally published in 1919 as Bulletin 61 of the Bureau of American Ethnology.

Giglio, Virginia. *Southern Cheyenne Women's Songs.* Norman, OK: University of Oklahoma Press, 1994. This book contains songs, dances, and cultural background information gathered from contemporary Cheyenne families. It also provides a comparison of traditional literature of interest to ethnomusicologists and children's songs and game songs of interest to the classroom teacher. A companion recording is available separately.

Heth, Charlotte, ed. *Native American Dance: Ceremonies and Social Traditions.* Washington, D.C.: Smithsonian Books, 1992. This is a beautifully told series of essays covering specific music and dance traditions from four cultures. It's told by members of the culture.

Laubin, Reginald, and Gladys Laubin. *Indian Dances of North America.* Norman, OK: University of Oklahoma Press, 1977. This is a classic work on Native American dance written by dancer Reginald Laubin. It contains descriptions of dances, cultural background information, and numerous photographs, but no notated songs.

McAllester, David P. "North American Native Music." In *Music of Many Cultures,* edited by Elizabeth May. New York: Schirmer Books, 1992. This is a scholarly overview of Native American music with particular emphasis on the southwestern United States.

McAllester, David P., and Edwin Schupman. "Teaching the Music of the American Indian." In *Teaching Music with a Multicultural Approach*, edited by William M. Anderson. Reston, VA: Music Educators National Conference, 1991. This book contains lectures and demonstrations presented as part of the 1990 MENC Symposium on Multicultural Approaches to Music Education in Washington, D.C.

Parker, Lisa A. *Wapato Indian Club: Traditional Dances and Stories of the Yakama Indian Nation*. Wapato, WA: Wapato Indian Club, 1994. This is a collection of nine songs and dances performed by the Wapato Indian Club at the 1994 World Conference of the International Society for Music Education. The accompanying tape features tribal elders. Available from the Wapato Indian Club, PO Box 38, Wapato, WA 98953.

Tiller, Veronica. *Discovering Indian Reservations*. Denver, CO: Council Publication, 1992. This state-by-state reference guide lists Native-owned or Native-related businesses, reservations, and museums. It also contains a listing of major cultural events.

Turtle, Eagle Walking. *Indian America*. Santa Fe, NM: John Muir Publications, 1991. This state-by-state reference guide lists Native-owned or Native-related businesses, reservations, and museums. It also contains a listing of major cultural events.

DISCOGRAPHY

Basin and Plateau/California
ISHI: *The Last Yahi*. This was recorded from 1911–1914. Wild Sanctuary.
Songs of Love, Luck, Animals, and Magic. Nightwork NW 297.
Songs of the Paiute, Washoe, Ute, Bannock, Shoshone. Library of Congress LC 38.
Starting Over (Yampaciki Singers). Sounds of America Records SOAR 155. Available from Sounds of America Records, PO Box 8207, Albuquerque, NM 87198.
Utes—War, Bear, and Sun Dance Songs. Canyon Records CR 6113.

Contemporary
Circle. Performed and produced by Keith Secola. Available from Akina Productions, PO Box 1595, Tempe, AZ 85280. This is a country music recording.
Creations Journey. Smithsonian Folkways SF 40410. This is a musical anthology of contemporary pieces.
Dreaming in Color. Performed by Songcatcher. A & M Records 31454-0247-2. Songcatcher, a Seattle band, combines traditional sounds, topics, and languages with a bit of grunge and a little jazz.
Heartbeat: Voices of First Nation's Women. Smithsonian Folkways SF CD40415. This is a collection of women's songs.
Old Time Chicken Scratch. Performed by the Gu Achi Fiddlers. Canyon Records CR 8092. This is a "chicken scratch" music recording.
Plight of the Redman. Performed by Tom Bee & XIT. Sounds of America Records SOAR 101-CD. Available from Sounds of America Records, PO Box 8207, Albuquerque, NM 87198. This is a rock music recording.
Makoce Wakan. Performed by Red Thunder. Eagle Thunder Records 3-7916-2-H1. c/o Koch Intertribal, 2 Tri-Harbor Court, Port Washington, NY 11050. This is a rock music recording.
Spirit Horses. Performed by Nakai and DeMars. Canyon Records CR 7014. This is an orchestral music recording.
Southern Scratch, Volume 1. Canyon Records CR 8093. This is a waila, or "chicken scratch," music recording.
Yazzie Girl. Performed by Sharon Burch. Canyon Records CR 534. This is a folk rock music recording.

Weavings. Performed by Nakai and Jackalope. Canyon Records CR 7002. This is a jazz-fusion music recording.

Eastern

Ceremonial Songs and Dances of the Cherokee, Volumes 1 and 2. Indian Sounds Recordings IS 9001, 9002. Available from Indian Sounds Recordings, PO Box 6038, Moore, OK 73153.

Contemporary Micmac Songs. Performed by Sarah "Flower" Michael. Sunshine Records Limited SSCT 4163. Available from Sunshine Records Limited, 275 Selkirk Ave., Winnipeg, Manitoba, R2W 2L5 Canada.

Honoring the Ancient Ones. Performed by the Arawak Mountain Singers. Sounds of America Records SOAR 154. Available from Sounds of America Records, PO Box 8207, Albuquerque, NM 87198.

Iroquois Social Dance Songs, Volume 1. Iroqrafts 001. Available from Iroqrafts, Oshweken, Ontario, NOA 1 MO Canada.

Micmac Songs. Performed by Free Spirit. Sunshine Records Limited SSCT 4093. Available from Sunshine Records Limited, 275 Selkirk Ave., Winnipeg, Manitoba, R2W 2L5 Canada.

Red Thundercloud. Performed by the Catawba tribe. Hilljoy Records. This is the only recording of this tribe in existence.

Seneca Social Dance Music. Folkways Ethnic FE 4072.

Native American Flute

Buffalo Spirit. Performed by Fernando Cellicion. Indian Sounds Recordings IS 5062. Available from Indian Sounds Recordings, PO Box 6038, Moore, OK 73153.

Canyon Trilogy. Performed by R. Carlos Nakai. Canyon Records CR 610.

Dreamcatcher. Performed by Kevin Locke. Earth Beat Records EB 2995.

Dreams from the Grandfathers. Performed by Robert Tree Cody. Canyon Records CR 554.

Songs of the American Indian Flute, Volumes 1 and 2. Performed by John Ranier, Jr. Red Willow Songs.

Traditional and Contemporary Indian Flute. Performed by Tom Ware. Indian Sounds Recordings IS 5050. Available from Indian Sounds Recordings, PO Box 6038, Moore, OK 73153.

Northern Plains

Crow Grass Dance and Owl Dance. Sound Chief SC 116. Available from Indian House Records, PO Box 472, Taos, NM 87571.

Intertribal Powwow Songs. Performed by Kicking Women Singers. Canyon Records CR 6178.

Mandan-Hidatsa Songs. Performed by the Mandaree Singers. Canyon Records CR 6114.

Plains Chippewa/Metis Music from Turtle Mountain. Smithsonian Folkways SF 40411. This recording also includes fiddle tunes of French and Scottish origins and folk songs of French origin.

Rabbit Songs of the Lakota, Volume 5. Performed by Porcupine Singers. Canyon Records CR 6191.

Northwest Coast and Alaska

Chemiwci Singers. Performed by the Chemiwci Indian School of Salem, OR. Canyon Records CR 6121.

Indian Music of the Pacific Northwest. Folkways Ethnic FE 4523.

Songs and Stories of the Yup'ik Eskimo. Performed by Drums across the Tundra. Wild Sanctuary.

Songs of the Warm Springs Reservation. Canyon Records CR 6123.

Stick Game Songs. Performed by Joe Washington Lummi. Canyon Records CR 6124.

Southern Plains

Hand Game of the Kiowa, Kiowa-Apache, and Comanche, Volumes 1 and 2. Indian House Records IH 2501 and IH 2502. Available from Indian House Records, PO Box 472, Taos, NM 87571.

These Plains hand game songs were recorded on location at a tournament between the "Road Runners" and "Billy Goat Hill" hand game teams.

Intertribal Songs of Oklahoma. Performed by Southern Thunder. Indian House Records IH 2081. Available from Indian House Records, PO Box 472, Taos, NM 87571.

Kiowa Gourd Dance, Volume 1. Indian House Records IH 2503. Available from Indian House Records, PO Box 472, Taos, NM 87571.

Round Dance Songs with English Lyrics. Performed by Ware/Moore. Indian Sounds Recordings IS 1004. Available from Indian Sounds Recordings, PO Box 6038, Moore, OK 73153.

Songs of the Comanche, Cheyenne, Kiowa, Caddo, Wichita, Pawnee. Library of Congress LC 39.

Southwest

Hopi Social Dance Songs, Volume 2. Canyon Records CR 6108.

Music from Zuni Pueblo. Performed by Chester Mahooty. Tribal Music International TMI 008. Available from Tribal Music International, 449 Juan Tomás, Tijeras, NM 87059.

Music of New Mexico: Native American Traditions. Smithsonian Folkways SF 40408.

Navajo Social Dance Songs. Performed by the Turtle Mountain Singers. Indian House Records IH 1523. Available from Indian House Records, PO Box 472, Taos, NM 87571.

Round Dance Songs or Taos Pueblo, Volume 1. Indian House Records IH 1001. Available from Indian House Records, PO Box 472, Taos, NM 87571.

Songs of the White Mountain Apache. Canyon Records CR 6165.

Yaqui Ritual and Festive Music. Canyon Records CR 6190.

Editor's Note: All recordings are available from Canyon Records and Indian Arts, 4143 North 16th Street, Phoenix, AZ 85016; telephone: 602-266-4823.

FILMOGRAPHY

American Indian Dance Theatre: Dances for the New Generations. 1993. Available from PDR Productions, 219 East 44th Street, New York, NY 10017. This video contains songs and dances from the northwest coast, New England, New York, Oklahoma, and the Great Plains. Not only does this video show performances by the American Indian Dance Theatre, it also shows members of the troupe learning the dances from tribal leaders around the country.

American Indian Dance Theatre: Finding the Circle. 1989. Produced by WNET/Thirteen, Maryland Public Television. Available through PDR Productions, 219 East 44th Street, New York, NY 10017. This is a performance by the American Indian Dance Theatre for the Great Performances public television special. Narration provides the cultural background for each dance. Many tribes are represented from across the United States, and the video shows pow-wows and intertribal songs and dances.

Entering the Circle. 1994. Available from American Orff-Schulwerk Association, PO Box 391089, Cleveland, OH 44139. This is a videotape of a session presented at the 1994 AOSA Conference by J. Bryan Burton. This video contains demonstrations of several dances, an overview of cultural contexts, and a display of representative instruments.

Into the Circle: An Introduction into Oklahoma Pow-wows and Celebrations. Available from Canyon Records, 4143 North 16th Street, Phoenix, AZ 85016. This video describes and gives background information on the pow-wow traditions in Oklahoma. A number of dances are shown in actual performance situations.

The Native Americans. 1994. Available from Turner Home Entertainment, One CNN Center, Atlanta, GA 30303. This well-documented and well-produced series is based on the book of the same name. Tribal elders, musicians, and historians provide insights and performances including stories, songs, and dances. There are six volumes in this series; each focuses on a specific region: 3214 *The Nations of the Northeast;* 3215 *The Tribal People of the Northwest;* 3216 *The*

Tribes of the Southeast; 3217 *The Natives of the Southwest;* 3218 *The People of the Great Plains, Part One;* and 3219 *The People of the Great Plains, Part Two.*

Songs of Indian Territory: Native American Musical Traditions of Oklahoma. Available from Canyon Records, 4143 North 16th Street, Phoenix, AZ. Songs and dances are described and shown on film. A number of tribes from Oklahoma are portrayed.

Teaching the Music of the American Indian. 1990. Available from Music Educators National Conference, 1806 Robert Fulton Drive, Reston, VA 22091. This video features highlights of the American Indian portion of the MENC 1990 Conference on Multicultural Music. David McAllester, Edwin Shupman, and Native American musicians and dancers are featured.

Thunder in the Dells. 1992. Produced for the Wisconsin Winnebago people showing their history and culture. Several songs and dances are presented as part of the narrative. Available from Ootek Productions, S12229 Round River Trail, Spring Green, WI 53588.

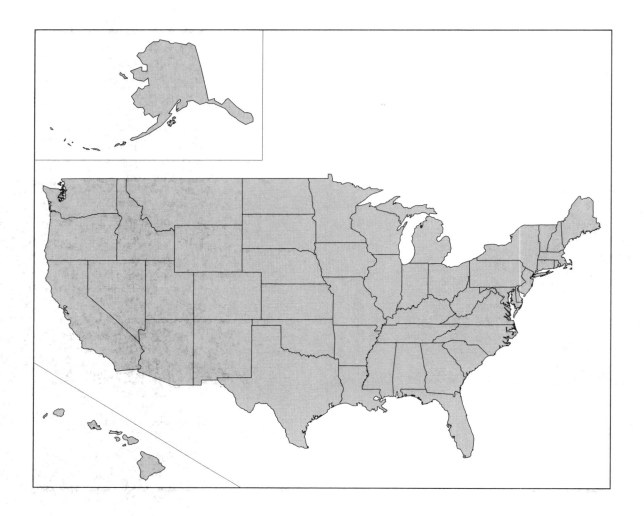

Map of the United States

AFRICAN AMERICAN MUSIC

by James A. Standifer and Linda Miller Walker

The music of African Americans, rich in variety and yet representing a unique tradition, has had considerable influence on contemporary music. It is not inappropriate to speak of the melody, rhythm, texture, form, and timbre of African American music in the ways in which we describe American music in general. There are, however, significant differences in the elements and structure of this music that are largely derived from the contributions of the African heritage of African Americans. This heritage has indelibly shaped African Americans' musical behavior and has produced a unique American music.

African American music is set apart from other American musics because of the African American history of slavery and the countless strictures imposed by that system. This period caused the people to develop new ways to express their reactions to what was going on in their lives. African forms of music were once prohibited among slaves, so the slaves were encouraged to practice a new music that blended the sounds of their homeland with the styles practiced by their colonial masters.

An especially important concept of African American music is its rhythm. The

African influence in African American music is shown in the rhythmic hand clapping, "hot" rhythms, and the use of strong metric and polymetric effects. To truly experience and understand the nuances of the music, both the listener and performer must become involved in the music's rhythm. By singing, providing body percussion sounds, and moving and dancing, the essence of African American music begins to emerge.

It is difficult to listen to the music of African Americans without wanting to move in response to its infectious rhythms. Dance, movement, and music-related activities such as hand clapping, feet stamping, and the chanting of speech patterns (known as rapping) are important for a clear understanding of African American music. This kinetic sense permeates all African American folk music traditions, and it is an integral part of customs associated with work, worship, and entertainment.

As in African culture, African American music allows ample opportunity for improvisation. Much reciprocity exists between dance and music, because the music will often shape a dance and, in turn, a dance will often shape the music. In the church, for example, religious fervor will often determine the movements of the worshipers, just as their movements will often influence the power and dynamics of the service.

In the African tradition, dance- and music-related movements are often functional. They are done for specific reasons, perhaps to honor a birth or celebrate a successful hunt or harvest. In the African American culture, these functions are replaced by more contemporary ones of a social or religious nature. Black dance, for example, often mixes the sacred with the profane. Dance is a part of the practices of certain fundamentalist religious groups, and dance movements are created by youngsters on the playground and elsewhere in response to contemporary popular music. Rhythm games played by African American children are derived from the Black musical tradition. Melodies, phrases, and lyrics of these games encourage physical movement of limbs and torso. One may see children engaged in such rhythmic activities during recess or after school, while jumping rope or simply playing on the sidewalk. The older layer of dance movements and the musical characteristics of those movements, however, remain alive.

An awareness of African American music in its various forms is critical to understanding and appreciating the development of the African American culture in the last few centuries. An active and physical involvement in these traditions will provide dividends unavailable through any other approach.

For at least the last two centuries, there have been two dominant musical traditions in America: the musical traditions or aesthetic of white people of the Western world and the musical traditions of black people transplanted to the New World. The major arts institutions in America were founded on a European approach to the arts, in which the primary concerns are more reflective than immediate. The traditional music performed in American concert halls and the exhibitions displayed in American museums often celebrate the creative talents of European creators. African American arts traditions more often than not focus on immediacy and a "nowness" of this time and this country.

African American music, at least that most closely associated with folk music traditions, is seldom divorced from everyday life. Generally, performing groups are large and often broken up into sections (for example, a percussion section, a melodic instrument and choral section, and dancers, with physical movement by all those involved). The audience and onlookers constitute a significant and complementary part of the music performance. They are not passive receivers but active participants who involve themselves as singers, hand clappers, or voluntary dancers. In short, the musical behavior of African

Americans is similar to that of their African ancestors; it is an extension of the activity of their daily lives. It may also, however, be similar to that of their European ancestors. This is especially true of their behavior in concert audiences. The tradition of this behavior is ostensibly passive, more reflective than immediate, and more interpretive than creative.

Before slavery was abolished in the United States and for a short time thereafter, communal gatherings, such as the "praise meetings" that took place in slave quarters, were the only organized forms of musical expression. Although that has changed, these gatherings continue to function as the wellspring of African American musical behavior. Throughout African American history, the church and praise meetings have been the environments in which most of the musical behaviors of African American people were born and nurtured. Religious expression and African American musical behavior almost from the start were one and the same; both manifested themselves in the experience of singing and in the behavior of being "hit by the spirit." This behavior consisted of shouting, dancing, arm-waving, screaming and hollering, swaying back and forth, moaning, fainting, and so on. It began in African musical behavior and existed in clandestine slave gatherings. As African Americans were converted to Protestant sects such as the Baptist and Methodist churches, these behaviors were integrated into the worship services.

This behavior and this music result from a fusion of the African and American experiences. It is generally agreed that the hymns of Dr. Watts and the a cappella moaning style typical of these hymn arrangements (for example, the hymns "Amazing Grace" and "Must Jesus Bear the Cross Alone?") are evidence of this fusion. These hymns were highly favored by the slaves and were probably the first hymns sung by them in the New World. These rugged eighteenth-century English hymns were altered by the African Americans, and a style of song emerged that has various names: surge-singing, lining-out, long meter, or "Dr. Watts style." In this style, a leader recites a line of text, followed by the congregation singing the same line of text in a slow, deliberate style. This manner of presentation permits intricate embellishment and improvisations on the basic tune by both leader and congregation as well as much sliding among the basic tones.

These hymns motivate the participants to "get happy." Thus, the style of singing, the text, and the emerging sounds have produced unique musical behaviors that truly represent African Americans. These musical behaviors include making a melodic idea and then reshaping that idea melodically or rhythmically, making the music reflect a feeling or mood by "bending" the tones so that they imitate sounds of man or nature. Alternately, performers will sometimes take a vocal sound and recreate it to sound instrumental (or vice versa).

African American music in this sense is inextricably tied to a belief that the concern of the aesthetic being is to reflect or emulate reality. But African American music is also an escape from involvement in the complexities of reality. It is important to understand that African American music and deeply felt responses to it are the accomplishment and, most significant, the *operation* of creating. The *process* is immensely more important than the result. One African American music scholar, Jimmy Stewart, put it succinctly when he said:

> What results there from (the operation of creating) is merely momentary residue of that operation—a perishable object and nothing more, and anything else you might imbue it with (which white aesthetic purports to do) is nothing else but mummification. The point is—and this is the crux of our opposing conception of being—that the imperishability of creation is not in what is created, is not in the art product, is not in the "thing" as it exists as an object, but in the procedure of its becoming what it is.[1]

Finally, there is the question of perceptual experience among cultures. It is erroneous to assume, because the African American and European American cultures are so integrally related in experiences and are interchanged so easily by individuals because of their use of similar musical elements, processes, and structures, that similar connotations or associations are evoked in musical encounters within each culture. Similar concepts may be characterized differently in different cultures or even within a single culture, not because association is inconstant, but because the concept is viewed in different ways. Also, each individual ethnic group and even each individual is apt to bring to that experience different "cultural baggage"—that is, different cultural backgrounds and experiences.

The African American existence "between the traditions" of the European American and the African cultures permits the establishment of a kind of sonic flexibility in the mind and ear. This, in turn, makes possible more efficient moves to other, more specific music styles and behavior such as blues, ragtime, rap, rhythm and blues, and jazz. Using tonal memory has always been crucial to the musical behavior among black people, and they have used it in highly successful ways in their attempts to accommodate the scales, modes, harmonic progressions, and other distinctive elements of the two dominant musical traditions of America. These elements do not remain constant from culture to culture. What does remain constant is the way the mind, operating in the context of a culturally established grammar, selects, organizes, evaluates, and perhaps reinterprets the musical materials presented to it.

One may generalize that some of the selection and use of music elements by African Americans are due, in large part, to the long historical consequence of the way slavery was practiced in America and the ensuing introduction of the slaves into the enslaving society. These selections of elements, the forms such environmental factors have engendered (including almost all the well-known forms of African American music), and the seemingly uninhibited responses to the dynamic processes of these musics may be directly traceable to the general mode of musical behavior among Africans. This mode is a highly active, improvisatory, and provocative involvement in musical activities and a refusal to differentiate these activities from the realities of everyday life.

General characteristics

African American music has its roots in Africa, especially West Africa. The early history of Africa is replete with slave trade activity. Countless Africans were captured and shipped to America (among other places). Those blacks who survived the long, arduous voyage were the ancestors of present-day African Americans.

Music, music-related behaviors, and other life patterns were the only cultural traditions the Africans brought with them. But in the slave camps, these traditions were often practiced under fearful and tragic circumstances. Musicologist Eileen Southern has reported:

> A...common practice was to force slaves to sing and under the most tragic circumstances. On the slave ships loaded with human cargo, captured Africans were frequently made to dance and sing during their "airings" on deck, the reluctant ones among them being stimulated by the sting of the whip. In the slave pens of the States, slaves were often forced to sing and dance prior to being put up for sale on the auction block.[2]

These circumstances and similar ones inspired countless African American musicians to create music that is currently treasured the world over. There were, however, times of play and entertainment in the slave camps, and many equally creative recreational styles of African American music developed during this time.

Some of the most obvious characteristics of African American song can be loosely categorized in six topic areas. First, African American music has been directly influenced by the tonal languages of West Africa in its deliberate and direct use of various pitch inflections and gestures to communicate a wide range of emotions and experiences. Second, African American musicians commonly use African vocal techniques in which the musician functions as a storyteller and communicator either verbally (as exemplified by contemporary "rap") or with vocables and instrumental sounds ("scat," using the voice to imitate instrumental sounds). Third, musicians use instrumental sounds to imitate the human voice or to provide reciprocal imitation with singers. Fourth, musicians often use African scales or melodic resources such as the tonal alterations and patterns of blues scales. A fifth African musical characteristic prevalent in the music of African Americans is polyrhythmic layering of rhythmic patterns and the preponderance of syncopation. Finally, African American musicians characteristically use improvisation as an important means of truly individualizing the total musical experience.

There are many vocal and instrumental performance traditions among African Americans. African American musicians perform in a variety of styles and produce sounds that are oriented toward the Western classical tradition. Other traditions exist, such as those in the Caribbean or Brazil, that show a significant African influence. Few African influences are found in other forms of American folk music traditions. This gives African American traditional music a unique place in American music—indeed, in world music.

When listening to African American music and observing the ways in which it is performed by African Americans, one can easily see that the slave in early American history was successful in adapting many of the major European musical characteristics in a process of assimilation that continues to the present day. These European characteristics include tonal language practices: the tendency toward regularity of pitch in the diatonic scale and aspects of the European melodic ideal, such as correctness of pitch, purity of tone, and the emphasis on the finality of melodies that have easily grasped melodic and structural devices. The most important characteristic may be the European "sound phenomenon": the method of creating and making music. The slaves were plunged into a musical environment that negated their musical history, but, as eminently musical people, they adapted to this environment. Their solution was to use what was appropriate for their musical ideal and to adapt those aspects of European music that were not. Although forbidden to use their own unique way of making music, they made similar changes in the process of music making as well. The result is African American music.

Melody

The use of "blue notes" is a common melodic trait that probably results from the blending of African and European cultures. The term "blue note" refers to altering the third and seventh degrees of the scale by slurring, sliding, swooping, groaning, moaning, and shaking. The blue tonality is the result of a partially flatted third or seventh. This may be an attempt to produce a tone foreign to the Western tonal system and possibly unique to the African tonal system as well as an avenue for the use, in a Western harmonic context, of the expressive characteristics of the tonal languages of Africa.

Pentatonic scales provide the pitches for many folk songs and children's songs. African Americans frequently use gapped scales as well, in which the melody in an otherwise major scale may be lacking the fourth or seventh degree; this may result in a hexatonic (six-pitch) scale. The intervallic structure of African American melodies varies, with frequent use of seconds, thirds, fourths, fifths, and sixths. Most spirituals are in the minor mode; the sixth and seventh tones may be raised.

Melodic ornamentation is a common stylistic device; syllabic song has little place in African American music. The more melismatic songs often use turns and the sliding and bending of pitches.

Rhythm

The distinctive features of African American rhythm are the syncopation, compound meter, accents on the second and fourth beats (as in gospels and rags), and anticipated beats that "beat the barline" by sounding slightly in advance of the regular pulse; the percussive style of performance practice that maintains the rhythmic pulse; the layering of several rhythmic patterns simultaneously; and the continuous rhythms. These ostinatos often exist in several layers that form a resultant sound that is quite different from the individual parts. The energy of the music is caught up in its rhythm and in its pulse.

Texture

In traditional African American music, a type of polyphony frequently results from the concurrent singing of the melody and the different rhythms of the hand-clapping that serve as accompaniment. The interplay between voices and instruments also provides interesting examples of counterpoint. Some vocal styles, including gospel, are set for a lead voice and a homophonic four-part ensemble. The texture of jazz as performed by African Americans ranges from heterophonic to polyphonic to melody with block-chord homophonic accompaniments.

Form

Perhaps the best-known formal structure of African American music is the African-derived call-and-response form. The interplay between a solo and group, vocally or instrumentally, often parallels question-and-answer structure. The lead musician is allowed, however, to use his or her voice to produce the unique and characteristic sounds that integrate speech, recitation, chant, and song and that are so prized in African American culture. Slurs, slides, and even shrill hollers are sometimes featured, and the responding group may even chant a refrain instead of singing. In call-and-response form, the leader's part will often overlap with the response part, producing an overlay of beginnings and endings with the group. This is especially true in the lining-out form of religious songs, which is still performed today in certain denominations such as the African Methodist Episcopal Church and the Black Baptist Church. Organ or piano music usually accompany gospel singing.

Vocal interjections are often used in African American vocal music, particularly in religious songs. For example, "Oh, Lord," "Sing it, children," or "Hallelujah" interjections can be melodic or rhythmic, and they occur spontaneously as the spirit or the impact of the music's content moves the individual.

Timbre

African American musicians have found a wide range of sound qualities in their voices and in their adaptation of European instruments. Their unique vocal techniques include nasal sounds, falsetto, shouting, and guttural tones (such as moaning and groaning, raspy tones, and a throaty quality). These techniques are considerably different from the norm of European folk and art musics.

The creative essence of African American music is its spontaneous variation. This music is thus an avenue to a very important goal of music education: the nurturing of creative musical expression. Teachers can help reinforce uniqueness of African American musical style by guiding students to sing a selected song as it is notated and to improvise on it. In doing so, the salient characteristics of the African American musical style may emerge through (1) the addition of melodic ornamentation, including slurs, slides, and bends, (2) accompaniment with hand-clapping patterns, (3) the use of vocal interjections, and (4) improvisations. Through performance will come an understanding of the elements that constitute the music of African Americans.

NOTES

1. Jimmy Stewart, "Introduction to Black Aesthetics in Music," in *The Black Aesthetic*, ed. Addison Gayle Jr. (Garden City, NY: Doubleday, 1971), 84.
2. Eileen Southern, from a presentation at the University of Michigan School of Music Musicology Conference in Ann Arbor, November 1984.

L E S S O N   1

■ Objectives

Students will:
1. Perform movements to an African American singing game with teacher assistance.
2. Demonstrate steady beat by imitating a leader.

■ Materials

1. "Sally Walker"
2. Medium-sized basketball or soccer ball

■ Procedures

1. Define beat as a steady, even pulse. Demonstrate "steady" by bouncing a ball on four even counts (bounce-catch, bounce-catch, bounce-catch, bounce-catch). Demonstrate "unsteady" by bouncing the ball one time and allowing it to stop on its own.
2. Relate steady beat in music to the heartbeat. Have the children feel and listen to their heartbeat to determine that it is steady.
3. Have the class form a circle and clap a steady beat with you. Sit in a squatting position in the center, sing "Sally Walker" (see figure 1), and clap the beat for students to imitate.
4. Teach the song by rote. When the students are able to clap a steady beat successfully

Sally Walker

Arranged and transcribed
by Emma Brooks-Baham

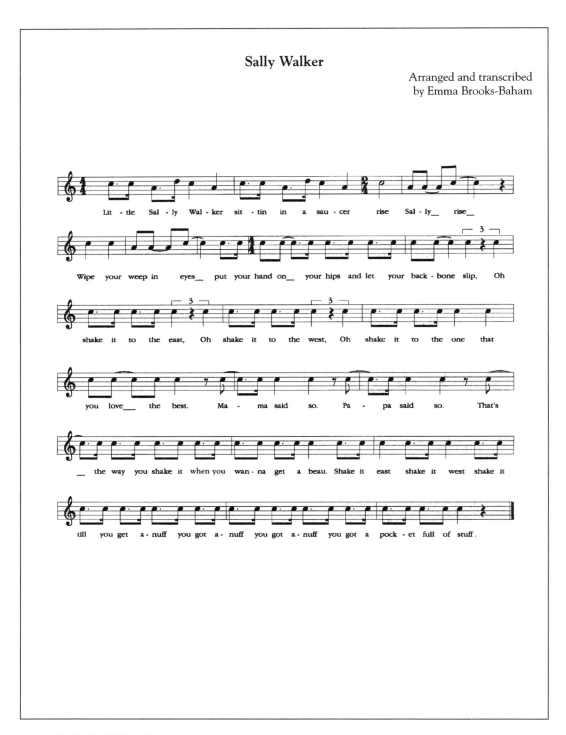

Figure 1. "Sally Walker"

while singing, choose one student to sit in a squatting position in the circle.

5. Have children hold hands, sing the song, and walk clockwise around the player who is squatting in the circle. On the words "Rise, Sally, rise," the center player should stand and dramatize words using motions to the beat. (The center player may do motions to the fast or slow beat.) Players in the circle will drop hands and imitate the center player's movements.
6. When the song ends, have the center player select another student from the circle to be "it."
7. Review steady beat and how it was used in the singing game.
8. Compare this song to other versions of it. See, for example, Peter Erdei and Katalin Komlos, *150 American Folk Songs to Sing, Read, and Play* (New York: Boosey and Hawkes, 1974).

LESSON 2

■ Objectives

Students will:
1. With teacher assistance, sing "He's Got the Whole World in His Hands" using proper phrasing.
2. Clap on beats 2 and 4 while singing the entire song.
3. Verbally identify the number of phrases in the song.

■ Materials

1. "He's Got the Whole World in His Hands"

■ Procedures

1. Tell the class that "He's Got the Whole World in His Hands" (see figure 2) is a spiritual. A spiritual is an African American folk song that has been handed down from generation to generation. The spiritual is also religious and expresses many emotions.
2. Teach the song by rote and model the appropriate place to breathe (after each phrase). Have the children sing one phrase at a time, after you. Remind the class that a "phrase" is a sentence in music.
3. Ask children how many phrases they sang (four). Put the four phrases together by singing the song in its entirety.
4. Tell the children they can accompany the song by clapping hands. Share with them the fact that in many African American Baptist churches, one hears hand clapping with most of the spirituals. What is generally heard is clapping on beats 2 and 4. Demonstrate this while singing the song.
5. Have the class practice clapping (only) as you sing the song in its entirety. When students can clap successfully, allow them to try singing and clapping simultaneously.
6. Review the meaning of a spiritual and a phrase in music.

Figure 2. "He's Got the Whole World in His Hands"

L E S S O N   3

■ **Objectives**

Students will:
1. Identify, with teacher assistance, the call-and-response form through listening and performance.
2. Sing "Long John," using the pentatonic melody that includes a minor seventh above the tonic as the basis. Introduce the related pentatonic scale and show students how it relates to the melody of "Long John."

■ **Materials**

1. Recordings:
"Long John" and "Michael, Row the Boat Ashore," from *Negro Prison Songs* (Tradition 1020)
The World of Popular Music: Afro-American, Album XLII, Code 4608 (Follett BS 12192)

■ **Procedures**

1. Discuss how singing, humming, or whistling can make a task seem easier. Which musical element can be associated most closely with work? (Rhythm.) Explore with the class some of the rhythms we produce while writing, erasing a chalkboard, or sweeping the floor. Lead the class in marking the pulse, tapping lightly as one student performs a task.

Figure 3. "Long John"

2. Explain that the work song, a dying tradition, was once prevalent among African Americans. It can still be heard in the southern prisons as the prisoners labor. Listen to several examples of prison songs from *Negro Prison Songs*, or listen to "Raise 'Em up Higher," a Texas State Prison song recorded on *The World of Popular Music: Afro-American*. Note that the words are derived from some experience other than work and that the singers use the call-and-response form.

3. Sing the song "Long John" (see figure 3; recorded on *Negro Prison Songs*). Ask the students to repeat the words and melody after you; they will discover that the call-and-response form can feature a response that is a preestablished phrase sung by a group or an imitation of the leader. Observe the melody's use of the pentatonic scale F, (G), A, C, D with the addition of E♭—a lowered seventh (compared to the diatonic major scale).

4. One work song from the mid-nineteenth century is "Michael, Row the Boat Ashore" (on *Negro Prison Songs*; see figure 4). It exemplifies both the call-and-response form and the use of words that take the minds of workers off their labors. Students may learn it in the way in which it was originally transmitted—orally, without notation.

Michael, Row the Boat Ashore

Mich- ael   row   the   boat   a-   shore,   Hal - le -

lu -   jah.   Mich - ael   row   the   boat   a -

shore,   Hal - le -   lu -   jah.

2.   Sister help to trim the sails, Hallelujah.
     Sister help to trim the sails, Hallelujah.

3.   Jordan River is chilly and cold, Hallelujah.
     Jordan River is chilly and cold, Hallelujah.

Figure 4. "Michael, Row the Boat Ashore"

L E S S O N   4

■ Objectives
Students will:
1. Sing "Joe Turner Blues" with teacher assistance, paying attention to style.
2. Verbally identify the "blue note" in this song.
3. Construct chords and create an accompaniment using the 12-bar blues progression.

■ Materials
1. Piano
2. Chalkboard
3. Overhead projector and transparency (optional)
4. Autoharps, omnichords, or guitars
5. Staff paper

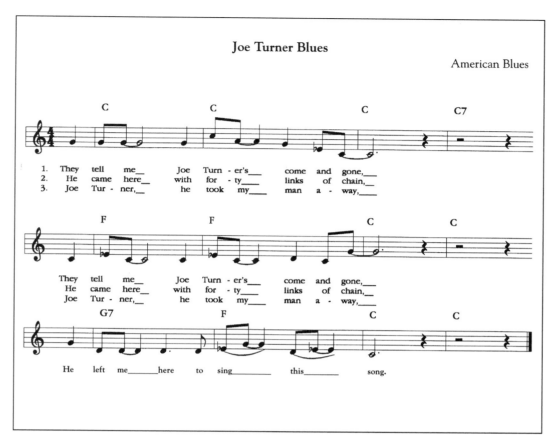

Figure 5. "Joe Turner Blues," in Barbara Staton et al., *Music and You,* Grade 4 (New York: Macmillan, 1988)

■ Procedures

1. Discuss the blues style. Tell students that blues is usually based on a 12-bar pattern in 4/4 meter. The harmony is a simple chord pattern: I (tonic), IV (subdominant), I, V₇ (dominant), I. Third, seventh, and sometimes fifth scale degrees are lowered and referred to as "blue notes." There are three types of blues. In *country blues,* which has been referred to as Mississippi Delta blues, the singer uses a falsetto voice to emphasize emotions, an unamplified guitar plays ostinato accompaniment, and introductions and endings are spoken. *City blues* is performed mainly by women. The form has been standardized with regular beginnings and endings, and more than two instruments accompany this style. *Contemporary blues* has added electric guitars and saxophones, and is written down. Vocalists (B. B. King, for example) sing in a shouting style.

2. Play "Joe Turner Blues" (see figure 5) on piano (melody and chords) and have students write down the chord progression heard and the number of measures between each change. Allow students to discuss their findings. Play the song again, write chord changes and measures on the chalkboard, and review 12-bar blues progression.

(The chord pattern is: C C C C$_7$ F F C C G$_7$ F C C; each chord is four beats in length.)

3. Play or sing the melody only, asking students to determine where the blue note (E♭) occurs.
4. Teach the song phrase by phrase and model the blues style of singing. When the students are comfortable with the melody, have them sing the entire song with you.
5. Review chord construction. Assign three to four students (in cooperative learning groups) to an Autoharp. Each member of the group is responsible for constructing the chords in the 12-bar blues progression. One student in each group is the composer (notates the chords on staff paper) or the performer (plays the accompaniment when the group is called upon). Tell the remaining students to practice singing words in the appropriate style, but without the piano. (Allow ample time to complete the task; performances may even take place during the next music class.)

L E S S O N   5

■ Objectives

Students will:
1. Develop, with teacher assistance, an understanding of the blues genre by reading and discussing blues texts about loneliness, hardship, and love.
2. Recognize how hollers and work songs are antecedents to the blues.
3. Point out characteristic vocal and instrumental styles after listening to examples.
4. Sing a blues song.
5. Perform an instrumental accompaniment to emphasize the formal and harmonic structure of the blues.
6. Trace the older blues form to the rhythm and blues genre of the 1950s and 1960s.

■ Materials

1. Recordings:
   The Rural Blues: A Study of Vocal and Instrumental Resources (RBF RP5)
   Mean Old Bed Bug Blues (Columbia G30818)
   The World of Popular Music: Afro-American, Album XLII, Code 4608 (Follett BS 12192)
2. Videos:
   Blues: Country to City (Program #5), *Jazz Gets Blue* (Program #6), and *Rhythm and Blues* (Program #7), from the series *From Jumpstreet: A Story of Black Music* (see Filmography)

■ Procedures

1. Discuss the meaning of the phrase "I've got the blues." What do you feel when you feel blue? (Lonely or depressed.) Read the following blues song verse: "You'll never miss your water till your well runs dry/You'll never miss your water till your well runs

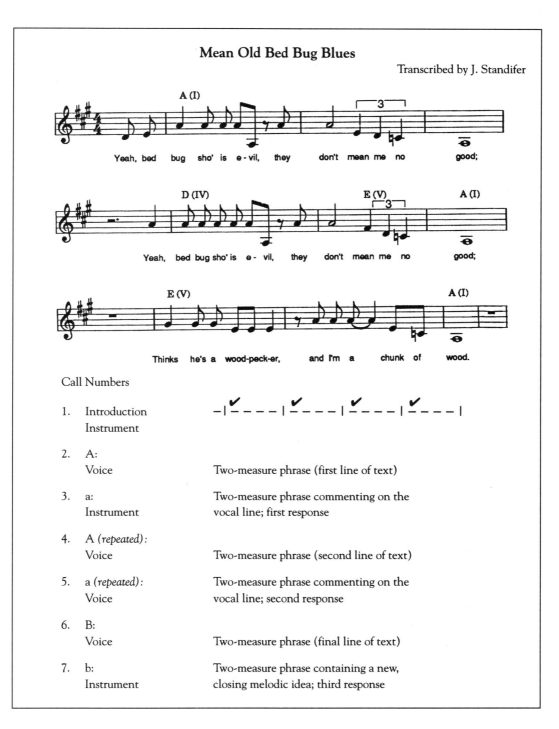

Figure 6. "Mean Old Bed Bug Blues"

dry/I never missed my baby till she said goodbye." What is the sentiment of the verse? Note the AAB form of the verse.

2. Play a recording of "Milk Cow Blues" (side two, band one on *The Rural Blues*) and listen for the falsetto and the tonal inflections of speech in the vocal quality that the singer has chosen for this song.

3. Listen to "Warm Up" (side three, band three of *The Rural Blues*) and explain the bottleneck guitar technique (determining pitches on the strings by sliding a bottle's neck over a section of the fingerboard rather than pressing the strings on the frets). This technique imitates the sound of African American vocal slides and slurs. Discuss the use of a solo voice with instrumental accompaniment and occasional vocal interjections, moans, and spoken commentary as characteristic of the blues. Point out the aspects of the holler and the work song, especially the flatted third and seventh scale tones, and the use of the flatted third and syncopation. Discuss other components of the blues, such as the use of solo voice with instrumental accompaniment, call-and-response between voice and instruments, and the use of occasional interjections, moans, and spoken commentary.

4. Listen to "Mean Old Bed Bug Blues" (see figure 6) by Bessie Smith. You can find it on the *Mean Old Bed Bug Blues* or on *The World of Popular Music: Afro-American*. Use the listening chart in figure 6 to demonstrate the AAB form and the interchange between the voice and instruments, or call-and-response technique, which is frequently encountered in African American music and in related music. There are three vocal phrases: the first two have the same text and melody, and the last has a new text and melodic phrase. The vocal phrase (the call) is answered each time by an instrumental phrase (the response), which comments on the vocal phrase. Each chorus, therefore, contains three call-and-response units.

   Make certain that the students know where the first beats fall in each measure (shown by check marks on the transcription). Try calling each number before the entrance of the corresponding material (or have a student call them). Direct the students' attention to events that demonstrate the music's stylistic elements as the events occur. If you ask the students to follow the music printed in the transcription, they will notice that some of the pitches will be a bit flatter and some of the rhythms a bit freer than the notation indicates. Each blues singer may give a slightly different rendition of any given melody on different occasions; the transcription given here is a close approximation of the performance by Bessie Smith on the recordings listed in the Materials section.

5. Teach "Mean Old Bed Bug Blues" to the students. Discuss how the singer is sad and lonely now that her husband has been sent to prison. Note the AAB form of the text and music. Sing the third degree of the scale as a lowered pitch, just as it is sung on the recording.

6. If your students play guitar, have them learn a guitar accompaniment to the blues. The chords shown in figure 6 can be used to give a solid harmonic structure to any 12-bar blues. If you study other blues compositions and the students perceive differences in detail, these differences can themselves be a subject for class discussion.

7. Although acoustic blues is still performed, as well as the more urban style of electric blues, a more contemporary style has developed with rhythm and blues. The roots of rock (and soul) music are found in rhythm and blues, or "R and B" style. This "blues with a big beat" is best demonstrated with the 1950s music of Chuck Berry, Fats Domino, and Ray Charles, whose recordings are available in large record stores and libraries.

LESSON 6

■ Objectives

Students will:

1. Identify, with teacher assistance, the form of ragtime music by raising their hands when the form occurs in different sections of the song.
2. Identify the use of syncopated melodies against steady accompaniment patterns by tapping and chanting.
3. Compare the form of two rags heard in class.

■ Materials

1. Recordings:
   Piano Rags by Scott Joplin (Nonesuch H-712 48), or see Basal series texts
   The World of Popular Music: Afro-American, Album XLII, Code 4608 (Follett BS 12192)
2. Film: *Scott Joplin*, Pyramid, 15 minutes, color, 1977
3. Video: *Early Jazz* (Program #8), from the series *From Jumpstreet: A Story of Black Music* (see Filmography)
4. "The Riches of Ragtime" by Patricia K. Shehan, *Music Educators Journal* 73, no. 3 (1986): 22–25
5. Piano

■ Procedures

1. Explain that ragtime music was developed by itinerant African American pianists, such as Scott Joplin, who traveled in the Midwest from 1890 to 1920, playing a music based on a mixture of formal European and informal African American folk traditions. Emphasize that ragtime music was fully composed before it was performed, unlike the oral traditions of work songs and blues.
2. Show the film *Scott Joplin*.
3. Play a recording of "The Entertainer" or "Maple Leaf Rag." Focus on the even left-hand chords by tapping a steady beat while listening. Listen also to the right-hand melody for the syncopated rhythm shown in figure 7.
4. Have the class say the chant in figure 7 to demonstrate the characteristic syncopation of ragtime melodies. Have students pat the rhythm of the chant on their laps. Divide the class and have one group clap and chant the words "rag time" to steady eighth notes.
5. Play the themes of the "Maple Leaf Rag" on the piano (see figure 8). Sections A, B, C, and D should be repeated until the students are familiar with their sounds. Explain that the most common ragtime form is AABBACCDD. Write that scheme on the chalkboard and play the recording, asking students to raise their hands every time they hear a new section. Point to the letters of the sections as they occur.
6. Have the students listen to "Pegasus," a classic rag written in 1919 by James Scott (1886–1936). This composition is recorded on *The World of Popular Music: Afro-American*. As they listen, have the students follow each section of the piece and write down the form (Introduction/A/B/C/Bridge/B). Notice that the bridge section features a return of the introductory material. Have the students compare the form of "Pegasus" to "Maple Leaf Rag."

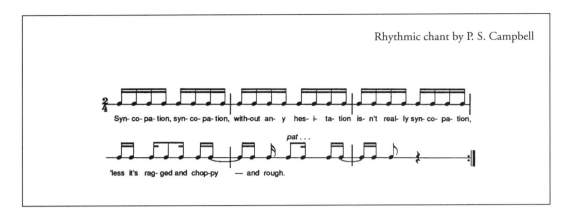

Figure 7. Syncopation example

Figure 8. Themes from "Maple Leaf Rag"

LESSON 7

■ **Objectives**

Students will:
1. Sing a spiritual.
2. Identify the religious and vocal significance of spirituals and gospel songs in African American culture.
3. Learn to identify nonverbal signals as they are reflected in African American culture and African American musical expression.

■ **Materials**

1. Recordings:
   The Fisk Jubilee Singers (Folkways FP-72)
   The World of Popular Music: Afro-American, Album XLII, Code 4608 (Follett BS 12192)
   Walking in Space (A & M Records SP 3023)
2. Video: *Gospel and Spirituals* (Program #3), from the series *From Jumpstreet: A Story of Black Music* (see Filmography)

■ **Procedures**

1. Give students a brief history of spirituals and gospel music:

   Spirituals developed during slavery as a form of religious expression and covert commentary on bondage. Traditionally, spirituals were orally transmitted folk songs that synthesized African melodic and rhythmic practices and Protestant hymns. Spirituals fall into three broad categories: fiery, up-tempo call-and-response chants; sorrowful songs with slow, sustained, long-phrase melodies; and syncopated, segmented melodies performed up-tempo with swinging rhythms and short phrases. Traditional spirituals are performed without accompaniment, are melodically and harmonically simple, and have simple rhythms that are often syncopated with hand clapping and foot tapping.

   Spirituals became the first African American music to gain international acclaim through the success of the Fisk Jubilee Singers. Around 1900, when the influence of romantic nationalistic composers was at its apex, spirituals were used as source material for extended classical compositions by several African American composers, including William Grant Still and Nathaniel Dett.

   Gospel music is also a family of performance styles, including soloist with accompanying group, male quartets, song sermons/holiness shouting, country gospel, balladeering, rhythm and blues- and soul-influenced gospel, and progressive gospel. Gospel music is generally performed with accompaniment, including guitars, drums, and an organ. It is drawn from secular music forms and is up-tempo, syncopated, and rhythmically complex, often using tambourines and body percussion to provide counter rhythms. Gospel music is characterized by a wide variety of vocal attacks, including moans, wails, shouts, and falsetto. It is based on texts drawn from the Bible and from life experience and frequently uses Black vernacular language. Gospel is also characterized by intensely emotional, communal participation through call and

There's a Great Camp Meeting

Figure 9. "There's a Great Camp Meeting"

response. Not all gospel music is fast and rhythmically hard-driving; some is ballad-like and rhythmically simple.

2. Describe the origin of the spiritual as a religious song genre in which slaves expressed their hope for a better life after death. Although they were sung during the period of slavery, spirituals gained popularity during religious camp meetings. The Western world took note of the spiritual when the Fisk Jubilee Singers of Fisk University in Nashville, Tennessee, performed these songs around the country and in Europe from the 1870s to the end of the nineteenth century.

3. Sing "There's a Great Camp Meeting" (see figure 9). Call attention to the call-and-response setting that alternates between the leader and the chorus and to the syncopations in the melody. After listening to "There's a Great Camp Meeting," have students listen to African American composer Thomas Kerr's composition for piano, "Easter Monday Swagger," which is based on the spiritual. Kerr's work is recorded on *The World of Popular Music: Afro-American*.

4. Listen to "There's a Great Camp Meeting" (side two, band two) and "Rocking Jerusalem" (side one, band three) on *The Fisk Jubilee Singers*. Compare the distinctly different musical and textual contents of spirituals with those of the blues examples studied in Lesson Three.

5. Define the gospel song as a religious form that originated early in the twentieth century. (Gospel songs use a biblical text; music based on a secular text is called "rhythm and blues.") Listen to "O Happy Day" on Quincy Jones's *Walking in Space* or any other gospel song that students may wish to share with the class. When distinguishing gospel music from spirituals, point out the following differences: (a) the music is composed, unlike folk music, which is not written down; (b) the music requires instrumental accompaniment rather than a cappella performance; (c) the music uses highly ornamented, often improvised melodies rather than a straightforward rendition of the printed notation; and (d) the text is about contemporary moral issues, not Bible stories. Both spirituals and gospel songs are religious and vocal in nature, but can be readily identified by these traits.

6. Test students on the knowledge they've gained from this lesson. Use both essay and multiple choice questions.

LESSON 8

■ Objectives

1. Students will hear examples of gospel music and perceive the following characteristics:
- Gospel music is often up-tempo and syncopated.
- Gospel music often involves counter rhythms produced by instruments and body percussion.
- A prevailing rhythmic characteristic of gospel music is the rhythmic accent falling on what is often considered to be the weaker beat in other music, as shown in figure 10.
- Gospel music includes vocal qualities such as wails, shouts, falsetto, vibrato, and sliding to and from various pitches.

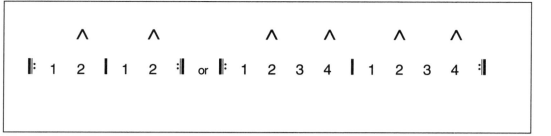

Figure 10. Prevailing rhythmic characteristic of gospel music

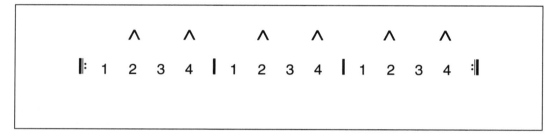

Figure 11. Rhythmic pattern

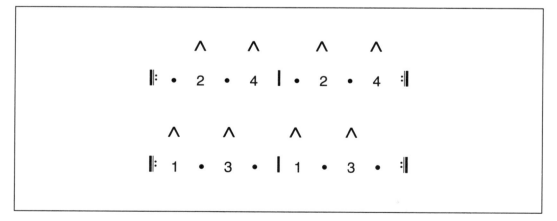

Figure 12. Hand- and foot-clapping pattern

- Gospel often involves intensely emotional communal participation through the use of call and response, which is a two-part performance structure in which the second part answers and sometimes overlaps the first.

■ Materials

1. Recordings:
   Ten Years of Gold by Aretha Franklin (Atlantic SD 18204)
   Oh Happy Day by the Edwin Hawkins Singers (Buddah BDS 5070)
   Walking in Space by Quincy Jones (A & M Records SP 3023)
   Please Be Patient with Me by Albertina Walker and James Cleveland (Savoy 14527)
2. Video: *Gospel and Spirituals* (Program #3) and *Rhythm and Blues* (Program #7), from the series *From Jumpstreet: A Story of Black Music* (see Filmography)

■ Procedures

1. Have students clap the pattern in figure 11. To achieve an accented beat, students should involve their entire bodies in making the clapping motion or movement, especially using their shoulders and total arm lengths. Students should note the regularity of the accented beat and may recall seeing and hearing this pattern in the performances of James Cleveland and the Mighty Clouds of Joy. This pattern may be clapped 1-2-1-2-, accenting the second beat.
2. Have students repeat the clapping experience, this time clapping only on the accented beats while simultaneously tapping their feet on beats 1 and 3. The dots in figure 12 indicate silence. Again, students should carefully note the accented beats and concentrate on achieving them by using their bodies emphatically.
3. Ask students to improvise a version of the pattern shown in figure 13. First, have the entire class do each part separately. This may be done in echo or call-and-response fashion. Then have students do the examples in various combinations, for example, Parts A and B, Parts A and C, Parts B and C, or Parts A, B, and C. The third step is for students to repeat the result as accompaniment to an appropriate gospel recording or song played in class. Ask students to discuss the similarities and differences between their improvisation and what they hear and/or observe in audio and video examples. Then have students transfer the rhythm clapping patterns to percussion instruments typically used as accompaniment to gospel music (tambourines and drums, for example). Finally, ask students to select specific rhythm and blues recordings, for example, "Respect" and "Baby I Love You" on *Ten Years of Gold*. Compare and contrast the sound, beat, and feeling of the rhythm and blues example with that of gospel.
4. Two call charts or listening guides, one for the Edwin Hawkins Singers' rendition of "Oh, Happy Day" and the other for Quincy Jones's interpretation of this same composition, follow. The chart for the Edwin Hawkins Singers' example has three basic components: it illustrates the form, content, and dynamic changes of the recording. Each of these parts may be used in separate listening experiences, or they may be used all at once.
   a. Have students compare and contrast characteristics of these examples with those heard in the video example, *Rhythm and Blues*.

b. Compare the rendition of the Edwin Hawkins Singers with that of Albertina Walker and James Cleveland.
c. Encourage students to improvise a rhythmic pattern using the strong 1 2 3 4 of the Quincy Jones example as a basic pulse.
d. Lead students to discover the use of syncopation in the Quincy Jones example. Permit students to sing in harmony along with the recording.

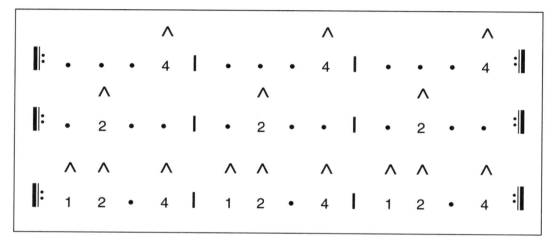

Figure 13. Rhythmic pattern

Figure 14. Piano and rhythm section in introduction

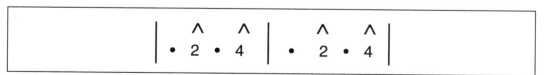

Figure 15. Clapping in accompaniment

CALL CHART

"Oh, Happy Day," from *Oh, Happy Day* (Buddah BDS 5070).
Side a, band b (4: 59); performed by the Edwin Hawkins Singers.

Form	Call Number	Content	Dynamics
Intro	1.	Piano and rhythm section in introduction (see figure 14)	f
A	2.	Soloist: "Oh, happy day...when Jesus washed my sins away...... Choir responds: "Oh, happy day...when Jesus....................	mp
B	3.	Full choir predominates: "He taught me how to watch, fight and pray......fight and pray! and..........................ev-ry-day.................everyday!	ff
A	4.	Soloist, as in Step 2: "Oh, happy day"............................. Choir responds: "Oh, happy day..................................	mp
B	5.	Full choir, as in Step 3 "He taught me........., fight and pray.............fight and pray! and....................ev-ry-day.....................every day!	ff
A^1	6.	Soloist and choir repeating: "Oh, happy day"................... (a) Soloist and choir: Improvising on basic melody and accompaniment (b) Clapping in accompaniment (as shown in figure 15) (c) Soloist and choir, slowing: "When Jesus washed......my sins away.......................	mp ff ff mp
Summation	7.	Soloist and ensemble in summation on: "It's a happy day, Oh Lord, Hmmmmm, Good God,..Oh yes,... Choir: "Oh, happy day."	mp

A^1 indicates material based on A and improvised parts.

CALL CHART

"Oh, Happy Day," from *Walking in Space* (A & M Records SP 3023).
Side 2, band 4 (3: 35); performed by Quincy Jones.

**Call
Number**

1.   Beat 1-2-3-4/1-2-3-4/etc.
     Bass guitar, electric piano, rhythm guitar, and drums in background anticipate
        entrance of melody in Step 2.

2.   Flute begins melody (legato).
     Other instruments continue to play softly in the background.
     Note the pattern, as shown in figure 16.

3.   Voices enter with "Oh, happy day" and repeat this phrase four times over the
        other instruments. There is a strong pulse, plus accents. A strong accent leads
        to Step 4.

4.   Brass *ff*, with blaring voices in long notes; loud, fast-moving bass guitar;
        accents, strong pulse; pause.

5.   Flute with legato melody, as in Step 2.
     Soft voices in the background on the same pattern as shown in Step 2; strong
        accent leads to Step 6.

6.   Reentry of *ff* brass with blaring voices in long notes. Fast-moving bass in
        background.

7.   Flute trill; flute, now higher in pitch, with legato melody.
     Instruments accompany.
     Subdued voices repeating "Oh, happy day" to fade out.

Figure 16. Rhythm pattern

Music Perception Test for Gospel and Spirituals

Directions: A musical selection will be played two times. Review the questions below and keep them in mind during the first listening. On the second listening, circle those responses that correctly describe the musical event you have heard.

1. This musical example consists of:
   A. Several instruments for accompaniment
   B. No instruments for accompaniment
   C. Rhythm section only for accompaniment

2. The music makes me want to count:
   A. 1-2-3
   B. 1-2-3-4
   C. 1-2-3-4-5

3. Beat accents seem to be on:
   A. The first beat
   B. The second beat
   C. The third beat
   D. None of the beats

4. The text is:
   A. Sacred
   B. Secular
   C. A mixture of A and B
   D. Neither sacred nor secular

5. The music rhythm has a:
   A. Regular beat
   B. Irregular beat
   C. Very weak, subtle beat

6. The music seems:
   A. Intensely emotional and up-tempo
   B. Lacking in overt emotion
   C. Laid back, with weak beats

7. The form of the music is:
   A. Call and response
   B. Through composed
   C. ABA

8. This composition is:
   A. Gospel music
   B. A spiritual
   C. Rhythm and blues

L E S S O N   9

■ **Objectives**

Students will:
1. Differentiate between gospel and spiritual styles without teacher assistance.
2. Discuss the messages (lyrics) found in gospel songs.
3. Identify instrumentation used in various gospel songs.

■ **Materials**
1. Recording: "Why We Sing" (words and music by Kirk Franklin, Gospocentric, Inc.);

also use examples from Lessons 7 and 8

2. Video: *Gospel and Spirituals* (Program #3) from the series *From Jumpstreet: A Story of Black Music*

3. "Mellonee Burnim on African American Music" by Patricia Shehan Campbell, *Music Educators Journal* 82, no. 1 (1995): 41–48

■ Procedures

1. Discuss gospel music. Gospel is called "gospel" because many song texts are biblical, based on the first four books of the New Testament. Unlike the spiritual (which was born in rural cotton fields), gospel has its roots in the revival meetings of urban settings. When black people migrated to cities during the twentieth century, they found that spirituals did not fit easily into their new lifestyles. A more expressive, unique music was needed, one which did not resemble spirituals or white gospel songs.

2. Gospel music is different from spirituals in the following ways: (a) the music is composed (unlike folk music, which is not written down); (b) it requires instrumental accompaniment rather than a cappella performance; (c) it uses highly ornamented, often improvised melodies rather than a straightforward rendition of the printed notation; and (d) the text is about contemporary moral issues, not biblical stories. Both spirituals and gospel songs are religious and vocal in nature, but gospel incorporates jazz rhythms and blues singing into religious music. The use of drums, guitars, tambourines, triangles, piano, and/or organ is acceptable in the church music form.

3. Thomas Dorsey (1899–1993) had tremendous influence on the gospel tradition and respect that slowly grew for the music. Among his many contributions (including the composition of more than 450 songs), he is well known for "Precious Lord, Take My Hand," which has been published in twenty-six languages.

4. Modern gospel emerged during the period of Martin Luther King Jr.'s leadership and has existed side by side with historic gospel. A few of the many famous gospel singers during that time were Aretha Franklin, the Staple Singers, Mahalia Jackson, James Cleveland, the Soul Stirrers (featuring Sam Cooke), and the Drinkard Singers (featuring Dionne Warwick). Have students bring in names and recorded examples of gospel music and gospel artists (both black and white).

5. Play several gospel songs and point out the salient features that make them gospel. Compare these to the spirituals used in Lessons Seven and Eight.

6. Play a gospel song and have the students focus on the lyrics/text. Ask them what they think is the song's message. Is it sacred? Why or why not? Play the song a second time to verify the correct answers.

7. Play the song again and have the students write down which instruments have been used. Ask them which instrument is playing the melody and which is playing the harmony.

8. Have students listen to, sing with, and accompany with hand claps the commercial gospel hit "Why We Sing." Have them compare and contrast it with other gospel songs, such as those by Dorsey or the Staple Singers.

9. Evaluate students' knowledge using the music perception test found in the previous lesson on gospels and spirituals.

L E S S O N   1 0

■ **Objectives**

Students will:
1. Create, without teacher assistance, appropriate words and a rap rhythm (maximum length is two minutes).
2. Add accompaniment using their voices/instruments.
3. Perform their rap from memory in front of the class.

■ **Materials**

1. Manuscript paper and pencils
2. "U Can't Touch This" by M. C. Hammer, Rich James, Alonzo Miller (1990), Bust It Publishing (BMI)/Jobete Music Co., Inc.
3. "Knowledge is King" by Kool Moe Dee (1989 by M. Dewese, P. Harris), Willesden Music Inc./Kool Moe Dee Music
4. "It's Like That" by Run-D.M.C. (1984, L. Smith, J. Simmons, D. McDaniels), Protoons, Inc./Rush-Groove (ASCAP)

■ **Procedures**

(Implementation of this lesson may require two–three music class periods.)

1. Involve students in a ten- to fifteen-minute discussion of rap music. What is rap? Is it music? Why or why not? How does it differ from other music? What is the performance practice? Can it be notated on a musical staff? (Suggestion: Avoid issues of racism, sexism, and profanity. Keep the discussion on students' perspectives about the musical or nonmusical qualities of rap.)
2. Play each of the above rap songs. As a class, analyze the rhythm (beat, accents, meter, syncopation, dotted notes?), melody (pitches, melodic contour, major, minor?), texture (homophonic, monophonic, polyphonic, heterophonic?), form (binary, ternary, rondo, theme and variation?), expressive elements (dynamics, tempo), and tone quality (discuss vocal timbres, identify instruments).
3. Give the following instructions: "Before the end of class, you will be assigned to a group to work on a special project during the next music class. Each group will be given manuscript paper and pencils to create their own rap music. Begin to discuss a theme of interest to all group members, and be prepared to discuss your group theme with me during the next class. It's a good idea to have two or three themes ready, since your themes must be approved before you begin to write the lyrics. Your rap piece will be analyzed for rhythm, melody, texture, form, expressive elements, and tone quality. Be sure to think about these elements as you create the lyrics and background music (which may use voices or instruments—for those of you who play). Your final product, which will be performed in front of the class, should be two minutes long, or less."

Integrating music with other studies

1. Explore poetry and literature for a fuller understanding of the African American experience. Read excerpts from the poetry of Langston Hughes and Paul Dunbar and the short stories and novels of James Baldwin (including *Go Tell It on the Mountain*) and Richard Wright's *Native Son*. Also introduce the class to James Baldwin's "Notes of a Native Son," which provides much useful information for interpreting Wright's book (see Bibliography).

2. For examples of African American folk tales presented in a local dialect, read the Uncle Remus stories by Joel Chandler Harris (see Harris's *Uncle Remus, His Songs and Sayings*, listed in the Bibliography). These tales are set in the context of the culture of the people in the Georgia Sea Islands, who, even in the twentieth century, retain many traditions from the period of slavery. The songs of Bessie Jones, collected in *Step It Down* by Jones and Beth Lomax Hawes (see Bibliography), are further examples of this regional culture.

3. The visual arts of African Americans are exemplified by the patchwork quilts and basketry of the rural people of the southern United States. Search for examples of these traditions in the collected volumes of American folk art such as Stephanie Miller's *Creative Patchwork* or Robin Franklin and Tasha Lebow Wolf's *"Remember the Ladies": A Handbook of Women in American History* (see Bibliography). Show your class the videotape *A Gift of Hearts and Hands* (see Filmography) or the book that accompanies it, *Hearts and Hands: The Influence of Women and Quilts on American Society,* by Elaine Hedges and Julie Silva.

4. On a map, trace the migration of African peoples in the eighteenth and nineteenth centuries from the west coast countries of Dahomey, Nigeria, Ghana, and the Ivory Coast to the seaports of Charleston, South Carolina, and throughout the south (to Atlanta, Georgia; Richmond, Virginia; Montgomery, Alabama; and Jackson, Mississippi). Trace the northern migration during the years following the Civil War (up the Mississippi River to Memphis, Tennessee; St. Louis, Missouri; and Chicago). Point out cities with large African American communities, including those previously noted, as well as Detroit, Cleveland, Washington, D.C., New York, Philadelphia, Boston, and Los Angeles. Suggest the historical significance of the industrial revolution, which provided jobs for African Americans in the factories of urban areas.

BIBLIOGRAPHY

Baldwin, James. *Notes of a Native Son*. New York: Dial, 1963. This is an excellent source that can be used in the study of Richard Wright's *Native Son*.

Bennet, Lerone. *Before the Mayflower: A History of the Negro in America*. Chicago: Johnson, 1966.

Berendt, Joachim-Ernst. *Jazz: A Photo History*. Translated by William Odom. New York: Schirmer Books, 1979. This striking visual history of jazz features stories and photographs of New Orleans, spirituals and gospels, blues, jazz performers, big bands, bebop, cool, and jazz in Europe and Japan. It includes an excellent discography.

Boyer, Horace. "Contemporary Gospel," *The Black Perspective in Music* 7, no. 1 (1979): 5–58.

Boyer, Horace. "Charles Albert Tindley: Progenitor of Black-American Gospel Music," *The Black Perspective in Music* 11, no. 2 (1983): 103–132.

Brooks-Baham, Emma. *A Model for Collecting Children's Singing Games for Use in Incorporating Movement in Elementary Music Instruction*. Unpublished doctoral dissertation. University of Washington, 1980.

Brooks, Tilford. *America's Black Musical Heritage*. Englewood Cliffs, NJ: Prentice-Hall, 1984. This comprehensive, indexed volume on African American music covers forms before 1900, the development of jazz, and African American composers.

Campbell, Patricia Shehan. "Mellonee Burnim on African American Music," *Music Educators Journal* 82, no. 1 (1995): 41–48.

Courlander, Harold. *Negro Folk Music, USA*. New York: Columbia University, 1963.

Davis, Nathan. *Writings in Jazz*. 3d ed. Scottsdale, AZ: Gorsuch Scarisbrick, 1985. This book covers jazz, blues, religious styles, minstrelsy, and the musics of Chicago, Kansas City, and other landmark cities in the history of African American music. It contains good discussions of jazz-rock fusion and women in jazz, a bibliography, a discography, and a list of examples for suggested listening, with all recordings categorized according to musical style.

DeLerma, Dominique-Rene. *Black Music in Our Culture*. Kent, OH: Kent State University, 1970.

Erdei, Peter, and Katalin Komlos. *150 American Folk Songs to Sing, Read, and Play*. New York: Boosey and Hawkes, 1974.

Feather, Leonard. *The New Edition of The Encyclopedia of Jazz*. New York: Bonanza Books, 1960. This reference work includes most major jazz performers and their works and gives comprehensive answers to most questions about this subject area.

Fox, Sidney, Barbara Reeder Lundquist, and James Standifer, comps. *The World of Popular Music: Afro-American*. Chicago: Follett, 1975. The songs discussed here include "Oh Happy Day," "Rockin' Jerusalem," "There's a Great Camp Meeting," and other recordings discussed in this chapter. This book is available from Follett Publishing Company, Department DM, 1010 West Washington Boulevard, Chicago, IL 60607. Also see the recordings that accompany this book, which are listed in the Discography.

Franklin, Robin, and Tasha Lebow Wolf. *"Remember the Ladies": A Handbook of Women in American History*. Ann Arbor: University of Michigan School of Education's Program for Educational Opportunity, 1980. This source includes information about women of the colonial period, the revolutionary era, the early nineteenth century, pioneer and Native American women, women during the Civil War era, women in the years from 1880 to 1920, and women during the period from 1920 to the present. It also includes a reading list with details about resources on women's contributions to the artistic developments of American society.

Fulton, Eleanor, and Pat Smith. *Let's Slice the Ice: A Collection of Black Children's Ring Games and Chants*. St. Louis: Magnamusic Baton, 1978. This collection contains several interesting examples of games and chants. See especially "This Away, Valerie" (pp. 22–23), "Who Stole the Cookie from the Cookie Jar?" (p. 52), and "Bluebells and Cockle Shells" (p. 37).

Harris, Joel Chandler. *Uncle Remus, His Songs and His Sayings*. New York: Penguin, 1982. This source contains the legends, songs, and sayings of Uncle Remus, using the text of the first edition (1880) of Harris's attempt to record traditional stories of his time.

Hine, Darlene, ed. *An Encyclopedia of African American Women in History*. Brooklyn, NY: Carlson Publishing, Inc., 1993.

Hughes, Langston. *Ask Your Mama: Twelve Moods for Jazz*. New York: Knopf, 1969.

Hughes, Langston. *Selected Poems of Langston Hughes*. New York: Knopf, 1959.

Hughes, Langston, and Anna Bontemps, eds. *The Poetry of the Negro—1746–1949*. Garden City, NY: Doubleday, 1945.

Jones, Bessie, and Beth Lomax Hawes. *Step It Down*. New York: Harper & Row, 1952. This book includes children's songs and games from the Georgia Sea Islands.

Lanker, Brian. *I Dream a World: Portraits of Black Women Who Changed America*. New York: Stewart, Tabori, and Change, 1989. This book contains photos of and interviews with noteworthy women.

Levine, Toby, and James Standifer. *Jumpstreet Humanities Project: Learning Package: Curriculum Materials for Secondary School Teachers and Students in Music, Language Arts, History, and the Humanities*. Washington, DC: Greater Washington Education Telecommunications

Association, 1981. See especially the multicultural unit on music, dance, and poetry on pages 155–72.

Miller, Stephanie, comp. *Creative Patchwork*. Edited by Liz Goodman and Susan Joiner. New York: Crescent Books, 1973.

Morgenstern, Dan. *Jazz People*. Englewood Cliffs, NJ: Prentice-Hall, 1976. This book contains excellent photos and some scholarly text.

Neff, Robert, and Anthony Connor. *Blues*. Boston: David R. Godine, 1975. Blues musicians talk about themselves and their art in this book.

Oakley, Giles. *The Devil's Music*. New York: Harcourt Brace Jovanovich, 1976. This historically sound primer on the development of the blues includes an annotated bibliography and discography and numerous photographs.

Oliver, Paul, Max Harrison, and William Bolcom. *The New Grove Gospel, Blues, and Jazz (with Spirituals and Ragtime*. 2d ed. New York: W. W. Norton and Company, 1986. This book contains discographies, bibliographies, and artist histories.

Ricks, George. *Some Aspects of the Religious Music of the U.S. Negro: An Ethnomusicological Study with Special Emphasis on the Gospel Tradition*. Unpublished doctoral dissertation. Northwestern University, 1960.

Roach, Hildred. *Black American Music: Past and Present*. Boston: Crescendo, 1976.

Rose, Tricia. "Fear of a Black Planet: Rap Music and Black Cultural Politics in the 1990s," *Journal of Negro Education* 60, no. 60 (1991): 280.

Shehan, Patricia K. "The Riches of Ragtime," *Music Educators Journal* 73, no. 3 (1986): 22–25.

Southern, Eileen. *The Music of Black Americans: A History*. New York: Norton, 1971. This is a well-documented history of all aspects of African American music from the African past to the mid-twentieth century.

Standifer, James A., V. Butcher, and Toby Levine. *From Jumpstreet: A Story of Black Music*. Ann Arbor: University of Michigan School of Education's Program for Educational Opportunity, 1980. A secondary school teaching guide designed to be used with the television series *From Jumpstreet* (see Filmography for more information), this publication contains a complete lesson guide for each of the series' programs, focusing on blues, gospel, dance, jazz, soul, concert music, and other forms. Bibliographies, discographies, and photographs are provided.

Stanley, Lawrence, ed. *Rap: The Lyrics*. New York: Penguin Books, 1992. According to Stanley, "*Rap: The Lyrics* is a complete guide to a phenomenon that has transformed our culture, giving musical voice to the youth of today and compelling the rest of America to listen." The book contains the lyrics of more than one hundred songs, featuring artists like Big Daddy Kane, Ice T, Kool Moe Dee, LL Cool J, M. C. Hammer, Queen Latifah, Salt-n-Pepa, and 2-Live Crew.

Stearns, Marshall W. *Jazz Dance: The Story of American Vernacular Dance*. New York: Macmillan, 1968. Stearns discusses a wide variety of dances in America and their historical place in our music culture.

Tirro, Frank. *Jazz: A History*. New York: Norton, 1977. This well-balanced and well-illustrated history of African American music styles and their development contains excellent music examples, an annotated bibliography, and a discography.

Work, John Wesley. *Folk Songs of the American Negro*. New York: Negro Universities Press, 1915. Reprint. Westport, CT: Greenwood Press, 1969. The author directed the Fisk Jubilee Singers, who introduced this folk music to the world. The book includes examples of prominent spirituals, work songs, blues, hollers, and other African American songs. It includes excellent discussions of each of the song types with definitive materials about the origins of these musics gleaned from Work's research in the area of African American music and its practice at Fisk University's music program and with the Fisk Jubilee Singers. The volume also contains an excellent bibliography and index of song titles.

Wright, Richard. *Native Son*. New York: Harper & Row, 1940. In the Afterword of this book, John Reilly states: "This novel has become a classic; it is dramatic, unsentimental, and uncompromisingly realistic. The main character, Bigger Thomas, is a character to shock everyone: the liberal who believes himself a friend of the Negro cause is disappointed...while many Negroes recognize that oppression makes Bigger their brother."

DISCOGRAPHY

Chuck Berry's Golden Hits. Mercury 8262561.

The Complete Works of Scott Joplin. Audiophile AP 71-72. This is the most important complete collection of Joplin's ragtime works.

Deep South Country Blues. Flyright Label, Album 102. This record contains examples of blues from the 1920s and 1930s.

Eubie Blake Blues and Rags: His Earliest Piano Rolls, 1917–1921. Biograph BLP 10110, Vol. 1. This is an excellent source of the late Eubie Blake's compositions as they were originally recorded on piano rolls. Its selections include "Charleston Rag." The record is available from Biograph Records, PO Box 109, Canaan, NY 12029.

The Fisk Jubilee Singers, Directed by John W. Work. Folkways FP-72. This record includes performances of "There's a Great Camp Meeting" and "Rockin' Jerusalem."

Heliotrope Bouquet Piano Rags (1900–1970). Nonesuch H 71257. This record includes piano rags from the early years of the form up to more recent examples.

Mean Old Bed Bug Blues. Columbia G30818. This recording contains examples of thirty-three of Bessie Smith's best-known blues performances of songs such as "You've Been a Good Old Wagon," "Yellow Dog Blues," and "Saint Louis Blues."

Music Down Home: An Introduction to Negro Music, USA. 4 vols. Folkways FA 2691 A, B, C, D, 1965. This record contains a broad sample of work songs, blues, spirituals, and related folk musics of African Americans. Excellent notes and complete texts to all songs are included.

Negro Blues and Hollers. Library of Congress AFS-L59. This record is a collection of field hollers and rural blues from the southern United States.

Negro Folk Music of Alabama, Vol. 1. Folkways FE 4417. This record includes Alabama field hollers, work songs, and blues.

Negro Prison Songs. Tradition 1020. This is a recording of songs from southern United States penitentiaries sung by African Americans.

Negro Work Songs and Calls. Library of Congress AAFS-L8.

Oh Happy Day. Buddah BDS 5070. This recording is by the Edwin Hawkins Singers.

Piano Rags by Scott Joplin. Nonesuch H-712 48. This is an assortment of Joplin's ragtime piano works, including "Maple Leaf Rag."

Please Be Patient with Me by Albertina Walker and James Cleveland (Savoy 14527).

Porgy and Bess. London OSA 13116. This is a production of Gershwin's opera with some material cut from the original score. It includes, however, the best-known arias and interesting performances of "Strawberry Woman" and "Crab Man." The record includes a booklet that provides the text of all the scenes that are included in this release and photographs of the cast and sets of the original 1935 production.

The Rural Blues: A Study of Vocal and Instrumental Resources. RBF RP5. This recording includes selections for unaccompanied voice and voice with acoustic instruments.

Scott Joplin—1966: Classic Solos Played by the King of Ragtime Writers and Others from Rare Piano Rolls. Biograph BLP-10060. This recording was made from piano rolls labeled "Played by Scott Joplin himself!" Available from Biograph, PO Box 109, Canaan, NY 12029.

The Smithsonian Collection of Classic Jazz. P6 11891. Distributed by Norton, 500 Fifth Avenue, New York, NY 10036. This set of six records contains samplings of the jazz styles by the greatest performers, including Jelly Roll Morton, Louis Armstrong, Duke Ellington, and John Coltrane.

Step It Down. Rounder Records 8004. This record includes children's songs and games from the Georgia Sea Islands. It is designed to accompany *Step It Down*, the publication by Bessie Jones and Beth Lomax Hawes (see Bibliography).

The Story of the Blues. 2 vols. Compiled by Paul Oliver. CBS 6618, 66232. Volume I covers blues from the 1920s, 1930s, World War II, and the postwar years. Volume 2 features guitarists, women blues musicians, pianists, and ensembles.

Ten Years of Gold. Atlantic SD 18204. This is an Aretha Franklin recording.

Walking in Space. A & M Records SP 3023. Side one of this album is a tribute to the Broadway musical *Hair.* Side two includes the gospel tune "Oh Happy Day," written by Edwin Hawkins, in a primarily instrumental version of the tune played by excellent jazz performers.

The World of Popular Music: Afro-American. Album XLII, Code 4608, Follett BS 12192. This record includes "Oh Happy Day," "Rockin' Jerusalem," and "There's a Great Camp Meeting," instrumental compositions such as Thomas Kerr's "Easter Monday Swagger" (based on "There's a Great Camp Meeting"), and many other interesting and useful selections. It also includes student and teacher books (with explicit lessons that use the recorded examples) and a poster. This is a very useful resource for any class devoted to African American music and history.

The World of Popular Music: Jazz. Album XL, Code 4628, Follett BS 23539. This recording includes examples that demonstrate African American styles, blues, ragtime, spirituals, Dixieland, swing, bop, and cool jazz.

FILMOGRAPHY

The Black Experience as Expressed through Music. Four VHS videotapes, 60 minutes each. Los Angeles: Los Angeles Public Schools, Music Division, 1978. This series consists of programs on gospel, spirituals, jazz, and ragtime. (There are two thirty-minute programs on each tape.) One program includes an interview with Eubie Blake, who performs many of his own compositions and talks about his career. For information, contact Betty Cox, Beem Foundation, 3864 Grayburn Avenue, Los Angeles, CA 90008, phone: 212-291-7252.

Forever Free: The Story of Blind Tom Bethune. VHS, 30 minutes. A teleplay by Kathleen McGhee Anderson, 1987. This program relates the life story of the blind African American piano genius, Blind Tom Bethune. For more information, contact Betty Cox, Beem Foundation, 3864 Grayburn Avenue, Los Angeles, CA 90008, phone: 212-291-7252.

From Jumpstreet: A Story of Black Music. Washington, DC: Greater Washington Educational Telecommunications Association, 1981. (Telephone 703-998-2851.) This series of thirteen thirty-minute television programs was hosted by writer and playwright Oscar Brown, Jr., and produced for secondary school audiences by WETA-TV. Brown explores the black musical tradition from its African sources to its present place in American music. The program's locations were chosen from a variety of areas in which black music flourishes. It was written primarily for the secondary school level, but it has much information that is relevant to other educational levels. It also has very inclusive, up-to-date bibliographies and discographies. National Public Radio has made available a ten-part audiotape series of *From Jumpstreet.* For more information, call 202-822-2670. Preview videocassettes (3/4" only) are available from GPN PO Box 80669, Lincoln, NE 68501, phone: 800-228-4630.

A Gift of Hearts and Hands. Videotape, 1 hour, color. This is a PBS program about the influence of black and white women on American society through the art of quilting. It includes many news clips and still photographs that match the quilt patterns shown, bringing home the meaning of each quilting pattern as it relates to historical events such as women's suffrage, the fight for freedom and emancipation by courageous African American women like Harriet Tubman, and the underground railroad. A book, *Hearts and Hands: The Influence of Women and Quilts on American Society* by Elaine Hedges and Julie Silva, accompanies the videotape. For more information, write The American Experience #112, Hearts and Hands, Box 322, Boston, MA 02134.

Porgy and Bess. Two cassettes or video or four-sided laser disc. This performance was shown on

American Playhouse and Great Performances. Phone 800-888-8574 to order.

Porgy and Bess. A ninety-minute video documentary on the sixty-year odyssey of *Porgy and Bess* to air on PBS in 1996. Funded by NEH, NEA, and the Ford Foundation. Phone project director and producer James Standifer at 313-764-8338 or WNET at 313-560-2023 for more information.

Scott Joplin. Pyramid, 15 minutes, color, 1977. This film gives a brief introduction to the life and works of the most famous of all ragtime composers.

Videotaped Interviews with Prominent Black Musicians and Others Associated with the Development of Black Music in the U.S. VHS. Ann Arbor: University of Michigan Afro-American Music Collections, Oral History Section, the N.C. Standifer Archive. This series consists of more than 250 videotaped interviews with prominent musicians, including Count [William] Basie, Eubie Blake, Anne Brown, William Dawson, Todd Duncan, Katherine Dunham, John Hammond, Alberta Hunter, Andy Kirk, William Grant Still, and Marylou Williams. For more information, call the University of Michigan School of Music, Afro-American Music Collection, at 313-764-5429, or the University of Michigan Center for African and Afro-American Studies at 313-764-5513.

Map of the United States

ANGLO-AMERICAN MUSIC

by Ellen McCullough-Brabson

Before any discussion of Anglo-American music can take place, the term Anglo-American must be defined. Who is an Anglo-American? According to the dictionary, an Anglo-American is a United States citizen who is of English descent and culture and speaks the English language. The American "white" population includes Anglo-Americans, as well as other Western European and Eastern European subpopulations. Therefore, Anglo-Americans represent only a part of the population designated "white," an ethnic category used in census surveys. But the definition of Anglo-American remains blurred. Any attempt to group Anglo-Americans within the set of white Americans would result in a very fuzzy line due to many generations of intermarriage among the subpopulations. In fact, many Americans think of themselves as simply "American," without any hyphenation. Similarly, an attempt to distinguish Anglo-American music from other American musical forms would result in an even vaguer line. Nonetheless, an argument can be made that there is a genre of music that clearly illustrates Anglo-American influence.

What is traditional Anglo-American music? It can be defined simply as music based on a Western European model that uses English lyrics. Traditional Anglo-American music has at its foundation English, Irish, and Scottish ballads and songs. These tunes were often turned into something uniquely American, the products of which the whole country shared and called its own. Nettl supports this idea: "The oldest and fullest folk music tradition of the White Americans came from Great Britain. Many of the American songs came from England and Scotland, and upon them was superimposed a native body of folk song, created in America in the British pattern but endowed with the special qualities of American culture and personality."[1]

Therefore, a colorful and rich potpourri of traditional Anglo-American music evolved and is still performed today. Is traditional Anglo-American music a Southern Appalachian mountain ballad? A group of cloggers from Oregon? Shape-note singers at a Sacred Harp Convention in Alabama? A dulcimer player performing a sweet song? A lively bluegrass fiddle tune? A cowboy singing a night-herding song to his cattle? All these examples, and many more, illustrate the wide variety of sounds that conjure up an image of traditional Anglo-American music.

Due to the complexity of the topic and the incredible number of musical examples that could be presented to describe and define traditional Anglo-American music, only selected genres can be examined in this chapter. Southern Appalachian Mountain music, shape-note singing, and cowboy music have been selected to illustrate the wide spectrum of diverse music that we call traditional Anglo-American.

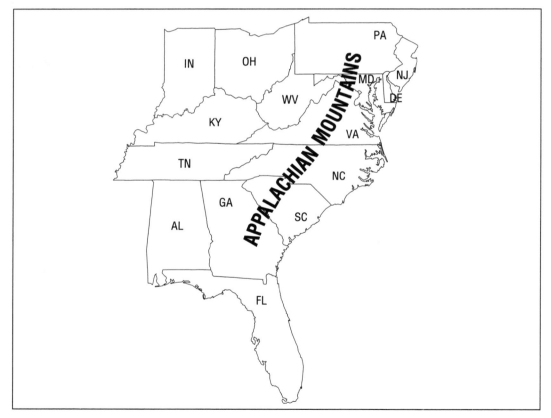

Figure 1. Map of Appalachia

SOUTHERN APPALACHIAN MOUNTAIN MUSIC

Have you ever heard of a gee-haw-whimmy-diddle or a flipperdinger? Have you churned butter, brewed sassafras tea, or listened to a "Jack" tale? These traditions (and many others) are indicative of the culture and the customs of the peoples of the Southern Appalachian Mountains.

The Southern Appalachian Mountains extend through parts of Virginia, West Virginia, North Carolina, South Carolina, Tennessee, Alabama, Georgia, and Kentucky (see figure 1). This extensive region is part of the oldest mountain range on the North American continent. This area, often called "the everlasting hills," is known for its beautiful terrain, bluegrass and country music, coal mining, and (in some sections) acute poverty.

Appalachia is often thought of in terms of physical geography only. However, many people who live in this area have a strong sense of cultural identity and refer to themselves as Appalachians, pronouncing the third syllable with a short "a" (as in "add") rather than with the long "a" of the academically preferred pronunciation. The difference may seem insignificant, but the residents of this area value their regional pronunciation as they try to define accurately and authentically their importance in the cultural makeup of the United States. Their ethnic composition is a mixture of Scotch-Irish, English, Welsh, German, French, African, American, and Cherokee, as well as other European nationalities. Regrettably, this rich culture is sometimes labeled with a negative stereotype—"hillbilly"—propagated by the mass media.

In the history of the Southern Appalachian Mountains, music has been an integral part of its culture. In the early seventeenth century, immigrants from parts of the British Isles (England, Scotland, and Wales) began to arrive in America and settle in this area, bringing their music with them. Many of the immigrants were illiterate laborers, servants, and farmers, however, so the music was not written down. Instead, it was passed orally from generation to generation. In the seclusion of the Southern Appalachian Mountains, the pioneers kept much of their music intact for many years. In fact, many of the people now living in the mountains are direct descendants of the first English settlers and continue to pass on their musical heritage in the same manner as their ancestors did.

Cecil Sharp, an English scholar and musician, discovered this reservoir of Anglo-American music when he first visited the Southern Appalachian Mountains in 1916 in search of British folk songs. He found many songs from the British Isles that were still being sung by the mountain people, seemingly untouched by the passage of three centuries. Sharp was amazed at the isolation of the area. He wrote, "There are but few roads—most of them little better than mountain tracks—and practically no railroad. Indeed, so remote and shut off from outside influence were, until recently, these sequestered mountain valleys that the inhabitants have for a hundred years or more been completely isolated from all traffic with the rest of the world."[2]

Sharp, with his assistant Maud Karpeles, collected 1,612 songs in forty-eight weeks of travel through the rugged Appalachian terrain during the years 1916–1918. Sharp wrote down the melodies and Karpeles copied the texts, and in 1932 Sharp published a two-volume set, *English Folk Songs from the Southern Appalachians*, containing 968 of these tunes. Because the purely oral transmission of these songs had led inevitably to some changes in interpretation by individual performers or local communities, there were many variants in tunes and texts.

The modern world, through such industries as coal mining, has since intruded into Southern Appalachia. Nonetheless, the old songs continue to be sung and passed on. Traditional Southern Appalachian Mountain music is still being performed today and is a significant part of the cultural heritage of the United States. It has formed the basis for many contemporary styles of music, such as country and bluegrass. Like a patchwork quilt from the same region, Appalachian music blends a wide spectrum of color, texture, and personal expression. It is a vibrant component of the musical heritage of the United States, a musically valid and interesting art form, and it offers an intriguing study of human feeling expressed through sound. It provides a natural springboard for the examination of other American musics.

The music and traditions of the Southern Appalachian Mountains are essential ingredients of the heritage of the United States and are, therefore, a meaningful part of a complete multicultural curriculum. Cecil Sharp supported this idea when he said, "Remembering that the primary purpose of education is to place the children of the present generation in possession of the cultural achievements of the past so that they may enter as quickly as possible into their racial inheritance, what better form of music or of literature can we give them than the folk songs and folk ballads of the race to which they belong, or of the nation whose language they speak?"[3]

Form

Ballads, songs, and play-party games are frequently used forms for the traditional vocal music from the Southern Appalachian Mountains. There is much use of repetition in each of these song types. A ballad is a song that tells a story. Appalachian ballads are traditionally performed by a solo, unaccompanied voice, even in the rather common case of a text that contains dialogue. No matter what the theme of the ballad, it is delivered in a detached, objective manner. Cecil Sharp commented on this unique style of Appalachian ballad singing:

> "During the performance the eyes are closed, the head upraised, and a rigid countenance maintained until the song is finished. A short pause follows the conclusion, and then the singer relaxes his attitude and repeats in his ordinary voice the last line of the song, or its title."[4]

Ballads are traditionally performed at home for family and friends and sometimes at public events. The focus is on the song, not the singer, and the singers are never conscious of the audience. Although delivered in an objective manner, the singing of the ballads is a very personal experience. No two singers would ever sing the same song in exactly the same way. Sometimes the same tune is sung with different texts.

Ballads have been written about a wide variety of topics: romance, humor, tragedy, happiness, religion, the supernatural, heroes, and historical events. An example of a ballad that may have been based on a historical event is "Wraggle-Taggle Gypsies." This ballad tells the story of a woman who is enticed to leave her husband, riches, and home to run away with the gypsies. Her husband is outraged and searches for her. There are various endings to this story, but, in one instance, there is a battle in which many are killed. This ballad may have been written about a real event that occurred in the seventeenth century, when a gypsy named Johnny Faa was killed in England when he defied many laws of the land.

An example of a humorous ballad is "The Farmer's Curst Wife." It is the story of a man who gives his wife to the devil. She creates so many problems for the devil, however, that he quickly gives her back to the farmer.

"Barbara Allen" is a ballad about love and tragedy. The heroine rejects a man who deeply loves her. He dies of a broken heart, and soon after, Barbara dies of sorrow. The ballad lyrics traditionally end by describing an image of a rose growing from the lover's grave and a thorn from Barbara's. The roses and thorns entwine as they reach upward.

The functions of the ballads varied. Because a large proportion of the population was illiterate, ballads were a source of entertainment. In addition, some ballads were used to illustrate and transmit the ideals of socially acceptable behavior: A person in a ballad who did not behave correctly was punished in some manner.

Francis James Child, an American scholar, grouped British ballads in a collection of 305 "genuine" songs (of popular origin) and gave each one a number. The texts (but not the music) of these ballads, collectively known as the "Child ballads," are contained in Child's five-volume work, *The English and Scottish Popular Ballads* (see Bibliography). Although the title for a ballad may vary in different localities, it can always be identified by a Child number.

There were also ballads native to America that covered a wide range of topics. According to one source, "These tales of murder and other crimes, true and false lovers, disasters, tragedies, and other adventures in the lives of sailors, lumberjacks, cowboys, soldiers, and even common citizens are the New World's contribution to oral-tradition balladry."[5] An example of a ballad based on an identifiable event is "Lily Schull," about the 1903 murder of a woman in Tennessee by her jealous boyfriend, Finley Preston.

In addition to the ballads, there are other styles of Anglo-American vocal literature. Cecil Sharp collected many types of music that contained only a fragment of a story or no story at all. He classified these as "songs" and described them as more emotional and passionate than a ballad. They portrayed a personal experience, rather than an objective narration of an event, and used texts shorter than those of ballads. Love is a popular theme of the songs, and the texts are often sung in the first person. Song melodies are built along more elaborate lines than are ballad tunes, and they are often sung as unaccompanied solos.

Another category of vocal music is the play-party game. Although these games may be thought of as children's songs, they actually provided recreational and social activities for young rural adults. Because dancing was once considered socially unacceptable, the euphemism "playing games" was frequently substituted for the word "dancing." Movements to the games, often very simple, were insignificant; the primary function of the dance was the selection of partners. Jealousy was not uncommon.

Melody

The melodies of the traditional ballads and songs from the Southern Appalachian Mountains are rich and varied. Some are complex, haunting, and beautiful; others are simple. Many are built on brief melodic fragments with ranges that may extend to an octave or more. Pentatonic and modal scales are frequently used, and melodies usually end on the tonic.

When Cecil Sharp studied the Anglo-American songs, he discovered much use of the pentatonic (five-note) scale. Sharp suggested that the use of this scale can be attributed to the influence and popularity of pentatonic melodies used in the northern parts of

England and Scotland. All modal forms of the common pentatonic scale (which is formed by the black keys on the piano) are used in this music; that is, any one of the five notes of the scale may serve as the tonic. Examples of traditional Appalachian pentatonic songs are "What'll I Do with the Baby-O," "Skin and Bones," and "The Mocking Bird." (See Patricia Brown's *The Mountain Dulcimer*, listed in the Bibliography, for printed versions of these songs.) Another good example of a pentatonic tune is "Sourwood Mountain," which is discussed further in Lesson Three.

Modal melodies are based on the diatonic modes. Each mode is known by a Greek name and is defined by its characteristic half- and whole-step patterns. The most prominent modes used in the traditional ballads and songs are Ionian (the "white note" scale starting on C), Dorian (starting on D), Mixolydian (starting on G), and Aeolian (starting on A). The Ionian mode, also known as major, is the most frequently used mode in Anglo-American folk tunes. The song "Go Tell Aunt Rhody" is an example (see figure 2). "Skin and Bones" may be played in the Dorian mode as well as in Aeolian or Phrygian (see Patricia Brown's *The Mountain Dulcimer*, listed in the Bibliography, for a printed version of this song). The Mixolydian mode is used for "Old Joe Clarke," and the Aeolian or minor mode is the basis for the "Wraggle-Taggle Gypsies" (see *Exploring Music* by Eunice Boardman, Beth Hardis, and Barbara Andress, listed in the Bibliography, for this example). The Phrygian (starting on E), Lydian (starting on F), and Locrian (starting on B) modes are rarely found in Appalachian music.

Appalachian music is usually based on a four-phrase melodic structure, although some irregular phrase lengths do occur. Melodies usually vary from one phrase to the next.

Rhythm

The rhythm of traditional Appalachian ballads and songs depends on the lyrics. Texts are usually balanced, four-line stanzas that rhyme at the ends of lines two and four, although this pattern may be altered by repeating the last line. Lines with three and four stressed syllables often alternate. Some refrain lines are composed of nonsense syllables.

Appalachian music commonly uses both duple and triple meters, but the meter may change frequently to accommodate the text or the singer. Sometimes the singer

Figure 2. "Go Tell Aunt Rhody"

will sustain a note of the melody (usually a weaker accent), which sometimes disguises the rhythm. This breaks up the monotonous regularity of the phrase and creates the effect of improvisation.

Texture

Monophonic texture is usually used when performing traditional Appalachian music. Ballads and songs are commonly sung by a solo, unaccompanied voice; fiddle tunes are also played without accompaniment. A dulcimer is used occasionally to harmonize by providing a countermelody, drone, or chordal accompaniment. Polyphonic and homophonic textures are more common in contemporary performances of Appalachian music. In these performances, the dulcimer may play a countermelody instead of a harmonic accompaniment. The singer and the dulcimer accompaniment may exchange melody and countermelody. The song "Go Tell Aunt Rhody" illustrates this type of accompaniment. Appalachian music also can be homophonic, using chordal accompaniments on the guitar, banjo, dulcimer, or a combination of these instruments.

Preserving the oral tradition of Southern Appalachian Mountain music is essential; thus, the expressive use of dynamics and interpretation of a selection are not written down but are left to the discretion of the individual performer. Because most traditional music is unaccompanied, the dynamic range is typically *piano* or *mezzo forte*. Instrumental music that accompanies dancing is louder.

Timbre

A discussion of Southern Appalachian Mountain music would be incomplete without the mention of some of the instruments that are commonly used. The mountain dulcimer, fiddle, banjo, and limberjack are colorful instruments that contribute richly to the musical whole.

The Appalachian or mountain dulcimer is one of the oldest American folk instruments still in use. Although the origin of the dulcimer remains a mystery, it was played in the Southern Appalachian Mountains as early as the eighteenth century. The word "dulcimer" is derived from the Latin "dulcis" (sweet) and the Greek "melos" (sound). Dulcimers can be constructed in a variety of forms, but the most familiar design is that of an elongated violin. It is a fretted instrument with either three or four strings. On a three-string dulcimer, the first treble string is used to play the melody, and the second treble and bass strings are used to play drones. The frets are arranged to yield a diatonic scale, making it possible to play in all seven diatonic modes by emphasizing a different pitch center.

To play the dulcimer, the performer holds the instrument across his or her lap and plucks the strings with a quill or pick held in the right hand, while the left hand stops the strings to change the pitches. Sometimes a "noter" (a small dowel) is used to play the melody. The noter is used to slide from fret to fret without leaving the string, which produces a whistling sound. Occasionally, snake rattles are placed inside the body of the instrument to make the strings sing out more and to strengthen the sound.

When the settlers arrived in America from the British Isles, they brought the violin with them. It was a favorite instrument, used to accompany communal social dancing, and was commonly called the fiddle. Until the twentieth century, fiddle playing was usually unaccompanied. Most music for the fiddle was handed down through an oral tradition for at least two centuries; more recently, written transcriptions have become available. Many of the Appalachian fiddlers were musically illiterate, and they did not follow traditional playing style. Rather than holding the violin in the manner of a classical violinist, fiddle players often held the instrument against the chest and grasped the bow some distance up from the frog. In some instances, steel strings were used on the fiddle to provide a more percussive sound, or rattlesnake rattles were put inside the instrument to create the same effect. Many tunes were played that an Appalachian audience would have associated with specific texts. "Old Joe Clarke," "Sourwood Mountain," and "Eliza-Jane" are a few examples that can be found in many compilations of Appalachian music.

The banjo was commonly used in the Southern Appalachian Mountains in the nineteenth century. It was modeled after an African instrument, the *halam*, and was brought to America by black slaves. Since there were so few blacks living in this region, however, the banjo was probably introduced by traveling minstrel shows or by whites who learned it from blacks living on plantations. The common banjo has frets and five strings and is plucked with either the fingers or a pick.

The limberjack is a rhythm instrument native to the Southern Appalachian Mountains (see figure 3).[6] It is usually constructed in the shape of a small man with a stick stuck into his back. When played, it is suspended over a board. The performer sits on one end of the board and hits the free end. As the board moves up and down, the limberjack goes "flying" in all directions. The motions of the limberjack imitate the movement and sounds of Appalachian clog dancing (basically a flat-footed walk with embellishments).

Figure 3. Two limberjacks

NOTES

1. Nettl, Bruno. *Folk Music in the United States: An Introduction.* Detroit: Wayne State University Press, 1974.
2. Cecil J. Sharp, *English Folk Songs from the Southern Appalachians* (London: Oxford University Press, 1983), vol. 1: xxii.
3. Sharp, *English Folk Songs,* vol. 1: 2.
4. Sharp, *English Folk Song: Some Conclusions,* 4th rev. ed. (Belmont, CA: Wadsworth, 1965), 134.
5. Charles Hamm, *Music in the New World* (New York: Norton, 1983), 60.
6. Limberjacks can be obtained from William R. Saling, Upper Sarahsville Studio, Route One, Box 308, Caldwall, OH 43724.

L E S S O N   1

■ Objectives

Students will:
1. Listen to and sing "Mister Frog Went A-Courtin' " and accompany the song on a dulcimer.
2. Identify the characteristics of a ballad.
3. Listen to two recordings of "Mister Frog Went A-Courtin' " and describe similarities and differences in the performances.
4. Draw selected scenes from the ballad and create their own picture book for the song.
5. Locate the Southern Appalachian Mountains on a map of the United States.

■ Materials

1. A picture book of "Mister Frog Went A-Courtin' "(You may want to make one, or you can use *Froggie Went A-Courting* by Chris Conover (New York: Farrar, Straus and Giraux, 1986)
2. A map of the United States
3. Crayons
4. Paper
5. Dulcimer, if available (If it is not available, sing the song as an unaccompanied melody.)
6. Recordings:
   "Mister Frog Went A-Courtin,' " from *Old Mother Hippletoe: Rural and Urban Children's Songs* (New World Records 291)
   "A Frog He Would A-Wooing Go," from *Brave Boys: New England Traditions in Folk Music* (New World Records 239)
7. Film: *Frog Went A-Courtin'* (see Filmography)

■ Procedures

1. Introduce a ballad as a song that tells a story. Explain why and how many ballads were preserved in the Southern Appalachian Mountains. Locate this area on a map of the United States.
2. Sing the song "Mister Frog Went A-Courtin' " for the students, without

Mister Frog Went A-Courtin'

Appalachian Song

Mis-ter Frog went a-court-in' and he did ride, Um-
hm! Um-hm! Mis-ter Frog went a-court-in' and he did ride,
Sword and pis-tol by his side, Um-hm, Um-hm.

2. He said, "Miss Mouse, are you within?"
Um-hm, Um-hm!
"Oh yes, Sir, here I sit and spin."

3. He took Miss Mouse upon his knee,
Um-hm, Um-hm!
And he said, "Miss Mouse, will you marry me?"

4. Oh, where will the wedding supper be?
Um-hm, Um-hm!
Away down yonder in a hollow tree.

5. Now Mister Frog was dressed in green,
Um-hm, Um-hm!
He ate so much it made him sick.

6. The first came in was a little white moth,
Um-hm, Um-hm!
He spread out the tablecloth.

7. The next came in was a bumblebee,
Um-hm, Um-hm!
With a fiddle on his knee.

8. The next came in was a little flea,
Um-hm, Um-hm!
To take a jig with the bumblebee.

9. The next came in was a pesky old fly,
Um-hm, Um-hm!
He ate up the wedding pie.

10. The next came in was a little red ant,
Um-hm, Um-hm!
She always says, "I can't, I can't."

11. The next came in was a fluffy yellow chick,
Um-hm, Um-hm!
And Miss Mouse looked like a queen.

12. The next came in was an old tomcat,
Um-hm, Um-hm!
He swallowed Miss Mouse as quick as a rat.

13. Then gentleman Frog swam, over the lake,
Um-hm, Um-hm!
But he got swallowed by a big fat snake.

14. There's bread and cheese upon the shelf,
Um-hm, Um-hm!
If you want any more, you can sing it yourself.

Figure 4. "Mister Frog Went A-Courtin' "

accompaniment (see figure 4). Ask them to join in on the "um-hm."

3. Tell the history of the song. "Mister Frog Went A-Courtin'" is an Anglo-American children's song that has existed for more than four hundred years. It was passed on from one generation to the next by oral tradition rather than by music notation. This accounts for the many variations of tune and text; in the case of this song, there are more than two hundred variants. In some accounts of the story, the mouse and the frog live happily ever after, rather than being swallowed. The different endings probably reflect the society in which they were sung. When there were good times for the common people, the song had a happy ending. When the times were bad, however, the ending was sad. Another variation of the song suggests that Miss Mouse represented Queen Elizabeth I of England and Mister Frog was the French ambassador to the English court, le Duc d'Alencon, who wanted to marry her. The song was used as a social protest against the marriage.

4. Use a homemade or printed storybook of "Mister Frog Went A-Courtin'" to illustrate the lyrics. Teach the song to the students.

5. If a dulcimer is available, tune it to the Ionian mode (the strings of the dulcimer should be tuned to D_3, A_3, and A_3). Have a student accompany the song by playing the open strings to the beat.

6. Have the students listen to the two recorded versions of "Mister Frog Went A-Courtin'." Discuss similarities and differences (for example, rhythm, lyrics, melody, and texture).

7. Have the students draw selected scenes from the song and create their own storybook. A mural could also be drawn on a large piece of paper.

Extension of Lesson One

1. Show a film of "Mister Frog Went A-Courtin'" (see the Materials section). Sing along with the film.

2. Write new verses to the song.

3. Stage a minidrama of the song with solos and chorus.

4. Make puppets and use them to dramatize the song.

5. Discuss oral tradition and play the "gossip game." One person creates a simple story (about three sentences) and whispers it to the next person, who whispers it to the next, and so on. This continues until everyone has heard the story. The last person speaks the story out loud. The last version will probably be quite different from the first. This activity will show how a song can also undergo radical changes as it is transmitted orally over time.

L E S S O N 2

■ Objectives

Students will:

1. Answer contemporary and traditional riddles.

2. Listen to and sing "The Riddle Song."

The Riddle Song

Appalachian Song

I brought my love a cher - ry that has no stone,

I brought my love a chick-en that has no ___ bone,

I told my love a sto - ry that has no end.

I brought my love a ba - by and no cry - en.

2. How can there be a cherry that has no stone?
How can there be a chicken that has no bone?
How can there be a story that has no end?
How can there be a baby with no cryen?

3. A cherry when it's blooming, it has no stone.
A chicken in the shell, it has no bone.
The story of I love you, it has no end.
A baby when it's sleepin', has no cryen.

Figure 5. "The Riddle Song"

3. View pictures from the Southern Appalachian Mountains.
4. Identify the pentatonic scale and the phrase structure used in "The Riddle Song."
5. Sing and move to the play-party game "Goin' to Boston."

■ **Materials**

1. Selected riddles (see, for example, *American Folk Tales and Songs* by Richard Chase (New York: Dover Publications, 1971) and *Way Down Yonder on Troublesome Creek: Appalachian Riddles and Rusties* by James Still (New York: Putnam, 1974))
2. Twelve pictures from the Southern Appalachian Mountains (see, for example, *Where Time Stood Still: A Portrait of Appalachia* by Bruce Roberts and Nancy Roberts (New York: Crowell-Collier Press, 1970))
3. The play-party game "Goin' to Boston," which is available in *Singing Games and Play-party Games* by Richard Chase (New York: Dover Publications, 1967)
4. Recording: "The Riddle Song," from *Edna Ritchie, Viper, Kentucky* (Folk-Legacy Records FSA-3)

■ Procedures

1. Ask the class a variety of riddles. Explain that these are an old tradition in many cultures, including Appalachia.
2. Sing, unaccompanied, "The Riddle Song" (see figure 5). Point out that there are four statements, four questions, and four answers. Riddle songs were once very popular in the British Isles. The correct answer to a riddle could mean a great fortune, a "yes" to a marriage proposal, or a life saved. In the United States, ballads with riddles were neither as widespread nor as complex as in the British Isles. "The Riddle Song," as sung in the Southern Appalachian Mountains, contains a melodic sequence in its first two phrases and is built on a pentatonic scale.
3. Have the class listen to the recording of "The Riddle Song." As the students are listening, show the twelve pictures from the Southern Appalachian Mountains (one for each phrase).
4. Teach the students "The Riddle Song." Study the pentatonic scale used in the song. Have the students identify the number of phrases.
5. Sing and illustrate the play-party game "Goin' to Boston." Teach the song and motions to the students.

Extension of Lesson Two

1. Learn other play-party games. Several of these games are printed in Richard Chase's *Singing Games and Play-party Games* and his *Old Songs and Singing Games* (see Bibliography).
2. Read about the Ritchie family in *Singing Family of the Cumberlands* (see Bibliography).
3. Listen to other dulcimer recordings such as *The Appalachian Dulcimer by Jean Ritchie: An Instruction Record* (Folkways FI 8352); *Edna Ritchie, Viper, Kentucky* (Folk-Legacy Records FSA-3); and *Larkin's Dulcimer Book* (Ivory Palaces Cassette IPC 7007) (see Discography).
4. Make a dulcimer and learn how to play it. See the Bibliography for more information.
5. Create an accompaniment for "The Riddle Song" using Orff instruments.

L E S S O N 3

■ Objectives

Students will:
1. Listen to the story "Sody Sallyraytus" and play a "bear's roar" instrument for sound effects.
2. Listen to and sing "The Wraggle-Taggle Gypsies" and watch a puppet dramatization of the story.
3. Listen to "Gypsy Davy" and compare it with "The Wraggle-Taggle Gypsies."
4. Discuss the importance of oral tradition in the Southern Appalachians.
5. Identify a Child ballad.
6. Use a limberjack to accompany a recording of "Sourwood Mountain."
7. Move to the beat of "Sourwood Mountain" and imitate the motions of the limberjack.

■ Materials

1. Finger puppets that represent one male and two female gypsies, the lady and lord of the manor, and a servant
2. "Sody Sallyraytus" in *Grandfather Tales* by Richard Chase (Boston: Houghton Mifflin, 1948)
3. Limberjacks
4. Recordings: *Folk Music of the United States: Anglo-American Ballads* (Library of Congress AFS-L1 and AFS-L12 or AFS-L21)

■ Procedures

1. Tell the tale "Sody Sallyraytus." Ask a selected student to play the "bear's roar" instrument for sound effects. You can construct one from an empty paper oatmeal container. Punch a hole in the closed end, insert a four-foot-long piece of string through the hole, and tie the string around a used match stick to hold it. The match stick should be held against the inside of the box. Wet a piece of cloth, grasp the string with the wet cloth, and run your hand along the string. It will make a sound like a bear's roar.
2. Sing "The Wraggle-Taggle Gypsies" (see figure 6). If you are teaching younger students, act out the story with finger puppets.
3. Teach the song "The Wraggle-Taggle Gypsies" to the students. Listen to "Gypsy Davy" on *Folk Music of the United States: Anglo-American Ballads* (Library of Congress AFS-L1). Discuss the way this tune and text vary from "Wraggle-Taggle Gypsies" and examine the term "oral tradition." Discuss characteristics of ballads (as explained in the beginning of this chapter) and explain why "The Wraggle-Taggle Gypsies" is a Child ballad.
4. Introduce the limberjack, a rhythm instrument from the Southern Appalachian Mountains. After showing students how to play the limberjack, have a student play it as an accompaniment to the recording of "Sourwood Mountain" as the students sing along (see figure 7); it is recorded on *Folk Music of the United States: Anglo-American Ballads* (Library of Congress AFS-L12 or AFS-L21). Record number L12 is a field recording sung by I. G. Greer of Thomasville, North Carolina, to a dulcimer accompaniment by Mrs. I. G. Greer; record number L21 is played on the banjo by Rufus Crisp. The limberjack can dance to the solo part of the song, and the students can sing the chorus. Have different groups sing the solo and the chorus. Explain that this type of singing is termed "call and response."
5. Have the students imitate the movements of the limberjack, as described in the introduction to this section, by moving to the beat of "Sourwood Mountain." You can lead by swinging your arms, hands, or elbows, or by lifting your knees.

Extension of Lesson Three

1. Have the students make their own limberjacks. A good description of the materials needed and the methods of making a limberjack can be found in *Foxfire 6* edited by Eliot Wigginton (New York: Doubleday, 1980).
2. Read other stories from the Southern Appalachian Mountains. You can find these in *American Folk Tales and Songs* by Richard Chase (New York: Dover Publications, 1971) or *Jack Tales* by Richard Chase (Boston: Houghton Mifflin, 1943).

The Wraggle-Taggle Gypsies

1. There_ were three gyp - sies a - come to my door,

And down - stairs ran this-a-la-dy, O!

The one sang high, and an-oth-er sang low,

And the oth-er sang, "Bon-ny, bon-ny Bis - cay, O!"

2. Then she pulled off her silk finished gown.
   And put on hose of leather, O!
   The ragged rags about our door,
   And she's gone with the wraggle-taggle gypsies, O!

3. It was late last night when my lord came home,
   Inquiring for his lady, O!
   The servants said on every hand,
   "She's gone off with the wraggle-taggle gypsies, O!"

4. O saddle me my milk-white steed,
   And go fetch me my pony, O!
   That I may ride and seek my bride,
   Who is gone with the wraggle-taggle gypsies, O!

5. O he rode high, and he rode low,
   He rode through wood and copses, too,
   Until he came to a wide-open field,
   And there he espied his a-lady, O!

6. What makes you leave your house and land?
   What makes you leave your money, O?
   What makes you leave your new-wedded lord?
   I'm off with the wraggle-taggle gypsies, O!

7. What care I for my house and land?
   What care I for my money, O!
   What care I for my new-wedded lord?
   I'm off with the wraggle-taggle gypsies, O!

8. Last night you slept on a goose-feather bed,
   With the sheet turned down so bravely–O!
   Tonight you'll sleep in a cold, open field,
   Along with the wraggle-taggle gypsies, O!

9. What care I for a goose-feather bed,
   With the sheet turned so bravely–O?
   For tonight I'll sleep in a cold, open field,
   Along with the wraggle-taggle gypsies, O!

Figure 6. "The Wraggle-Taggle Gypsies"

Figure 7. "Sourwood Mountain"

3. Learn a simple dance to "Sourwood Mountain." See the textbook *Music* by Elizabeth Crook, Bennett Reimer, and David S. Walker (Parsippany, NJ: Silver Burdett Ginn, 1981) for the music and dance steps.
4. Have the students make their own finger puppets for "The Wraggle-Taggle Gypsies."

L E S S O N   4

■ **Objectives**

Students will:
1. Observe a clogging demonstration.
2. Identify characteristics of clogging.
3. Dance the clogging step.

■ **Materials**

1. *Clog Dance in the Appalachians* by Jerry Duke (San Francisco: Duke Publishing, 1984)
2. Recording: *Appalachian Clog Dancing and Big Circle Mountain Square Dancing* (Educational Activities AR 53)

■ **Procedures**

1. Give a brief history of clogging. Clogging originated as a combination of foot movements and was brought to America by the early settlers. Many regional styles of clog dancing evolved and are popular in the United States today.
2. After learning the clogging steps from *Clog Dance in the Appalachians*, demonstrate how to clog. A good method for learning to clog is to pretend that you have just stepped, with the tip of each shoe, on two wads of gum. Try to get the gum off the left shoe first: Raising your heel slightly, shuffle the ball of your foot with a quick forward-and-backward motion, moving a few inches in front of your body. Keep the ball of your foot in constant contact with the floor so that it makes two distinct sounds as you move it forward and backward for the "shuffle." Then step in place with your left foot. These two movements are called the "shuffle-step" and are performed in the rhythm shown in figure 8. Another variation, the "shuffle-step-step-step," is performed in the rhythm shown in figure 9 (L represents the left foot, R the right).
3. Teach the students these simple clogging steps as they stand in place. Ask them to emphasize the rhythm of the dance with the sounds of their feet striking and shuffling along the floor. The explanations describing the clog step on *Clog Dance in the Appalachians* are clear and precise.
4. If possible, invite dancers from the community to give a clogging demonstration.

Figure 8. Shuffle step

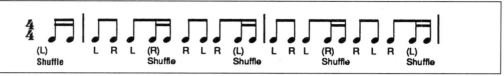

Figure 9. Shuffle-step-step-step

L E S S O N   5

■ **Objectives**

Students will:
1. Listen to "Old Joe Clarke" and identify Mixolydian mode in the verse and chorus of the song.
2. Sing "Old Joe Clarke" and create new verses.
3. Accompany "Old Joe Clarke" with a limberjack.
4. Clog to "Old Joe Clarke."

■ **Materials**

1. Limberjacks
2. Recording: "Old Joe Clarke," from *Going Down the Valley: Vocal and Instrumental Styles in Folk Music from the South* (New World Records 236)

■ **Procedures**

1. Have the students listen to the recording of "Old Joe Clarke" (see figure 10) and identify the mode of the tune as Mixolydian.
2. Teach the students "Old Joe Clarke." Once the song has been mastered, create new verses. Discuss the humor of the lyrics and the use of exaggeration techniques.
3. Listen to another version of the song; a good source is the recording that accompanies *The Music Book* by Eunice Boardman and Barbara Andress (New York: Holt, Rinehart and Winston, 1981). Ask the students to compare and contrast the two recordings, paying special attention to the melodies. How is variety created in each one?
4. Accompany "Old Joe Clarke" with a limberjack. For variety, have the students play the limberjack only on the verse or the chorus.
5. Clog to a recording of "Old Joe Clarke."

Extension of Lesson Five

1. Listen to other recordings of traditional Appalachian instrumental music on *The Appalachian Dulcimer by Jean Ritchie: An Instructional Record* (Folkways FI 8352) and *Brave Boys: New England Traditions in Folk Music* (New World Records 239). Ask the students to identify the instruments on each recording.
2. Listen to the fiddle in bluegrass music. Some good recordings are *Hills and Home: Thirty Years of Bluegrass* (New World Records 225) and *The Great Bill Monroe and His Bluegrass Boys* (Harmony HS 11335).
3. Invite a fiddler from the community to visit your class and perform for the students.

Figure 10. "Old Joe Clarke"

LESSON 6

■ **Objectives**

Students will:
1. Sing "Ev'ry Night when the Sun Goes Down" in a call-and-response fashion.
2. Listen to two or more of the following songs: "Barbara Allen," "The Devil's Nine Questions," "House Carpenter," "The Farmer's Curst Wife," and "Gypsy Davy."
3. Complete worksheets for each song.
4. Identify and discuss characteristics of traditional Anglo-American ballads.

■ **Materials**

1. Listening worksheets
2. Recording: *Folk Music of the United States: Anglo-American Ballads* (Library of Congress AFS-Ll)

■ **Procedures**

1. Sing the song "Ev'ry Night when the Sun Goes Down" (see figure 11). The teacher should sing the lead, and the students should echo the response. A dulcimer can be used to play the echo.
2. Listen to recordings of "Barbara Allen," "The Devil's Nine Questions," "House Carpenter," "The Farmer's Curst Wife," and "Gypsy Davy" on *Folk Music of the United States: Anglo-American Ballads* (Library of Congress AFS-L1). Ask the students to complete worksheets for each song, or copy the worksheet format on the board.

Listening worksheet: (circle the correct answer)

A.	1.	accompanied	unaccompanied
	2.	woman's voice	man's voice
	3.	refrain line	no refrain line
		nonsense syllables	no nonsense syllables
	4.	strict meter	flexible meter
	5.	rhyming scheme	rhyming scheme
		(phrases 1 and 3)	(phrases 2 and 4)

B. Give a brief summary of the story line.

3. Identify and discuss characteristics of traditional Anglo-American ballads as explained in the beginning of this chapter. Remember to refer to the presence of these musical characteristics in traditional Southern Appalachian Mountain music.

Extension of Lesson Six

1. Listen to other recordings of traditional vocal music of the Southern Appalachian Mountains. You can find good examples on *British Traditional Ballads in the Southern Mountains* (Folkways 8352) and *Edna Ritchie, Viper, Kentucky* (Folk-Legacy FSA-3).

Figure 11. "Ev'ry Night when the Sun Goes Down"

2. Identify contemporary songs that are ballads (for example, "The Wreck of the Edmund Fitzgerald" (Reprise, 1976, by Gordon Lightfoot)). Ask the class to compare and contrast other contemporary ballads with traditional Anglo-American ballads.

LESSON 7

■ Objectives

Students will:
1. Listen to a recording of Jean Ritchie playing "Go Tell Aunt Rhodie" and identify the tone color of the dulcimer.
2. Listen to a brief history of the origin of the dulcimer.
3. Observe a dulcimer performance and recognize the number of strings on the dulcimer, the picking scoop, the noter, the pick, and the nonequidistant fretboard.
4. Listen to the Mixolydian dulcimer tuning and identify the pattern of half and whole steps used for the Mixolydian mode.
5. Sing "Old Joe Clarke" and discover that it is in the Mixolydian mode.
6. Listen to the Ionian tuning and identify the pattern of half and whole steps used for the Ionian mode as the same as that of a major scale.
7. Sing "Go Tell Aunt Rhodie" with dulcimer accompaniment.
8. Sing "Go Tell Aunt Rhodie" with a countermelody accompaniment played on the dulcimer.
9. Sing "Go Tell Aunt Rhodie" with a chordal accompaniment played on the dulcimer.
10. Take turns playing the open strings on the dulcimer to accompany Appalachian songs, such as "Go Tell Aunt Rhodie," "Old Joe Clarke," "Every Night when the Sun Goes Down," and "Sourwood Mountain."
11. View the video, *Discovering American Folk Music*, and identify the dulcimer.

■ Materials

1. Recording of *The Appalachian Dulcimer: An Instructional Record* by Jean Ritchie (Folkways FI 8352)
2. Dulcimer
3. Modal tuning diagram
4. "Go Tell Aunt Rhodie" notation
5. "Go Tell Aunt Rhodie" countermelody notation
6. "Go Tell Aunt Rhodie" chordal arrangement notation
7. Video: *Discovering American Folk Music*

■ Procedures

1. Have the students listen to a recording of Jean Ritchie playing "Go Tell Aunt Rhodie" and identify the tone color of the dulcimer. Ask the students to guess the name of the song. Mention to them that this tune is a traditional "first" song for beginning dulcimer players to master.
2. Present a brief history of the dulcimer:

One of the oldest American folk instruments still in usage, the dulcimer is known to have been played in the Southern Appalachian Mountains in the early part of the nineteenth century. Although the dulcimer has gained in popularity since its revival in the 1960s, it is no wonder that this instrument is sometimes confused with other instruments or even remains unknown. Some of the reasons for this are that (1) the exact origin of the dulcimer is a puzzle; (2) the word "dulcimer" is sometimes used to describe similar instruments, such as the hammered dulcimer; (3) the dulcimer is not widespread in the United States; and (4) it is often given other names.

Although the exact origin of the dulcimer is a mystery, some tentative conclusions have been drawn. Both Jean Ritchie, renowned dulcimer player, and Charles Seeger, noted musicologist, surmise that the dulcimer probably evolved from the Pennsylvanian German zither, a popular instrument played by the German settlers in the Southern Appalachian Mountains during the eighteenth century. The dulcimer was possibly influenced by European instruments such as the Norwegian *langeleik*, Swedish *hummel*, and German *scheitholt*.

The first dulcimer players in the Southern Appalachian Mountains may have selected the word "dulcimer" to describe their instrument because it was mentioned in the King James version of the Bible (Daniel 3:10). Although the instrument mentioned in the Scriptures was not the same as the Appalachian dulcimer, the term might have been selected to persuade the church to sanctify its use. If the church thought that the dulcimer were sinful, it would have been banned. Another probable source for the derivation of its name is from Greek and Latin, subjects that were taught in the Southern Appalachian Mountain schools. The Latin word "dulce" means sweet, and the Greek word "melos" means sound. "Sweet sound" is an excellent description of the dulcimer's tone color. It was not uncommon for the mountain people to name their daughters Dulcimre, which means "sweet one." The dulcimer is also called the "mountain dulcimer," "lap dulcimer," and "Appalachian dulcimer." But no matter what name you may choose to call this instrument, there is one thing certain: the dulcimer makes a lovely, magical sound to your ears.

3. Play the dulcimer for the students and have them identify the strings, picking scoop, noter, and nonequidistant fret fingerboard. Explain that there are several dulcimer shapes and that the dulcimer may have three or four strings.

4. Tune the dulcimer to Mixolydian tuning (see figure 12) and play the Mixolydian mode. Ask the students to sing along on the syllable "la." Demonstrate the pattern of half and whole steps with an emphasis on the flatted seventh. Sing "Old Joe Clarke" and lead the students to discover that the song is in the Mixolydian mode.

5. Tune the dulcimer to the Ionian mode. Ask the students to sing along on the syllable "la." Lead the students to discover that the Ionian mode has the same pattern of half and whole steps as a major scale.

6. Play "Go Tell Aunt Rhodie" on the dulcimer and teach the students the words of the song. Ask them to join in with the singing as you play it on the dulcimer (see figure 13.)

7. Demonstrate the countermelody on the dulcimer (see figure 14). Have the students sing the melody of "Go Tell Aunt Rhodie" as you play the dulcimer countermelody.

8. Demonstrate the dulcimer chordal accompaniment to "Go Tell Aunt Rhodie" (see figure 15). Have the students sing the melody of the song as you play the chordal accompaniment.

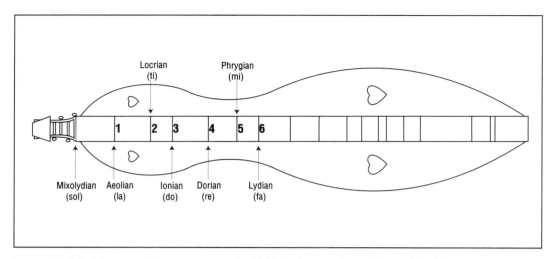

Figure 12. Modal tuning diagram, copyright 1982 by Ivory Palaces Music. Used by permission.

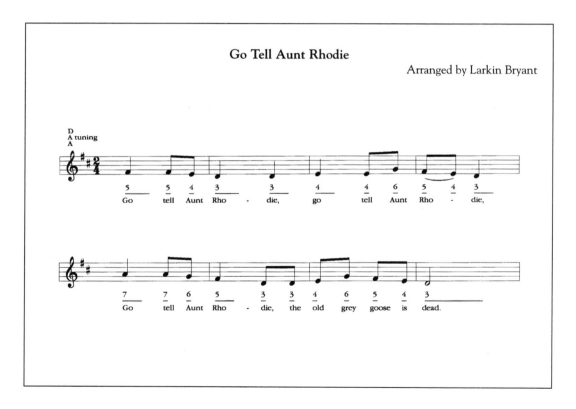

Figure 13. "Go Tell Aunt Rhodie" in Ionian mode, copyright 1982 by Ivory Palaces Music. Used by permission.

Figure 14. "Go Tell Aunt Rhodie" countermelody, copyright 1982 by Ivory Palaces Music. Used by permission.

Figure 15. "Go Tell Aunt Rhodie" chordal accompaniment, copyright 1982 by Ivory Palaces Music. Used by permission.

9. Select a student to play the open strings of the dulcimer to accompany a traditional Appalachian song, such as "Go Tell Aunt Rhodie," "Old Joe Clarke," "Ev'ry Night when the Sun Goes Down," and "Sourwood Mountain."
10. View the video *Discovering American Folk Music* and identify the dulcimer and other traditional American instruments featured in the film.

Extension of Lesson Seven

1. Listen to a variety of traditional and contemporary dulcimer sound recordings.
2. Make a dulcimer from a dulcimer-making kit. See the Bibliography for more information.
3. Research the dulcimer artist Jean Ritchie.
4. Take a survey of your friends and family and discover how many of them know what a dulcimer is.

Integrating music with other studies

Social studies

1. Lead the class in a discussion about the coal mining industry and how it has affected the land and the people who live in the Southern Appalachian Mountains.
2. Listen to several protest songs about the coal mining industry: "Black Waters," words and music by Jean Ritchie, Geordie Music Publishing, 1971, and "West Virginia Mine Disaster," words and music by Jean Ritchie, Geordie Music Publishing, 1971. These songs are recorded on *Clear Waters Remembered* (Sire/London Records).
3. Investigate traditional customs and crafts of the Southern Appalachian Mountains. A good source is *The Foxfire Book* edited by Eliot Wigginton (New York: Anchor Books, Doubleday, 1972).
4. Interview an older person in the community who can share something about his or her musical past. This is an example of oral history.
5. Examine stereotypes. Discuss the following statements and draw conclusions from them. Are stereotypes fair representations?

    a. People who live in cities are unfriendly.
    b. All snakes are harmful.
    c. Teenagers are troublemakers.

6. Read *Grandfather Tales* by Richard Chase (Boston: Houghton Mifflin, 1948) and *Jack Tales* by Richard Chase (Boston: Houghton Mifflin, 1943), and discuss the role of storytelling in a society.

Geography

1. Locate the Southern Appalachian Mountains on a map of the United States. Compare the topography and location of the Southern Appalachian Mountains with the entire Appalachian range.
2. Examine photographs of the land and people of the Southern Appalachian Mountains. You can find these photographs in *Where Time Stood Still: A Portrait of Appalachia* by Bruce Roberts and Nancy Roberts (New York: Crowell-Collier Press, 1970).
3. Compare and contrast the terrain of the Southern Appalachians with the type of environment in which you live.

4. Read poems that describe the geography of the area. You can find examples in *A Jesse Stuart Reader: Stories and Poems Selected and Introduced by Jesse Stuart* by Jesse Stuart (New York: McGraw, 1963).
5. Read *The Dollmaker* by Harriette Arnow (New York: Macmillan, 1954) and discuss the differences, as illustrated in the book, between living in rural Appalachia and post-World War II Detroit.
6. Discuss how geography played a role in the traditional ballad lyrics and explain how geography influenced the preservation of the ballad. How does the isolation of an area affect the music? Does it produce more melancholy, soulful tunes? You can find this information in *English Folk Songs from the Southern Appalachians* by Cecil Sharp (London: Oxford University Press, 1952).

History
1. Examine the history of the Southern Appalachian Mountains as told through music. Follow the growth of Anglo-American music as it influenced bluegrass and country music. See the *New Grove Dictionary of American Music* edited by H. Wiley Hitchcock and Stanley Sadie (New York: Macmillan, 1986), especially the article titled "Country Music," and "Appalachian Folk Music: From Foothills to Footlights" by Peggy Langrell, *Music Educators Journal* 72, no. 7 (March 1986): 37–39 for more information.
2. Historical figures have played a role in Appalachian ballads, as discussed in Lesson One. What contemporary songs have been written about recent figures and events?

Visual and performing arts
1. Draw a mural representing the story line of a ballad.
2. Select a ballad and present it as a drama.
3. Create a picture book illustrating the story line of a ballad.
4. Listen to a movement from any recording of *Appalachian Spring* by Aaron Copland and create a dance to a portion of it.

SHAPE-NOTE SINGING

Shape-note singing has been described as singing by letter. You open your mouth and let the "letter" fly! Actually, shape-note singing is a pedagogical tool developed in the early eighteenth century to teach people how to sight-read music through the use of unconventional shape-note music notation. In place of the usual round noteheads, shape-notes are used as a visual clue to sight-singing. The shapes consist of a triangle for "fa," a circle for "sol," a rectangle for "la," and a diamond for "mi" (see figure 16). The use of the four solmization syllables—"fa," "sol," "la," and "mi"—was derived from an English music system already in use. Shape-notes are also called "character," "patent," or "buckwheat" notes. Singers using this method do not have to worry about keys, lines, or spaces in order to read music; thus, music-reading is simplified. Except for the actual notehead shapes, standard musical notation is printed to indicate rhythms, meter signatures, and key signatures.

Shape-note singing is often associated with traditional Anglo-American sacred and secular songs. However, it should be noted that African Americans have also participated in this form of music making. Although shape-note singing was once considered the domain of the rural South, it can be found all over the United States today.

The shape-note system is based on a moveable "do." No matter what key signature or clef sign is used, scale degrees have the same note syllables and the shapes and intervals between them remain constant. Accidentals are represented by the syllables "fi," "si," and "li" for sharps and "say," "lay," and "may" for flats. A seven-shape notation system that uses a separate shape for each solmization syllable was developed after the four-shape notation and is still used by some shape-note singers.

Shape-note music is sung a cappella and in three- or four-part harmony. Alan Lomax, folklorist and musicologist, described shape-note music as "a choral style ready-made for a nation of individualists."[1] All parts have independent and interesting lines, not just the tenor melody. The melodic tenor part is sung by men and women in octaves. The treble part may also be sung by men and women, but the alto line is sung only by women and the bass line is sung only by men.

Shape-note singers include trained and untrained voices, and they sing for the sheer joy of singing. There are no auditions, no rehearsals, and no audience. Because singers tend to sing at the top of their lungs, the singing is very loud. One shape-note singing newsletter described the dynamics in shape-note singing as, "Loud is good, and louder is better!" Tradition and practice dictate when to sing softly, if ever.

A hollow square is the standard seating arrangement for shape-note choirs. All rows face the center. The tenors and altos face each other. The basses are on the tenors' left and the treble singers are on the tenors' right. This formation is used because the singing is done for the pleasure of the singers, not for some separate audience or congregation. The song leader stands in the center, faces the tenors, and conducts the beat. A singer is welcome to try different parts and to move around the room to figure out which part he or she wants to sing. Newcomers are encouraged to stand in the middle of the circle so that they can be immersed in the sound. Once a song has been selected, the shape-note syllables are sung first so that people can learn their parts, and then the words to the song are sung. The leader may give encouragement and shout, "Look at the notes! The shapes will guide you!" A song may be sung in any key that fits the crowd and feels comfortable to the singers. For example, early in the morning the conductor may lower the pitch and then gradually raise it as the day goes on. One shape-note leader said that if the pitch is too high, you bring your book down lower so that the notes "look lower." Singers need to watch the leader because the leader decides whether or not to take any repeats in the music.

Singers are also encouraged to "sing with authority." According to Hugh McGraw of Georgia, a Smithsonian Institution "Master Traditional Artist," in the early days of shape-note singing the singers never used the book once they had learned the tunes. To "do or sing with authority" meant to do it from memory. McGraw said that you really need to take care of your songs to do that. Now everyone uses the book.

Shape-note singing has been described as "majestic" and "of the folk." George Pullen Jackson, author of *White Spirituals in the Southern Uplands*, said, "This is democratic music making. All singers are peers. At the moment selection and exclusion enter, at that moment this singing of, for and by the people loses its chief characteristic."[2]

History of shape-note singing

The musical life of the New England colonists was a sorry state of affairs; they sang abysmally. There were very few books available and very few music readers. Jackson writes, "In the seventeenth-century church they sang few tunes, and the few they did were tolerated rather than prized and fostered. The spoken gospel was the thing. 'Part singing' sank to one part, the droned melody which church folk could sing, to their own satisfaction at least, without any musical instruction at all."[3] In addition, the leader "lined out" the text of the tunes. The leader sang a line of a psalm and the congregation echoed the line by rote. This type of singing produced inaccuracies in rhythm and pitch.

A solution was discovered in the early eighteenth century: the singing school. Singing schools, modeled after those in England, were led by a singing master with the purpose of teaching people how to sing. A singing master would go to a community and teach once or twice weekly for a few weeks to a month. New song texts were compiled and written by the singing-school masters, many of whom preferred writing their own books rather than using those that came from England. These new books rejuvenated the early Anglo-American musicians because many were published with new tunes and used music notation. People were not just performing by rote anymore. However, sight-singing remained difficult for most people.

In 1721, the Reverend John Tufts wrote America's first music textbook, *An Introduction for the Singing of Psalm-Tunes*. Tufts put sol-fa syllables on the staff and used a simple rhythmic notation that accompanied them. This text was a predecessor to the first shape-note publication. Although it is not known for sure who invented shape notes, the first publication to use shape notes was *The Easy Instructor* by William Little and William Smith. It was published in Albany, New York, in 1798. This text used four syllables, each with a different shape, as an aid to sight-singing and music reading. It was a set system for interval and pitch recognition. Many books were published that featured the four-shape musical notation during the late eighteenth and mid-nineteenth centuries. Although the four-shape method was widely used, a seven-shape notation was created that was preferred by some shape-note singers. This system was published in 1846 in Philadelphia by Jesse B. Aikin and called the *Christian Minstrel*. This book was very popular but was not used as much in the South. Other seven-note systems were devised. In the late nineteenth and early twentieth century, shape-note gospel hymnody developed using Aikin's seven-shape notation.

Although shape-note singing flourished during the late eighteenth to the mid-nineteenth century, the North gradually began to reject this sight-singing method. The North embraced European music, a music they considered more musically sophisticated than the tunes using shape notes. Because of this, Lowell Mason, the father of music education, promoted solmization based on the European musical tradition. Nonetheless, shape-note singing survived and flourished in the South, particularly in the rural areas, where it eventually became associated with Southern country folk.

One of the most popular shape-note books was *The Sacred Harp: The Best Collection of Sacred Songs, Hymns, Odes, and Anthems Ever Offered the Singing Public for General Use*. This text was published in Philadelphia in 1844 by Benjamin Franklin White and E. J. King. It has been in continuous use ever since. Although there have been several revisions and appendices added since then, it is often referred to as a "living tradition" because new life (in the form of new songs) is continually added to it. The title of the book, *The Sacred Harp*, does not refer to an instrument. The term "harp" is an "old timey" word for hymnal.

The Sacred Harp contains over six hundred songs including hymns, anthems, fuguing tunes, and choral works. Smith divides the songs into five main genres:

> "...plain tunes (homorhythmic settings of metrical psalms and hymns); fuguing tunes, similar to plain tunes, but with at least one passage in which the voices enter one after the other in free imitation; anthems (through-composed pieces often based on scripture); 'set pieces' which may have secular texts; and canons."[4]

The melody of shape-note tunes is often modal and nondiatonic, such as "Amazing Grace." The songs have three- or four-part harmony that includes chords with parallel fifths and octaves but without thirds. *The Sacred Harp* has some music from the colonial period and includes texts by authors such as Isaac Watts, William Couper, and Charles Wesley. Composers such as William Billings are also represented. The introduction at the beginning of the book is dedicated to "All lovers of Sacred Harp music, and to the memory of the illustrious and venerable patriarchs who established the traditional style of Sacred Harp singing and admonished their followers to 'seek the old paths and walk therein.' "[5]

In 1845, the Southern Musical Convention was formed by Benjamin Franklin White to encourage the use of Sacred Harp singing. Today, a century and a half later, shape-note conventions are still being held in the United States. There is a section in the beginning of *The Sacred Harp* that describes the organization and conduct of singings and conventions. It gives details regarding officers, committees, minutes, and information about socialization activities such as dinners and lunches. There is also a source, the "Directory and Minutes of Sacred Harp Singers," that gives a schedule of regular singings and conventions, minutes of other meetings, and the addresses and names of other sacred harp singers.[6]

Early editions of *The Sacred Harp* actually had "a set of don't." For example, the 1869 copy states:

> "a cold or cough, all kinds of spirituous liquors, violent exercise, too much bile on the stomach, long fasting, the veins overcharged with impure blood etc., etc., are destructive to the voice of one who is much in the habit of singing."[7]

In addition, it admonishes:

> "all affectations should be banished, for it is disgusting in the performance of sacred music, and contrary to that solemnity which should accompany an exercise so near akin to that which will, through all eternity, engage the attention of those who walk in climes of bliss."[8]

In 1923, African American musicians from southeastern Alabama composed and arranged tunes for the *The Colored Sacred Harp*. This book is still being used today by Black Americans in churches, schools, and conventions.

Shape-note singing is a vivid part of Anglo-American musical tradition and heritage. The fact that shape-note singers still gather together in all parts of the United States to raise their voices in joyous song is a tribute to its creative inventors and its longevity. Shape-note musicians continue to express the spirit and sentiment of the inventors when they sing lyrics from hymns such as, "Amazing grace, how sweet the sound."

Figure 16. Shape notes

NOTES

1. From notes located inside the following album jacket: *White Spirituals from the Sacred Harp: The Alabama Sacred Harp Convention* (New World Records NW 205).
2. George Pullen Jackson, as quoted in the *Desert Harmony: An Occasional Newsletter of the New Mexico Shape-Note Singers*, no. 2 (October 1994), 2.
3. George Pullen Jackson, *White Spirituals in the Southern Uplands* (Hatboro, PA: Folklore Associates, Inc., 1964), 6.
4. Kathryn Smith, "Shape-Notes: Historical Perspective and Reflections on an Early American Solfège Tradition," in *Bulletin of the International Kodály Society* 19, no. 2 (Autumn 1994): 33.
5. *The Sacred Harp: The Best Collection of Sacred Songs, Hymns, Odes, and Anthems Ever Offered the Singing Public for General Use* (Breman, GA: Sacred Harp Publishing Company, Inc., 1991), 5.
6. Kathryn Smith, "Shape-Notes," 36.
7. George Pullen Jackson, *White Spirituals in the Southern Uplands*, 98.
8. Ibid., 98.

LESSON 8

■ **Objectives**

Students will:
1. Listen to "Singing School," from *The Social Harp: Early American Shape-Note Songs* (Rounder CD 0094), which features shape-note singers, and discuss the singing style.
2. List musical characteristics of shape-note singing.
3. View the shape-note musical notation for "Happy Birthday, Anita" and practice chanting each part with the "sol-fa" syllables.
4. Sing each line of "Happy Birthday, Anita" with shape-notes.
5. Sing one or more lines of "Happy Birthday, Anita" with the traditional words.
6. View the shape-note musical notation for "Welcome, Welcome, Ev'ry Guest" and sing it using the shape-note notation.
7. Sing "Welcome, Welcome, Ev'ry Guest" in a four-part round.
8. Watch the segment on shape-note singing featured in the video *Amazing Grace with Bill Moyers*.

■ **Materials**

1. "Happy Birthday, Anita" music in shape-note music notation
2. "Welcome, Welcome, Ev'ry Guest" music in shape-note music notation
3. Video: *Amazing Grace with Bill Moyers* (PBS Home Video, PBS 102)
4. Recording: *The Social Harp: Early American Shape-Note Songs* (Rounder CD 0094)

■ **Procedures**

1. Play a recording of shape-note singing. Ask the students to identify musical characteristics representative of this singing style.
2. Show the students shape-note music notation. Give a brief history of shape-note singing and explain how the system works. Arrange the chairs in a traditional shape-note singing set-up that is used for a singing school or shape-note convention.
3. Using the tenor line first, practice singing each part of "Happy Birthday, Anita" (see figure 17) with shape notes. Combine several or all of the lines. Once the shape notes have been mastered, sing the song using the traditional words with two or more parts.
4. Sing each line of "Welcome, Welcome, Ev'ry Guest" using shape notes (see figure 18). Practice singing it as a round. Sing the song with the words. The song "Welcome, Welcome, Ev'ry Guest" is a singing exercise found in the "Rudiments of Music" section in *The Sacred Harp*.
5. Watch the shape-note singing segment found in the video *Amazing Grace with Bill Moyers* and discuss the singing, the singers, the leader, the room set-up, and any other details that are observed.

Extension of Lesson Eight

1. Take a simple melody and rewrite it using shape notes.
2. Try to find shape-note singers who may live in your community and attend a shape-note singing session.

Happy Birthday, Anita

Arranged by Hugh McGraw

Figure 17. "Happy Birthday, Anita"

3. If there is a shape-note singing group in your community, interview a singer.
4. Listen to recordings of Anglo-American and African American shape-note singers and compare the singing styles. For example, listen to the recordings *The Social Harp: Early American Shape-Note Songs* (Rounder CD 0094) and *The Colored Sacred Harp: Wiregrass Sacred Harp Singers* (DIDX 018902).

Figure 18. "Welcome, Welcome, Ev'ry Guest," copyright 1991 by the Sacred Harp Publishing Company. Used by permission.

THE COWBOY AND HIS MUSIC

The image of the American cowboy is highly romanticized. Most of us think of a handsome, virile man (like Clint Eastwood) who rides a horse, saves a damsel in distress, gets rid of all the bad guys, and gallops off into the sunset while playing his guitar and singing a tune. While some cowboys may have some, if not all, of these traits and may have performed a few, if not all, of the aforementioned good deeds, the life of a cowboy involves much more work and grit than what Hollywood has portrayed.

The cowboy profession is an old one, as attested by Biblical scriptures that describe people taking care of cattle. There were even cowherders, often referred to as cowkeepers, in the early seventeenth-century American colonies. Cows in the colonies were branded, earmarked, and driven to market. If it had not been for events that occurred at the close of the Civil War, the cowboy might never have been in the limelight of the American public.

The cowboy came into prominence during 1866–1890 (see figure 19). At the end of the Civil War, there was a food shortage in the East that caused a demand for cattle and meat. The East looked westward to Texas, land of the rugged longhorn cow, for the perfect solution to the East's problem. Cattle were transported by cowboys from Texas to the railheads that took the cows eastward. These early American cowboys were Anglo-Americans, Blacks, and Spanish *vaqueros*. The famous cattle drives began as cowboys delivered the herds via the Sedalia and Baxter Springs, Chisholm, Western, and Goodnight/Loving Trails to the East, West, and Northwest. After 1890, the railroads took over the cattle transportation industry, and barbed wire took over the open-grazing plains. The cattle drives ceased for the most part, and the cowboy adapted his lifestyle to working on a ranch.

Trail drives were a major affair and usually included a crew comprised of a trail boss, cook, and eight to ten cowboy riders, as well as a chuck wagon and many horses. It was a hard life; the cowboys herded 1,500 to 3,000 cattle up the trail. During the early part of the drive, they would travel from twenty to thirty miles per day to wear down the animals and then they would average from ten to fifteen miles per day after that. Cowboys had to control cattle stampedes, fight Indians, ford streams, find strays, save cows sinking in bogs, stand guard, ride, rope, brand, and protect their horses from stumbling into prairie dog holes. And all of these tasks were performed in every kind of weather imaginable. Needless to say, a cowboy had to handle a horse and cattle with expertise. A cowboy's most prized possessions were his hat, boots, horse, and saddle.

In spite of the cowboy's romantic image, the cowboy's life was often boring and lonely. There were days of drudgery and routine on the ranch, as well as the days of the long trail drives. Langmore states:

> "Another observer of hundreds of ranches recalled that the men were so bored that they often memorized the labels on canned goods, then recited them to their surprised visitors without warning or request. 'Condensed milk is prepared from…' went one ditty, while 'Of Peaches' was the favorite on another ranch."[1]

Cowboys also spent this time writing poetry and creating toasts, prayers, and epithets. For example, a favorite toast goes, "Up to my lips and over my gums; look out guts, here she comes!"[2] If mundane routine was a part of the cowboy's life, how did the romanticization of the cowboy materialize? A big part of the cowboy mystique was generated from Hollywood's B-rated cowboy movies that were produced in the middle part of the twentieth century.

Gene Autry and Roy Rogers were two Hollywood cowboy stars who defined the cowboy image for many Americans. They were handsome heroes who championed good over evil and upheld noble and virtuous values. Harris and Rainey examined the myth and reality of the cowboy image portrayed in early cowboy films:

> "Most B-westerns had within them elements of both reality and myth, for if the cowboy had been depicted solely as he actually was—a mostly drab, hard-working, hard-drinking, illiterate, shabbily dressed, over-sexed, and unambitious drifter—there would have been little audience for such movies. No, there had to be a bigger-than-life hero."[3]

In their book, *The Cowboy: Six-Shooters, Songs, and Sex*, Harris and Rainey questioned the following:

> Cowless cowboys. Where did all the cows go? And why did we call them cowboys when, in fact, most of the time they were marshals or Texas Rangers or just drifters? Only in a majority of Westerns was the cowboy star ever depicted as a working cowboy.

> Well-lodged hats. Yes, neither gravity, force, or 'all hell turned loose' seemed to be able to separate a cowboy's fancy stetson from his head. It was an interesting phenomenon when you stop to think about it.

> Full musical orchestrations. I never could figure out where all the music was coming from out there on the desert when Gene Autry or Roy Rogers was riding along singing to his horse. I could have sworn that either the whole Lawrence Welk orchestra or Bob Wills and his Texas Playboys were hidden behind a boulder somewhere.[4]

The romantic image depicted in films is also found in traditional cowboy music.

Photo by W. H. Cobb

Figure 19. Unidentified cowboy (circa 1900). Photo courtesy of The Albuquerque Museum.

Cowboy music

What is cowboy music? Is it music that cowboys sing? Is it music that others sing about cowboys? Or is it music with lyrics that describe what cowboys do? Probably the best answer to the question is "all of the above." Cowboy music did not stop with the end of the cattle drives; today, traditional cowboy music is performed side by side with contemporary tunes and lyrics.

The two most widely used and well-known sources for traditional cowboy music are N. Howard "Jack" Thorp's *Songs of the Cowboys* and John A. Lomax's *Songs of the Cattle Trail and Cow Camp*. Many of the songs found in these collections are well known and include such titles as "Goodbye Old Paint," "I'm Going to Leave Old Texas Now," "My Home's in Montana," "Whoopee Yi-Yi-Yo, Git along Little Dogies," "O' Bury Me Not on the Lone Prairie," "The Old Chisholm Trail," and the "Night-Herding Song." Most of these songs can still be found in elementary and middle school music texts, and a majority of them are transmitted by oral tradition at camps, meetings, and other types of gatherings.

Although there is some disagreement as to whether or not cowboys sang to their cattle during the day as they worked, there is a consensus that they did sing to their herd at night. One cowboy stated:

> "One reason I believe there was so many songs about cowboys was the custom we had of singing to the cattle on night herd. The singing was supposed to soothe them and it did; I don't know why, unless it was that a sound they was used to would keep them from spooking at other noises…The two men on guard would circle around with their horses at a walk, if it was a clear night and the cattle was bedded down and quiet, and one man would sing a verse of a song, and his partner on the other side of the herd would sing another verse; and you'd go through a whole song that way, like 'Sam Bass.' I had a cracker jack of a partner in '79. I'd sing and he'd answer, and we'd keep it up like that for two hours."[5]

Cowboys would often sing hymns to their cattle during night-herding, although it has been stated that they might not have always felt the message of the words. In addition to singing quiet songs to the herd in the evenings, cattle calls were also used to communicate.

Cowboy songs were mainly sung for entertainment around the campfire and in bunkhouses, dancehalls, and saloons. The lyrics to many of the tunes were unprintable because they quite graphically described certain parts of the human anatomy, with nothing left to the imagination. Jim Bob Tinsley states, "The repertoire of the cowboy included hymns, bawdy ditties, familiar ballads, cowboy songs of communal authorship, popular songs of the day, and poems that had been put to music with either original or borrowed tunes."[6] Some cowboy singers yodeled and used falsetto singing. Bruno Nettl describes this vocal characteristic and the form often used in cowboy music: "In some of them, the stanzas are followed by a falsetto refrain with meaningless syllables for a text. Others have no strophic structure but simply an alternation of a falsetto phrase with one sung in a normal voice."[7]

The majority of cowboy songs were sung unaccompanied, unlike the image of the singing cowboy on his horse projected in the old cowboy movies. Favorite instruments were the fiddle, banjo, guitar, accordion, harmonica, and jew's harp. Cowboys also enjoyed dancing where they could act wild, rowdy, and crazy.

There is a close connection between cowboy poetry and cowboy song. In the early cowboy collections, both cowboy poems and songs were printed, many without musical notation. Some poets set their poems to music. Often they became so popular through oral tradition that the poet was long forgotten, even though the song became a permanent part of the cowboy repertoire. Some cowboys today prefer to just speak the words of a cowboy song; a good voice is not always needed, just an exceptional memory.

Logsdon suggests that the romanticization of the cowboy image was due in part to the early collection of songs. When the songs were transcribed, the words were often changed to fit the modified tunes in order to appeal to the general public. He states:

> The origin of cowboy songs has been of limited concern for the second, third, and fourth generation of cowboys and collectors who accept the romantic image of the cowboy and protect it. However, the first generation of cowboys only sang a few occupational songs, which were mostly lyrical. Most of the great ballads or narratives came from the second generation or, as stated previously, from the noncowboy.[8]

Logsdon also rejects the idea that cowboys' work songs were sung to the gait of a horse:

> It is highly improbable that much singing was done on horseback except at a slow walking pace. Also, the work was hard, dusty, nonrhythmic activity, and to think that a cowboy, face covered with a kerchief, eating dust, trailing cattle, could sing is ludicrous. Horseback riding is not conducive to singing. However, musical yells were used for driving cattle.[9]

The American cowboy of the twentieth century is alive and well. He can be found working on a ranch or riding in a rodeo. His music can also be heard at cowboy symposiums where poetry is recited, music is performed, and dancing is featured. There are also cowboy country music artists who perform dance music for the two-step, waltz, schottische, and line dance. Although the lyrics of a contemporary popular song warn, "Mama, don't let your babies grow up to be cowboys," some would say that the romantic and noble image of the cowboy is an important part of Americana and, indeed, much needed in our contemporary world.

NOTES

1. Bank Langmore, *The Cowboy* (New York: William Morrow and Company, 1975), 17.
2. John A. Lomax and Alan Lomax, *Cowboy Songs and Other Frontier Ballads* (New York: Macmillan, 1938), 63.
3. Charles W. Harris and Buck Rainey, *The Cowboy: Six-Shooters, Songs, and Sex* (Norman, OK: University of Oklahoma Press, 1976), 23.
4. Ibid., 23–24.
5. E. C. Abbott ("Teddy Blue") and Helena Hunington Smith, *We Pointed Them North: Recollections of a Cowpuncher* (Norman, OK: University of Oklahoma Press, 1955), 223.
6. Jim Bob Tinsley, *He Was Singin' This Song* (Orlando, FL: University Presses of Florida, 1981), 17.
7. Bruno Nettl, *An Introduction to Folk Music in the United States* (Detroit, MI: Wayne State University Press, 1962), 52.
8. Charles W. Harris and Buck Rainey, eds., *The Cowboy: Six-Shooters, Songs, and Sex* (Norman, OK: University of Oklahoma Press, 1976), 131. Guy Logsdon is a contributing author for the book.
9. Ibid., 132.

LESSON 9

■ Objectives

Students will:

1. Sing "Old Texas" in a call-and-response style.
2. Brainstorm and list facts they know about cowboys.
3. Listen to a brief history of the American cowboy.
4. Discuss the American cowboy image as portrayed by the media.
5. Listen to "Cattle Calls" and follow the iconic notation that outlines the sounds.
6. Listen to "Cattle Call" sung by Tex Owens and identify the falsetto and "normal" singing style.
7. Dance to "Cotton-Eyed Joe."
8. Listen to "Back in the Saddle Again" and "Streets of Laredo" and compare and contrast the two songs.

■ Materials

1. Music notation for "Old Texas"
2. Recording of "Cattle Calls," from *Cowboy Songs, Ballads, and Cattle Calls from Texas*, performed by Sloan Matthews, AAFS L28, side 1, band 6
3. Recording of "Cattle Call," from *Back in the Saddle Again: American Cowboy Songs*, performed by Tex Owens, New World Records NW 314/315, side 3, band 4
4. Recording of "Cotton-Eyed Joe" and dance instructions
5. Recording of "Back in the Saddle Again," from *Back in the Saddle Again: American Cowboy Songs*, performed by Gene Autry, New World Records NW 314/315, side 3, band 8
6. Recording of "Streets of Laredo," from *Back in the Saddle Again: American Cowboy Songs*, performed by John G. Prude, New World Records NW 314/315, side 1, band 5

■ Procedures

1. Have the students sing "Old Texas" in a call-and-response style (see figure 20). Discuss the lyrics of the song and ask questions such as, "Why were the cowboys going to leave Texas?" "What significance was there in fencing the cattle range?"
2. Have the students brainstorm facts about the American cowboy. Make a list of their ideas.
3. Present a brief summary of the history of the American cowboy with an emphasis on the cattle drives. Show pictures of cowboys and cattle drives or an excerpt from the television movie, "Lonesome Dove."
4. Analyze the romanticized image of the cowboy and the media's influence on our perception.
5. Listen to "Cattle Calls" and have the students create their own iconic notation for each call. Use the "Cattle Call" visual for a comparison of what they heard.
6. Listen to "Cattle Call" and identify the use of falsetto singing, a characteristic vocal timbre used in some cowboy songs.
7. Dance to "Cotton-Eyed Joe," a country music favorite. Students should form a double circle of partners, all facing counterclockwise. Partners should stand side by side, holding right hands in right hands and left hands in left. Throughout the A section, have the students do the following movement while alternating left and right feet:

brush, kick, step, step step.

   Throughout the B section, repeat the following pattern, alternating right and left feet, moving the circle forward counterclockwise: step forward with the left foot, close right to left heel, step forward with the left foot. (These patterns are based on directions from Barbara Staton, et. al. *Music and You*, Grade 5 (New York: Macmillan, 1988), 269.)

8. Listen to "Back in the Saddle Again" and compare and contrast this song with "Streets of Laredo." Make a list of similarities and differences.
9. View a Gene Autry movie and critique and analyze the romantic image that is projected.

Extension of Lesson Nine

1. Watch a contemporary cowboy western movie or television show and list stereotypical images.
2. Examine nineteenth- and twentieth-century works of art that depict the American cowboy.
3. Listen to cowboy country music artists and compare and contrast their songs with traditional cowboy music.
4. Dance the waltz to a country music tune.
5. Read cowboy poetry.

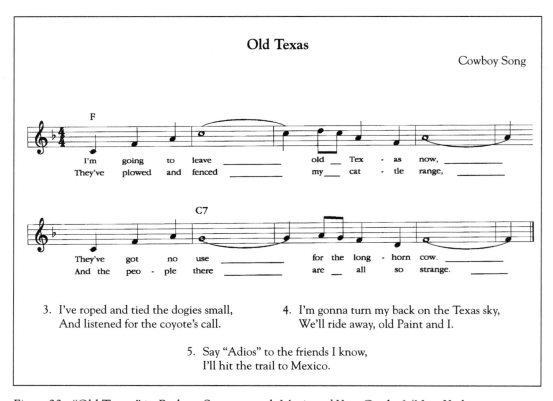

Figure 20. "Old Texas," in Barbara Staton, et. al, *Music and You*, Grade 6 (New York: Macmillan, 1988)

SOUTHERN APPALACHIAN MOUNTAIN MUSIC
BIBLIOGRAPHY

Armstrong, Randall. "The Adaptable Appalachian Dulcimer." *Music Educators Journal* 66, no. 6 (February 1980): 39–41. This article provides information about the dulcimer and how to play it.

Arnow, Harriette. *The Dollmaker.* New York: Macmillan, 1954. This is a touching story about an Appalachian woman and her family who move to Detroit.

Bennett, George E. *Appalachian Books and Media for Public and College Libraries.* Morgantown, WV: West Virginia University Library, 1975. This annotated bibliography includes picture books, folklore and music, films, videotapes, phonograph recordings, and periodicals.

Boardman, Eunice, and Barbara Andress. *The Music Book.* New York: Holt, Rinehart and Winston, 1981. This book contains lessons with selected Appalachian songs.

Boardman, Eunice, Beth Landis, and Barbara Andress. *Exploring Music.* New York: Holt, Rinehart and Winston, 1975. The lessons in selected grade levels of this textbook contain Appalachian songs.

Botkin, B. A. *The American Play-Party Song.* New York: Frederick Ungar, 1963. This book contains many detailed discussions of play-party games.

Brown, Patricia. *The Mountain Dulcimer.* Woods Hole, MA: N.P., 1979. This is an excellent resource with visual aides for learning how to play the dulcimer.

Brown, Tom. "Sugar in the Gourd: Preserving Appalachian Traditions." *Music Educators Journal* 70, no. 3 (November 1983): 52–55. The author describes an innovative project to help keep the Appalachian musical heritage alive.

Bryant, Larkin. *Larkin's Dulcimer Book.* Memphis, TN: Ivory Palaces Music Publishing, 1982. This book presents a logical, easy method for playing the dulcimer. An excellent audiotape accompanies the book.

Campbell, Olive, and Cecil J. Sharp. *English Folk Songs from the Southern Appalachians.* New York: Putnam, 1917. This is a collection of ballads and songs from the Southern Appalachian Mountains.

Chase, Richard. *American Folk Tales and Songs.* New York: Dover Publications, 1971. This is a compilation of folk tales, songs, and riddles.

Chase, Richard. *Grandfather Tales.* Boston: Houghton Mifflin, 1948. This collection of stories indigenous to the Southern Appalachian Mountains includes "Sody Sallyraytus."

Chase, Richard. *Jack Tales.* Boston: Houghton Mifflin, 1943. This book contains traditional stories from Appalachia about a boy named Jack.

Chase, Richard. *Old Songs and Singing Games.* New York: Dover Publications, 1972. This is an excellent collection of songs, ballads, carols, folk hymns, rounds, singing games, play-party games, and country dances from the Southern Appalachian Mountains.

Chase, Richard. *Singing Games and Play-party Games.* New York: Dover Publications, 1967. This is a book of folk games, children's singing games, and boy's singing games.

Child, Francis James. *The English and Scottish Popular Ballads.* New York: Dover Publications, 1965. This is a collection of the Child ballads.

Conover, Chris. *Froggie Went A-Courting.* New York: Farrar, Straus and Giraux, 1986. This book contains both the music for the ballad and charming illustrations of it.

Cooperative Recreation Service. *Songs of All Times.* Burnsville, NC: World Around Songs, 1957. This publication contains representative songs and ballads from the Southern Appalachian Mountains.

Crook, Elizabeth, Bennett Reimer, and David S. Walker. *Music.* Parsippany, NJ: Silver Burdett Ginn, 1981. The lessons in selected grade levels in this textbook contain Appalachian songs.

Duke, Jerry. *Clog Dance in the Appalachians.* San Francisco: Duke Publishing, 1984. This book gives a history of clogging and a variety of clogging styles.

Hamm, Charles. *Music in the New World*. New York: Norton, 1983. A discussion of Anglo-American music is included in this book.

Hitchcock, H. Wiley, and Stanley Sadie, eds. *The New Grove Dictionary of American Music*. New York: Macmillan, 1986. This reference work is a good source of information on many aspects of American music.

Karpeles, Maud, ed. *Eighty English Folk Songs from the Southern Appalachians*. Cambridge, MA: MIT Press, 1968. An interesting introduction to this collection provides information about how Karpeles and Cecil Sharp collected these folk songs.

Landeck, Beatrice, Elizabeth Crook, and Harold C. Youngberg. *Making Music Your Own*. Morristown, NJ: Silver Burdett, 1971. Selected grade levels in this textbook contain a variety of Appalachian songs.

Langrell, Peggy. "Appalachian Folk Music: From Foothills to Footlights." *Music Educators Journal* 72, no. 7 (March 1986): 37–39. The author describes the roots of traditional Appalachian music and its influence on country music.

Langstaff, John. *Frog Went A-Courtin'*. New York: Harcourt Brace, 1955. This is a colorful picture book of this old Anglo-American ballad.

Lomax, Alan. *American Ballads and Folk Songs*. New York: Macmillan, 1964. This collection contains a wide variety of traditional tunes and texts.

Marsh, Mary Val, Carroll Rinehart, and Edith Savage. *The Spectrum of Music with Related Arts*. New York: Macmillan, 1980. Selected grade levels in this book contain a variety of Appalachian songs.

Nettl, Bruno. *Folk Music in the United States: An Introduction*. Detroit: Wayne State University Press, 1976. This is a discussion of Southern Appalachian Mountain music.

Ritchie, Jean. *The Dulcimer Book*. New York: Oak Publications, 1974. The author presents a history of the dulcimer and clear, simple instructions on how to play it.

Ritchie, Jean. *Singing Family of the Cumberlands*. New York: Oxford University Press, 1955. This book includes interesting vignettes from the life of the Ritchie family as seen through the eyes of Jean Ritchie.

Roberts, Bruce, and Nancy Roberts. *Where Time Stood Still: A Portrait of Appalachia*. New York: Crowell-Collier Press, 1970. This publication contains excellent pictures of the region and its people.

Seeger, Charles. "The Appalachian Dulcimer." *Journal of American Folklore* 72 (January–March 1958): 40–51. This is a discussion of the history and construction of the dulcimer.

Seeger, Ruth. *American Folk Songs for Children*. Garden City, NY: Doubleday, 1948. This is an excellent resource with songs and notes on how to teach them.

Sharp, Cecil J. *English Folk Song: Some Conclusions*. 4th ed. Belmont, CA: Wadsworth Publishing, 1965. The author discusses musical characteristics of English folk songs and Southern Appalachian Mountain music in this book.

Sharp, Cecil J. *English Folk Songs from the Southern Appalachians*. London: Oxford University Press, 1952. This is a classic and timeless collection of ballads and songs from the Southern Appalachian Mountains.

Still, James. *Way Down Yonder on Troublesome Creek: Appalachian Riddles and Rusties*. New York: Putnam, 1974. This is a collection of Appalachian sayings and riddles.

Stuart, Jesse. *A Jesse Stuart Reader: Stories and Poems Selected and Introduced by Jesse Stuart*. New York: McGraw, 1963. This book contains a variety of literature by an Appalachian author.

Wigginton, Eliot, ed. *The Foxfire Book*. New York: Anchor Books, Doubleday, 1972. Written by high school students from Appalachia, this book contains a wealth of information about traditional Appalachian customs and ways of doing things.

Wigginton, Eliot, ed. *Foxfire 6*. New York: Doubleday, 1980. This book includes a description of the process of making a limberjack.

DISCOGRAPHY

Anglo-American Ballads. Folkways 2037. This record contains excellent representative recordings.

Appalachian Clog Dancing and Big Circle Mountain Square Dancing. Educational Activities AR 53. This is a demonstration record by Glenn Bannerman with clear instructions on how to clog.

The Appalachian Dulcimer by Jean Ritchie: An Instruction Record. Folkways FI 8352. This record provides excellent playing instructions and models of dulcimer playing.

Brave Boys: New England Traditions in Folk Music. New World Records 239. This record features Gail Stoddard Storm singing "A Frog He Would A-Wooing Go."

British Traditional Ballads in the Southern Mountains. Vol. 1. Folkways 8352. Selected Child ballads are featured in this recording by Jean Ritchie.

Child Ballads Traditional in the United States (I) and (II). Library of Congress, AAFS L57, AAFA L58. This is an excellent resource for traditional ballads sung by untrained singers, edited by Bertrand H. Bronson. "The Two Sisters," "Lord Bateman," and "The Devil and the Farmer's Curst Wife" are included.

Children's Songs and Games from the Southern Mountains. Folkways FC 7054. Features Appalachian music for children as sung by Jean Ritchie.

Edna Ritchie, Viper, Kentucky. Folk-Legacy Records FSA-3. This record includes "The Riddle Song."

Folk Music of the United States: Anglo-American Ballads. Library of Congress, AFS-L1, AFS-L12, and AFS-L21. This contains an excellent variety of traditional ballads and singers, edited by Alan Lomax.

Going Down the Valley: Vocal and Instrumental Styles in Folk Music from the South. New World Records 236. This recording includes "Old Joe Clarke."

The Great Bill Monroe and His Bluegrass Boys. Harmony HS 11335. This is a recording of classic bluegrass music at its best.

Hills and Home: Thirty Years of Bluegrass. New World Records 225. This is a representative sample of bluegrass music.

I'm On My Journey Home: Vocal Styles and Resources in Folk Music. New World Records 223. I. N. Marlor sings "Barbara Allen" on this recording.

Larkin's Dulcimer Book. Ivory Palaces Cassette IPC 7007. This is a good introduction to the dulcimer.

Oh, My Little Darling: Folk Song Types. New World Records 245. Several Anglo-American ballads are featured on this recording.

Old Mother Hippletoe: Rural and Urban Children's Songs. New World Records 291. This recording features Almeda Riddle singing "Mister Frog Went A-Courtin'."

Richard Chase Tells Three "Jack" Tales from the Southern Appalachians. Folk-Legacy FTA-6. Three stories are told on this record, taped before a live audience of children.

FILMOGRAPHY

American Patchwork: Appalachian Journey. PBS Home Video. PBS 300.

End of an Old Song. Produced by John Cohen. Macmillan Films, 34 MacQuesten Parkway South, Mt. Vernon, NY 10550. 16mm, 26 minutes, black and white. This film features mountain songs from North Carolina.

Fine Time at Our House: A Film on Old-Time Mountain Music. Produced by Lois Tupper and Boston University, 1972. Available from Lois Ann Tupper, 60 Chilton Street, Cambridge, MA 02138. 16mm, 30 minutes, color. This film presents mountain people who sing and play their music as they go about their daily lives.

Frog Went A-Courtin'. Produced and distributed by Weston Woods Studios, 389 Newtown Turnpike, Weston, CT 06883. 16mm. 12 minutes, color. This is a sing-along performance by John Langstaff.

Froggie Went A-Courtin'. Produced and distributed by Barr Films, 3490 East Foothill Boulevard, Pasadena, CA 91107. 16mm, 6 minutes, color. This is a dramatization of the ballad.

A Froggie Went A Courtin'. Produced and distributed by Lucerne Films, 37 Ground Pine Road, Morris Plains, NJ 07950. 16mm, 4 minutes, color. This is an animated version of the song.

Music Makers of the Blue Ridge. Produced by David Hoffman, National Educational Television, 1966. Available from NET Film Service, Indiana University Audio-Visual Center, Bloomington, IN 47401. 16mm, 45 minutes, black-and-white. This film features folk music and folk dances.

Music of Many Mountains. M-12a, Mountain Music; M-12b, Tommy Jarrell; M-12c, Taylor and Stella Kimble; M-12d, Mountain Music. These videotapes are available from Broadside T.V. and Videomaker, 204 East Watauga, Johnson City, TN 37601.

Tomorrow's People. Produced by Appalachian Educational Media Project, PO Box 743, Whitesburg, KY 41853. 16mm, 25 minutes, sound. The music of Appalachia is presented without narration in this film.

DULCIMER MUSIC
DISCOGRAPHY

The Appalachian Dulcimer by Jean Ritchie: An Instruction Record. Folkways FI 8352. Available from Smithsonian/Folkways Recordings, c/o Office of Folklife Programs, L' Enfant Plaza, Suite 2600, Washington, D.C. 20560.

Appalachian Dulcimer Duets: Neal Hellman. Kicking Mule Records, Inc. KM 222. Available from Kicking Mule Records, Box 158, Alderpoint, CA 95411.

Doug Berch: English and Scottish Dances, Songs and Airs for Dulcimer. Kicking Mule Records, Inc. KM 232, available from Kicking Mule Records, Box 158, Alderpoint, CA 95411.

Dulcimer Duets, Rounds, and Ensembles by Lois Hornbostel. Mel Bay, MB 94041C. Available from Lois Hornbostel, 3309 Old Montgomery Place Road, Monroe, NC 28110.

Dulcimer Four: Leo Kretzner and Jay Leibovitz. Traditional Records, TR-018. Available from Traditional Records, PO Box 8, Cosby, TN, 37722.

Edna Ritchie, Viper, Kentucky. Folk-Legacy Records, FSA-3. Available from Smithsonian/Folkways Recordings, c/o Office of Folklife Programs, L'Enfant Plaza, Suite 2600, Washington, D.C. 20560.

Elizabethan Music for Dulcimer by Randy Wilkinson. Kicking Mule Records, Inc. KM226. Available from Kicking Mule Records, Box 158, Alderpoint, CA 95411.

Fiddle Tunes for Dulcimer: Mark Nelson. Kicking Mule Records, Inc. KM 218. Available from Kicking Mule Records, Box 158, Alderpoint, CA 95411.

Fingerpicking Dulcimer: Tanita Baker. Kicking Mule Records, Inc. KM 218. Available from Kicking Mule Records, Box 158, Alderpoint, CA 95411.

Larkin's Dulcimer Book. Ivory Palaces, IPC 7007. Available from Ivory Palaces Music Publishing Company, Inc., 3141 Spottswood Avenue, Memphis, TN 38111.

Lois Hornbostel: Vive le Dulcimer! Kicking Mule Records, Inc. KM 235. Available from Smithsonian/Folkways Recordings, c/o Office of Folklife Programs, L'Enfant Plaza, Suite 2600, Washington, D.C. 20560.

Mountain Dulcimer and Psaltery Instrumentals by Terry Rockwell and Mary Ann Samuels. Traditional Records, TRC-019. Available from Traditional Records, PO Box 8, Cosby, TN 37722.

Note. For information on dulcimer-making kits, contact: Appalachian Mountain Dulcimers, Warren A. May, College Square, Berea, KY 40403; Backyard Music (Dulcimer Kits, Dulcimers, Workshops, Group Discount Prices), David Cross, 509 South 44th Street, Philadelphia, PA

19104; Cripple Creek Dulcimers, The Dulcimer Shop, PO Box 284, Cripple Creek, CO 80813; Green River Dulcimers, Bill Walker, Elkhorn, KY 42733; or Hughes Dulcimer Company, 4419 W. Colfax Avenue, Denver, CO 80204.

SHAPE-NOTE SINGING

BIBLIOGRAPHY

Desert Harmony: An Occasional Newsletter of the New Mexico Shape-Note Singers. No. 2 (October, 1994).

Eskew, Harry. "Shape-note Hymnody." *New Groves Dictionary of Music and Musicians,* Stanley Sadie, ed. 223–228.

Jackson, George Pullen. *White Spirituals in the Southern Uplands.* Hatboro, PA: Folklore Associates, Inc., 1964.

Hitchcock, H. Wiley. *Music in the United States: A Historical Introduction.* 2d ed. Englewood Cliffs, NJ: Prentice-Hall, 1974.

The Sacred Harp: The Best Collection of Sacred Songs, Hymns, Odes, and Anthems Ever Offered the Singing Public for General Use. Bremen, GA: Sacred Harp Publishing Company, Inc., 1991. For more information, contact Hugh McGraw at 770-537-2283 or 770-562-3221.

Smith, Kathryn. "Shape-Notes: Historical Perspective and Reflections on an Early American Solfège Tradition." *Bulletin of the International Kodály Society* 19, no. 2 (Autumn 1994): 30–40.

DISCOGRAPHY

The Colored Sacred Harp: A Songbook by Nineteenth Century African-Americans. (CD notes) Wiregrass Sacred Harp Singers. New World Records. DIDX 018902. Available from New World Records, 701 Seventh Ave., New York, NY 10036.

Fasola: 53 Shape-Note Hymns: All Day Sacred Harp Singing, Houston, Mississippi. Smithsonian/Folkways 4151. Available from Smithsonian/Folkways, c/o Office of Folklife Programs, L'Enfant Plaza, Suite 2600, Washington, DC 20560.

The Social Harp: Early American Shape-Note Songs. (CD notes) Performed by Southern Traditional Singers. Rounder CD 0094. Available from Rounder Records, One Camp St., Cambridge, MA 02140.

FILMOGRAPHY

Amazing Grace with Bill Moyers. PBS Home Video, PBS 102.

THE COWBOY AND HIS MUSIC

BIBLIOGRAPHY

Allen, Jules Verne. *Cowboy Lore.* San Antonio, TX: The Naylor Company, 1950.

Bell, William Gardner. *Will James: The Life and Works of a Lone Cowboy.* Flagstaff, AZ: Northland Press, 1977.

Billington, Ray A. *America's Frontier Culture.* College Station, TX: Texas A&M University Press, 1977.

Brookings, George L. *70 Years Cowboy on the Frontier.* Washington State: G. L. Brookings, 1987.

Cannon, Hal. *Cowboy Poetry: A Gathering.* Salt Lake City, UT: Gibbs M. Smith, Inc., 1985.

Cook, James H. *Longhorn Cowboy*. Norman, OK: University of Oklahoma Press, 1942.

Davis, Tom. *Be Tough or Be Gone: The Adventures of a Modern-Day Cowboy*. Alamosa, CO: Northern Trails Press, 1984.

Fife, Austin, and Alta Fife. *Ballads of the Great West*. Palo Alto, CA: American West Publishing Company, 1970.

Finger, Charles J. *Sailor Chanties and Cowboy Songs*. Girard, KS: Haldeman-Julius Company, 1923.

Hall, Douglas Kent. *Working Cowboys*. New York: Holt, Rinehart, and Winston, 1984.

Harris, Charles W., and Buck Rainey, eds. *The Cowboy: Six-shooters, Songs, and Sex*. Norman, OK: University of Oklahoma Press, 1976.

Langmore, Bank. *The Cowboy*. New York: William Morrow and Company, 1975.

Lomax, John A., and Alan Lomax. *Cowboy Songs and Other Frontier Ballads*. New York: Macmillan Company, 1938.

Martin, Russell. *Cowboy: The Enduring Myth of the Wild West*. New York: Stewart, Taborit, Chang Publishers, 1983.

Neil, J. M., ed. *Will James: The Spirit of the Cowboy*. Casper, WY: Nicolaysen Art Museum, 1985.

Ohrlin, Glenn. *The Hell-Bound Train*. Urbana, IL: University of Illinois Press, 1973.

Savage, William W. Jr., ed. *Cowboy Life: Reconstructing an American Myth*. Norman, OK: University of Oklahoma Press, 1975.

Texas Cowboy Artists Association. *The Texas Cowboy*. Fort Worth: Texas Christian University Press, 1984.

Thorp, N. Howard (Jack). *Songs of the Cowboys*. Lincoln, NE: University of Nebraska Press, 1984.

Tinsley, Jim Bob. *He Was Singin' This Song*. Orlando, FL: University Presses of Florida, 1981.

White, John. *Git Along, Little Dogies*. Urbana, IL: University of Illinois Press, 1975.

DISCOGRAPHY

Asch Recording 1939–1945, Volume 2. ASCH AA 3/4.

Back in the Saddle Again: American Cowboy Songs. New World Records 314/315.

Cowboy Songs, Ballads, and Cattle Calls from Texas. AAFS L28.

String Band Instrumentals: The New Lost City Ramblers. FA 2492.

FILMOGRAPHY

The American Cowboy Collection: Do You Mean There Are Still Real Cowboys? (PBS 388).

Buckaroo Bard (PBS 389).

Cowgirls (PBS 390).

On the Cowboy Trail (PBS 391).

A Salute to the Cowboy (PBS 392).

Map of Central America, South America, and the Caribbean Islands

LATIN AMERICA AND THE CARIBBEAN

by Dale A. Olson

L atin America is a vast area that stretches from the southern border of the United States through Mexico in North America, through Central America and the Caribbean, to Cape Horn at the southern tip of South America. Many of the inhabitants of the Caribbean basin are of northern European or African descent, so the term "Caribbean" (a geographic term) is often used separately from Latin America, even though many people from the Caribbean are also "Latinos." In our context, however, the term "Latin America" will include the Caribbean area. There are so many countries included in this vast region that not all of them can be included in this chapter.

Latin Americans are not all of one race or ethnic group. They can be separated into five large groups as follows: (1) descendants of the original Native Americans, commonly called Indians, who inhabited this region before the arrival of Columbus; (2) peoples of African descent, mainly from Western and Central Africa; (3) peoples of European descent, mainly Spanish and Portuguese, but also French, Dutch, Italian, British, and others; (4) peoples of Asian descent, mainly Chinese, Japanese, Indians, and Javanese;

and (5) peoples who are mixtures of any of these groups.

Latin America's geography and culture are tremendously varied. Although it is impossible to make sweeping statements that describe the music and way of life of the many peoples living in Latin America, it can be said that contemporary Latin American music and culture is the direct result of certain shared historical influences.

In the late fifteenth century, for example, Europeans invaded the region now called Latin America and maintained control of it for about four hundred years. In some places, such as the Caribbean islands, most of the Native Americans did not survive the European domination. But in certain parts of Central and South America, some Native American cultures survived by retreating into the dense jungle interiors or the vast mountain reaches. The Europeans also brought in large numbers of African slaves to work on the islands and the coastal areas of Latin America, and after the slaves obtained their freedom, they were replaced by hired workers from other far-off lands. In Guyana, Jamaica, and Trinidad, the Europeans brought in Asian Indian and Chinese laborers; in Brazil and Peru, many Japanese were imported as laborers. Many of these workers never returned to their native lands after their contracts ran out.

Contemporary Latin America is the product of the influences of several cultures. Many of these diverse groups handed down and maintained their customs, beliefs, and culture patterns for generations. Not only do these cultures contain original traits from their past, but the fact that they came together in similar geographical regions under similar historical circumstances caused many of them to interact, mix, blend, and create new and unique cultural patterns. It is more accurate to describe Latin America as an area comprising many cultures rather than just one.

It was only in Latin America that the musics and cultures of the Aztecs, Mayas, and Incas blended with the musics and cultures of the Spanish. No other geographic region has provided us with such a mixture of African music and Spanish/Portuguese music. Moreover, the steel band of Trinidad bears a resemblance to some African percussion ensembles, but it was born in a new environment using a new set of instruments: oil drums. These examples help illustrate how Latin American musics have a flavor all their own.

The Native American peoples of Latin America, as in North America, probably began arriving in the Western Hemisphere from northern Asia about fifty thousand years ago. During the last Ice Age, a land bridge connected the regions known today as Alaska and Russia, allowing ancient hunters to follow game across the Bering Strait. These hunters brought their music with them; melodies were probably sung or played on bone flutes by the shamans (medicine men) to magically lure game animals. The descendants of these native peoples spread throughout the Americas, touching nearly every inhabitable corner of Mexico, Central, and South America. In the few areas, such as the Amazon rain forest, where Native Americans were not heavily influenced by the African and European newcomers to the Western Hemisphere, their music exists much as it did thousands of years ago.

The traditional musics of the Native Americans are used for curing illnesses; causing rain; making the land, animals, and people fertile; enhancing the harvest; hunting and making war; and praising the gods. Much of their music is purely vocal; when instruments are used, they are traditionally made from natural substances such as bone, clay, bamboo, hollowed sticks, and shells, as well as silver and gold.

African slaves were brought to Latin America from western and central Africa by the first Spanish and Portuguese conquerors and colonists. They worked mainly in sugarcane fields and gold mines as replacements for the enslaved Native Americans who had died of disease. The slave owners believed they had completely converted their African slaves to Christianity, and although the slaves were treated harshly, the Africans were often allowed to live together and perform music after working hours. Many of them also continued to worship their African gods and performed their music for worship at the same time that they venerated the Catholic saints. Today, in many regions of Latin America, particularly in Brazil and in the Caribbean (especially Cuba, Haiti, and Trinidad), the African and European religions fused to become new syncretic religions that continue to be important to the descendants of the African slaves. Also among the important attributes of this Afro-Latin American culture are various types of musics and dances for entertainment, as well as work songs.

The primary Euro-American influence in Latin America is that of the Spanish and the Portuguese, although British influence is prevalent in portions of the Caribbean. Near the beginning of the European exploration of the Western Hemisphere, Pope Alexander VI in 1494 designated an imaginary line, known as the Line of Demarcation, decreeing that everything west of the line belonged to Spain and everything east belonged to Portugal. This led to the formation of Spanish (Hispanic) America and the Portuguese-speaking country of Brazil. These European conquerors, settlers, and religious men brought their music, along with the other aspects of their culture.

In some parts of South America, European music has remained somewhat intact since the colonial period and is still found in certain regions of Chile, Argentina, Colombia, and Brazil. In other regions, Catholic missionaries taught European music directly to the Native Americans and to some of the African slaves. In some areas, European music was learned by listening to the settlers. Thus, a tremendous and complex mix of musics began in Latin America from the time of the earliest European migrations.

The Asian presence in Latin America is the result of events in the late nineteenth and early twentieth centuries, when East Indians, Javanese, Chinese, and Japanese were brought to British, Dutch, Spanish, and Portuguese lands after African slaves had been granted their freedom. Although Asians' presence in many regions of Latin America is substantial (there are more than one million Japanese and their descendants in Brazil alone), their musics have not blended extensively with the Native, African, and European musics.

By far, the largest number of Latin Americans belong to a mixed culture of one type or another. Many Latin American countries have terms for their people of mixed heritage, such as mestizo (mixed, basically Native American and Spanish), mulato (African and European), and zambo (African and Native American). Some countries have no designation for their racial and cultural mixing, since they are almost completely mixed, whereas in Brazil, the terms "branco" (white) and "negro" (black) are social rather than color distinctions.

As the races have often mixed in Latin America, so have their musical characteristics. This musical mixing is obvious in the festivals that exist in all Latin American and Caribbean countries. Most of these festivals, such as the carnivals in Trinidad and Brazil, are joyful celebrations in which people of all social classes participate for several days. The people who perform as festival musicians or dancers earn great prestige; they often spend most of their year and much of their money in preparation for the festival events and competitions.

Native Americans

The principal Native American ethnic or cultural groups in Latin America share many distinctive musical characteristics in their use of melody, rhythm, texture, timbre, dynamics, and form. Native Americans commonly use descending melodic lines that combine short musical motives. The choice of cadential intervals varies from culture to culture: minor thirds are used by some ancient cultures in Venezuela, Colombia, Chile, and the Andes; major thirds are used by many Andean groups; major seconds were used by Carib groups in Venezuela; and microtones (intervals smaller than those used in Western music) were probably used by ancient cultures in Peru, Colombia, and Mexico. Melodic range also varies among cultures: some groups use one-note recitation; some use ranges of a minor third; and others expand to a perfect fourth or fifth. Scales may be of various types, including microtonal (with intervals smaller than those found in Western music), bitonic (two-toned), tritonic (three-toned), tetratonic (four-toned), and pentatonic (five-toned).

Native American cultures often use specific melodies and rhythmic styles for specific functions. Religious songs may include slow-paced songs and free rhythms; dances and lullabies may contain measured rhythms. Most Native American dances are set in duple meter. The Andean dance form known as the *wayno* can be interpreted as being in an additive meter based on 1/4 (or as 2/4 with an occasional 3/4 measure).

Native American musicians also associate specific tone colors with specific purposes. Often, for example, they use a "masked" vocal tone when a song is used to communicate with supernatural powers. In instrumental music, they often emphasize a "buzzing" timbre, using drums equipped with snares and the buzzing sound of native clarinets. Both flutes and human whistling are used to produce a contrasting "whistle" sound.

Many native cultures of Latin America use monophonic textures that are often accompanied by a rhythm instrument such as a rattle or drum. However, some perform multipart music in freestyle rounds or canons as well as parallel melodies. Some cultures sing certain special songs mentally when addressing the supernatural, never singing them aloud. Songs used for curing illnesses or other supernatural songs may be sung very softly, and many cultures follow a dynamic of decreasing volume as melodies descend.

The song text determines the form as well as the dynamics of most religious vocal music. This through-composed music often sounds repetitious to Euro-Americans because the detailed and lengthy texts have to be sung precisely. Native American musicians, on the other hand, often model their dance music in strophic forms, using repetitions necessary for the dance itself.

Afro-Latin Americans

The Afro-American subcultures of Latin America have their own distinctive organization of the elements of music. Although they often use scale forms common both to Europe and Africa (including major, minor, modal, and pentatonic scales), they almost always use African-derived call-and-response patterns that alternate between a high-pitched solo singer and an equally high-pitched choral response, as in, for example, the Colombian *cumbia* and the Puerto Rican *plena*. This responsorial technique produces the most common vocal texture; many performances include the additional textures of hand clapping and other sounds that accompany dancing, such as yells, shouts of encouragement, foot stomping, and talking. The element of call-and-response also provides the singers with a basic strophic form in which the text of the call changes constantly because of improvisation and the choral response repeats predetermined phrases.

In drum ensembles, only one drum improvises while the others maintain steady rhythmic patterns or ostinatos. Afro-Latin American musicians most often base their music on duple meters with a very fast pulse or rhythmic density (number of notes per minute). As in traditional African drumming, percussion ensembles display a complex layering of rhythms such as two against three or three against four, creating a wealth of syncopations and cross rhythms.

Afro-Latin American vocal music is often deep-chested, raspy, or gravelly. The instrumental music typically uses resonant drums and sympathetic buzzes produced by attachments to instruments or sounds rich in overtones such as the steel drums of Trinidad. Drummers and groups of singers typically perform at high volume levels, and idiophonic ensembles such as the steel band use dynamic nuance as part of their stylistic language.

Euro-Latin Americans

Euro-Latin American music throughout Latin America shows varying degrees of European characteristics. In certain isolated coastal or highland regions of South America, such as the Colombian Pacific coast and southern Chile, musicians use modal melodies of European Renaissance origin. The most common scale forms, however, are the diatonic major or minor scales, and the "Andalusian cadence" (the chord progression A minor, G, F, and E) is found throughout heavily Hispanic areas such as parts of Venezuela or Colombia, showing the influence of Moorish music on Spain. Euro-Americans generally prefer stepwise, lyrical melodies.

These descendants of the first Europeans in the New World also use some rhythmic practices imported from their homelands. They use dual meter, for example, in two different ways: the 6/8 against 3/4 hemiola, called "colonial rhythm," and an alternation between 6/8 and 3/4, called *sesquiáltera*. Colonial rhythm is commonly found in the Spanish jota, the Chilean *cueca*, the Peruvian *marinera*, the Argentine *zamba*, and the Venezuelan *joropo*. *Sesquiáltera* is found in Chile, in Mexico's *son-jarabe* and mariachi styles, in Puerto Rico and Cuba, and was immortalized by Leonard Bernstein in the *West Side Story* song "I Like to Be in America." Euro-Latin Americans also use somewhat simpler duple meters in lullabies and dances and triple meters for waltzes.

The texture of Euro-Latin American music ranges from unaccompanied vocal solos, including lullabies, work songs, *desafío* or challenge songs, and ballads; to vocal solos, accompanied by a stringed instrument such as guitar, harp, or lutes or guitar-like instruments; to vocal duets in parallel thirds, accompanied by European-derived instruments; to ensembles of European-derived musical instruments, such as harp, guitar, and violins. Singers of some cattle songs have a Spanish *cante jondo* style of singing, using deep chest tones and solo guitar music that features alternating plucking (*punteado*) and strumming (*rasgueado*) styles.

Musicians in this culture group commonly use volume to intensify the mood of the music and also use dynamics expressively in ballads. Both vocal and instrumental musicians use strophic forms with a binary structure, which consists of even or uneven measures of two alternating sections that repeat with slight variations.

Mixed American

Latin America contains a great diversity of mixed races, mixed cultures, and mixed musical styles and forms. Many of the musical characteristics of the Native Americans, Afro-Latin Americans, and Euro-Latin Americans can be found in a rich variety of combinations throughout the area.

LESSON 1

Objectives

Students will:

1. Explain what a panpipe is and which cultures use them in their music.
2. Identify the principle of interlocking parts as exemplified in Peruvian and Bolivian panpipes (the *siku*).
3. Define the term "syncopation" and identify syncopated passages in the music.
4. Explain why Peruvian and Bolivian panpipe music is important as a surviving tradition.

Materials

1. Recordings:
   Kingdom of the Sun, Peru's Inca Heritage (Nonesuch H-72029)
   Mountain Music of Peru (Folkways FE 4539) (also Smithsonian/Folkways CD SF 40020, vol. 1, and SF CD 40406, vol. 2, reissues)
   Instruments and Music of Bolivia (Folkways FM 4012)
2. Photos of the Andes of Peru and Bolivia from *National Geographic* (vol. 144, no. 6, December 1973; vol. 161, no. 3, March 1982; vol. 162, no. 1, July 1982) or other sources

Procedures

1. Show or display pictures of the Andes of Peru and Bolivia. Discuss the cultures of the Peruvian and Bolivian Andes, and explain that the regions of southern highland Peru and most of highland Bolivia lie at very high elevations, where the air is thin, temperatures are often very cold, and wood is scarce. The llama is the chief beast of burden. The two Native American languages spoken there are Quechua and Aymara, and these are the names given to the people as well. The great Quechua-speaking civilization of the Incas captured many other civilizations in its military conquests. Today, music is used by both cultures for religious and festive dancing. The most important instruments are cane flutes (including panpipes) and drums (see figure 1). The Spanish conquered the Native Americans in the 1500s, and today many of the people are of mixed blood (mestizos).
2. Play a recorded example of Peruvian or Bolivian panpipe music to demonstrate the principle of interlocking musical parts, a technique in which two musicians (or multiples of two) play alternate notes of a single melody on a pair of panpipes. These two players consist of the *ira* (leader) and the *arka* (follower). The interlocking musical parts can be clearly heard on *Kingdom of the Sun* (side one, band four; and side two, band two) and *Mountain Music of Peru* (side four, band five; CD vol. 2, 15). Discuss the listening example, and have the class generate a definition for the term "interlocking parts."
3. Discuss the term "syncopation." The basic "short-long-short" Andean syncopation is very common in *siku* panpipe music and is found in the song "Waka Waka" and in the listening examples in the Materials section. Teach it aurally with the syllables "dot-da-dot" while patting in a steady duple pulse. Have the students sing "dot-da-

Figure 1. Peruvian *sikuri* (panpipes), played by *Aconcagua,* an Andean music ensemble from Florida State University in Tallahassee

dot" while the teacher claps a steady rhythm; then have the students both sing and clap.

4. Discuss the importance of *siku* music by pointing out that the present panpipe traditions in Peru and Bolivia are continuations of ancient traditions: panpipes constructed from cane, silver, gold, and clay have been found in 3,000-year-old desert tombs. Explain that panpipe traditions are also found in Ecuador, the Amazon rain forest, Africa, Europe (Romania), Melanesia, and ancient China. Point out these places on a world map and list the countries on the chalkboard. Discuss how panpipes are made by the Native Americans from their local materials (cane or bamboo and string), and explain how we can make them from modern materials: polyvinyl chloride (PVC) plastic tubing and glue.

5. Andean *siku* panpipes can be constructed from a 12' length of 1/2"diameter PVC plastic tubing according to the following instructions:

    a. Measure for and mark out lines on a 36", 3/8" diameter dowel (see figure 2).

    b. Measure the PVC tubing according to the dimensions shown, and cut it with a saw (using a miter box, if possible). Sand the blowing edges inside and outside until smooth.

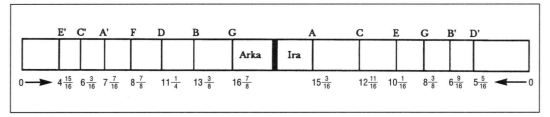

	E'	C'	A'	F	D	B	G		A	C	E	G	B'	D'
							Arka	Ira						
0 →	$4\frac{15}{16}$	$6\frac{3}{16}$	$7\frac{7}{16}$	$8\frac{7}{8}$	$11\frac{1}{4}$	$13\frac{3}{8}$	$16\frac{7}{8}$		$15\frac{3}{16}$	$12\frac{11}{16}$	$10\frac{1}{16}$	$8\frac{3}{8}$	$6\frac{9}{16}$	$5\frac{5}{16}$ ← 0

Figure 2. Constructing *siku* panpipe, part 1

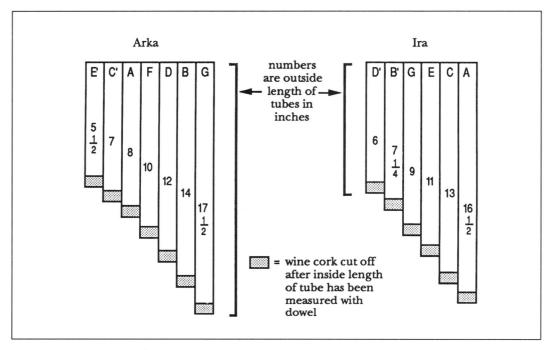

Figure 3. Constructing *siku* panpipe, part 2. **Caution:** The PVC cement vapors are toxic. Use the glue outdoors ONLY.

c. Using medium sandpaper, remove the printing on the PVC tubes; this will slightly roughen the edges of the tubes to be glued, making the glue hold better.

d. Insert a cork into the bottom of each properly measured PVC tube. Old wine corks that are tapered are easy to insert; new corks must be compressed many times in a vise for them to be pliable enough to be inserted. Measure the internal length of each tube from the open end to the cork, and compare with the proper mark on the dowel. Cut off the excess cork (the cut-off portion of the cork can be your next plug).

e. Place the tubes into two sets (as shown in figure 3) on a flat surface covered with waxed paper, and place a one-quarter-inch wide bead of PVC glue (see **Caution**) along the sanded edge of each tube that is to be joined. Glue and join the tubes

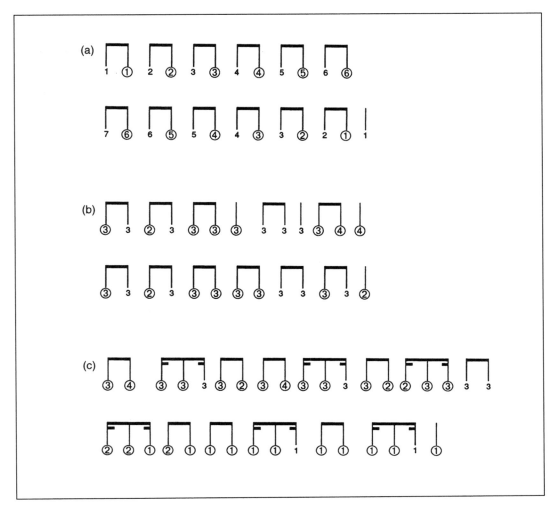

Figure 4. (a) the scale, (b) "Mary Had a Little Lamb," and (c) "Waka Waka"

       one by one; then let the glue dry according to the manufacturer's instructions, or for approximately two hours.

6. Using a marking pen, write numbers on each tube. Beginning with the longest tube of each half at your right, draw at the top of the tubes the numbers 1–6 on the half with six tubes (the *ira*) and 1–7 on the half with the seven tubes (the *arka*) from right to left, or longest tube to shortest tube. Next, on the *ira* half of the instrument only, draw a circle around each number.

7. With the longest tubes to your right, practice playing each half of the panpipe by blowing as you would across a bottle, using the attack "tu" or "pu." Give each note a forceful attack with support from the diaphragm. Sustaining notes is not a part of the *siku* tradition, and the notes of a melody are commonly shared between two players,

so you should not become dizzy or short of breath when performing the panpipes. The sound will be loud and breathy.

8. Introduce the simple notation system used in the music examples for this lesson. In this system, developed by Dale A. Olsen, the numbers with circles are for the six-tubed *ira*, and the numbers without circles are for the seven-tubed *arka*. Study and play the examples in figure 4: (a) the scale, (b) "Mary Had a Little Lamb," and (c) "Waka Waka" (a portion of a piece from the *Aymara* tradition).

LESSON 2

Objectives

Students will:

1. Identify pan-Andean music and the following musical instruments that form a typical pan-Andean ensemble: *siku, kena,* guitar, *charango, bombo.*
2. Play music of the pan-Andean tradition using the *siku* constructed in Lesson One, a Western flute or recorder to substitute for the Andean *kena* flute, and guitars. The students will learn how European harmony combines with Native American-derived instruments.

Materials

1. Recordings:
   Pukaj Wayra: Music from Bolivia (Lyrichord LLST 7361 or LYRCD 7361)
   Urubamba (Columbia KCC 32896)
   Inti-Illimani 3: Canto de Pueblos Andinos (Monitor MFS 787)
   La Flûte Indienne (Olympic Atlas Series 6160)
2. Book: *Sounds of the World: Music of Latin America: Mexico, Ecuador, Brazil* (Reston, VA: Music Educators National Conference, 1987)
3. Optional musical instruments: Set of *siku* panpipes, as constructed in Lesson One, guitar, *charango,* or ukulele, *bombo* or bass drum, and an Andean *kena* flute or a Western flute or recorder

Procedures

1. Present a cultural and historical perspective: Pan-Andean music came about as a result of the racial and cultural mixing of the people of the Andes. Some of the musical instruments from the Andes of Ecuador, Peru, Bolivia, northern Argentina, and northern Chile have been joined with Spanish instruments such as the guitar and other guitar-like instruments. These combined instruments have formed a musical idiom that reveals the mixed cultural heritages of the Andean people. Today, many pan-Andean ensembles from Chile and other countries are living and performing outside of their native lands. Some of the best-known performing groups are *Quilapayun* (Paris), *Angel Parra* (Mexico), and *Grupo Aymara* (New York).
2. Play several selections from the recordings listed, choosing examples that use all the instruments instead of just guitar. Point out the following musical instruments and

discuss their musical characteristics with the students. (You should be able to recognize the instruments after repeated listenings to the recordings.)

a. The *siku* has a breathy quality and is played with the interlocking note technique discussed in Lesson One.

b. The *kena* is a vertical, end-blown flute with a ductless, notched mouth piece. Like the *siku*, these flutes have been found in ancient graves in the coastal regions of Peru and were made from human, llama, or pelican bones and clay, gold, silver, and cane. Today, the *kena* is played alone by llama herdsmen (men and boys), by men in *kena* ensembles, and in ensembles with guitars, *charangos*, violins, mandolins, and harps. The *kena*, made with only six finger holes and one thumb hole, was often traditionally played to sound the notes of a pentatonic scale. In modern pan-Andean music, however, the musicians play in the natural minor and major, and they even play some chromatic notes by using cross-fingerings and partially covering the finger holes. The *kena* is played using a fast vibrato mostly in the high register; this style is favored in Andean Native American music. Sometimes the tunings do not correspond to European tuning—the instrument is not out of tune, but is just tuned to correspond to Andean cultural traditions. *Kena* players use many ornaments similar to mordents in European music, and they sometimes slide (glissando) from one note to the other.

c. The *charango* is a stringed instrument based on the guitars and guitar-like instruments brought by the Spaniards to the New World (see figures 5 and 6). Because wood is scarce in the Andes mountains, the Native Americans of Peru and Bolivia constructed these small guitars using armadillo shells as resonators. Today, it is illegal to kill armadillos in Bolivia, so the *charango* is often made entirely from wood. A typical *charango* has ten metal or nylon strings, arranged into five double courses (a double course consists of two strings, placed side by side, that are tuned to the same pitch and played together). Some varieties may use triple courses and substitute geared metal tuners for the traditional straight, wooden, violin-type pegs. *Charango* players use both the *rasgueado* and *punteado* playing styles, sounding the strings with their fingernails. The instrument is tuned to be played in a very high range, and, in Chile, the instrument is often called *chillador*, which means "screamer"; players must use fast strums and play melodies in the characteristic range of the instrument (an octave or two above the guitar).

d. The *bombo* is a large, double-headed bass drum. It usually resembles a European Renaissance drum in shape and is also similar to those depicted in paintings about the American Revolution. The term may also be used to describe drums of Native American origin that are similar to Western marching band bass drums. The *bombo* is usually played with only one padded stick when accompanying *siku* orchestras and two padded sticks when accompanying a modern pan-Andean ensemble (one is used to strike the wooden body or the rim of the drum).

e. The guitar player usually strums but can also pick; often a guitar or a *guitarrón* (large guitar) will play bass notes and fast runs. The instrument used is always a nylon-stringed Spanish guitar.

3. After listening to several examples, discuss the structure of the pan-Andean ensemble. Explain that this ensemble is organized according to the different sounds of the instruments and according to how the instruments are played. For example, high-pitched instruments play the melody and a parallel melody a third lower. Low-pitched

Figure 5. Andean *charangos*. The middle *charango* is from Bolivia; the other two are from Peru.

instruments such as the guitars play harmony, and the *charango* plays either accompaniments in the middle register or jumps to the top register when it plays the melody.

4. *An optional project for this lesson could be the following:*

a. Construct a *kena* flute from PVC tubing, tuned in A minor, according to figure 7 and the following instructions:

Cut a 15 1/2" section of 3/4" PVC tubing. Using a rat-tail file, make a notched mouthpiece on one end; drill five 3/8" holes in the front and a 1/4" hole in the back of the *kena*, and smooth the edges of the finger holes with a knife, sandpaper, or a file. Instead of drilling, you can make the finger holes by burning through the tubing with a soldering gun or a heated metal nail or rod. The holes can then be filed to the necessary roundness and size (see figure 7).

Figure 6. Back view of *charangos:* left, *charango* with box resonator; middle, with wood resonator; and right, with armadillo shell resonator

b. Learn to play the *kena.* Blow it as you would a Western flute (except that the *kena* is end-blown) by focusing the airstream against the sharp edge of the notch. Learn the notes according to the fingering chart in figure 8, and notice that the notes basically correspond to a transposed alto recorder or a clarinet in the lower register. Learn "Mary Had a Little Lamb" on the *kena* in both the lower and upper octaves (see figure 9).

5. Organize a pan-Andean music ensemble using a *siku,* a *kena* (a flute or a recorder may be substituted), a *charango* (you may use a treble ukulele), a guitar, and a *bombo* (you may substitute a bass drum). Professional ensembles usually use only one instrument for each part, but students may double any of the parts if more instruments are available. Learn the piece in figure 10, which is in the style of the Andean music of

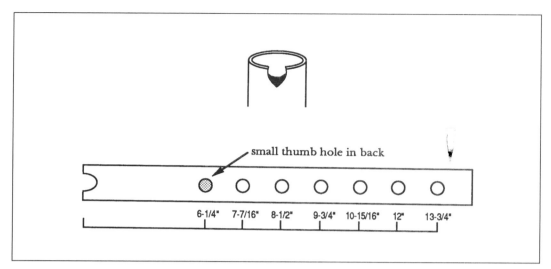

Figure 7. Constructing a *kena* flute

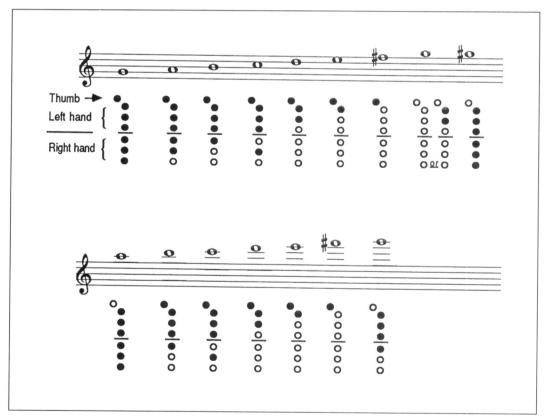

Figure 8. Fingering chart for *kena*

Figure 9. "Mary Had a Little Lamb"

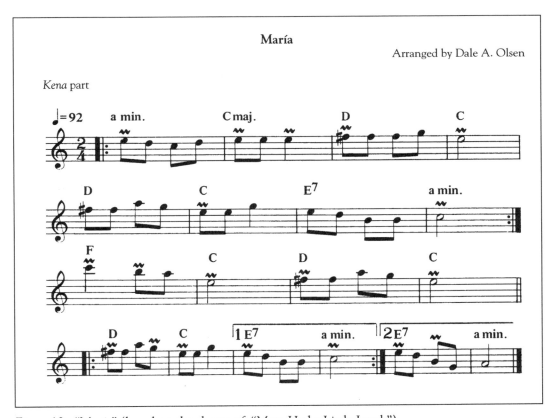

Figure 10. "María" (based on the theme of "Mary Had a Little Lamb")

Siku part

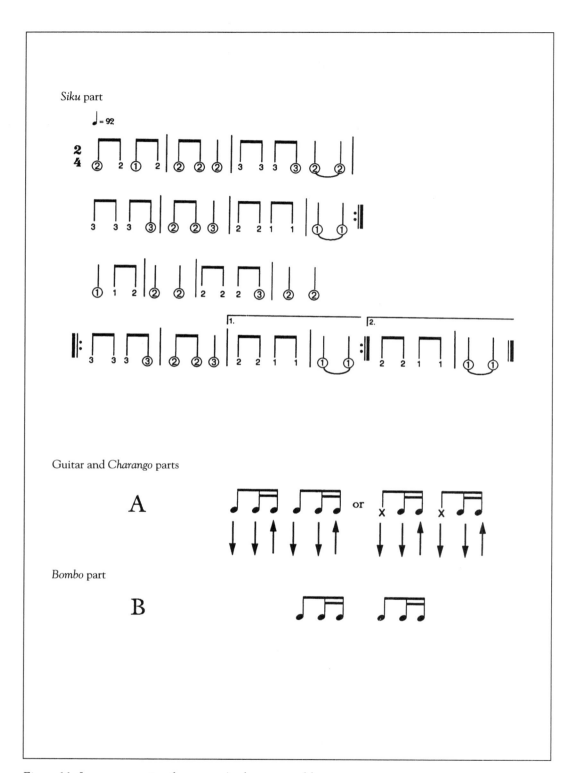

Guitar and Charango parts

Bombo part

Figure 11. Instrumentation for a pan-Andean ensemble

southern Peru and northern Bolivia. In the *kena* part, ornaments like mordents are indicated above their corresponding notes. The *siku* part, written in parallel thirds below the *kena* part, is given in Olsen notation, and the guitar and *charango* parts should be played with the *wayno* strum as shown in figure 11: the X-shaped note heads indicate stopping the strings with the palm of the hand immediately after strumming them with the fingernails.

L E S S O N   3

■ Objectives
Students will:
1. Imitate rhythmic patterns created by the teacher or taken from the drum performance on "Oshossi," from *Afro-Brazilian Religious Songs: Cantigas de Candomble/Candomble Songs from Salvador, Bahia* (Lyrichord LLST 7315), using percussion instruments or by striking the body.
2. Study and perform some of the layered and interlocking rhythms of the drum ensembles of Brazil, Haiti, Cuba, Suriname, and Venezuela using classroom percussion instruments.
3. Combine three different rhythmic ostinatos written in TUBS (Time Unit Box System) notation to produce a composite ensemble pattern.
4. Improvise patterns in a small-group setting.

■ Materials
1. Recordings:
   Afro-Brazilian Religious Songs: Cantigas de Candomble/Candomble Songs from Salvador, Bahia (Lyrichord LLST 7315)
   Amazonia, Cult Music of Northern Brazil (Lyrichord LLST 7300 or LYRCD 7300)
2. Book: *Sounds of the World: Music of Latin America: Mexico, Ecuador, Brazil* (Reston, VA: Music Educators National Conference, 1987)
3. Classroom drums, preferably bongos or congas
4. Claves, triangles, sticks, tins, bottles, spoons, or other available percussion instruments
5. Question and answer sheets (optional)

■ Procedures
1. The teacher should play line A (the quarter-note pulse) of figure 12 on a drum. Have the class imitate it, using their bodies as instruments by tapping, clapping, clicking, or stamping.
2. Play line B of figure 12 on a triangle. Ask the students to imitate it using bottles and spoons while saying the vocable "mm" on the rests.
3. Play line C of figure 12 on the claves, and instruct the students to imitate it using sticks. Students again say "mm" on the rests.
4. Divide the class into three sections, assigning one section line A, the second section

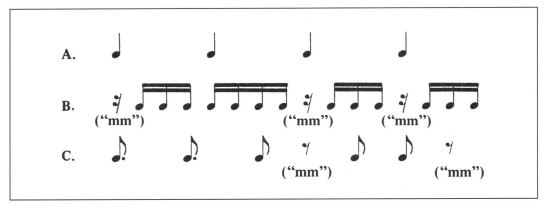

Figure 12. Rhythms

Figure 13. A large *mina* drum. *Laures* (sticks) are used to strike the body of this Northeastern Venezuelan drum.

Figure 14. A *curbata* drum from Northeastern Venezuela

line B, and the third section line C. Begin with one section, and then add the other sections to form a layered texture.

5. After the composite rhythm is successfully achieved, discuss the activity by asking students the following questions:
   a. Did we all perform the same rhythmic pattern after we divided the class?
   b. Did our different patterns fit together?
   c. How did we put them together?

6. *Drum ensemble.* In Afro-Latin America, the drum ensemble is important to both secular and religious festivals (see figures 13 and 14). Using a three-drum ensemble is common. One drummer provides a time-line with a simple ostinato that may vary only slightly; another answers with interlocking phrase patterns influenced by the other drummers; the third drummer usually improvises by bringing cross rhythms, syncopations, irregular phrase lengths, and rhythmic excitement to the performance. Certain rhythms are usually associated with specific occasions.

   Discuss the terms "time-line," "ostinato," "rhythmic layering," "interlocking rhythms," and "composite pattern." Ask the class which parts of the world have drum ensembles that use these principles.
   a. *Time-line*—a steady rhythmic pattern that is repeated throughout a performance. It serves as a foundation or organizing principle for the entire rhythmic structure.

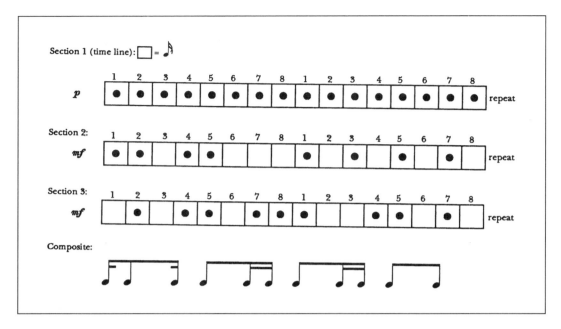

Figure 15. TUBS notation

It is usually played by idiophones such as the claves or cow bell and is sometimes played in a drum ensemble as a rhythmic ostinato. Sometimes more than one percussion instrument may be used to play the time-line.

   b. *Ostinato*—a repeated rhythmic pattern that may be changed slightly during the performance but never loses its basic form.

   c. *Rhythmic layering*—the principle of creating a dense texture in which more than one rhythmic pattern occurs simultaneously. If the parts enter at different points, the layering effect becomes more evident.

   d. *Interlocking rhythms*—rhythms that fit together as they progress through time. If the drums or instruments have various pitches or textures, the interlocking effect is easier to detect.

   e. *Composite pattern*—the total rhythmic phrase that emerges as the drummers play ostinatos and improvised patterns together.

7. Play a recording of an Afro-Latin American drum ensemble performance ("Oshossi," from *Afro-Brazilian Religious Songs: Cantigas de Candomble/Candomble Songs from Salvador, Bahia*). List students' answers to the following questions on the board:

   a. Is there more than one drum playing?

   b. Do you hear a steady pattern that you could imitate?

   c. Does the steady pattern ever change?

   d. What else do you hear? Do you hear voices, clapping, other instruments, or a foreign language?

   e. Can you tell which instrument or instruments play the time-line?

   f. Can you guess what kind of occasion this music is being played for?

g. Can you guess what country this music comes from?

8. Show the students the example of TUBS notation in figure 15, and explain how to read it. Explain that the notation gives them three different rhythmic ostinatos that they must put together to produce a composite pattern. Lead students in counting eight-beat "measures" slowly. Students should play their percussion instruments when specified by the boxes marked with dots; when the parts are secure, increase the tempo.

9. Divide the class into three sections. Section one establishes the time-line using sticks or claves, section two plays the second rhythmic layer using sticks and tin cans, and section three plays the third rhythmic layer using bottles and spoons. The rhythms should be precise and the ostinatos regular.

10. If possible, select one student from each group, and encourage them to perform the composite pattern as a solo group using three drums. As an alternative, play the recording again and have the class perform improvised patterns or ostinatos along with the drum ensemble on the recording.

11. Introduce the idea of improvisation by having students experiment with hitting the drum in various ways, such as with sticks, hands, or fingers, in the middle of the membrane, on the edge, or on the side. Incorporate these new techniques for given measures at prescribed times.

This lesson was contributed by Selwyn Ahyoung.

L E S S O N   4

■ Objectives

Students will:
1. Define the terms "marimba," "ostinato," and "call and response."
2. Identify the sound of an African-derived ensemble from Colombia or Ecuador that includes the marimba, drums, and a rattle.
3. Identify the stylistic characteristic of parallel thirds in a marimba melody.
4. Identify the call-and-response technique and sing a song using that principle.
5. Explain how music functions as an aspect of Afro-Latin American daily life, especially for entertainment and religious celebrations; perform an *arrulo* and simulate a *currulao*.

■ Materials

1. Recordings:
   In Praise of Oxalá and Other Gods: Black Music of South America (Nonesuch H72036)
   Afro-Hispanic Music from Western Colombia and Ecuador (Folkways Records FE 4376)
2. Photo of a marimba or a marimba ensemble
3. If possible, a Western marimba or any type of xylophone

■ Procedures

1. Discuss the region of the Pacific lowlands or littoral of Colombia and Ecuador: it is a

tropical rain forest between the Andes mountains and the Pacific Ocean. The region stretches from the border of Colombia with Panama into Ecuador, and much of the area can only be reached by boat. African slaves were brought into the region to work in gold mines, and after the gold was gone, the whites left and the blacks stayed. Today, there are about five thousand blacks living in the area. Buenaventura, Colombia, the only town of any size, has drawn some of the inhabitants from the rain forest, but others continue living in the jungle, where they grow bananas and catch fish. The majority of the population is very poor.

2. Explain how music functions as an aspect of daily life, for both entertainment and for religious celebrations. (Refer to the contexts and words of the songs given on the record jacket.) Mention that Afro-Latin Americans use songs to emphasize social relationships and to venerate Catholic saints.

   a. Discuss the secular song and dance festival called *currulao* (marimba dance), which is often performed on weekends by the blacks of the Pacific lowlands of Colombia and Ecuador. The typical song text of a *currulao* is sung by a man about his imagined freedom to leave his wife whenever he wishes, while a woman may boastfully sing about her ability to keep her husband. Listen to the *currulao* from *In Praise of Oxalá and Other Gods* (Nonesuch H72036) (side two, band five), and note the driving, forceful rhythm of this energetic dance, which simulates a contest between a man and a woman. This song uses a marimba ostinato, probably because the context is secular and therefore more African and perhaps because the example comes from a small, isolated village in which African elements have been retained.

   b. Discuss the religious songs performed to honor a saint on a special day; these songs are commonplace among blacks in this area. Known as *arrullos,* these songs are usually sung by women using the call-and-response technique and are accompanied by marimba, drums, and rattles. Read the information and the text on "San Antonio," from *In Praise of Oxalá and Other Gods,* and play the example.

3. Show a picture of a marimba to the class (see figure 16). If possible, bring a marimba to class and demonstrate how to play it and its scale (playing only the diatonic keys on a chromatic instrument). Define the marimba as an African-derived struck idiophone consisting of many slabs of hard wood placed in descending order from right to left. An Orff diatonic marimba works very well in this context.

4. Play an example of Colombian marimba music, using the records listed for this lesson. Point out the sounds of the marimba, the drums, and the rattle.

5. Demonstrate the principles of ostinato and parallel thirds on a marimba, piano, or xylophone, and ask students to identify examples. Either improvise your examples or perform them from (a) the secular song and (b) the marimba melody from a religious song in the examples shown in figures 17 and 18.

6. Demonstrate the call-and-response technique and discuss this technique with the students. Show how to sing responsorially by using the religious song "San Antonio," from *In Praise of Oxalá and other Gods,* as a guide; the words are in Spanish and English on the record's back cover. Learn the song by ear or use the following excerpt as shown in figure 19.

7. Play the marimba melody of the religious song "San Antonio" on the marimba or

Figure 16. When suspended in a marimba house, the marimba is played by two men with four mallets.

Figure 17. Secular song

Figure 18. Religious song

Figure 19. Excerpt from "San Antonio"

piano while the students sing the vocal call-and-response of the song.

8. Using phrases from "San Antonio," have students demonstrate the call-and-response technique by individually singing a call while the rest of the class sings a response.

9. Have the students write a brief report about the musical and cultural characteristics of both secular and religious music making among the blacks of the Pacific lowlands of Colombia and Ecuador.

10. Have the students create their own tunes and perform them on xylophones, Orff instruments, or marimbas.

L E S S O N   5

■ Objectives

Students will:

1. Describe the background and social context of calypso and steel band music from Trinidad and Tobago.
2. Describe the instruments in a steel band.
3. Sing and play a simple tune that illustrates the calypso style, and create a text based on the tune.
4. Perform two rhythmic accompaniment patterns characteristic of the calypso.

■ Materials

1. Recordings:
   The Hammer (Windham Hill Records, WD-0107 DIDX 1658)
   Pan All Night. Steel Bands of Trinidad and Tobago (Delos International, DE 4022)
   Trinidad Carnival. Steel Bands of Trinidad and Tobago (Delos International DE 4012)
   Calypso Travels, Lord Invader, and His Calypso Group (Folkways FW 8733)
   Sparrow, the Greatest (Charlie's Records JAF1007)

2. Books:
   Calypso Calaloo: Early Carnival Music in Trinidad by Donald R. Hill (Gainesville, FL: The University Press of Florida, 1993)
   Tropical Hammer Steel Drum Crafters Presents Tom Reynolds, Steel Drums: Steel Drum Manual by Thomas Bibik (Ferndale, MI: Thomas Bibik, 1993).
   Catalog:
   Everything for the Steel Band. 1996 catalog. Available from Panyard, Inc., 1216 California Avenue, Akron, OH 44314-1842

3. Claves, sticks, hand drums, brake drums, cowbells, bongos, congas, or other unpitched percussion instruments; Orff xylophones and metallophones or other melodic instruments

4. Photos of the Trinidad carnival, a calypsonian, a steel band, or a Caribbean setting [Examples can be found in "Trinidad and Tobago," in *Isles of the Caribbean* (Washington, DC: National Geographic Society, 1980), 10–41.]

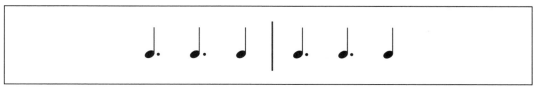

Figure 20. Bass line rhythmic pattern found in *soca*

■ **Procedures**

1. Show or display photos of Trinidad or the Caribbean.
2. Discuss Trinidad and its location. Mention that it is an island that contains a rich heritage of traditions. Trinidad, the home of the steel band, lies close to Venezuela in the Caribbean and was discovered by Columbus in 1498. The culture of Trinidad has been influenced by the Spanish, French, British, West Africans, and East Indians. The British ruled for a time beginning in 1797; Trinidad became independent in 1962.
3. Study the music styles calypso and *soca* as well as the steel band.
   a. Calypso is a very popular type of song in the Caribbean islands, especially in Trinidad, where this art form developed around the turn of the century. Calypso has a long history that dates back as far as African slave songs: One of the earliest forms of calypso was the *lavway*, made up of a call and response. Modern forms of calypso contain more lines of text, which may be silly, serious, or humorous, and describe news, world events, and village happenings. Many of the texts are political, containing protest themes and social commentary, and may contain double or hidden meanings in their texts as well. Calypsos are composed particularly for the carnival season but are also sung year-round. The melodies, as well as the accompaniments played by brass, pop, or steel bands, have syncopated, dance-like beats, and the tunes include several verses and catchy refrains. Professional calypsonians carefully stage their performances; they wear dazzling outfits and dramatize their songs. There is usually a backup chorus that sings the refrain lines in harmony. *Soca* is a new form of calypso that evolved during the 1970s. It is influenced by the East Indian musical rhythms of Trinidad and United States soul music and is called soul calypso or *soca* for short. Its beat is slightly different from

Name of instruments	Number of pans
Single tenor or lead (ping-pong)	1
Double tenor	2
Double second	2
Quadraphonic	4
Triple guitar	3
Triple	3
Cello	3
Tenor bass	4
Bass	6–9

Note: In addition, a steel band often uses a drumset, congas, brake drum, cowbell, and many other percussion instruments, depending on the style of music being performed.

Table 1. Pans

Figure 21. Selwyn Ahyoung (left) and Dale A. Olsen (right) with steel drums

Figure 22. "Ambakaila" excerpt

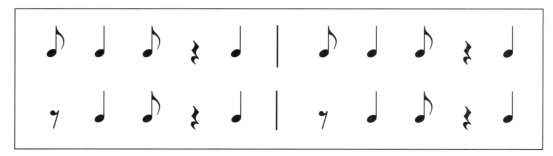

Figure 23. Accompaniment patterns to be used for "Ambakaila"

the traditional calypso beat. Figure 20 shows a typical bass line rhythmic pattern.

b. The steel band is an instrumental ensemble comprised entirely of percussion instruments that specializes in calypso, reggae, and pop music, but it can also play classical and religious music. The instruments used in the band, called "pans," are made from fifty-five-gallon oil drums (see figure 21). Although pans were first created in Trinidad in the late 1930s, their percussive ancestors may be traced to Africa, and they have since spread to all parts of the world. Many American high schools, colleges, and universities now have steel band ensembles, and groups can also be heard in many large cities in the United States, Canada and Europe. Every steel band needs a good arranger and a good tuner, for its overall sound depends on how well the pans are made and maintained. The making of pans is a complex process requiring skill and patience. The oil drums must be cut into different lengths, as pans come in different ranges and have to be grooved, tempered, and tuned. The spaces on the top surface of the pans, separated by grooves, are tuned to produce different pitches. Generally, the larger the note surface, the lower the pitch; the larger the pan, the lower its range. Pans are played with sticks of varying lengths, covered at one end with some type of rubber tubing. A small band consisting of eight players may be made up of the instruments shown in table 1. The pans are listed in table 1 in descending order of their ranges, from the highest to the lowest. In Trinidad, traditional steel bands may contain as many as 150 players, whose instruments are placed on stands in brightly decorated, mobile metal frames. These bands have become famous for their fantastic and elaborate calypso arrangements created for carnival street dancing and the Panorama, an annual steel band competition. Players used to hang instruments around their necks and carry them through the streets.

4. Play a recording of a modern calypso. Have the class listen for the words and for any repeated accompanying rhythmic patterns.

5. Sing the tune "Ambakaila," an old *lavway* melody, as shown in the figure 22 excerpt. The text is: "O Lawd, de glorious morning come/Ambakaila." The song was sung about the "glorious morning" ("J'ouvert morning") of the stick fight that usually occurred on the first day of Carnival, or on the Monday before Shrove Tuesday. *Ambakaila* is a corruption of the term *en bataille la,* meaning "in battle." At first, students should sing only the response "Ambakaila," but they may gradually join in on the call as well. Clap the basic accompaniment pattern of the calypso, and have the students follow in rote imitation as they continue to sing the tune and accompany themselves on percussion instruments. Ask the class to practice the following two rhythmic accompaniment patterns (shown in figure 23) of the calypso and use them for "Ambakaila."

6. Pass out transcriptions of "Ambakaila" and have some students play the tune on melody instruments.

7. Have students improvise other words for the call-and-response format of "Ambakaila," such as "Oh Lord, my pocket got a hole/in de center."

8. Have students play "Ambakaila" and harmonize the tune using the tonic, subdominant, and dominant seventh chords.

This lesson was contributed by Selwyn Ahyoung with revisions by Darren and Jennifer Duerden.

LESSON 6

■ **Objectives**

Students will:

1. Identify the sound of Euro-Latin American music from Chile and Argentina that features the guitar, the most important Spanish-derived instrument.
2. Identify the two Spanish-derived guitar techniques, the *rasgueado* (strumming) style and the *punteado* (picking) style.
3. Identify the three European-derived meters known as *ritmo colonial* (colonial rhythm, or bimeter), *sesquiáltera* (alternating meter), and European triple meter (waltz time).
4. Perform three notated examples in small ensembles with guitars and recorders or flutes as a long-term or follow-up project.

■ **Materials**

1. Recordings:
   Traditional Chilean Songs (Folkways FW 8748)
   Songs of Chile (Folkways FW 8817)
   Argentina: The Guitar of the Pampas (Lyrichord LLST 7235)
2. Book: *Sounds of the World: Music of Latin America: Mexico, Ecuador, Brazil* (Reston, VA: Music Educators National Conference, 1987)
3. Musical instruments (optional): guitar (the parts to be played call for strumming only), flute or recorder (to be played using Western notation)

■ **Procedures**

1. Show Chile and Argentina on a map and discuss the two countries, emphasizing that they lie in the southern portion of South America and that they show the strongest European influence of all the Latin American countries. Chile and the much larger Argentina are separated by the Andes mountains. Both countries are famed for their cowboys, known as gauchos in the Argentine pampas or plains and as *huasos* in the central valley of Chile. These South American cowboys are highly regarded for their singing and guitar playing.
2. Play two of the recorded examples for this lesson. Point out the times when the guitar is strummed (*rasgueado* style) and picked (*punteado* style). In the second selection, have students indicate the style of playing.
3. Discuss the three most important European-derived meters or rhythms, which are "colonial rhythm" (bimeter), the Spanish *sesquiáltera* (alternating meter), and triple meter (waltz time).
4. Play recordings that illustrate colonial rhythm. Some good examples are "Tonada," from *Argentina: The Guitar of the Pampas*; "Dos Puntas tiene el camino," from *Songs of Chile*; and "Los Gallos," from *Traditional Chilean Songs*. As you play the recordings, clap a quarter-note pulse in three for 3/4 time and then follow with a dotted-quarter-note pulse in two for 6/8 time to show that the two meters are related. Explain that at times the melody is strictly in 3/4 time while the guitar accompaniment is strictly in 6/8 and that the music as a whole can be heard in either meter. Divide the class into two sections, and have one section clap 3/4 and the other 6/8 simultaneously.

5. Play the recordings that illustrate *sesquiáltera*, using "Si Yo Volviera a Quererte," from *Traditional Chilean Songs* and "Despedimiento del Angelito" from the same recording. Clap in three for 3/4 for the measures that stress three, and clap in two for 6/8 for the measures that stress two. Emphasize that this is an alternation rather than a superimposition and that it often involves the guitar part as well as the melody.
6. Play the recorded waltz example, "La Golondrina," on *Traditional Chilean Songs*. Clap in three.
7. Play and discuss selected examples of songs that employ colonial rhythm, *sesquiáltera*, or waltz time rhythms and *punteado* or *rasgueado* performance techniques.
8. If time permits, teach the following three songs shown in figures 24, 25, and 26. If your students can read Western notation, have them perform in small ensembles. The melody, chord changes, and strumming patterns are indicated in the transcriptions; perform the examples several times so the students understand the European-derived meters.

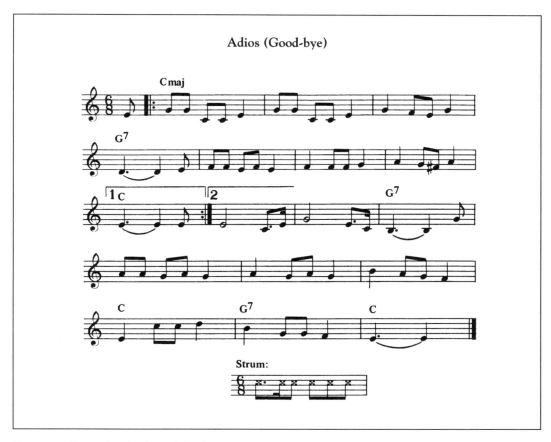

Figure 24. Example of colonial rhythm

Dices que me quieres, macho
(Tell Me You Love Me, Tiger)

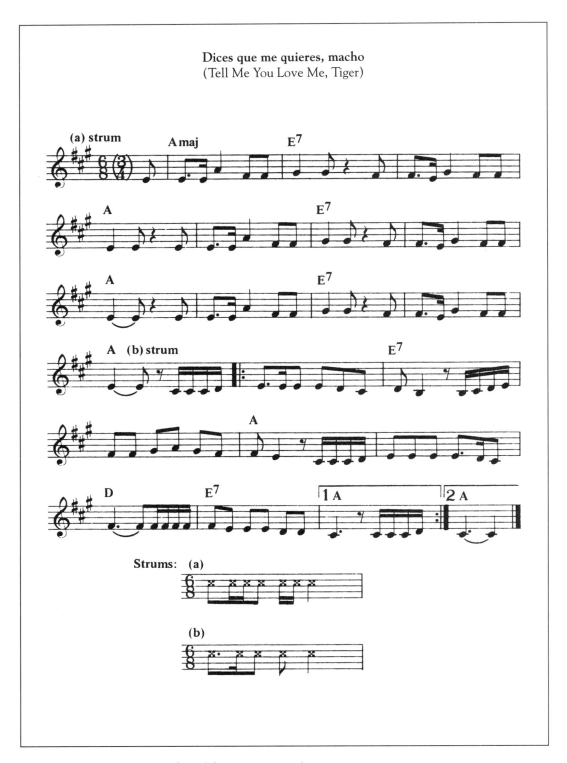

Figure 25. Example of *sesquiáltera* (alternating meter)

Vals Chilote (Waltz from Chile)

Figure 26. Example of triple meter (waltz time)

Figure 27. The Salsa Florida Orchestra, Florida State University, Tallahassee

L E S S O N   7

■ **Objectives**

Students will:
1. Identify the instruments, sound, and musical techniques of a salsa orchestra.
2. Identify the African-derived characteristics of salsa music and perform one of them.
3. Identify the musical characteristics of salsa music that are Spanish-derived.

■ **Materials**

1. Recording: *Cachao Master Sessions, Volume 1* (Crescent Moon Records, Epic Records Group, CineSon EK 64320)

■ **Procedures**

1. Discuss the origin of salsa music in Cuba in the 1940s and how it spread to the rest of the Spanish-speaking Caribbean (especially San Juan in Puerto Rico) and to Miami and New York City (these three centers are known collectively as the "salsa triangle"). Salsa is an Afro-Cuban music that developed in the nightclubs of Havana, Cuba, and was influenced by American jazz from the swing era (see figure 27). The term "salsa," which means "hot sauce," was applied (probably by non-Latinos) because the music is rhythmically spicy, energetic, and appropriate for dancing. Afro-Cuban percussion is an important part of salsa, featuring such skin drums as the congas, bongos, and *timbales*, and other instruments like claves (sticks), cowbells, and even wooden boxes. Salsa has its greatest appeal among people from the Spanish Caribbean or those with Caribbean roots.

2. Make up a call-and-response pattern, and have the students sing a simple response.
3. Play a short excerpt chosen from the suggested recording of salsa music that contains call-and-response patterns (they all do).
4. Teach the following African-derived elements:
    a. The bell tone or clave beat, which is provided by the bell or claves in a rhythmic pattern or ostinato that repeats every two measures (claves are two 1 1/2" hardwood dowels that are struck together, making a loud, sharp, and resonant sound)
    b. Layered texture, consisting of rhythmic and melodic ostinatos (repeated patterns)
    c. Instrumental improvisation
    d. The use of African-derived drums in the ensemble
    e. The use of call-and-response texture
    f. The *montuno* improvised vocal section, which includes African-styled praise texts about women, personages, events, or places
    g. Use of the music for dancing, with a great deal of audience participation by hand clapping, singing along, and yells of excitement (two of the most common dance forms are the rumba and mambo)
5. Teach the following Spanish elements of salsa:
    a. Singers use the Spanish language, often to tell a story about a place or person, much like the ballad in American music.
    b. The music is constructed with Western harmony.
    c. Certain Western instruments are used as part of the ensemble (piano, bass, guitar-type instruments, trumpet, saxophone, flute, etc.).
    d. The music uses traditional formal structures, such as ABA.
6. Play "Lindo Yambo," from *Cachao Master Sessions, Volume 1* and introduce some of the major instruments and techniques in a salsa ensemble. They are presented on the recording in the following order:

Rumba Introduction

   a. claves (two and three beat)
   b. wood block
   c. two wooden boxes (these were used historically when drums were prohibited)
   d. *tres* = guitar-type instruments with six strings in three double courses (*tres* means three and refers to the courses)
   e. chorus (try singing along)
   f. *trompeta* = trumpet
   g. solo male singer (reads words from liner notes)

Rumba *Montuno* Section

   h. *bajo* = bass
   i. trumpet (again)
   j. cowbell
   k. call and response (singer improvises and chorus sings "morena" [brown-skinned girl])
   l. full percussion
   m. *trombón* = trombone
   n. saxophone
   o. *flauta* = flute
   p. trumpet (again)

7. This overall texture can be termed "layering." This means that many levels of sound

occur at the same time. This technique is very much like African ensemble music (layers of ostinatos with constant variation).

   a. Ask the children to stand and dance to the *montuno* section of this rumba music.

   b. Ask the class to determine what else is happening musically during the introduction and what its purpose might be (perhaps nondance, presentation of words). Explain that the melody instruments improvise solos during the *montuno* section, and everybody plays many ostinatos.

   c. Continue by playing any examples from this recording; using a "discovery and discussion" process, explain the following to the students:

     (1) When the singer enters, he and a male chorus sing in a call-and-response manner while the instruments play ostinatos.

     (2) The vocal part is followed by the melody instruments playing several ostinatos together, layered one on top of the other.

     (3) The ostinatos are followed by improvised solos on individual instruments. When the improvisation begins, this is often called the *montuno* section (listen for the cowbell in this section).

     (4) This style continues until the end of the performance, with different instruments taking solos, including the singer (this time also improvising during the *montuno* section), and with chorus response.

8. Above all, this music is meant to be danced to.

L E S S O N 8

■ Objectives

Students will:

1. Learn a traditional circle game, a *rueda* (roo-EH-dah), from Puerto Rico.
2. Identify the dynamic accents in the song by adding appropriate movements.
3. Learn to sing this Puerto Rican song in Spanish.

■ Materials

1. Space in the classroom for the children to form one or several circles

■ Procedures

1. "A La Limón" is one of the many traditional *rueda* songs that Puerto Rico and other Hispanic countries assimilated from Spain (see figure 28). As in other cultures, Puerto Rican children sing while walking around in a circle holding hands. This in Spanish is called a *rueda*. The title "A La Limón" may be roughly translated as "in the manner of a lemon," but it does not have a specific meaning except its association with a *rueda* game. This one is particularly appropriate for smaller children. While singing the first phrase, which mentions the broken-down fountain, children usually jump and pretend to fall like the fountain. For a classroom situation, a small jump or gesture should be enough to accent the normally unstressed second beat and corresponding syllable in the fourth measure while continuing the flow of the song.

2. Using an example the children know, such as "The Mulberry Bush" or "Looby Loo,"

Figure 28. "A la Limón"

explain to them that children all over the world do singing games. Tell them that this one is in Spanish and comes from Puerto Rico. Instruct them to keep the beat to the song (while you sing) by stepping in place by their seats. Sing the first verse at a moderate tempo. If the students are not independent at finding the beat, help them by stepping as you sing. After the activity, give the translation of the lyrics and repeat the first verse until they can do the beat accurately and independently.

"A la Limón"

1. A la limón, a la limón, que se rompió la fuente,
   A la limón, a la limón, mandadla a componer,
   Hurrí, hurrí, hurrá, la reina va a pasar,
   Hurrí, hurrí, hurrá, la reina va a pasar.

2. A la limón, a la limón, no tenemos dinero,
   A la limón, a la limón, pues mandadlo a hacer,
   Hurrí, hurrí, hurrá, la reina va a pasar,
   Hurrí, hurrí, hurrá, la reina va a pasar.

3. A la limón, a la limón, de qué se hace el dinero,
   A la limón, a la limón, de cascarón de huevo,
   Hurrí, hurrí, hurrá, la reina va a pasar,
   Hurrí, hurrí, hurrá, la reina va a pasar.

Phonetic Pronunciation

1. Ah lah lee-MOHN, ah lah lee-MOHN, keh seh rohm-peeOH lah fooEHN-teh,

   Ah lah lee-MOHN, ah lah lee-MOHN, mahn-DAD-lah ah kohm-por-NEHR

   Oo-RREE, oo-RREE, oo-RRAH, lah reh-EE-nah vah ah pah-SAHR. (repeated)

2. Ah lah lee-MOHN, ah lah lee-MOHN, noh teh-NEH-mohs dee-NEH-roh,

   Ah lah lee-MOHN, ah lah lee-MOHN, poo-ehs mahn-DAD-loh ah-CEHR,

   Oo-RREE, oo-RREE, oo-RRAH, lah reh-EE-nah vah ah pah-SAHR. (repeated)

3. Ah lah lee-MOHN, ah lah lee-MOHN, deh KEH seh AH-ceh ehl dee-NEH-roh,

   Ah lah lee-MOHN, ah lah lee-MOHN, de kahs-kah-ROHN deh oo-EH-voh,

   Oo-RREE, oo-RREE, oo-RRAH, lah REH-ee-nah vah ah pah-SAHR. (repeated)

Translation

1. *A la limón, a la limón*, the fountain broke down,

   A la limón, a la limón, have it fixed,

   Hurrí, hurrí, hurrá, the queen is passing by,

   Hurrí, hurrí, hurrá, the queen is passing by.

2. *A la limón, a la limón*, we do not have money,

   A la limón, a la limón, then make some,

   Hurrí, hurrí, hurrá, the queen is passing by,

   Hurrí, hurrí, hurrá, the queen is passing by.

3. *A la limón, a la limón*, what is money made of,

   A la limón, a la limón, of eggshell,

   Hurrí, hurrí, hurrá, the queen is passing by,

   Hurrí, hurrí, hurrá, the queen is passing by.

3. Having previously prepared the room for the activity, instruct the students to form a circle, or two or three circles, depending on the number of students and the space available. Have them face the inside of the circle and instruct them to step to the beat once more, still in place. Sing the song again.

4. Ask the children if they notice a sound that would be louder than the others. Sing the first phrase and have them raise their hands when they hear the loud sound. Tell them that this is an accent and have them say the word. Still staying in their place, have them make a small jump in the accent as you sing the first phrase. Repeat until the children have enough familiarity with the music to jump on the accent and not before or after.

5. Begin combining the steps by having the children stay in their place, step to the beat, and jump on the accent while you sing.

6. Instruct them to hold hands while walking to the beat of the song in one direction and jumping on the accent. Sing the song again.

7. Review the lyrics and melody of the first verse with them, mapping the stepwise motion and leaps of the melody as needed. (At this point, they have heard the song many times.)

8. For closure, have them perform the *rueda* game, singing and moving together.

Possible extension of Lesson Eight

Have a few children stand in the middle of the circle and play the pulse on a hand drum while dancers revolve around them.

This lesson was contributed by Milagros Agostini Quesada.

LESSON 9

■ **Objectives**

Students will:
1. Perform the basic step for the *plena*.
2. Learn the refrain of the *plena* "A Ti Na Má" in Spanish.
3. Identify meter, form, and singing style of the *plena* after singing "A Ti Na Má" and performing the *plena's* basic step.
4. Learn a basic *güiro* or maracas rhythm to accompany the song.

■ **Materials**

1. *Güiros* (one or two), or maracas (two or three) and hand drums (two or three)
2. Map of the Caribbean

■ **Procedures**

1. Give students the following information:
   The *plena* is a song-dance from Puerto Rico (indicate Puerto Rico on the map of the Caribbean). It originated in the southern coast of the island during the beginning of this century. It narrates or comments on something, and for this reason it served an important social function, that of propagating news and important happenings in the communities. Some of its most important musical characteristics include the use of duple meter, verse and refrain in call-and-response style, and the use of triplets and syncopation. Although its instrumentation has changed throughout the years, nowadays it uses mostly percussion instruments with two or three melodic ones. The traditional percussion instruments that accompany the *plena* are two hand drums covered with goat skin, but conga drums are used by some groups. The *güiro* is sometimes added.
2. Following the steps listed below, teach the basic *plena* step to the beat, focusing on the duple meter.
   a. Keep a beat at a moderate tempo by tapping your feet. Instruct the students to join you. Begin counting "1, 2" to group the beats into duple meter, a characteristic of the *plena*.
   b. When the students are feeling the beat, begin modeling the *plena* step, which consists of extending your right foot one step forward, then retracing one step back in place beside the left foot. One step forward is taken with the left foot, then one back in place beside the right foot. The forward step is done to beat

one, and the step back in place to beat two. Eight pairs of the step for a total of sixteen measures will make one sequence, after which a change of direction takes place. A pair consists of one step right-forward, and one step back in place, one step left-forward and one step back in place.

    c. The change of direction consists of extending your foot one step to the side with the right foot, and then one step back to the original position. One step to the side is taken with the left foot, and then one step back to the original position. The step to the side is done to beat one, and the step to the original position to beat two. Practice a sequence of four pairs of side-steps for a total of eight measures. A pair consists of one step to the right side, and one step back to the original position, one step to the left side, and one step back to the original position. Follow with a repetition of the first sequence of forward steps and alternate with the sequence of side steps, finishing with the forward steps in the following sequence: eight pairs of forward steps, four pairs of side steps, and eight pairs of forward steps. Do this once or twice or until students are successful at following the step sequences.

3. Using the following procedure, introduce the refrain of the *plena* "A Ti Na Má" (see figure 29) in Spanish while students perform the *plena* step:

    a. Tap your feet to the duple meter as in step #1 (a) and instruct the students to perform the steps with you.

Figure 29. "A Ti Na Má"

b. Sing the refrain twice while doing the eight pairs of forward steps. Follow by singing the verse and doing the four pairs of side steps. Repeat the refrain twice and finish with the last statement of the words "a ti na má." Practice until the students change accurately and on the beat from the forward step to the side step as the refrain or the verse is sung.

c. Give the translation and instruct the students to sing the refrain on signal. Go over the complete sequence, with the teacher singing and doing the steps to the verse and the refrain while signaling the students to sing in the refrain.

"A Ti Na Má"

Verse

Dale la leche al nene,

acurúcalo que tiene frío,

dale la leche al nene,

acurrúcalo que tiene frío.

Refrain

A ti na má, te quiero.

A ti na má;

A ti na má, te quiero.

A ti na má.

Pronunciation for verse

DAH-leh lah LEH-cheh ahl NEH-neh;

Ah-koo-ROO-kah-loh keh tee-EH-neh FREE-oh;

DAH-leh lah LEH-cheh ahl NEH-neh;

Ah-koo-ROO-kah-loh keh tee-EH-neh free-oh.

Pronunciation for refrain

Ah TEE nah MAH, teh kee-EH-roh

Ah TEE nah MAH.

Ah TEE nah MAH, teh kee-EH-roh

Ah TEE nah MAH.

Translation for verse

Feed the baby,

And cradle him because he is cold.

Feed the baby,

And cradle him because he is cold.

Translation for refrain

Only you, I love you

Only you,

Only you, I love you

Only you.

d. Divide the class into two groups. One group will do the dance steps while the second group sings the refrain. Review briefly the sequence of steps. Perform the song in call-and-response style in the following sequence:
- Students sing the refrain twice (with teacher's help) while the teacher and some students do the forward step.
- Teacher sings the verse and does the side step while the group of students do the steps.
- Same as the beginning, finishing with the last statement of words "a ti na má."

4. Label the activity by introducing the word *plena* (PLEH-nah). Tell the students how to pronounce it.

5. Instruct the students to exchange activities so that both groups get to sing and do the steps. Before performing the *plena* once more, draw the students' attention toward the form and meter by asking: Is the music the same or different when we change the steps? Do the same number of people sing all the time? Is the *plena* in duple or triple meter? Sing the song once and have the students answer the questions at the end of the performance. The following characteristics of "A Ti Na Má" are typical of the *plena* and should be discussed and/or explained:
a. Verse and refrain (AB form)
b. Call-and-response singing style by soloist and chorus
c. Duple meter
d. Double statement of the refrain at the beginning

6. Teach a basic rhythmic pattern for the *güiro* or maracas by following the procedure listed below:
a. Show the instruments and explain that both the *güiro* and/or maracas are of Indian or African origin. Explain that two Puerto Rican hand drums are used for the *plena,* while the *güiro* is added sometimes. Demonstrate how the instruments are played. The *güiro* is played by holding the instrument with the left hand and scraping the body with the metal scraper in any of the patterns included in figure 30. If using the maracas, use any of the patterns included in figure 31.
b. Repeat the refrain of "A Ti Na Má." Model the hand movements for playing the *güiro* by pretending to hold the instrument and going through the motions "down-up, down-up" (or the chosen rhythm) with the right hand. Do the same with the maracas, pretending to hold one in each hand and going "left-right, left-right" or in the chosen rhythm. Add the movement of the hand drum to the beat. Instruct the students not to sing but to imitate the movements until they can do them with precision. Distribute the instruments to a group of students and have them practice the patterns briefly.

7. Guide the students in a final performance of the song with instrumental accompaniment by doing the following:
a. Sing the *plena* and add the instruments in the following manner:
- Singers and teacher begin the refrain on signal.
- During the second statement of the refrain, start signaling the instruments beginning with the hand drum(s).
- Add the *güiro* and/or maracas in any order as the singing proceeds from verse to refrain.
b. After the performance, and for closure of the lesson, review the following:
- Name of the musical form and country of origin.
- The meter, form, and singing style of the *plena.*

This lesson was contributed by Milagros Agostini Quesada.

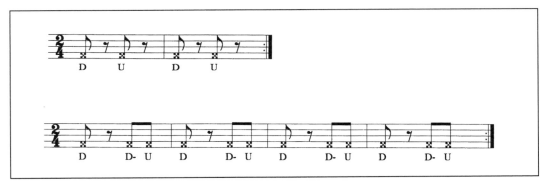

Figure 30. Güiro rhythms

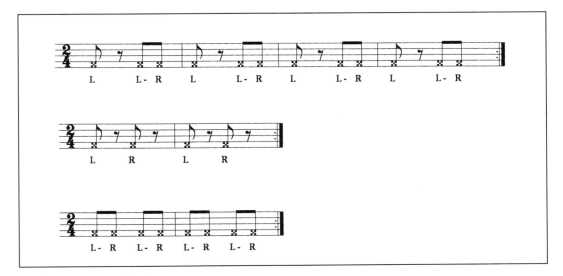

Figure 31. Maracas rhythms

LESSON 10

■ Objectives

Students will:
1. Play an instrumental accompaniment to the beat of the Mexican dance "Jarabe Tapatío," using different percussion instruments for the different sections.
2. Determine if the sections are the same or different and how many sections the dance has.
3. Identify the main families of instruments used in the mariachi ensemble.

■ Materials

1. Maracas, rhythm sticks, tambourines, hand drums

2. Recording: *Bailes Regionales de México con El Mariachi Vargas de Tecalitlán* (RCA 9607-2-RL)

■ **Procedures**

1. The musical style and instrumental group known as the mariachi is one of the best-known types of Mexican music. Its origin can be traced back to the 1800s. The ensemble's modern instrumentation consists basically of two trumpets, two or three violins, a guitar, and two purely Mexican instruments called the *vihuela* and the *guitarrón*. The guitar and *vihuela* provide harmony, while the *guitarrón* adds rhythmic punctuation and plays bass notes. Sometimes the mariachi members add singing to their performance depending on the type of music they are playing. The *jarabe* is a type of dance form played by the mariachi that does not include singing. There are different types of *jarabes*, in many instances, labeled according to their place of origin. For example, the "Jarabe Tapatío" originated in the state of Jalisco. *Tapatío* refers to people or things from Jalisco. *Jarabes* are characterized by contrasting sections, usually four or five. Meter and tempo changes may occur from section to section. *Sesquiáltera* or the alternation of duple and triple meter can also be found in the *jarabes*. The particular combination of string and brass instruments in the mariachi allows for contrasts in tone color within sections by playing these instruments antiphonally.

2. Before playing "Jarabe Tapatío," introduce the activity by stating that the music to be heard is a dance from our Mexican neighbors. It is known in the United States as "The Mexican Hat Dance" because a big sombrero or hat is thrown on the floor and a couple dances around it.

3. Play the excerpt the first time and have the students find the beat by clapping or tapping to the four sections of the dance, helping and modeling as necessary. The first, third, and fourth sections can be clapped in duple or quadruple meter, the second in triple. A slow bridge connecting the third and fourth sections should not be clapped. If the students are competent with the beat, focus the activity on meter and have them identify the metric feeling of each section.

4. For the second listening, tell the students they will pretend to be playing different instruments by doing with their hands the movements required to play them. Show them the instruments, and, depending on the students' previous experience with these, give them their names and/or demonstrate or review how they are played. Explain to the students that they will be changing their movements as the music changes and that they should listen for these changes and imitate your movements. If the students lack the physical maturity to perform the wrist action needed for the maracas, have them hold one maraca with one hand and hit it against the opposite hand. Play the dance. While doing the beat, model the movements for playing the following instruments:
    a. Rhythm sticks
    b. Hand drums
    c. Maracas
    d. Tambourines
    After the activity, draw their attention to the different sections by asking: Why did we change our movements? Was the music the same or different every time we changed movements? According to the students' background, discuss the musical

aspects that change. (The character of the music changes for each section. The melodic rhythm, tempo, and meter change in section two.)

5. For the third time the music is played, add the different instruments to the beat of each section. Before playing the excerpt, be sure the students know the instruments they are playing and how to play them by having them practice briefly. Tell them to remember the number of times the music and their instruments change. After the performance, ask which instruments they were playing, how many times they changed instruments, and how many sections the music has. (*Jarabes* have four or five sections of music. This one has four.)

6. Display pictures or illustrations of brass and string instruments on opposite sides of the room. Play part of the "Jarabe Tapatío." Have the students point at the instruments playing at a given time, strings (violins, guitars, *viheulas*, and *guitarrónes*) or winds (trumpets), helping as necessary.

7. Play an excerpt of "Las Chiapanecas" and ask the students whether or not a mariachi is playing. Ask why or why not. Play another excerpt of the piece in which the violins and trumpets play antiphonally. Without your help, have the students point at the pictures back and forth as the instruments are heard in the music.

8. Review the following questions:
   a. Are the sections in the dance the same or different?
   b. How many sections are heard?
   c. Are strings (violins, guitars, *vihuelas*, and *guitarrónes*), winds (trumpets), or both heard in the mariachi from Mexico?

This lesson was contributed by Milagros Agostini Quesada.

LESSON 11

■ Objectives

Students will:
1. Learn a step to the dance "Las Chiapanecas" as performed by a mariachi group.
2. Identify the meter, form, and instruments used in the dance after performing the step.
3. Sing a short section of "Las Chiapanecas" in Spanish.
4. Learn the song "Mambrú se Fue a la Guerra."

■ Materials

1. Recording: *Bailes Regionales de México con El Mariachi Vargas de Tecalitlán* (RCA 9607-2-RL)

■ Procedures

1. Teach a waltz-like, in-place step to "Las Chiapanecas," using the following procedure:
   a. Establish a beat and meter at a slower tempo than that of the music by tapping your foot on the downbeat and clapping twice each time (tap, clap, clap). Instruct the students to join you. Begin counting "1, 2, 3" to group the beats into

triple meter.

b. When the students are feeling the beat, begin modeling the step by slightly flexing your knees at every downbeat until the students can follow you with precision. Take a step slightly to the right in the downbeat and follow with a step slightly to the left at the next downbeat. Add a swinging motion to the steps by moving your torso from side to side as you move your feet.

c. Once the students can perform these movements successfully, add a step after the downbeat with the left foot, keeping it slightly in back of the right, and follow with the right foot to complete the waltz-like step RLR to each measure of the music (one foot movement for each beat). Follow with the same pattern to the left, or LRL, and alternate patterns for each measure. Practice by counting aloud, and gradually increase the tempo until it matches the tempo of the recorded example. The form of this dance is ABCABC. Thirty-two steps will be added to each of the A and C sections.

2. Explain to the students that for the short, second section of "Las Chiapanecas," they will stand in place and clap at the appropriate time. Demonstrate this activity by clapping to the upbeat of the third phrase and the downbeat of the fourth in section B. Have the students practice briefly by standing in place and clapping to this section.

3. Begin combining the activities with the music by doing the following:

   a. Review the sequence of steps and clap in order.

   b. Play the first ABC sections of "Las Chiapanecas," and help the students begin in time by counting the introduction (eight measures) and modeling the step before signaling them to move to section A. Signal them to stand in place and clap to the B section and return to the waltz-like step for the C section. After the performance, ask the students whether the music is in duple or triple meter. Explain that dances from Mexico have different meters and sometimes combine triple and duple meters. They are part of the forms usually played by the type of ensemble they just heard. This group is called a mariachi (mah-ree-AH-chee). Explain that although Mexico has many different types of music, this group has become very representative of Mexican music. Have the students repeat the word "mariachi" after you.

4. To teach the lyrics of the C section and focus the students' attention on the type of instruments used in the mariachi, do the following:

   a. Play this section of the dance and introduce the Spanish lyrics to the students by singing with the record (see figure 32). After singing, give the translation. Go over the pronunciation of the second phrase (measures 5–8) with the students as needed. Have them sing this phrase with you and practice briefly.

Lyrics for Section C of "Las Chiapanecas" (*Las Cheeah-pah-NEH-kahs*)

Ya no tenemos penas, ya estamos alegres,

Vengan a bailar, a bailar, a bailar.

Phonetic Pronunciation

Iah noh teh-NEH-mohs PEH-nahs,

Iah ehs-TAH-mohs ah-LEH-grehs,

VEHN-gahn ah bahee-LAHR, ah bahee-LAHR, ah-bahee-LAHR.

Figure 32. Section C of "Las Chiapanecas"

Translation

> We are not sad anymore, now we are happy,
>
> Come and dance, come and dance, come and dance.

   b. Play the C section and sing with the record in the following sequence: Teacher will sing the first phrase. Students will sing the second phrase with teacher's help. Teacher will sing the third phrase.

   c. Practice the pronunciation of the first and third phrases with the students. Have the students practice singing these new phrases as needed. Play the excerpt again and exchange the sequence.

   d. Before playing the excerpt one more time, draw the students' attention to the instrumentation of the mariachi by asking which instruments are prominent in this piece. In this particular section, the strings (violins, guitar, *vihuela*, and *guitarrón*) and wind instruments (trumpets) play antiphonally following the sequence that was established in the singing part. Display illustrations of brass instruments and strings that also include the guitar, and have the students choose the ones they just heard. Show pictures or illustrations of the Mexican *guitarrón* and *vihuela*. Explain that the combination of violins, guitars, *vihuelas*, *guitarrónes*, and brass instruments gives the mariachi its particular tone color.

5. Briefly review the step and play the dance, giving a counting introduction. Tell the

Figure 33. "Mambrú se Fue a la Guerra" (syllables in original version are *do re mi, fa sol la*)

students to remember how many different sections the piece has. Have the students do the steps and sing to "Las Chiapanecas" upon signal. After the performance, ask them to determine the form of the dance (ABC). Review the meter, the instruments used in the mariachi ensemble, and its country of origin.

6. Introduce the song "Mambrú se Fue a La Guerra" shown in figure 33, following these steps:

   a. Explain that the song is originally from Spain, but that in Mexico and some other Spanish-speaking countries, it is a traditional song for children. The title refers to the duke of Marlborough, written and pronounced "Mambrú" (mahm-BROO) by the Spaniards. He was a well-known army general and politician from England who mingled in Spanish politics of the times.

   b. Read the translation. Sing the phrase "que dolor, que dolor, que pena," and have the students map the melody. The teacher should model or help as needed. Instruct the students to map the melody of this phrase when they hear it in the song. (Depending on students' background and/or ability, during this first listening have them raise their hand when they hear the phrase or map the melody). Sing the song for the students.

"Mambrú se Fue a La Guerra"

1. Mambrú se fue a la guerra, que dolor, que dolor, que pena,
   Mambrú se fue a la guerra y no se cuando vendrá,
   Que do re mi, que fa sol la, no se cuando vendrá.*

2. Si vendrá por la Pascua, que dolor, que dolor que pena,
   Si vendrá por la Pascua o por la Trinidad,
   Que do re mi, que fa sol la, o por la Trinidad.

3. Allá viene un barquito, que dolor, que dolor, que pena,
   Allá viene un barquito que noticias traerá,
   Que do re mi, que fa sol la, que noticias traerá.

4. Es que Mambrú se ha muerto, que dolor, que dolor, que pena,
   Es que Mambrú se ha muerto y ya no volverá,
   Que do re mi, que fa sol la, y ya no volverá!

   *syllables used in this popular version may be substituted with *do re si, si do la*,
   the correct solfeggio syllables for the corresponding pitches (see figure 33)

Phonetic Pronunciation

1. Mahm-BROO seh foo-EH a lah GEH-rah, keh doh-LOHR, keh doh-LOHR,
   keh PEH-nah,
   Mahm-BROO seh foo-EH a lah GEH-rah ee noh seh coo-AHN-doh vehn-DRAH,
   Keh doh reh mee, keh fah sohl lah, noh seh coo-AHN-doh vehn-DRAH.

2. See vehn-DRAH pohr lah PAHS-kooah, keh doh-LOHR, keh doh-LOHR,
   keh PEH-nah,
   See vehn-DRAH pohr la PAHS-kooah, oh pohr lah tree-nee-DAHD,
   Keh doh reh mee, keh fah sohl lah, oh pohr lah tree-nee-DAHD.

3. Ah-JAH vee-EH-neh oon bahr-KEE-toh, keh dohLOHR, keh dohLOHR,
   keh PEH-nah,
   Ah-JAH vee-EH-neh oon bahr-KEE-toh, ke noh-TEE-seeas trah-eh-RAH,
   Keh doh reh mee, keh fah sohl lah, keh noh-TEE-seeas trah-eh-RAH.

4. Ehs keh Ma-hm-BROO seh ah moo-EHR-toh, keh doh-LOHR, keh doh-
   LOHR, keh PEH-nah,
   Ehs keh Mahm-BROO seh ah moo-EHR-toh ee IAH noh vohl-veh-RAH,
   Keh doh reh mee, keh fah sohl lah, ee iah noh vohl-veh-RAH.

Translation

1. Mambrú left for war, how painful, how painful and sorrowful, (repeated)
   Mambrú left for war and he will not come back; que do, re, mi,
   que fa sol la, and he will not come back.

2. Will he come back for Christmas, how painful, how painful and sorrowful,

Will he come back for Christmas or for Easter, que do re mi,

que fa sol la, or for Easter.

3. A little ship is approaching, how painful, how painful and sorrowful,

A little ship is approaching, what news will it bring? que do re mi,

que fa sol la, what news will it bring?

4. Mambrú has died, how painful, how painful and sorrowful,

Mambrú has died and will not come back que do, re mi, que fa sol la,

And he will not come back!

c. Go over the melody of the same phrase with the students, practicing just with the syllable "loo" if necessary. Practice the pronunciation as needed, and integrate the melody and lyrics of that phrase. Sing the complete song again, and signal the students to sing this phrase with you.

d. Teach the phrase that utilizes the solfeggio syllables by following the same basic procedure. When they can sing it correctly, sing the song while signaling the students to sing both known phrases.

e. Go over the pronunciation of the remaining phrases, numbers one and two, and practice singing them. Proceed to sing the complete song.

Extension of Lesson Eleven

Teach a guitar accompaniment for this song. If students do not have enough background and cannot change chords readily, assign each chord to a different group of students, signaling the changes. Use either the "down-up" (two quarters) strumming pattern for each duple measure or just the "down" strumming for each measure if the students are less experienced. Make sure the students strum all the chord strings when going down. As psychomotor preparation, practice the wrist action by having the students do the strumming movements while the group sings the song. The Autoharp may substitute for the guitar without detracting from the style or authenticity of the song. If the Autoharp is used, or if the students know the B7 chord on the guitar, transcribe the song to A major.

This lesson was contributed by Milagros Agostini Quesada.

Integrating music with other studies

Musical events in Latin America are seldom isolated phenomena. These events nearly always relate to a particular aspect of culture such as ritual, celebration, devotion, entertainment, or work; classes should not, therefore, study any aspect of culture without thinking about the music that may accompany it and form an integral part of it. All of the musical styles discussed in the lessons in this chapter have their own cultural contexts; it is unlikely that the music would be performed outside of that context, or that the context would take place without music. Students might develop an awareness of the cultural background of musical traditions in social science classes such as history, geography, psychology, and sociology. Include a discussion of the following facts about these cultural contexts in the lessons of this chapter, in other lessons dealing with the music of other cultures, or in one lesson that emphasizes music as it relates to culture in general.

Siku panpipe music of Peru is performed during festive celebrations on feast days and other religious holidays.

Afro-Latin American drumming exists in various contexts, including secular, social ones, and religious festivals of the Catholic calendar or rituals of African derivation.

The Colombian marimba is also performed for both secular and religious occasions such as the social *currulao* dance and the festival of Saint Anthony.

Calypsos of Trinidad and Tobago and elsewhere in the Caribbean are often songs of derision and ridicule that regulate social behavior. They also provide joyful rhythms during the annual carnival fete, which provides a release before the solemn celebration of Lent.

The European-derived musics of many Latin American countries function as entertainment or for dancing. In the lonely life of the farmer, rancher, or cowherd, such as the *vaquero* of Venezuela, the gaucho of Argentina, and the *huaso* of Chile, music serves to break the solitude.

Pan-Andean music reflects the cultural past and heritages of many of its music makers and listeners. Much pan-Andean music functions as a vehicle for protest against racial, social, and political oppression.

One of the happy musics in Latin America is salsa. It inspires even the most inhibited people to dance and have a good time, and the texts speak about happy times and merry-making. Certain musics developed as they did because of the geographies and histories of certain areas. Search for examples of this concept, such as these that follow:

1. Afro-Latin American musics developed along the hot, humid coastal regions of Latin America and the Caribbean. These were the areas where slaves worked on sugar, cotton, and coffee plantations, and they were also areas that were topographically similar to the African homelands of the slaves. In these areas, people of African descent had natural materials with which to construct instruments similar to African drums and marimbas.

2. In cattle-grazing regions that are similar to cattle-grazing regions in Spain and Portugal, many South American cowboys sing songs similar to those sung in the Old World.

3. Geography also determines what materials are available for musical instrument construction. The *charango* of Bolivia and Peru, for example, was made from an armadillo shell because of the scarcity of wood in the high elevations of the Andes mountains.

4. History affects musical development. The Bush Negroes of Suriname have retained a greater amount of African music and culture than any other African-derived culture in the Americas because of an event in history: when the area known today as Suriname was traded by the British for the present Manhattan Island, which was owned by the Dutch, many slaves took advantage of the political confusion and escaped from the plantations into the jungles to establish their own African-type villages and to preserve their culture.

5. More recently, the steel band tradition of Trinidad and Tobago was made possible by the discarded oil drums left on Caribbean beaches during World War II.

   In the area of visual arts, there are two ways that Latin American music can be studied:

   a. The instruments themselves are often works of art and have earned places in museums. The beautiful ceramic instruments of the pre-Columbian cultures of Peru, Ecuador, Colombia, Costa Rica, Panama, and Mexico, for example, are highly valued as art objects. Modern musical instruments are also often constructed and designed with visual beauty in mind.

b. Musical instruments and musical events are often depicted in sculptures and in painting. Much can be learned about the musical contexts of ancient Latin American cultures from this "music iconography" on ceramic pots, such as those found in Peru and Mexico. Modern painting can also be an important source for seeing the contexts of music. Many paintings in Haiti and Brazil, for example, are important sources that illustrate the roles of musical instruments in daily life.

Students can also be brought to understand the relationship of folk music to art music. Music from the oral traditions of Latin America (folk, ritual, and indigenous music) has often provided composers in the European art tradition with sources for musical inspiration. In Brazil, Heitor Villa-Lobos is the best-known composer who has been inspired by the folk music of his native land; in Mexico, Carlos Chavez has been similarly inspired, as has been the Argentine composer Alberto Ginastera. Indeed, each Latin American country seems to have its Aaron Copland who has been inspired by the folklore of his or her native land. The interest in this so-called folk music is so great, and musicians of such caliber have given their attention to its composition and performance, that it has become art music in the best and truest sense of the word.

***Integrating music with other studies** was contributed by Selwyn Ahyoung.*

BIBLIOGRAPHY

Behague, Gerard. "Brazil." In *The New Grove Dictionary of Music and Musicians*, vol. 3. New York: Macmillan, 1980. A comprehensive discussion of the folk and popular music of Brazil.

Behague, Gerard. "Latin American Folk Music." In *Folk and Traditional Music of the Western Continents* (4th ed.), edited by Bruno Nettl. Englewood Cliffs, NJ: Prentice Hall, 1990.

Bergman, Billy. *Hot Sauces, Latin and Caribbean Pop*. New York: Quill, a division of William Morrow, 1983. A short, well-written book including articles on "Reggae" (Bergman), "Reggae After Marley" (Schwartz), "Soca" (Bergman), and "Salsa and Latin Jazz" (Leymarie).

Bibik, Thomas. *Tropical Hammer Steel Drum Crafters Presents Tom Reynolds, Steel Drums: Steel Drum Manual*. Ferndale, MI: Thomas Bibik, 1993. Available from Thomas Bibik, 800 W. Drayton, Ferndale, MI 48220.

Hill, Donald R. *Calypso Calaloo: Early Carnival Music in Trinidad*. Gainesville, FL: The University Press of Florida, 1993.

Isles of the Caribbean. Washington, DC: National Geographic Society, 1980. Special Publications Division. A popular introduction to the Caribbean with several pages about and excellent pictures of Trinidad's carnival.

Olsen, Dale A. "Folk Music of South America—A Musical Mosaic." In *Musics of Many Cultures: An Introduction*, edited by Elizabeth May. Berkeley: University of California Press, 1980. A survey of Spanish and Portuguese-derived, African-derived, Native American-derived, and nationalistically determined folk music of South America.

Olsen, Dale A. "Symbol and Function in South American Indian Music." In *Musics of Many Cultures: An Introduction*, edited by Elizabeth May. Berkeley: University of California Press, 1980. A survey of the music of Native South Americans.

Olsen, Dale A., Daniel Sheehy, and Charles A. Perrone. *Sounds of the World—Music Of Latin America: Mexico, Ecuador, Brazil*. Reston, VA: Music Educators National Conference, 1986.

Perrone, Charles A., and Enlyton de Sá Rego. *MPB: Contemporary Brazilian Popular Music*. Albuquerque, NM: Latin American Institute, 1985.

Roberts, John Storm. *Black Music of Two Worlds*. New York: Morrow Books, 1972. An easily readable book that provides an introduction to the music of Africa and discussions about the black musics of North America, Central America, South America, and the Caribbean.

Roberts, John Storm. *The Latin Tinge: The Impact of Latin American Music on the United States*. (2d ed.) Tivoli, NY: Original Music, 1985. An informative book that focuses on Latin American and Caribbean popular musics in the United States.

Sadie, Stanley, ed. *The New Grove Dictionary of Music and Musicians*. 20 vols. New York: Macmillan, 1980. This extensive publication contains informative articles on the music of many Latin American countries.

Stevenson, Robert. *Music in Aztec and Inca Territory*. Berkeley: University of California Press, 1968. Portions of this book give historiographic details about the music of the Andes.

DISCOGRAPHY

African and Afro-American Drums. Ethnic Folkways Library FE 4502. Although somewhat outdated, this is still a good survey of African-derived drumming in the Americas.

Afro-Brazilian Religious Songs: Cantigas de Candomble/Candomble Songs from Salvador, Bahia. Lyrichord LLST 7315. Contains songs and drumming examples pertaining to Afro-Brazilian religious ceremony.

Afro-Hispanic Music from Western Colombia and Ecuador. Ethnic Folkways Library FE 4376. A very important recording. Music collected and text written by Norman Whitten, one of the foremost authorities on African-derived music from the west coast of Colombia.

Amazonia. Cult Music of Northern Brazil. Lyrichord LL6T 7300. Contains good examples of songs and drumming pertaining to Afro-Brazilian religious ceremony.

Argentina: The Guitar of the Pampas. Lyrichord LLST 7253. This album contains concert music for guitar, composed by Abel Fleury in a folk style and performed by Roberto Lara, a leading South American guitarist.

Bailes Regionales de México con El Mariachi Vargas de Tecalitán. RCA 9607-2-RL.

Batucada Number 3, the Exciting Rhythm of the Wild Brazilian Carnival. Philips 6482 002. Excellent recording featuring samba rhythms and percussion improvisations, with individual examples of samba instruments.

Black Orpheus (movie sound track). Fontana 67520. Has excellent examples of samba music and other popular musics from Brazil.

Cachao Master Sessions, Volume 1. Crescent Moon Records, Epic Records Group, CineSon EK 64320. 1994. A division of Sony Music. This company is located at 550 Madison Ave., New York, NY 10022-3211.

Calypso Travels. Folkways Records FW 8733. An outdated recording, but still important because it features Lord Invader and his Calypso Group; many song texts are included.

The Columbia World Library of Folk and Primitive Music: Venezuela. Vol. 9, Columbia Masterworks SL212. Collected by Alan Lomax, this old album contains important examples of Venezuelan traditional musics of many types.

Fiestas of Peru, Music of the High Andes. Nonesuch Explorer Series H-72045. This contains mestizo music from Peru, including music of carnivals and festivals, featuring brass bands and traditional ensembles.

The Hammer. Windham Hill Records, WD-0107 DIDX 1658. Performed by Andy Narell.

Historic Recordings of Mexican Music, Volume 1: The Earliest Mariachi Recordings 1906–1936. Folklyric Records 9051.

Historic Recordings of Mexican Music, Volume 2: Mariachi Coculense de Cirilo Marmolejo 1933–36. Folklyric Records 9052. Volumes 1 and 2, which include informative record notes, are distributed by Down Home Music, 10341 San Pablo Avenue, El Cerrito, CA 94530.

In Praise of Oxalá and Other Gods, Black Music of South America. Nonesuch Explorer Series H-72036. The best anthology of African-derived music of South America, with examples from Colombia, Ecuador, and Brazil (including *candomblé* and *capoeira*).

Instruments and Music of Bolivia. Ethnic Folkways Library FM 4012. Contains many examples of panpipe orchestras from Bolivia.

Inti-Illimani 3: Canto de Pueblos Andinos. Monitor Records MFS 787. An accessible and inexpensive recording by one of Chile's greatest pan-Andean ensembles.

An Island Carnival—Music of the West Indies. Nonesuch 72091. This record is well recorded and documented, but the title is a complete misnomer; it has nothing to do with Carnival in the Caribbean. It contains, however, many examples of small groups performing secular and sacred music, including village bands, bamboo bands, cocoa-lute bands, and Hindu epic songs.

Kingdom of the Sun, Peru's Inca Heritage. Nonesuch Explorer Series H-72029. Good examples of mestizo music from Peru, including panpipe music.

Mountain Music of Peru. Folkways FE 4539. This two-record set is the best collection of Peruvian highland music on an American label, including panpipes and flutes of diverse types, guitars, *charangos*, and more, with informative notes.

Music from the Land of Macchu Picchu. Lyrichord LLST 7294. Contains diverse musics from Peru, including black traditions for comparison with Brazil and the Caribbean.

Music of Mexico: Sones Jarachos. Arhollie 3008. Includes texts, translations, and informative notes. Distributed by Down Home Music, 10341 San Pablo Avenue, El Cerrito, CA 94530.

Music of the Incas: "Ayllu Sulca." Lyrichord LLST 7348. This record contains excellent examples of ensemble music from Ayacucho, Peru, performed by Antonio Sulca on the harp, with his family ensemble playing violins, mandolins, and *kenas*.

Pan All Night. Steel Bands of Trinidad and Tobago. Delos International DE 4022. Caribbean Carnival Series.

The Piñata Party Presents Music of Peru. Folkways Records FW 8749. This music shows some recent roots of pan-Andean music; also included are Peruvian harp duets.

Pukaj Wayra...Music from Bolivia. Lyrichord LLST 7361. A good recording by a Bolivian pan-Andean ensemble.

Songs and Dances of Brazil. Folkways FW 6953. A survey of some of the lyrical musical forms of Brazilian popular music of several decades ago.

Songs of Chile. Folkways FW 8817. Traditional Chilean folksongs, with guitar accompaniment, sung by two Chilean girls; contains good examples of Spanish-derived music.

Sparrow, The Greatest. Charlie's Records JAF 1007. This album contains recent calypsos by one of Trinidad's most famous singers. Available from Original Music, RD #1, Box 190, Lasher Road, Tivoli, NY 12583.

The Steel Drums of Kim Loy Wong. Folkways Records FI 8367 and FS 3834. This is an outdated recording with inferior sound quality, but it still provides an important documentation of steel band, especially when accompanied by Pete Seeger's booklet by the same name.

Traditional Chilean Songs. Folkways Records FW 8748. Sung by Chilean folksinger Rolando Alarcón with guitar accompaniment, this is a good album for Spanish-derived music; it includes song texts in Spanish and English.

Trinidad Carnival. Steel Bands of Trinidad and Tobago. Delos International, DE 4012. Caribbean Carnival Series.

Urubamba. Columbia Records KCC 32896. An excellent album of pan-Andean music produced by Paul Simon with the same group that performed "El Condor Pasa" for Simon and Garfunkel's album *Bridge over Troubled Waters*.

Viracocha, Legendary Music of the Andes. Lyrichord LLST 7264. The selections on this record contain three harp performances from Cuzco, Peru, and music by other Peruvian ensembles during festivals.

NORTHERN IRELAND

SCOTLAND

IRELAND

UNITED KINGDOM

NORWAY

SWEDEN

FINLAND

DENMARK

ESTONIA

LATVIA

LITHUANIA

BYELARUS

NETHERLANDS

BELGIUM

GERMANY

POLAND

UKRAINE

Atlantic Ocean

LUXEMBOURG

CZECHOSLOVAKIA

SLOVAKIA

MOLDOVA

FRANCE

SWITZERLAND

AUSTRIA

HUNGARY

SLOVENIA

CROATIA

ROMANIA

PORTUGAL

ANDORRA

BOSNIA

YUGOSLAVIA

BULGARIA

SPAIN

ITALY

MONTENEGRO

MACEDONIA

GREECE

Mediterranean Sea

ALBANIA

NORTH AFRICA

Map of Europe

CHAPTER 6

EUROPE

by Patricia Shehan Campbell

What comes to mind when you think of Europe? Do your images include the Eiffel Tower in Paris, St. Peter's Cathedral in Rome, and London's Big Ben clock tower? Do you envision boats on the Rhine or Danube rivers, the breathtaking Alps of Switzerland, the Côte d'Azur of southern France, the islands of Greece, and the fjords of Norway? Do you harbor thoughts of European sidewalk cafes, galleries of great art, the music of concert halls and opera houses, and exquisite cuisine? This is classic Europe as seen on first tours and in travel brochures, but consider these scenes as well: shepherds and their flocks against the backdrop of rocky hills; village women en route to the central market for fresh vegetables, fruits, and grains; three-day wedding feasts and their great spreads of food, drink, and dancing; massive churches with onion-shaped towers rather than spires and steeples; and farms where sickles, scythes, and motorized combines work together. Such are the images of the "other Europe," the more ancient European cultural stratum still found in the rural areas and in the countries in the eastern regions.

Europe is a conglomerate of many images and many nations and is a land of great diversity. Viewed as a whole, Europe is perceived as the foundation of Western civilization. The now widespread Western traditions of governance, education, and the arts first developed in Europe, and European contributions to world progress continue today. Over the centuries, Greece, Italy, Spain, France, Germany, and other nations have emerged as world leaders in the arts, the humanities, and the sciences.

The continent of Europe is approximately the same size as the United States, including Alaska. It is outranked in size by all other continents except Australia, but it embraces a great diversity of climates, natural resources, and densities of population. Europe extends from the icy Arctic Circle in northern Scandinavia to the temperate climate of the Mediterranean countries of Spain, Italy, and Greece. The British Isles are its farthest western countries (beyond which is the Atlantic Ocean), and its eastern borders are flanked by the Asian continent and areas of the Black and Caspian seas. Europe is in close proximity to major cultural regions including North Africa and the Middle East. Despite a one-time history of isolationism, cultural exchanges among countries have allowed for fascinating new cultural manifestations.

European peoples vary in ethnic composition, language, and religion. For its size, Europe is the most polyglot area in the world. Celtic, Romance, Teutonic, Baltic, Slavonic, Hellenic, Turkic, and Finno-Ugric are some of the broad language classifications, which can be further distinguished by country or region. The Romance languages, for example, include Italian, French, Spanish, Portuguese, and Romanian, as well as Walloon (Belgium), Catalán and Galician (Spain), and Ladin (Italy). Another language group is Slavic, which can be classified into three groups according to regions in eastern Europe; for example, South Slavic alone is divided into six language groups. Is it any surprise that language has fostered national consciousness and political divisions throughout the continent?

Although there are similarities among European peoples, the cultural regions are distinctive in many ways. Some divide the continent along political boundaries, but the physical characteristics of the land itself may provide clearer borders between cultural regions. The British Isles share elements of the Germanic countries of continental Europe, but England, Scotland, Ireland, and Wales developed customs different from those of the mainland because of their somewhat remote island status. Three of the four Scandinavian countries—Norway, Sweden, and Finland—are separated from the continent by the Baltic Sea; their Nordic cultures are more similar to one another than to the rest of Europe.

The Mediterranean countries of Spain, Italy, and Greece share a more moderate climate than that of central Europe, and their cultural influences include North Africa and the Middle East. The Germanic countries of Austria, parts of Switzerland, Germany itself, and the Netherlands are united by language and location in the western portion of Europe, and the Alpine regions of the first three countries contribute similar customs beyond their political borders. Eastern European countries, including Poland, the Czech Republic, Slovakia, Hungary, Romania, Bulgaria, Russia, the Ukraine, Albania, and the smaller nations east of the Adriatic (Bosnia-Hercegovina, Croatia, Macedonia, Montenegro, Serbia, and Slovenia) remained agrarian societies well into the twentieth century; the rustic peasant life of this region still exists in many communities. The Romantic-Atlantic countries of France, Portugal, and Belgium, which complete the list of major European countries, are akin in location (all are coastal countries on the Atlantic) and language (from the Romance family).

Figure 1. Traditional line dance of Romania

The splendors of Europe are at hand, whether through the romance of transcontinental travel, staring out the windows of the great railway cars that link the cities and the villages, or through the more immediately accessible avenues of knowledge: the literature and the fine arts. Study of these cultural contributions is likely to lead to a deep understanding of Europe's people, and such study may just as surely transport the learner to this historical land of so many of our forefathers. In particular, a view of the music and the dance of these countries offers insight into both the diversity and the similarities among the people of Europe (see figures 1–4).

Characteristics of European musics

As languages differ among ethnic groups, so do music styles. European folk music can be divided into two genres: songs and dance music. Although some may view the traditional music of Europe as a single unit with common elements maintained across the continent, each region, country, and community has its own style, songs, and dances. Since all music consists of fundamental sonic elements (melody, rhythm, texture, form, and timbre), these are the elements evaluated when reviewing the styles of Europe as a whole and those of the six distinctive regions studied in this chapter: the British Isles, Scandinavia, Germanic western Europe, the Atlantic Romantic countries, the Mediterranean, and eastern Europe.

Figure 2. Ethnic heritage celebration (Macedonian) in midwestern United States

European traditional music has many unifying elements. Although we immediately hear differences between the musics of Sweden and Italy, they resemble each other far more than either one resembles Chinese or Native American music. What is so characteristic about European folk music?

Song structure is one important element of European music. Across the continent, the use of strophic form is widespread: melodies are sung more than once with different words for each repetition. The verse-by-verse and verse-chorus organization of songs reinforces the view of Europe as a distinct musical unit.

Meter is another facet common to European traditional music. Most songs and dance music are metric, so there is a regular and consistent recurrence in the accent patterns. Duple and triple meters (and even irregular meters such as 5/8 and 7/8) feature the repetition of accents in a cyclic manner. In songs, this meter is usually linked to the poetry. Music with no obvious metric pattern is rare in Europe.

Certain song genres are found in many parts of Europe. These include the narrative song, love songs, ceremonial songs, seasonal songs, and dance music. Song stories called ballads and their lengthier cousin, the epic, are prominent throughout the continent. Clearly, then, European music can be efficiently classified as songs and dance music.

There are instruments that are associated with the music of the various European countries, but several are so predominant throughout the continent that they can be referred to as pan-European instruments. There are perhaps three such instruments: the fiddle, the accordion, and the bagpipe. Although they vary in construction, size, and shape, their tone quality and principles for sound production do not. Other common European instruments include flutes, drums of various types, plucked lutes, and zithers.

Figure 3. Norwegian *lur* performer

Figure 4. Bulgarian *tapan* drummer

Certain instruments that are less widespread, including the Swiss *alphorn*, the double-reeds of the Mediterranean countries, and the Irish tin whistle, provide a means of distinguishing the music of a country or region.

The British Isles

Folk music in the British Isles of England, Scotland, Wales, and Ireland is somewhat related to the art music of western Europe, even though the British Isles are geographically separate from the continent. Folk songs, ballads, and dance tunes, like so many madrigals and art songs, are commonly organized into four-phrase melodies or four-line stanzas in duple or triple meters. Folk music of the British Isles has retained its modal structure to a greater extent than has folk music on the continent. The vocal melodies range from strictly syllabic English ballads to the Irish-Gaelic lyrical and melismatic songs of love and war. In fact, Irish music is essentially melodic, relying on ornamentation rather than harmony for its effects. Traditional instruments of the British Isles include fiddles, bagpipes, flutes, and harps. The following elements characterize music and songs in the British Isles:

Melody: Based in C, A, D, and G modes (Ionian, Aeolian, Dorian, and Mixolydian); syllabic vocal music in Britain, more decorative and ornamental music in Ireland

Rhythm: Duple and triple meter; jigs in 6/8, 9/8 ("slip jig"), and 12/8; reels and slow hornpipes in duple meter

Texture: Homophonic song (melody and chords) in Britain; heterophonic music in

Ireland, in which several pitched instruments may play simultaneous variations on the melody

Form: Many two-part binary folk songs (AB)

Genres: Jigs, reels, ballads, and love songs

Timbre: Fiddle, flute, tin whistle, Scottish highland bagpipe, smaller *uilleann* "elbow" bagpipe of Ireland, Irish *bodhran* (flat drum), Celtic harp, and concertina

Scandinavia

Denmark, Sweden, Norway, and Finland are referred to jointly as Scandinavia. Denmark, Sweden, and Norway share common linguistic elements, and Sweden, Norway, and Finland sit side by side, extending from the Arctic Circle into the Baltic Sea. Scandinavian folk music has been influenced by the cultivated traditions of Germany, and the villages maintain traits of an ancient musical tradition. The parallel fifths, or organum, of medieval church practice appear in the folk music of nearby Iceland. Only Albania shows similar early forms, probably because both areas were isolated from Europe's cultural mainstream for centuries. Modal folk tunes and major-minor melodies are prevalent. Stringed instruments, including the standard fiddle and the Norwegian *hardanger* fiddle, the Swedish *nyckelharpa*, the Finnish psaltery called *kantele*, and Scandinavian dulcimers, are frequently played to accompany songs and dances. Typical Scandinavian songs display the following elements:

Melody: Based in major, or mixing major and minor modes; arpeggios and triad-like figures

Rhythm: Duple and triple meter (including dances such as the *vals, hambo,* and *polska*); meter obscured by overlapping measures in much instrumental music

Texture: Homophonic (chordal) or polyphonic (independent and interwoven melodic lines)

Form: AB (binary) and ABA (ternary) forms

Genres: Dance music and love songs

Timbre: Fiddle (usually played in pairs or larger ensembles), *hardanger* fiddle (Norway), *kantele* psaltery (Finland), dulcimer, *nyckelharpa*, and flute

Germanic Western Europe

The rich folk music traditions in the Germanic countries of western Europe faded rapidly by the nineteenth century, when other forms, such as church and school songs, easy art and community songs, and popular hits and ballroom dances, grew in popularity. Music making had once been nurtured, but the industrialization of this region created a void of social functions including seasonal agrarian customs and gatherings for spinning, cornhusking, and other communal activities. Of the remaining folk songs of Germany, Austria, Switzerland, and the Netherlands, the most common consist of arpeggiated melodies set in major keys and in duple or triple time.

Strophic forms, a simple syllabic style, and elementary harmonic sequences characterize the music. In the alpine regions, there is a distinctive song style called *jodler*, whose melodies contain wide-ranging leaps and are cast in a major key. Germanic peoples who still use folkloric styles live in the mountainous regions of the area and share instruments like the *alphorn*, the accordion, the wooden hammered dulcimer, and the zither. Folk music of the Germanic countries generally follows these guidelines:

Melody: Songs mostly in major keys; triads and sixths used frequently in melodies

Rhythm: Duple and triple meter, with an emphasis on triple time in southern Germany (Bavaria), Switzerland, and Austria

Texture: Homophonic melody with chordal accompaniment; polyphonic song tradition

Form: Variety, with emphasis on AB (binary) and ABA (ternary)

Genres: Ballad, love song, *jodler*

Timbre: Alphorn (Switzerland), accordion, wooden hammered dulcimer, zither, occasional brass band, or rommel pot (Dutch friction drum)

Romantic-Atlantic Europe

France, Portugal, and Belgium are "Romantic-Atlantic" countries because they are coastal countries on the Atlantic and because their people speak languages of the Romance family. Of course, there are other countries that border the Atlantic Ocean, and there are other Romance-language nations; these three countries, however, share both geographic and linguistic elements. Folk songs in these countries are largely monodic and sung as solos. Chants and rounds are associated with the carnival days preceding Lent, "begging songs" with Christmas, and egg-rolling songs with Eastertide. There are songs whose rhythms and incantations arise directly from work such as wood-carving, shepherding, and spinning. Typical instrumental sonorities in this region include the drone of bagpipes, the grinding timbres of the hurdy-gurdies, and the noisy strains of village wind bands. Belgium also shares in the Germanic tradition, just as Portuguese music frequently sounds Spanish in flavor.

Melody: Mostly major melodies, both diatonic and pentatonic; often conjunct (stepwise)

Rhythm: Duple meter predominant; 6/8 in Brittany (France) and northern Portugal

Texture: Homophonic (melody and chordal accompaniment)

Form: AB (binary) and ABA (ternary) forms

Genres: Seasonal and love songs

Timbre: Bagpipe, hurdy-gurdy, pipe and drum, and concertina

Mediterranean Europe

North Africans and Middle Easterners have contributed to the music and culture of the Mediterranean countries of Europe—Spain, Italy, and Greece. Although these countries each make unique contributions to the world's music, there are elements that are similar among them. The florid melodies are unmistakably Mediterranean, as is the somewhat nasalized vocal timbre of the singers. Much of the music is metered, but there is also considerable use of the free and flexible rhythms associated with declamatory speech. When musicians play in ensemble, they frequently create simultaneous variations of the melody, particularly in Greece and in the southern portions of Spain and Italy. The world-famous genre of Spanish flamenco dance music exemplifies the passionate music of the Mediterranean. Among the instruments common in these countries are guitars or other types of plucked lutes (Greek *oud* and *bouzouki*), double-reeds, and percussion instruments such as castanets, spoons, tambourines, and rattles. Typical Mediterranean music makes use of these elements:

Melody: Frequent use of minor melodies, largely melismatic and decorative; augmented seconds

Rhythm: Occasionally free of meter; some use of irregular, yet isometric patterns including sevens and fives (5/8, 7/8, 11/8)

Texture: Heterophonic; polyphonic and chordal in northern Italy and Spain

Form: Through-composed, AB (binary) form

Genres: Love songs and dance music (in Spain, flamenco; in Italy, tarantella; in Greece, *tsamiko)*

Timbre: Lutes (guitar, Greek *oud, bouzouki*), double-reeds, bagpipes, percussion (especially idiophones)

Eastern Europe

Eastern Europe encompasses a large geographic area and numerous countries. From north to south, they are Poland, the Czech Republic and Slovakia, Hungary, Romania, Bulgaria, Albania, and the smaller nations east of the Adriatic once known collectively as Yugoslavia (Bosnia-Hercegovina, Croatia, Macedonia, Montenegro, Serbia, and Slovenia); Russia and the Ukraine are farther east and part of the Asian continental land mass. Eastern Europe is much less influenced by art music than is the rest of Europe, and traditional music is still quite prevalent. Bulgaria, Albania, Romania, and the six nations of the former Republic of Yugoslavia, known collectively as the Balkans, share certain style traits with the Mediterranean countries: melismatic singing, heterophonic texture, and irregular or free meter. The pentatonic melodies used by Hungarians are evidence of an ancient layer of musical culture in which pitches are transposed up or down a fifth. Parts of Poland and the Czech Republic show Germanic influences in the music's major tonalities, duple and triple meters, and use of anacruses. The farther east one moves, the more one will hear folk songs in older church modes, asymmetrical meters, and performances in the great polyphonic tradition. The following are elements common to eastern European styles:

Melody: Major, minor and modal; syllabic in northern and melismatic in southern areas; gypsy scale (augmented seconds of the Balkans)

Rhythm: Duple and triple in northern areas, asymmetrical and nonmetric music in the Balkans, little use of anacrusis

Texture: Heterophony or melody and drone in the Balkans, rich polyphony in the north

Form: Through-composed common in the Balkans; also AB (binary) and ABA (ternary) throughout the region

Genres: Epics, wedding song cycles, love songs, dance music (Hungarian csardas, Polish polka, Bulgarian *rachenitsa*, and Romanian hora)

Timbre: Lutes (plucked *tamburs* and *tamburitza* ensembles of Croatia and Serbia), *gaida* bagpipes (Bulgaria and Macedonia), accordions, *cimbaloms* (hammered dulcimers of Hungary), flutes, fiddles, and hand drums

L E S S O N   1

■ Objectives

Students will:
1. Sing a number of modes common to Irish songs.
2. Sing the song "Leaving Erin" first without and then with the characteristic melismas in the melody.
3. Accompany the song on guitar.
4. Identify the historical significance of the song's text.
5. Locate the British Isles and Ireland on a map.
6. Listen to examples of Irish jigs and tap the underlying pulse of the music.
7. Improvise jig rhythms, both vocally and on drums.
8. Identify traditional Irish instruments.

■ Materials

1. Guitar
2. Hand drum
3. Recording: *The Chieftains 8* (Columbia 35726)
4. Map of Europe

■ Procedures

1. Sing each of the four common modes of Irish music: Ionian (the diatonic mode on C), Aeolian (on A), Dorian (on D), and Mixolydian (on G). Have the students imitate you—rote learning is the most efficient means of teaching these modes. Repeat the modes a number of times, changing the rhythm of the scale from quarter notes, to eighth notes, to eighth-note triplets, to combined rhythm patterns in order to challenge the students while reinforcing the sound of the modes.
2. Sing the Irish American song "Leaving Erin" (see figure 5). Where there are triplets notated in the music, sing the circled pitch only (as a quarter note). Learn

Figure 5. "Leaving Erin"

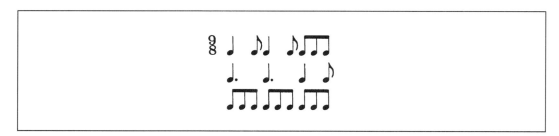

Figure 6. Jig-like patterns

the additional verses:

> Oh son, I loved my native land with energy and pride,
> Until a blight came o'er my crops—my sheep, my cattle died;
> My rent and taxes were too high, I could not them redeem,
> And that's the cruel reason why I left old Skibbereen.
>
> And you were only two years old and feeble was your frame,
> I could not leave you with my friends, you bore your father's name,
> I wrapped you in my woolen coat, and in the night unseen,
> I heaved a sigh, and bade goodbye to dear old Skibbereen.
>
> Oh father dear, the day may come, when in answer to the call,
> Each Irishman, with feeling stern, will rally one and all;
> I'll be the man to lead the van beneath the flag so green,
> When loud and high we'll raise the cry: "Remember Skibbereen."

3. Sing the song with the triplet figures added. Note the change from the rather syllabic setting of much of the melody to melismatic sections in which several pitches are sounded on one syllable. This is the typical Irish lyrical song style. The recording of "The Session," from *The Chieftains* 8 (Columbia 35726), contains more florid melismas in an instrumental setting.

4. Discuss the meaning of the text. The song is popular in Ireland and in Irish American communities. The harshness of the potato famine in Ireland and the dissatisfactions of the Irish with British rule brought about the migration of many Irish men and women to the United States and Canada in the mid-nineteenth century.

5. Locate Ireland on the map of Europe and note its relationship to Britain. Point out the division of Ireland and Northern Ireland, which today is still ruled by the British.

6. Listen to "The Session" for the metric structure and for the use of traditional Celtic instruments. Define a session as an informal meeting of musicians to play traditional Celtic tunes, keeping the music alive by improvising on familiar melodies. Use the following outline as a listening guide:

1. "Elizabeth Kelly's Delight," **A**
   9/8 jig
   flute

2. "Fraher's Jig," **B**
   12/8 jig
   bagpipe, fiddle,
   bodhran (large hand drum)

3. "Elizabeth Kelly's Delight," **A**
   9/8 jig
   bagpipe, flute

4. "Dinny's Delight," **C**
   12/8 jig
   fiddle, flute, bagpipe

5. "Fraher's Jig," **B**
   12/8 jig
   fiddle, flute, bagpipe

6. "Dinny's Delight," **C**
   12/8 jig
   bagpipe, flute

7. "Elizabeth Kelly's Delight," **A**
   9/8 jig
   fiddle, flute, bagpipe

7. Listen again, leading students in keeping the pulse of the music. Call attention to the heterophonic texture, in which the fiddle, flute, and bagpipe play slight variations of the same melody simultaneously.

8. Use a hand drum to keep a basic pulse. Lead students in performing subdivisions of the beat vocally on a neutral syllable such as "dee," "nah," or a combination of vocables. Ask students to imitate the jig-like patterns in figure 6 immediately after you play them.

9. Encourage the vocal improvisation of jig rhythms. For example, allow each student to contribute a spontaneously invented rhythmic pattern of one or two measures in length, followed by the group's imitation of it. As a challenge, suggest a melodic improvisation in 9/8 and 12/8.

10. Listen again to "The Session" for the jig rhythms, and ask students to distinguish between 9/8 and 12/8 by patting the leg on the first pulse and clapping on the remaining two 9/8 or three 12/8 pulses.

L E S S O N   2

■ **Objectives**

Students will:
1. Listen to the waltz tune "Vals from Orso" played by two fiddles.
2. Identify the arpeggiated melody as typical of Scandinavian folk music.
3. Clap the waltz pulse.
4. Dance a modified waltz step.
5. Play "Swedish Tune" on classroom instruments.
6. Locate Sweden and Scandinavia on a map of Europe.

■ **Materials**

1. Recording: *Folk Fiddling from Sweden* (Nonesuch H-72033)
2. Recorders
3. Autoharp
4. Map of Europe

■ **Procedures**

1. Define waltz as a dance in triple meter that developed in the ballrooms and community halls of early nineteenth-century Europe, especially in Germany and the Scandinavian countries. The Swedes call it *vals*.

2. Have students listen to "Vals from Orso" as played by a pair of fiddles. Keep the triple meter pulse through pat-clap-clap movements. Since the dance moves so quickly, try also a pat-clap-hold gesture. Note the melodic leaps in the arpeggios, the complementary and interweaving melodies of the two fiddles, and the three themes (the third of which characteristically shifts between major and minor keys).

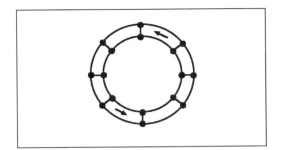

Figure 7. Formation of couples

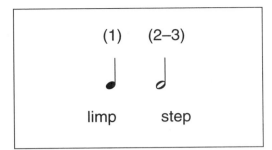

Figure 8. Limp step

3. Learn a modified waltz step like the following: Form an inner circle and an outer circle with students in couples (not necessarily boy-girl) (see figure 7). Warm up by practicing a "limp step," moving right-left, left-right, around a circle in order to feel the rhythmic pattern (as shown in figure 8).

Theme 1
   Section A: Couples face each other, feet together, weight on left foot, step in place (as shown in figure 9).
   Section B: Couple holds hands, as shown in figure 10. Repeat sections A and B four times, for a total of thirty-two measures: AB, AB, AB, AB.

Theme 2
   Shoulder hold: Dancers extend their arms and hold their partners' shoulders. They turn together in small circles with right-left, left-right steps. Repeat this step eight times for sixteen measures (as shown in figure 11).

Theme 3
   Couples promenade forward in skater's position with right-left, left-right steps; repeat eight times for sixteen measures (as shown in figure 12).

Theme 4
   Couples separate, forming inner and outer circles. The inner circle moves forward and then back again; the outer circle moves backward, away from the circle, and back in. Repeat four times for sixteen measures (as shown in figure 13). The form should go this way: Theme I, II, III, IV; I, II, III, IV; I.

4. Lead the students in playing "Swedish Tune" on recorders (see figure 14). Add an accompaniment, or ask a student to add an accompaniment on the Autoharp. Observe the arpeggiated melody and the fundamental chord structure.
5. Choose one or several students to perform the waltz steps while others play the "Swedish Tune."
6. Locate Sweden on a map of Europe. Note the countries that surround Sweden and name the Scandinavian countries. Locate Germany (to the south), where the language and culture, including the music components of melody and rhythm, bear a resemblance to expressions of Swedish culture. The form should go this way: Theme I, II, III, IV; I, II, III, IV; I.

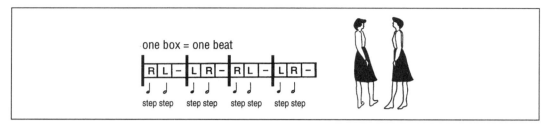

Figure 9. Section A

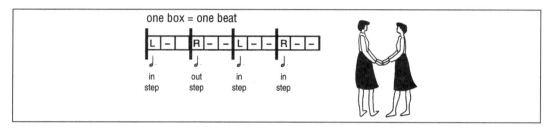

Figure 10. Section B

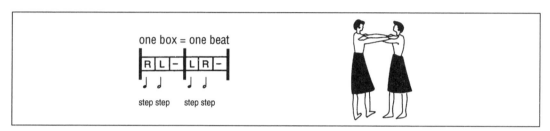

Figure 11. Shoulder hold

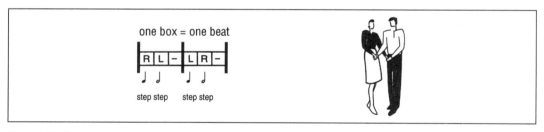

Figure 12. Promenade

Figure 13. Inner and outer circle

Figure 14. "Swedish Tune"

Figure 15. "The Cuckoo's Song"

L E S S O N   3

■ **Objectives**

Students will:
1. Listen to songs that feature the yodel.
2. Identify instruments of Austria and the alpine countries.
3. Sing an Austrian folk song.
4. Accompany the folk song with guitar or Autoharp.
5. Locate Austria, Bavarian Germany, and Switzerland on a map of Europe.

■ **Materials**

1. Recording: *Jodler und Schuhplattler* (Fiesta FLPS 1905)
2. Guitar
3. Autoharp
4. Map of Europe

■ **Procedures**

1. Play a recording from *jodlerer* (yodel songs) and *schuhplattler* (folk dances that feature the boot slapping of men). Call attention to the preponderance of triple meter and to the arpeggiated melodies in major keys. Many yodel songs are organized into a verse-refrain form, the refrain of which is usually the yodeling of syllables rather than words.
2. Sing "The Cuckoo's Song" in unison, adding the harmony if appropriate for the age level (see figure 15). The language is an alpine Austrian dialect of German.

   Pronunciation:
   > Vehn dehr goo-goo-shrite, ahft ees lahng-ees-tsite.
   > Veerd dehr schnee fehr-gehn, veern dee vees-lahn green.

   Translation:
   > When the cuckoo calls, early springtime falls.
   > Oh di lay le oh. Hoh di lay lee lay lee oh
   > All the snow will go, meadows green will grow.
   > Oh di lay le oh. Hoh di loh
   > Oh di lay le oh. Hoh di lay lee lay lee oh
   > Oh di lay le oh. Hoh di loh

3. While singing, add a pat-clap-snap gesture to keep the triple meter feeling.
4. Accompany the song on guitar or Autoharp.
5. On a map of Europe, locate the Germanic countries of Austria, Switzerland, and the southern part of Germany known as Bavaria. Discuss the possible reasons for the development of the yodel. Could it be that the Alps motivated people to sing from one mountain to the next for the pure enjoyment of the echo (in which case words were not necessary and the pitched cries of the arpeggiated melody collided into chords as they were bounced back to the singer)?

L E S S O N 4

■ **Objectives**

Students will:
1. Dance the *branle*, a French folk dance.
2. Recognize the division of dance music into musical themes and phrases.
3. Identify the sound of the concertina.
4. Locate France on a map of Europe.

■ **Materials**

1. Recording: *Dances of the World's Peoples, European Folk Dances, Volume 2* (Folkways FD 6502)
2. Map of Europe

■ **Procedures**

1. Play the recording of the *branle*, an old circle dance. The concertina (a small accordion) plays the melody, and a second, larger accordion plays the accompaniment. Keep the steady beat by patting or clapping softly with two fingers.
2. Teach students to dance the *branle*. The formation is a circle, with hands joined (as shown in figure 16). In the introduction, students bend their knees and bounce in place for sixteen beats. Follow these patterns for the dance, and repeat until the music's end:

   Part 1   Move in the circle—eight running steps to the right and then eight running steps to the left—for sixteen beats.

   Part 2   Standing in place, step and kick for sixteen beats, as shown in figure 17.

   Part 3   Step and kick, moving into the circle for eight beats and out of the circle for eight beats, as shown in figure 18.

   Part 4   Each dancer stands in place and alternately points the left foot over the right foot and the right foot over the left foot, as shown in figure 19.

   Repeat these steps as the dance music continues.

3. Locate France on the map of Europe. Cousins of the *branle* are found throughout France and in many parts of Europe. Along the Pyrenees in the south, the Basques dance a similar circle dance called the *sardana*, and throughout most of Europe, people enjoy the communal spirit of dancing in a circle.

Figure 16. Branle formation

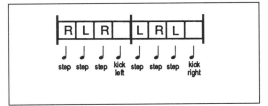

Figure 17. Procedure for Part 2

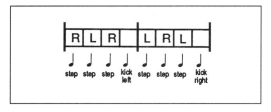

Figure 18. Procedure for Part 3   *Figure 19.* Procedure for Part 4

L E S S O N   5

■ **Objectives**

Students will:
1. Listen to examples of Spanish dance songs.
2. Recognize the importance and extent of dance music in Spain, including the fandango, seguidilla, and flamenco.
3. Play the Andalusian cadence on the guitar.
4. Play rhythmic ostinatos on the castanets.
5. Sing "Tío Pep."
6. Locate Spain on a map of Europe.

■ **Materials**

1. Guitar
2. Castanets
3. Recordings:
   "Seguidillas Guitano," from *Authentic Folk Music and Dances of the World* (Murray Hill S-4195)
   "Fandango de Comares," from *Spanish Folk Music* (Columbia World Library of Folk and Primitive Music: Spain, 91A-02001)
4. Map of Europe

■ **Procedures**

1. Listen to "Fandango de Comares," which features guitar, *bandurría* (large mandolin), castanets, and voice. Then listen to "Seguidillas Guitano" for the interplay of guitar and voice in the seguidilla, a flamenco-style dance song. Note the importance of guitar for both songs. Call attention to the melismatic melody of the seguidilla and to the shouts of joy and excitement.
2. Play the A minor, G major, F major, and E major chords in succession. This chord combination is known as the Andalusian cadence and is found in the music of southern Spain. Sing the root note as the cadence is played: A, G, F, and E. Listen again to "Seguidillas Guitano" for the cadence (see figure 20).
3. Listen for the castanets again on "Fandango de Comares." Ask several students to play the Andalusian cadence on guitars, while others first clap and later play castanets for the Spanish rhythms shown in figure 21.

Progression:

Guitar:

A m   G   F   E

Figure 20. Andalusian cadence

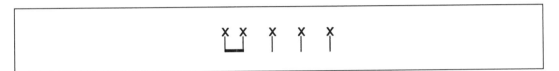

Figure 21. Spanish rhythms

4. Sing "Tío Pep," a folk song from central Spain (where the Andalusian sound is absent) (see figure 22). Note the use of melisma in the refrain (on the vocable "ah"). If guitar accompaniment is added, transpose to the key of D major. The text pronunciation is as follows:

> Lo tee-oh Pehp sehn vah Moo-roh, Tee-oh Pehp
> Day Moo-roh kaym pore-tah-rah, Tee-oh Pehp, Tee-oh Pehp.
> Oo-na tahr-tah-nah ee oon boo-roh Tee-oh Pehp
> Payr-nahr-sayn ah pahs-say-chahr Tee-oh Pehp, Tee-oh Pehp.

Translation:
> Old Uncle Joe's going to Muro, Uncle Joe.
> What will he bring back from town? Uncle Joe, Uncle Joe.
> A two-wheeled cart and a burro, Uncle Joe.
> So he can ride up and down, Uncle Joe, Uncle Joe.

5. Locate Spain on the map of Europe. Discuss the historical significance of Spain's proximity to North Africa, which is across the narrow Strait of Gibraltar. A report on the Moorish occupation of Spain over a five-hundred-year period can help students place the country and its culture in perspective. The North African–Middle Eastern influence on the music is found in the melismatic singing, the somewhat free and flexible rhythm, and the evolution of the guitar from its predecessor, the Egyptian ʿūd.

Figure 22. Tío Pepe

Figure 23. "Trugnal mi Yane Sandanski, lele"

LESSON 6

■ **Objectives**

Students will:

1. Listen to "Trugnal mi Yane Sandanski, lele," a Bulgarian work song in 7/8 meter.
2. Sing a Bulgarian song in 7/8 with drone.
3. Play a Bulgarian song on recorders.
4. Perform a Bulgarian dance.
5. Identify the sound of the *gaida* bagpipes.
6. Locate Bulgaria and Macedonia on a map of Europe.

■ **Materials**

1. Recording: "Trugnal mi Yane Sandanski, lele," from *In the Shadow of the Mountain* (Nonesuch H-72038)
2. Recorders
3. Map of Europe

■ **Procedures**

1. Listen to "Trugnal mi Yane Sandanski, lele" (see figure 23) and tap the pulse of the 7/8 meter. Listen for the sound of the *gaida* bagpipes, the flute, and the various fiddles and lutes.
2. The teacher should give the translation for the song: "Yane Sandanski sets off walking about the Pirin Mountains. He has a carbine over his shoulder; he has a double cartridge-belt. Yonder comes a young shepherd. Yane asks him: 'Didn't you see my people from my fighting band?' The young shepherd replies: 'Oh, Yane, up in the mountain, at the high peak of the Pirin Mountains you will find them.'" Explain that Yane was fighting the Turks, who occupied Bulgaria and most of the Balkans for about five hundred years.
3. Sing "Trugnal mi Yane Sandanski, lele," first in unison and later with the addition of the drone accompaniment. Note the only change that occurs: in measure seven, there is a shift from D to C and back to D again at measure eight. The text pronunciation is as follows:

   > Troog-nahl mee Yah-neh Sahn-dahn-skee lay-lay
   > Poh-tah-yah Pee-reen plah-nee-nah
   > Zah-meht-nahl koo-sah kah-rah-bee-nah lay-lay
   > Pray-pah-sahl dvoy-ehn pah-trohn-dahsh

4. Play the Bulgarian dance song "Trgnala mi Rumjana" on recorders (see figure 24). The teacher should point out that the drone of the previous song and the harmony in thirds found in this song are characteristic of different regions of Bulgaria. Add to the recorders a chordal accompaniment on guitar or piano and a rhythmic pattern on a hand drum, as illustrated in figure 25.
5. Learn the following dance to accompany either 7/8 song: Have the students form a line with arms in a "W" (holding hands with arms crooked at elbow). Each dancer then steps to the right with the right foot and places the left foot behind the right.

Trgnala mi Rumjana

Figure 24. "Trgnala mi Rumjana"

Figure 25. Rhythmic pattern on hand drum

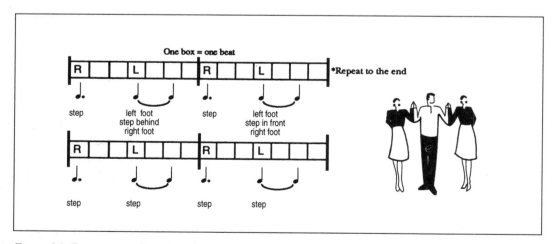

Figure 26. Dance steps for "Trgnala mi Rumjana"

Students step right again and then place the left foot in front of the right. For the third measure, they step right and then left, bringing the feet together; and in the fourth measure of the dance pattern, step left and then right, bringing the feet together again. This pattern is repeated to the end of the music (see figure 26 for a diagram of the dance steps).

6. Locate Bulgaria on the map of Europe. Discuss the isolation of the Balkan countries from the European mainstream and their close proximity to Turkey and Asia Minor.

L E S S O N   7

■ **Objectives**

Students will:
1. Sing a Hungarian folk song.
2. Identify aspects of melody and rhythm that are typical of Hungarian folk music.
3. Dance the csardas national dance.
4. Listen to Kodály's *Hungarian Rondo*.
5. Locate Hungary on a map of Europe.

■ **Materials**

1. Recording: Zoltán Kodály, *Hungarian Rondo* (Columbia MS 7034)
2. Map of Europe

■ **Procedures**

1. Sing the song "The Forest" (see figure 27). Note the way in which the melody seems to focus on C, the fifth of the key, especially at the beginnings and endings of phrases one, two, and four. Note also the dotted rhythms, especially in measures three, seven, and fifteen. These are characteristic sounds of Hungarian folk music.

2. Dance the national folk dance of Hungary, the csardas. Students form a circle, either holding hands or with arms resting on neighbors' shoulders, and step, slide, and stomp, alternating motion to the right with motion to the left (see figure 28).

3. Through the efforts of Zoltán Kodály and Béla Bartók, Hungarian peasant music was collected and became the inspiration for many of their compositions. Kodály's *Hungarian Rondo* features "The Forest" as the A theme and four other folk songs in the contrasting sections. You can guide students in their listening by calling their attention to these items:

> A *theme*—"The Forest" theme played in a straightforward manner by strings, especially violins
> B *theme*—second folk song, played in conversation by clarinet and violins; stretched rubato tempo
> A *theme*—"The Forest" theme, third and fourth phrases only, played by violins
> C *theme*—third folk song, csardas-style accompaniment with cellos representing the "oom-pah-pah" of the *cimbalom*; virtuosic, gypsy-sounding violin melody

Figure 27. "The Forest"

  A *theme*—"The Forest" for violin solo, partly minor harmony, fragments of melody, and
    slowing rubato tempo
  D *theme*—fourth folk song, strings sounding a syncopated accompaniment on the offbeats
  E *theme*—fifth folk song starting with bassoon and double bass; increased tempo with
    clarinet and then high strings on melody; drone-like reference to tonic
  A *theme*—"The Forest" theme, beginning with pulsing double bass drone; modulation of
    the theme and stretching of theme with slow tempo
  E *theme*—return to the fifth folk song; a festive dance ending

4. Locate Hungary on a map of Europe. Discuss the early origins of the people deep within the Russian interior and their migration westward to Hungary. Consider other
  events of a historical nature such as the Austro-Hungarian Empire and the Hungarian
  Revolution of 1956.

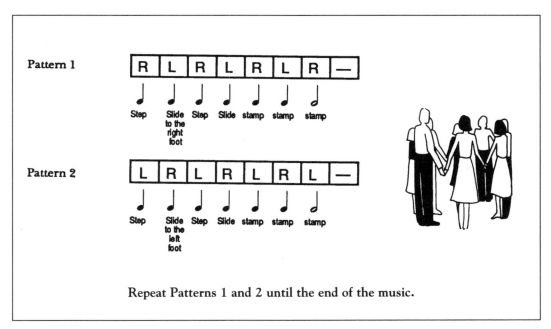

Figure 28. Csardas diagram

BIBLIOGRAPHY

Bartók, Béla, and Albert Lord. *Serbo-Croatian Folk Songs.* New York: Columbia University Press, 1951. A technical study of South Slavic traditional songs collected by Slavist Millman Parry. Transcriptions and texts of 205 women's songs with analysis.

Bronson, Bertrand Harris. *The Traditional Tunes of the Child Ballads.* Vols. 1–4. Princeton, NJ: Princeton University Press, 1959. The musical counterpart to the Francis James Child collection of English and Scottish ballads from the thirteenth to the nineteenth centuries. Tunes and texts are arranged by period for the study of ballads in England, Scotland, Ireland, and America.

Karpeles, Maud. *Folk Songs of Europe.* London: Novello, 1956. A fine collection of texts and notations for European folk songs, transcribed by the author.

Kodály, Zoltán. *Folk Music of Hungary.* London: Barrie and Jenkins, 1971. Collected by Kodály, these songs represent the oral traditions of the Hungarian people. Several black-and-white photographs and illustrations of instruments are provided.

Lawson, Joan. *European Folk Dance.* London: Pitman Publishing, 1972. A description of folk dances from all of Europe, with instructions on specific movements. Melodies of dance songs are provided. The text also includes chapters on the development of the dances and costumes.

Lord, Albert. *The Singer of Tales.* Cambridge, MA: Harvard University Press, 1960. The author summarizes years of fieldwork among the Yugoslav epic singers and discusses the nature of the oral tradition.

Nettl, Bruno. *Folk and Traditional Music of the Western Continents,* 3d ed. Englewood Cliffs, NJ: Prentice-Hall, 1990. This publication, which is an update of the 1973 version, is one of the most concise descriptions of European traditional music available. The author presents his thoughts on the character of European folk music and regional musics.

O'Canainn, Tomas. *Traditional Music in Ireland*. London: Routledge and Kegan Paul, 1978. The structure of traditional vocal and instrumental music is described, along with organological analysis of the *uilleann* pipes and fiddle. Excellent analysis of Sean-nos singing.

Rice, Timothy. *May It Fill Your Soul*. Chicago: University of Chicago Press, 1994. This is a description of music and music making in Bulgaria, including social and cognitive processes of music learning. Black-and-white photos, musical transcriptions, and a compact disc enhance descriptions.

DISCOGRAPHY

Authentic Folk Music and Dances of the World. Murray Hill S-4195 ("Seguidillas Guitano").

Bavarian Yodeling Songs and Polkas. Olympic 6115C. This recording includes songs and instrumental music with emphasis on the *jodler*, clog dancing, and polkas.

The Chieftains 8. Columbia 35726. A collection of Irish instrumental music, featuring the *uillean* bagpipe, tin whistle, fiddle, harp, concertina, and the *bodhran* drum. The recording includes descriptive liner notes.

Dances of the World's Peoples, European Folk Dances. Vol. 2. Folkways FD 6502. Dance music for the Italian tarantella, French *branle*, Greek *horo*, Irish reel, and assorted Bulgarian dances. A pamphlet for learning the dance steps is included.

Folk Fiddling from Sweden. Nonesuch H-72033. Fiddle tunes from rural Sweden are performed on two fiddles, including dance music for *vals*, *polska*, and *langdans*.

Folk Music from Norway. Heilo NCD7078. Fiddle tunes and dance music for string and accordion ensembles.

Greece Is...Popular and Folk Dances. EMI 14C 062-70007. Contact Rashid Sales Company, 191 Atlantic Avenue, Brooklyn, NY 11201. Twelve Greek dances performed on *bouzouki*, *santouri*, and *baglamas* are presented, along with an instructional pamphlet.

Hungarian Instrumental Music. Hungariton LPX 18045–47. The most complete collection of Hungarian instrumental music, this four-record set contains examples of every Hungarian instrument, from the *leaf* to the *cimbalom*. A descriptive pamphlet accompanies the recordings.

In Dublin's Fair City. Olympic 6169. The Guinness Choir sings favorite Irish tunes.

In the Shadow of the Mountain, Bulgarian Folk Music. Nonesuch H-72038. Songs and instrumental music of southwestern Bulgaria (Pirin-Macedonian) are presented. The recording includes the diaphonic song style and the *zurna*, *gaida*, and *gaydulka*.

Jodler und Schulplattler. Fiesta FLPS 1905. Yodeling songs and folk dances that feature the boot slapping of men.

Kodály, Zoltán. *Hungarian Rondo*. Columbia MS 7034.

Le Mystère des Voix Bulgares. Explorer CD 79165-2. Women's choral songs, including dance melodies in 7/8 and 10/8.

The Long Harvest, Ewan Maccoll and Peggy Seeger. Records 1 and 2. Argo ZDA 67. Write to 115 Fulham Road, London SW3. Traditional children's ballads are presented in English, Scottish, and North American variants, including "The Elfin Knight," "The Daemon Lover," and "Riddles Wisely Expounded." A pamphlet gives the text and origin of songs.

Music and Song of Italy. Tradition 1030 (Everest Records, 10920 Wilshire Boulevard, Los Angeles, CA 90024). This recording includes songs and instrumental music from various regions of Italy, with liner notes that describe the influences of Albania, the Moors, and the Germanic countries. The performance of an ancient polyphonic song of Sardinia is a jewel in itself.

Spain, World Library of Folk and Primitive Music. Columbia 91A-02001. This recording includes music from all regions of Spain, including Andalusia, the Pyrenees, Galicia, and the Mediterranean. The attached booklet provides a background for each recorded selection.

Spanish Folk Music. Columbia World Library of Folk and Primitive Music: Spain, 91A-02001 ("Fandango de Comares").

Swiss Yodeling Songs. Olympic 6171. Ten Swiss yodelers perform these traditional songs.

FILMOGRAPHY

Danzas regionales españolas, 15 minutes, color. 1966. Appropriate for junior high school. This film covers the cultural background of various regional dances of Spain, which are performed by professional and folk troupes.

Discovering Russian Folk Music, 22 minutes, color, 1975. This film presents choruses, plaintive songs, swirling dances, and magnificent dances; also traditional uses of music in Russian villages, cities, and churches.

European Culture Region, 23 minutes, color. 1966. Appropriate for junior high school. This film provides a survey of the influences of the Greeks, Romans, Christians, feudal city states, and merchant traders in the development of Europe. It also gives a geographical and economic overview of the continent. Note the stress placed on the relationship of economy to geography.

Folklore Dances of Yugoslavia, 47 minutes, color (ND). This film captures the music, dance, dress, and ways of life in the traditional cultures of the former Yugoslavia (Bosnia-Hercegovina, Croatia, Macedonia, Montenegro, Serbia, Slovenia).

Greece—the Land and the People, 11 minutes, color. 1977. For intermediate or junior high school. This film depicts the rich cultural background of Greece, which served as the trade center for southeast Europe, Africa, and Asia Minor. A Greek man and woman show the people, geography, industries, and agriculture in their homeland as well as the arts and sciences of its glorious past.

Irish Ways, 52 minutes, color, 1989, VHS. This film focuses on the daily life in Irish working class and business neighborhoods. The film's emphasis is on the political struggles of the Irish in their continued drive for the freedom of Ulster, but the film also provides a taste of music and other traditional cultural-artistic forms.

Singendes Deutschland, 16 minutes, black and white. 1952. For junior high school. Fifteen popular German songs are sung and illustrated with appropriate German scenes and dances.

Spanish Gypsies in Flamenco Songs and Dances, 10 minutes, color, 1948. Spanish gypsies hold a family festival in a Granada grotto, with traditional songs and dances.

Editor's Note. These films can be ordered from Audio-Visual Library Services, 3300 University Southeast, Minneapolis, MN 55414.

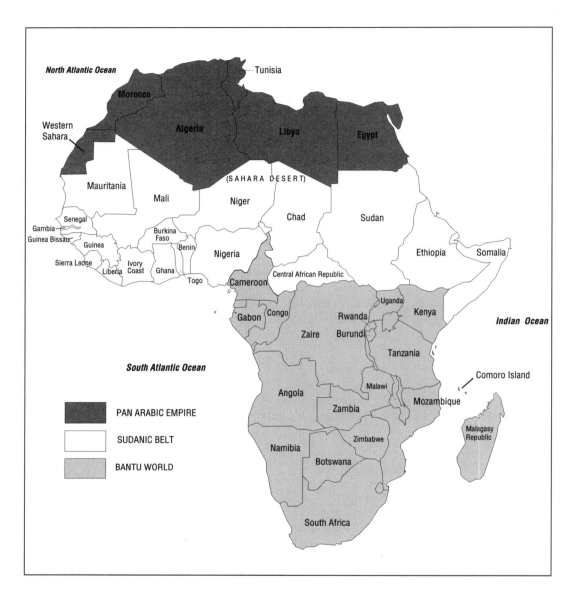

Figure 1. Geographic zones of Africa

African Continent

SUB-SAHARAN AFRICAN MUSIC

by Kazadi wa Mukuna and Elizabeth Oehrle

Africa is probably the least understood and the most misinterpreted area of the world today. Some misunderstandings result from assumptions made about African history and cultures by early scholars and colonial anthropologists. However, regional histories, such as those of the first and second Empires of the Congo in the fifteenth and sixteenth centuries,[1] the Empire of the Mandingo in Mali, the Zulu Empire under Shaka, the Luba Empire under Ilunga Kalala, the Empire of Sokoto, and the great wall of Zimbabwe, attest to powerful kingdoms that flourished well before the arrival of the white man on the continent.

From a historical perspective, in spite of several contacts Portugal made with the continent of Africa, it was only after the Berlin Conference in 1885 that the fate of the continent was decided.[2] The division of the continent into political regions gave rise to permanent contact with Europe and marked the beginning of the European domination of Africa. When countries were formed at the Berlin Conference, no consideration was given to the indigenous cultural clusters of the continent. Hence, it is not uncommon to encounter an ethnic group on both sides of a political boundary.

The continent of Africa can be approached in various ways. Geographically, there are three major areas: the Pan-Arabic Empire, the Sudanic Belt, and the Bantu World. The Pan-Arabic Empire was forged by the followers of Muhammad between the seventh and twelfth centuries. This territory covers the entire northern portion of the continent, extending to the south through the Sahara Desert. In addition to the shared Islamic religion, Arabic/Islamic/Middle Eastern musical styles have become characteristic of this geographical area. The Sudanic Belt begins with the *Sahel*[3] and extends laterally from the east to west coast, encompassing the countries of Mauritania, Mali, Niger, Chad, the Sudan, Ethiopia, Somalia, the Central African Empire, Nigeria, Burkina Faso, Togo, Benin, Ghana, the Ivory Coast, Guinea, Guinea Bissau, Liberia, Sierra Leone, Senegal, and Gambia. The Bantu World is the area that encompasses Cameroon, Gabon, the Congo, Zaire, Uganda, and Kenya to the north and the entire southern portion of the continent (see figure 1).

African languages are often organized into linguistic groups based on their syntactical similarities and semantic proximity. The Sudanese languages found in the Sudanic Belt are syntactically related to each other; their phrase structures follow similar rules. Those languages spoken within the Bantu World are identified by the presence of the suffix *ntu* in any word that refers to humans (*mu-ntu*, one person; *ba-ntu*, several people; *ki-ntu*, a small person, and so on). Unlike the Sudanese languages, the relationship between Bantu languages is at the semantic level. As a result, in this linguistic group, different ethnic groups can understand each other much more so than those in the Sudanese.

Racial groups

Racial distinctions in Africa are not based on the color of one's skin, but rather on the physical features of individuals. Among the most outstanding groups are the Pygmies, the Nilotics, the Bushmen, and the Huttentots.

The Pygmies were the first occupants of the Central African area. They lost this territory to the Bantu as the latter migrated southward from their homeland between Eastern Nigeria and Western Cameroon. The invasion of the Pygmies' territory by the superiorly armed Bantu resulted in the submission and assimilation of a large number of Pygmies and the subsequent mixing of the two races. This relationship gave birth to a midsize race known as the *Twa*, which is found today in a small cluster in Rwanda at the Rwanda-Zaire border. The Pygmies who were not subjugated by the Bantu continue to lead their nomadic lives scattered in such places as the Itury Forest in Zaire, the Central African Republic, and the Congo.

The Nilotics are the descendants of the ancient Egyptians who followed the Nile River at the demise of Egypt after the fourth dynasty (ca. 2400 B.C.).[4] They are found on the eastern coast of Africa in the areas surrounding the Nile, including Sudan, Ethiopia, Kenya, Tanzania, Rwanda, and Burundi. In Kenya, such groups as the Massay and the Luo belong to this racial group.

The Bushmen and Huttentots are two racial groups that live in the southern portion of the continent. Most are hunters and gatherers living a nomadic life in the southern deserts. Good examples of the Bushmen's life-style are captured on the film *Bitter Melon* (see Filmography). This film provides insight into the organization of the social structures of the groups and the processes of maintaining harmony within their communities.

The single, most important element that permeates all facets of life (social, religious, economic, political, and so on) is the African philosophy of existence. In contrast to much Western thought, which stresses individualism and the physical, African philosophy focuses on belonging, collectivism, and the conceptual. The individual is composed of both the physical and the spiritual. Africans believe that their identity is determined by those elements and individuals they share with the cosmos. Stated another way, Africans believe that individuals cease to exist conceptually when they are divorced from the cosmos—family, land, trees, animals, rivers, and so on—to which they belong and that belong to them. This concept can be summarized in the Luba saying: "I am because we are, and we are because I am," which is at the very core of all cultural expression. It has been carried out through language, the vehicle par excellence of this philosophy, and has had a major impact on all aspects of musical organization.

Characteristics of African music

African music began to intrigue foreign visitors by the fifteenth century. For five centuries, it has interested laymen and scholars alike, who discuss its many aspects, point out its uses, and underline the roles it fulfills in the daily lives of individuals and communities. Early historical documents contain accounts about African music. These accounts are often marked by the Eurocentrically tinted opinion of writers who discredit African music as noisy, monotonous, and lacking harmony. These writers do, however, provide valuable information about music events, dance, and musical instruments, many of which are no longer in use today. The descriptions of these early writers constitute, for the most part, the only source of empirical data used today by scholars in the historiography of African music.

In Africa, music brings the community together through entertainment by documenting oral tradition and expressing the world view of its creators. Music provides a channel of communication between the physical and spiritual worlds and serves as a didactic tool to pass on knowledge about the ethnic group from one generation to another. Musicians recite and sing poetry and praises and formulate airs on musical instruments to communicate over long distances.

Melody

African languages are predominantly tonal; that is, the meaning of each word is determined by the pattern of its tonal inflections. For example, although the linpala words "ekolo" and "ekolo" have the same spelling, they differ from each other when various tonal levels are applied to their syllables (E-ko-LO and E-KO-lo). Semantically, the first word means "basket," while the second one means "tribe." Any modification of these tonal sequences changes the meaning of the word or renders it meaningless. Therefore, to maintain the meaning of each word, the basic melodic pattern—the directions but not the sizes of the intervals—is determined by the linguistic tonal patterns of each word. However, the final melodic contour is determined by the artistic creativity of the individual composer to whose discretion the size of the intervals is left. In short, in the vocal music of Africa, the basic melodic pattern is determined by the linguistic tonal sequence of the lyrics, while the shape of the final melodic contour results from the combination of this factor with the artistic discretion of each individual composer.

A variety of tonal materials are present in African music. These are often conceived as a hierarchy of pitches arranged in different intervallic orders, commonly called modes.

The most common modes are pentatonic and are grouped into two major categories: hemi-pentatonic (with half-steps) and anhemi-pentatonic (without half-steps). In African music, the selection of musical instruments is often linguistically influenced. However, the tuning of instruments is culturally determined. The instrument maker's selection of the principal note from which the entire instrument is relatively pitched, the choice of the structure of the mode, and the preferred timbre of the instrument all influence the tuning process. There are two distinguishable tuning systems in Africa, based on the ability or inability of instruments to adapt to the vocal repertoire. For example, a xylophone that has been tuned in one modal structure cannot be modified to accompany songs that are not in the same modal system. Songs must be composed to fit the tuning system of the instrument and not vice versa. This is a "fixed" tuning system due to its inability to adapt to the song repertoire. On the other hand, a *kora* player from Mali wanting to expand his repertoire to include songs from the Senegal/Gambia tradition will have to learn how to retune his instrument before the performance.

One of the most predominant styles of singing in Africa is known as call and response (responsorial), in which the leader calls in the form of a question and the group responds with an answer. This singing style is reflected in the melodic structure that is often in two parts (question and answer). This is true even when a melody is performed as a solo or heterophonically. Although instrumental melodies are often linguistically derived, their performance follows a different set of aesthetic norms.

In some music traditions, such as the *hindehou* of the Pygmies and the *nshiba* (pan pipe) of the Luba, melodies are also performed in interlocking fashion. Thus, individuals sing or play their parts, which interlock with other parts to produce a total musical line.

Rhythm

The organization of African rhythm is governed by a different set of principles than the rhythm of Western music; most of the African rhythms are linguistically derived. In vocal music, the rhythm is dictated by the poetic rhythm. In most African languages, in a word with more than one syllable, the stress is often placed on the syllable preceding a semiconsonant such as "l," "m," "n," "s," "w," and "y." Musically, this is reflected in the following rhythmic organization: any syllable followed by a syllable beginning with a semiconsonant receives a longer note value than the syllable beginning with the semiconsonant. For example, with *kobenga* ("to call"), which is composed of three syllables (ko-be-nga), the poetic stress is placed on the second syllable, *be,* which is elongated as a result of the anticipated pronunciation of the third syllable, *nga,* beginning with the semiconsonant "n." The poetic stress suggests but does not dictate the final melodic rhythm, which is left to the artistic discretion of the composer.

The impact of the language is also felt in the instrumental rhythmic structure. Often, a phrase or a series of nonsense syllables is formulated in an instrumental rhythmic pattern, which serves as a memory and teaching aid.

The temporal aspect of instrumental music is divided into units of time that are organized patterns referred to as a time-line or standard pattern, such as the pattern in figure 2. In a composition, these patterns function as a measuring stick for musical phrases. While each pattern may appear simple individually, the difficulty in the understanding of the final rhythmic tapestry of a piece stems from the relationship created by its combination with other patterns. Each pattern contains holes that provide receptacles for other

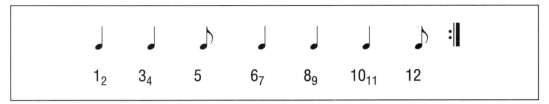

Figure 2. A time-line pattern

patterns, and so on. Although it may be perceived as a temporal part of the composition, the relationship between the patterns is also conceptualized as a melodic part. The super-imposition of any number of time-line patterns in an interlocking relationship constitutes what Meki Nzewi coined as an "ensemble thematic cycle," or a section of the composition in which all patterns are recycled, regardless of the number of times an individual pattern recurs before reaching a new starting point.[5] Its evolution is vital to the performance/composition process. This evolutionary process is based not on the repetition but on a recycling concept of each integral part. Thus, a time-line pattern is recycled but not repeated with each recurrence, thereby providing a same-but-different pattern to the total creative process of the performance/composition. During a performance, there is always an underlining density referent, felt but not always played, which provides the basic pulse of the composition or governs the internal relationship between time-line patterns in an ensemble thematic cycle.

Texture

Texture is perhaps the most misinterpreted element of African music. Taking into consideration the melodic construction just discussed, it is obvious that the linguistic association that dictates the direction of the intervals in the main melodic phrases also has the same impact on other vocal lines being sung at the same time. That is, voices singing the same words at different intervals result in parallel harmony, which is very common in the African vocal tradition.

Heterophonic texture is also common and is achieved when versions of the same melody are sung simultaneously. While parallel singing is found in most African singing, heterophonic singing is distinctive to particular ethnic groups. No two ethnic groups share a similar heterophonic style of singing. Each is unique and ethnically defined. For example, the style of heterophonic singing of the Tutsi in Rwanda is totally different from that of the Luba in Zaire.

A variety of musical instruments are found in Africa. In considering the types of musical instruments belonging to various cultural groups, it is important to consider two factors: the ecological condition of the geographic area in which the instrument is found, and the life-style of the group using the instrument. Ecologically speaking, the musical instruments a cultural group uses are often made from the raw materials that are available to them. Hunters and gatherers, for example, live in the rain forest where the materials necessary for making log drums are available, but since they live a nomadic life, they are most likely not going to include log drums in their music. This is also the case with the

Pygmies who live in the Itury Forest in Zaire, the Bambuti from the Central African Republic, and the Congo's Babenzele. In spite of the bountiful availability of large trees, their catalogs of musical instruments do not include log drums (membranophones or idiophones) because their nomadic life-style does not accommodate these unwieldy instruments.

On the other hand, settlers such as farmers and fishermen make use of their available materials. The musical instruments of these groups do contain instruments of varying sizes, some of which cannot be carried by the player during a performance. Examples include the slit drums found throughout the Bantu World and the *boma* found among the Ashante people in Ghana. This phenomenon accounts for the distribution of musical instruments in zones of cultural interaction, which are geographic areas that extend beyond political boundaries in which a cultural element and its variants are shared by its inhabitants. Musically, these areas are defined by a style of singing, a genre, a characteristic dance movement, or a musical instrument.

African instruments

The mbira (see figure 3) is one of the several names by which this idiophone (lamellophone) is known in Africa.[6] It is found across the entire Bantu World. Mbira usage extends into the Igbo land in Nigeria bordering with Cameroon and into the areas of the Central African Republic. Mbira players were known to make their own instruments according to personal specifications, varying the dimension, weight, style, ornamentation, and the materials for the keys. Today, this instrument is made by a craftsman who possesses

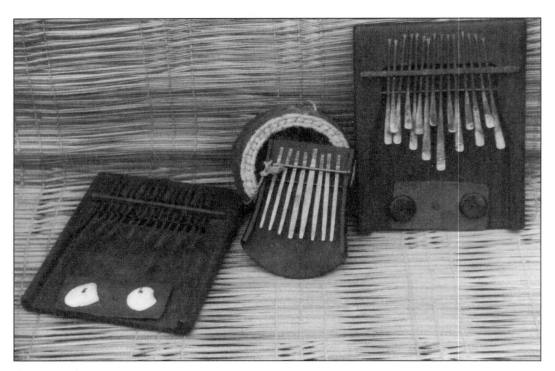

Figure 3. Mbira

Figure 4. Xylophone

Figure 5. Xylophone showing gourd resonators

the appropriate tools. The mbira is found in varying shapes and sizes, with or without sound boxes, and with a varying number of keys. Children use the inside of bamboo to fabricate the body of the mbira (which is shaped like a raft) and make the bark into keys. Among the adult population, the mbira is generally an instrument for individual entertainment and the accompaniment of songs during story telling. However, it is not unusual to encounter mbira ensembles, such as the *bisanji* among the Baluba in Zaire and the Shona in Zimbabwe. Among the latter, it is believed that the mbira was given to the founding fathers by the spirits. Therefore, a ceremony of ancestor invocation is not complete without the music of the mbira.

The xylophone, an idiophone with wooden keys, is used throughout the entire sub-Saharan Africa region, including the Bantu World and the Sudanic Belt (see figure 4). There are a variety of xylophones in Africa, and they differ in size, shape, the number of keys, and how they are tuned. Xylophones are also known by a variety of names, including *madimba, balafon,* and *amadinda.* On the xylophone, each key has a gourd attached underneath it that functions as its individual resonator (see figure 5). The lower the range of the pitch emitted by the key, the larger the gourd, and vice versa. Generally, each gourd is pierced, and the hole is covered with a membrane derived from the spider eggshell, which provides the sympathetic buzzing sound when the key is struck. However, among the Chopi of Mozambique (where the *timbila* xylophones are built differently), gourds are not used; rather, holes are fashioned in dried fruit resonators and are covered with a membrane derived from goat intestines. In spite of the many xylophones found throughout Africa, only the Chopi can boast an entire orchestra comprised of xylophones of varying sizes tuned to a single mother note. The ensemble, known as *Timbila,* performs the music, known by the same name, which accompanies an all-male dance also called the *timbila.* As with the mbira among the Shona in Zimbabwe, the Chopi believe that the xylophone was given to their founding fathers by the spirits. Hence, this instrument plays a vital role in the ancestral invocation ceremonies.

The *kora* is a stringed instrument with twenty-one strings that is often classified as a harp-lute (see figure 6). It is comprised of half a gourd, which serves as its resonator for the amplification of sound, and is covered with an animal skin. A long neck goes through the sound box. The twenty-one strings are arranged in two rows, with eleven strings on the left and ten on the right. There are twenty-one animal hide rings on the neck, one for each string, which also function as part of the tuning mechanism. Although its origin remains obscure, the *kora* is primarily the instrument of the *Mandingo* people of Mali, who used the instrument to entertain Kelefa Sane, a mid-nineteenth century Mandinka hero.[7] These *kora* players are known in Mandingo as *Jalolu* (singular: *Jali*) and referred to in French as *"griots."* The most renowned *jalolu* belong to the families of Suso, Konte, Diabate, and Kuyate. Senegal, Guinea-Bissau, Gambia, the northern Ivory Coast, Mali, and Niger constitute the zone of cultural interaction defined by the *kora.* Traditionally, the *kora* is best known for its accompaniment of epics, poetry, and praise singing. Today, the *kora* is also used for other forms of musical expression. To accommodate this adaptation, the *kora* may have an additional four strings.

The *inanga* is a trough zither with seven to nine strings strung from one single string (see figure 7). Its wooden soundboard is carved out of a piece of log. The *inanga* is found principally in the countries that surround Lake Victoria, including Tanzania, Uganda, Rwanda, and Burundi. It is primarily used to accompany praise- and epic-singing and is used by the Haya of Tanzania and at the court of Mutara in Rwanda.

Figure 6. Kora

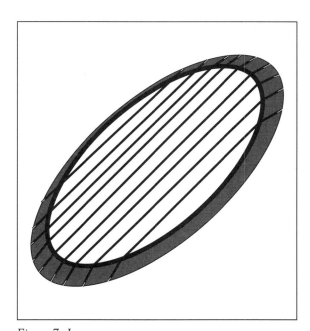

Figure 7. Inanga

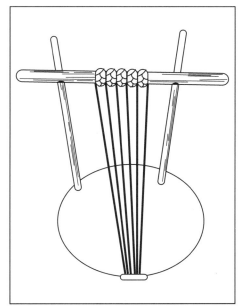

Figure 8. Krar

Figure 9. Shekere

Figure 10. Agogo

The *krar* is a chordophone found in the area extending from Egypt through the Sudan, Ethiopia, and Somalia to Kenya, Uganda, and Tanzania (see figure 8). This instrument is mentioned in the Bible as *kithara*—the harp that was played in the temple of Apollo. The *krar* has a sound box carved from wood. Two sticks are obliquely attached to the sound box, and a cross-bar placed on these sticks receives the hide rings, one for each of the strings. These rings not only retain the strings but also function as tuning pegs. As with the *inanga*, the *krar* is used to accompany songs and epics with simple ostinato formulae. *Krar* are found in various shapes, and their ornamentation styles vary among different cultures.

The *shekere* is a generic name for all rattles with an external net of beads over a gourd (see figure 9). Such rattles are found throughout the Sudanic Belt, particularly in Nigeria (where the name comes from) and in Ghana. In the Bantu World, gourd rattles contain dried seeds. The most common form of rattles in the Bantu World is a woven basket with a piece of gourd for a base and dried seeds or pebbles. This style of rattle is acoustically inferior to the *shekere* and is often used with smaller ensembles.

The *agogo* is a double bell made of iron and pitched high and low (see figure 10). The two bells, known as male and female, are welded together. In an ensemble, the *agogo* provides time-line patterns as part of rhythmic tapestry. This style of double bell is common in the Sudanic Belt zone and especially in Ghana and Nigeria. The style of double bell found in the Bantu World has a curved handle to which the bells are welded.

The *dundun*, a talking drum of the Nigerian Yoruba, is a two-headed membranophone with an hourglass-shaped shell (see figure 11). The two heads rest on the shell and are held in position with the hide strips strung between them. As a talking drum, the *dundun* is capable of producing a variety of tones comparable to those present in the Yoruba language. The *dundun* is sometimes confused with another two-headed, hourglass-shaped shell drum called the *dono* in Ghana. The *dono*, however, is found in the much

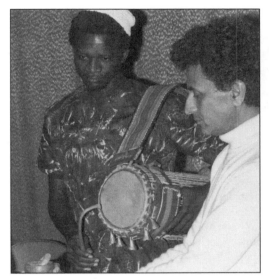

Figure 11. Dundun   *Figure 12. Atumpan*

broader geographical area extending throughout the Sudanic Belt. The *dundun* and the *dono* differ in the materials from which they are made and also in their playing techniques. The *dono*, which is often used as an integral part of the ensemble, is held under the arm pit and is squeezed with the arm to alter pitches. The *dundun*, on the other hand, is carried by a shoulder strap and is squeezed with the hand. Both instruments are struck with a curved mallet.

The *atumpan* is a set of male and female drums used as talking drums by the Ashante in Ghana (see figure 12). As a musical instrument, the *atumpan* is also used in a variety of speech modes. It is a principal instrument for communicating over long distances; it is used by the master drummer at the court to recite praises to the chief; and it is used at schools to indicate the changing of classes. A new set of *atumpan* drums is always carved and presented to the newly installed chief. They serve as the symbol of his authority; after his death, they are buried with him.

A variety of *aerophones* can be found in Africa. Their selection is determined by the available raw material in the area as well as by the livelihood of their users. Flutes are preferred by Nilotic shepherds. Horns made of elephant ivory predominate in areas where elephants are plentiful. Animal horns, gourds, and brass are also used to make side- and end-blown trumpets. Some of these horns are decorated with carved motifs.

The origin of the urban musical styles in Africa is rooted in a mixture of domestic and foreign musical materials. Urban music is an artistic expression that summarizes the world view of its people. It entertains and educates; sings praises to the land, its heroes, cities, rivers, and mountains; and chronicles the history and accomplishments of its people. As a product of the hybridization between European medium (instruments) and African content (traditional music cognition), urban music reflects the reality of the context in which it is created. Thus, the variety of styles, such as the *soukous* in Zaire, *high-life* in

Ghana, *Juju* in Nigeria, *Makossa* in Cameroon, *Marabi* in South Africa, *Kwela* in Malawi, *Chimurenga* in Zimbabwe, and *Zokela* in the Central African Republic, are but some of the most prominent.

NOTES

1. See Georges Balandier, *La Vie Quotidienne dans le Royaume du Kongo du XVI au XVIII Sciecle* (Monaco: Imprimérie Nationale, 1965). See also Jan Vansina, *Kingdoms of the Savanna* (Madison, WI: University of Wisconsin Press, 1964).
2. Portugal's first contact with Africa began in 1444 on the Goree Island and the mainland area known today as Lagos, Nigeria. Portugal's second and third visits were to the First Empire of Kongo in 1482 and again in 1493, when a diplomatic relationship was established between Portugal and the Empire of the Kongo.
3. *Sahel* is an Arabic word that means "border." The term also designates a political front that groups all formerly French colonies on the Sudanic Belt. *Sahel* also refers to the climate zone between the Sahara Desert and the Sudanic Belt, which receives less than twelve inches of rain per year.
4. For a complete account of how Egypt was dismantled, see Cheikh Anta Diop's *The African Origin of Civilization: Myth or Reality* (Westport, CT: Lawrence Hill, 1974).
5. Meki Nzewi, "Theoretical Content and Creative Continuum in African Music: The Culture Exponents' Definitions" (unpublished manuscript, Nsuka University, Nigeria, 1994), 18–20.
6. Other names for this idiophone include *kibiti, kisanji, likembe,* and *sanza.*
7. See Lucy Duran and Anthony King, "Kora," in *The New Grove's Dictionary of Musical Instruments,* Stanley Sadie, ed. (London: Macmillan Press, 1980), 461–463.

L E S S O N   1

■ Objectives
Students will:
1. Understand that a "metronomic sense" is an essential aspect of rhythm in African music.
2. Learn that in African music, accents often fall on pulses (beats) other than the first one.

■ Materials
1. Overhead projector and transparency
2. Xylophones

■ Procedures
1. The teacher begins to clap an even rhythmic pulse in moderate tempo with *no* accents (use a metronome if necessary). Students clap along with the teacher until an exact steady pulse is established. Do this several times but with different tempos each time, always striving for an exact metronomic pulse with *no* accents.
2. Clap eight pulses, accenting the first one, while students imitate. Do this several times. Vary the tempo—slow, medium, fast. Note that tempos of African musics are often quite fast, and only start to feel "African" when this is so. Thus, strive to establish a fast metronomic pulse of eight with the class from the start.

3. Clap six pulses, accenting the first one. Have students alter the accented clap to correspond with the number of fingers you hold up. For example, two fingers means accent the second pulse, five fingers means accent the fifth pulse, and so on. Then repeat, altering the tempo.

4. Write the numbers 1–8 on the overhead transparency, and ask a student to circle the pulse on which he or she would like the accent to occur. For example,

$$①\ 2\ ③④\ 5\ 6\ ⑦⑧\ :// \quad \text{or} \quad 1\ ②\ 3\ ④\ 5\ ⑥\ 7\ ⑧\ ://$$

Have students clap this pattern. Follow this procedure with six pulses and with twelve pulses.

5. Improvise a melody for the clapped rhythm using a pentatonic pitch set (for example, C D E G A) on a xylophone while the class claps the accented pulse patterns.

6. Show the following on the overhead transparency, revealing one line at a time:

$$1\ ②\ 3\ ④\ ⑤\ 6\ ://$$

$$1\ 2\ ③\ ④\ 5\ ⑥\ ://$$

$$①\ 2\ 3\ 4\ 5\ ⑥\ ://$$

a) Have the students clap the first line several times, accenting the circled numbers.
b) Clap the second and third lines several times, accenting the circled numbers.
c) Use other sounds for the same exercise.
d) Vary the tempo.
e) Combine the lines.
f) Follow the same procedure using eight and twelve pulses.

7. Divide the class into small groups and ask them to do the following:
a) Choose either 1–6, 1–8, or 1–12. Circle the numbers where you want the accents to occur, then decide on a tempo and body sound, and perform your pattern for the class.
b) Add an improvised melody/set of pitches to the rhythmic patterns on xylophones. Embellish the patterns with improvised rhythms that are layered over the basic six-, eight-, or twelve-beat patterns on drums.
c) Add dance/movement to one of the two preceding activities. Strive for fuller involvement of the body while performing.

8. Have students perform, analyze, and discuss each group's performance. They should begin to realize that African rhythms are often metronomic with accents appearing on pulses other than the first.

LESSON 2

■ **Objective**
Students will:
1. Understand that music making in Africa uses cross-rhythms.

■ **Materials**
1. Several xylophones
2. Overhead projector and transparency

■ **Procedures**
1. The simplest cross-rhythm is two against three. Write the following on the overhead transparency.

Left hand	Right hand
1	1
2	•
3	3
4	•
5	5
6	•

Count to six. Raise the right hand and beat pulses 1, 3, and 5 in the air on an imaginary wall.

2. Write the following on the overhead transparency.

Left hand	Right hand
1	1
•	2
•	3
4	4
•	5
•	6

Count to six. Raise the left hand and beat pulses 1 and 4 in the air on an imaginary wall.

3. Have half of the class clap the left-hand pattern (1 • 4 •) and the other half clap the right-hand pattern (1 • 3 • 5 •). It is very important to direct students to shift their listening back and forth between each of the patterns:

   a) Left-hand pattern   1 • • 2 • • (a two-beat pattern)
   b) Right-hand pattern   1 • 2 • 3 • (a three-beat pattern)
   c) Combined pattern   1 • 3 4 5 • (the resultant rhythm)

4. Show the students how to combine the two patterns. Alter the numbers as follows to indicate that students are playing two beats with the left hand while playing three beats with the right:

Left hand	Right hand
1	1
•	•
•	2
2	•
•	3
•	•

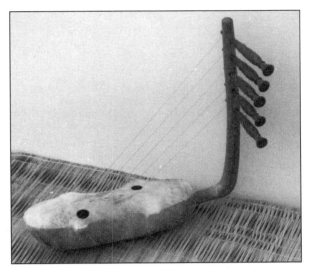

Figure 13. Kunki

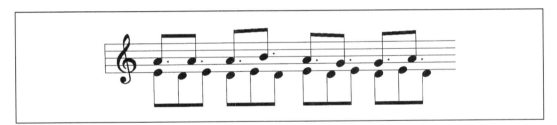

Figure 14. Kunki melody

When students are able to shift their listening from one pattern to another, they are beginning to experience the way Africans listen to music with varied and complex rhythmic patterns.

5. Divide the class into small groups. Have the students choose body sounds and perform an exercise of six pulses, with two against three. Encourage students to shift their listening between the two-rhythm patterns and the resultant rhythm.
6. Have select students form a circle. Each will clap either a two-beat pattern or a three-beat pattern. Following the example of the six pulses, the circle moves one step, left to right, as each person claps his or her chosen rhythm pattern.
7. An example of a piece played on the *kunki* (see figure 13), a harp-like instrument played in northern Zaire by the Azande people, is shown in figure 14. Note that the top melody is in two and the bottom is in three. Using xylophones, play the selection in figure 14 continuously while others perform the rhythms with body sounds.

L E S S O N 3

■ **Objectives**

Students will:
1. Experience repetitive rhythm patterns.
2. Experience several contrasting rhythms at the same time (polyrhythm).

■ **Materials**

1. Double bell or two cow bells of varying sizes
2. Recording: "Ewe Atsimevu," from *Master Drummer of Ghana, Mustapha Tettey Addy* (Lyrichord LLCT 7250)
3. Chalkboard

■ **Procedures**

1. Write the following on the chalkboard:

   Pattern A. ① 2 3 4 ⑤ 6 7 8 ⑨ 10 11 12

   Pattern B. ① 2 3 ④ 5 6 ⑦ 8 9 ⑩ 11 12

   Count to twelve and have the class clap Pattern A several times, and then Pattern B. Have half of the class clap Pattern A while the other half claps Pattern B. Set the tempo by counting twelve even counts. Direct the class to listen to each of the two rhythm patterns and the resultant rhythm and to note the overall polyrhythmic effect.

   A. 1 • • • 2 • • • 3 • • •   (a three-beat pattern)
   B. 1 • • 2 • • 3 • • 4 • •   (a four-beat pattern)
   C. 1 • • 4 5 • 7 • 9 10• •   (the resultant rhythm)

   Again encourage students to clap three against four and to shift their listening from one rhythm pattern to another.

2. Divide the class into small groups. Create pieces using three against four. Groups may choose either body, instrumental, or vocal sounds for their compositions.

3. Analyze and discuss each performance. Note how many students were able to shift their listening to hear the two-rhythm patterns and the resultant rhythm.

4. Form a circle with select students and let each student choose which pattern he or she will play. Following the example from the previous lesson, the circle will move one step, left to right, as each person claps his or her own pattern.

5. Have students listen to and perform with a shared sense of time (or "rhythmic lock" or "feeling") by playing two-rhythm patterns along with the recording of "Ewe Atsimevu" on *Master Drummer of Ghana, Mustapha Tettey Addy*. One rhythm pattern, in this case, is twelve pulses long, with low and high sounds distributed through the cycle, as shown in the following pattern. Have some members of the class play the bell pattern, using a two-toned bell or low and high sounds, while the others clap on pulses one, four, seven, and ten. Listen carefully to the repetitive and contrasting rhythm patterns.

   1 • 3 • 5 6 • 8 • 10 • 12 (double bell pattern)
   low high high high high high high
   1 • • 4 • • 7 • • 10 • • (clap)

L E S S O N 4

■ **Objective**

Students will:
1. Learn that African music uses a variety of scales, including ones with four and five tones.

■ **Materials**

1. Recorders, xylophones, tuned bottles (tuned to C, D, E, G, A), or voices
2. Chalkboard

■ **Procedures**

1. Write the numbers one through twelve on the chalkboard and circle several of them. Ask students how they might clap the accented numbers (loud, soft, fast, slow). Decide on one way, set the pulse by counting to twelve, and clap. Do this several times, changing the tempo and dynamics each time.
2. Sing or play on xylophones an A above middle C. Have the class sing the circled numbers on the note A using any syllable, such as *la*. Then sing the D above middle C. Divide the class and combine notes D and A using the same rhythmic pattern; the resultant sound is a drone-like open fifth.
3. Follow the same procedure with the notes A and E, allowing the students to decide which of the twelve pulses they will be accenting. Have students sing or play on xylophones, recorders, or tuned bottles, first in unison, and then in two parts. Have them do the same with the notes G and E (singing in unison and then in two parts).
4. Divide the class into four groups. Using the notes A, G, E, and D, allow the students to decide which of the twelve pulses they will accent. Have the students play or sing the accented notes.
5. Divide the class into small groups to create their own three- or four-part work, using instrumental, vocal, or tuned-bottle sounds. Analyze and discuss their compositions.
6. Form a circle. Invite each student to sing one of the four lines as the circle moves, left to right, to the music.
7. Using the pentatonic scale of C D E G A, repeat these exercises or improvise using C D E G A while the class sings one of the exercises.
8. Divide the class into small groups and ask each to create either a four- or five-pitch composition with movement for performance. Have students analyze and discuss what they hear.

L E S S O N 5

■ **Objectives**

Students will:
1. Learn the sixteen-pulse clapping pattern called *gome* (from the GA people in Ghana).

Figure 15. "Wateh Eh"

2. Learn the song "Wateh Eh" by rote. When students are able to sing accurately, add the clapping pattern. (Have the students play one pattern per measure, based on a sixteenth-note pulse, beginning at the "X".)

■ **Materials**

1. Recording: "Wateh Eh" and "Gome Drum and Songs," from *Master Drummer of Ghana, Mustapha Tettey Addy* (Lyrichord LLCT 7250)

■ **Procedures**

1. Teach the sixteen-pulse clapping pattern called *gome*, making sure that it is consistent, fluent, and automatic.
2. Teach "Wateh Eh" by rote (see figure 15). When students are able to sing accurately, add the clapping pattern. (Have the students play one pattern per measure, based on a sixteenth-note pulse, beginning at the "X.")
3. Listen to the recording of "Gome Drum and Songs" from *Master Drummer of Ghana, Mustapha Tettey Addy.*

Figure 16. "Manamolela," from *Choral Songs of the Bantu* by H. Williams. Copyright 1960 by G. Schirmer. Used by permission.

LESSON 6

■ **Objective**

Students will:
1. Experience a *Sutho* song from South Africa.

■ **Materials**

1. "Manamolela"

■ **Procedures**

1. Introduce "Manamolela," a *Sutho* work song from South Africa that is sung when the workers are hoeing (see figure 16). The workers are tired and they want to "take it slow." Though they are singing to their boss or foreman, the African word *Manamolela* appears along with the English lyrics.
2. Sing the top part several times. Invite the class to sing along until they are comfortable with the words and music. Pronounce "i" as in ee; "e" as in egg; "u" as in lute; "a" as in father; "kh" like the "ch" in Bach; "t'h" is a cross between t and th.

    Translation: *Manamolela, manamolela*
                      Won't you let us take it slow?
                      Won't you let us take it slow:
                      You know the day is long,
                      You know the day is long. *Manamolela, manamolela*
                      Helele re khat'hetsi
                      Helele re khat'hetsi
                      Ahere khat'hetsi!
                      Ahere khat'hetsi!

3. While the class sings the first part, you sing the second part, and eventually all will be able to sing this two-part song.
4. Divide the class into four groups. While two groups sing the song in two parts, the other two groups create cross-rhythms, using the twelve-pulse pattern (see Lesson 3).

LESSON 7

■ **Objectives**

Students will:
1. Sing the "Axe Blade Song" from Zambia and add a rhythmic accompaniment.

■ **Materials**

1. "Axe Blade Song"
2. Map of Africa
3. Overhead projector and transparency

Figure 17. "Axe Blade Song" from the Bemba tribe; new version. From A. M. Jones, "African Rhythm," *Africa: Journal of the International African Institute* 24 (1954): 37. Used by permission.

Figure 18. Resultant rhythm of combined Patterns A, B, and C

■ Procedures

1. Find Zambia on the map of Africa.
2. The "Axe Blade Song" is from the *Bemba* people who live in Zambia. Sing the song (shown in figure 17).
3. Add the rhythmic accompaniment to the song.
   a. Write the following two patterns on the overhead transparency. Divide the class in half, and have each group of students clap one of the patterns (which are a now-familiar pattern of two against three).

      Pattern A: ① 2 3 ④ 5 6 ⑦ 8 9 ⑩ 11 12

      Pattern B: ① 2 ③ 4 ⑤ 6 ⑦ 8 ⑨ 10 ⑪ 12

4. Add a third line to the other two and have the class clap it.

      Pattern C: ① 2 ③ ④ 5 ⑥ 7 ⑧ 9 ⑩ ⑪ 12

5. Then add these accents to the circled numbers, and have the students clap on the accented pulses.

      >   >   >   >   >
      1   4   6   8   11

6. Divide the class into three groups and have them clap Patterns A, B, and C together. Listen for the resultant rhythm, as shown in figure 18.
7. Combine the rhythms with the "Axe Blade Song."

L E S S O N   8

■ Objective

Students will:
1. Develop an awareness of African instruments and an appreciation of the fact that many Africans make their own instruments.

■ Materials

1. Enlarged photos of African instruments
2. Descriptions of each instrument
3. Recordings: See Discography—those recordings marked with asterisks feature the instruments discussed in this lesson

■ Procedures

1. Make copies of the photos of African instruments and display them around the

Figure 19. Boy with talking drum

Figure 20. Talking drum

Figure 21. Hand position for performance of talking drum

Figure 22. Amadinda xylophone

classroom. *Number each photo* to correspond with the description of the instruments you will be providing. Give each student a description of these instruments. The students will move around the room examining each picture and matching each description with the relevant picture. Recordings of these instruments are found in the Discography and are marked with an asterisk. The following are the instrument descriptions you will be giving to the students.

a. *The talking drum.* Imagine standing on a hill and speaking to people on another far-off hill by means of a special drum called the talking drum (see figures 19, 20, and 21). The Yoruba, Kongo, Ewe, Ashanti, Lozi, Ibo, Bechuana, and other African groups make use of the talking drum to announce important social events such as births, deaths, marriages, and special ceremonies.

Long before the telegraph and telephone were invented, Africans made use of different tones to communicate messages. These tones are imitative of tonal languages. Message drums from West Africa have an hourglass shape, are double headed, and have thongs that stretch from end to end. The drum, suspended from the shoulder, is held between the player's arm and body. It is squeezed to alter the tone as the player hits the drum with a drumstick shaped like the head of a crane's bill or with the hand.

For many, drums are synonymous with African music. They are generally made by people who live close to forests. In the wide, treeless plain areas of South Africa, for example, people find it difficult to obtain wood for drum making. This is certainly true for the Zulu and Xhosa who work in big cities like Johannesburg. For lack of wood, these groups of people use discarded metal containers such as old oil drums or even garbage cans, and they transform them into objects that can

Figure 23. Mangwilo xylophone

produce sounds. These drums may be single- or double-headed, and they are played either with the hand or with a large beater or stick. The Zulu also make percussive sounds by using their hide shields and beaters.

b. *Amadinda xylophone.* This wooden xylophone is found as far west as Sierra Leone and as far south as Mozambique (see figure 22). It varies in type and size; one of the largest is found in Uganda. There the Ganda tribe uses a single xylophone, the *Amadida,* which is played by three men simultaneously. Each musician plays on the end of the keys with two wooden sticks about thirty-five centimeters long. The music that they perform has been handed down to them by their forefathers.

c. *Timbila xylophone.* The Chopi of Mozambique play in xylophone orchestras of up to thirty or more *timbila* (see figure 4, shown earlier). This xylophone is constructed in five different pitches from treble to double bass. Gourds fitted with a thin membrane stretched across the opening are used as resonators. The music they perform is composed anew every year.

d. *Mangwilo xylophone.* In northern Mozambique, the *Mangwilo* xylophone is played by two people sitting on opposite sides of the instrument (see figure 23). This xylophone has seven keys made of logs, which are cut to shape and left to dry. The keys are then placed across two banana stems. The parts played by the two players interlock; thus, the players are named *Opachera* ("the starting one") and *Wakulela O* ("the responding one").

e. *Mbira.* Africa's unique instrument has over one hundred different names, including *nsansi, likembe, agidigbo,* and *kalimba,* and it comes in a variety of shapes. This instrument is common throughout the continent.

Look at figures 3 and 24. Figure 3 depicts three types of mbira. Figure 24

Figure 24. Mbira *vza vadzimu*

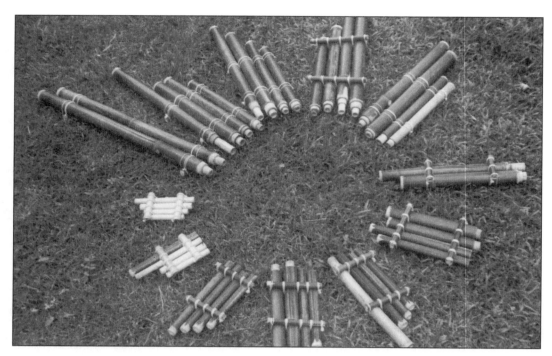

Figure 25. Pan-pipes

Figure 26. Kudu horns

Figure 27. Mouth bow

shows a young boy holding the mbira *vza vadzimu* from Zimbabwe. If you study figure 24, you will notice that the mbira has a number of metal tongues attached to a soundboard or sound box. Sometimes an additional resonator is used to increase the instrument's volume; thus, you will see the mbira *vza vadzimu* being played inside a large calabash. The player, usually an adult male, holds the instrument in his hands and plucks the tongues with both thumbs, or sometimes with the thumb and index finger. Metal bottle tops or shells may be attached to the board to add a rattling or buzzing sound. Though the mbira is usually played by men, today some women play the instrument as well.

f. *Pipes.* The pan-pipes are among the many aerophones, or wind instruments, found in Africa. In figure 25 you see a collection of pipes. Some are sets of four; others are sets of two. They are made of bamboo and are secured with plant fiber. Each player simultaneously plays his particular melodic pattern on his set of pipes, sings another melodic pattern, and dances. The players then must interpolate their particular parts into the music at the right moment.

One *Tswana* pipe ensemble consists of twenty-one pipes covering a range of five octaves. The pipes that this ensemble uses are made of metal, as these men are miners working for the Luipaardsvlei Estate and Gold Mining Company near Krugersdorp in South Africa. Pan-pipes are common in all parts of Africa, as are other wind instruments such as whistles (made of wood, metal, and clay) and flutes (both end-blown and transverse).

g. *Horns.* Horns and trumpets all over Africa are made of animal horns and tusks. They are picturesque in appearance, for some are straight, some are curved, and

Figure 28. Umakhweyana

Figure 29. Shekere

others are twisted. The instruments vary in size, from the small signal whistles of the southern cattle herders to the large ivory horns of the tribal chiefs of the interiors.

Kudu horns of varying sizes appear in figure 26. Players hold them sideways to their lips and blow single notes. When a set of *kudu* horns is played together, each player must interpolate his part into the music at the right moment.

h. *Mouth bow.* The simplest of the stringed instruments, or chordophones, is the mouth bow. It is shaped like a hunting bow and has one string. The mouth bow is played either by being plucked with the finger or struck with a thin stick. These particular bows make use of the open mouth as the resonator. In figure 27, the player uses a stick to which a small packet of seed is attached. The sound produced, though very soft, is often of a complex nature.

i. *Harp.* Harps are found in northern East Africa and on the west coast of Africa. Figure 13 shows a harp used by the Azande people from northern Zaire. The body of this five-stringed arched harp is made of wood across which antelope hide is stretched and secured. The five strings are fastened to five tuning pegs. The Azande people are famous for their beautifully carved harps, and harp music is used by boys and young men for walking songs, love songs, and topical songs.

j. *Umakhweyana bow.* This bow was often played by young unmarried Zulu women to accompany love songs, but today only the older women keep the music of this instrument alive by singing songs relevant to their own lives. (Young Africans have become more interested in Western instruments as greater prestige is attached to the playing of them.)

The *umakhweyana* is a gourd-bow, the stave of which is made from the wood of the acacia tree (see figure 28). It is made into an arch shape, and copper or

Figure 30. Idiophones

brass wire is stretched between the two ends. Another wire length is used to attach the gourd to the stave, and fibers or cloth forming a ring are placed between the gourd and the stave. The bow is held in the left hand, and the string is struck with a small stick or grass stalk held in the fingers of the right hand.

k. *Shekere*. This instrument is made from a gourd and covered with a woven net (see figure 29). Sound is created when the hollow gourd is struck by the beads surrounding it. In Ghana, it is known as *axatse*, and it is found in other African countries south of the Sahara.

l. Metal gongs, rattles, shakers, clapping sticks, and double bells are examples of other African instruments that produce sounds when they are struck or shaken. Such instruments are called idiophones (see figure 30).

After the students have completed the exercise:

• Discuss what they've learned about African instruments.

• Classify the instruments as aerophones (sound is produced by a vibrating column of air), chordophones (sound is produced by the vibration of strings), idiophones (sound is produced by striking or shaking), or membranophones (sound is produced by a vibrating membrane or drum head).

• Play recordings featuring African instruments.

• Make African instruments. To make your own African musical instruments, including some mentioned in this chapter, see *Music of Africa*, an educational videotape with an accompanying booklet (listed in the Filmography).

BIBLIOGRAPHY

Adzinyah, Abraham Kobena, Dumisani Maraire, and Judith Cook Tucker. *Let Your Voice Be Heard! Songs from Ghana and Zimbabwe*. Danbury, CT: World Music Press, 1986. These songs are from the *Akan* people of Ghana and the *Shona* people of Zimbabwe. A sixty-minute companion audiotape is included.

Amoaku, W. K. *African Songs and Rhythms for Children: Orff Schulwerk in the African Tradition*. New York: Schott, 1971. Fifteen Ghanaian songs with instrumental accompaniment. Companion recording Smithsonian/Folkways 45011.

Bebey, Francis. *African Music: A People's Art*. New York: Lawrence Hill, 1975. Written by an African musician and composer, this book provides an African's perspective on African music. It includes a discography and photographs.

Berliner, Paul. *The Soul of Mbira*. Berkeley: University of California Press, 1978. This class discussion of the mbira emphasizes the *Shona* music culture of Zimbabwe.

Brouckaert, Liz, comp. *Songs Sung by South African Children*. South Africa: Grassroots Educare Trust, 1990. Children's songs sung in Xhosa and Afrikaanse. An audiocassette accompanies the book.

Carrington, John F. *Talking Drums of Africa*. London: Carey Kingsgate Press, 1949. This definitive description of the message drumming of Africa includes illustrations about how it works and message phrases with English translations.

Chernoff, John Miller. *African Rhythm and African Sensibility*. Chicago: University of Chicago Press, 1981. This is a description of drumming in Ghana. The author discusses his personal experiences with the music and culture, and the book includes comments by master musicians.

Cooke, Peter. *Play Amadinda: Xylophone Music of Uganda*. Edinburgh: K & C Productions, 1990. Accompanying audiocassette. Contains instructions for making this instrument; also includes performance instruction.

Dietz, Betty Q., and M. A. Olantunji. *Musical Instruments of Africa.* New York: John Day, 1965. This book for students, especially for levels K–8, is about African musical instruments. It includes pictures and descriptions.

Jahn, Janheinz. *Through African Doors.* New York: Grove Press, 1969. This is an extremely readable description of the travels of a scholar in Africa.

Jessup, Lynne. *The Mandinka Balafon Book.* Available from West Music Company, 1208 Fifth Street, PO Box 5521, Coralville, IA 52241. This is a practical guide to the West African xylophone tradition. It includes several tapes.

Jones, Claire. *Making Music: Musical Instruments of Zimbabwe, Past and Present.* Academic Books, 1992. This is a good introduction to the musical instruments of Zimbabwe.

Makeba, Miriam. *The World of African Song.* Chicago: Quadrangle Books, 1971. This collection of songs from South Africa includes urban musical examples.

Musgrove, Margaret. *Ashanti to Zulu.* New York: Dial Press, 1976. This beautifully illustrated children's book contains pictures of people from different areas of sub-Saharan Africa.

Nketia, J. H. Kwabena. *African Music in Ghana.* Evanston, IL: Northwestern University Press, 1963. This study of music in Ghana includes an appendix with eighteen songs.

Nketia, J. H. Kwabena. *The Music of Africa.* New York: Norton, 1974. This textbook provides information on the organization of musical groups as well as the tonal, timbral, rhythmic, and formal characteristics of the music and some information on its contextual use.

Oehrle, Elizabeth. *A New Direction for South African Music Education.* 2d ed. Pietermaritzburg, South Africa: Shuter & Shooter, 1988.

Orff, Carl. *African Songs and Rhythms for Children: A Selection from Ghana* by W. K. Amoaka. Mainz: Schott, 1971.

Serwadda, W. Moses. *Songs and Stories from Uganda.* Available from West Music Company, 1208 Fifth Street, PO Box 5521, Coralville, IA 52241. Includes thirteen traditional story songs and a companion tape.

Titon, Jeff Todd, ed. *Worlds of Music.* 2d ed. New York: Schirmer Books, 1992. This is a survey of world music. The chapter on music in Africa/Ghana by James T. Koetting, which includes a look at contemporary music, is appropriate for use in a teaching unit. An audiotape is included.

Weinberg, Pessa. *Hlabelela Mntwanami—Sing My Child—Zulu Children's Songs.* Johannesburg: Ravan Press, 1984. A collection of Zulu children's songs with staff notation.

Williams, H. *Choral Folksongs of the Bantu.* London: Chappell and Co., no date.

DISCOGRAPHY

African Journey. Vanguard Nomad SRV73014/5. This recording, produced and recorded by Samuel Charters, includes musical examples from the area of West Africa and made famous by Alex Haley's *Roots.*

African Mbira: Music of the Shona People of Rhodesia. Dumisani Maraire, Nkosane Maraire, and Sukutai Chiora. Nonesuch Explorer Series H-72043. The mbira and the *hosho* (rattle) can be heard along with the three singers. The accompanying documentation is good.

African Music. Kaleidaphone KMA-1-10. These ten audiocassettes, recorded by Hugh Tracy and published originally by the International Library of African Music, are devoted to (1) strings, (2) reeds, (3) drums, (4) flutes and horns, (5) xylophones, (6) and (7) guitars, (8) music from Zimbabwe, (9) music from Tanzania, and (10) music from Uganda. They are well recorded and useful. These recordings are available through Paul Tracey, 340 Las Casas, Pacific Palisades, CA

90272. Recordings are accompanied by a book.

African Music from "The Naked Prey" (original soundtrack). Folkways 8454. Although this comes from a movie score, it contains excellent examples of traditional choral music from several cultures in southern Africa.

African Rhythms and Instruments, Volumes 1, 2, and 3. Lyrichord LYRCD 7328 (LLCT 7328), LYRCD 7338 (LLCT-7338), and LLCT 7339.

African Story-Songs—Told and Sung by Abraham Dumisani Maraire. Seattle: University of Washington Press, 1969. This selection of stories and *ngano* (*Shona* story-songs from Zimbabwe) includes record notes by ethnomusicologist Robert Kauffman. Additional stories from Zimbabwe are available on cassette tapes from Paul Tracey, 340 Las Casas, Pacific Palisades, CA 90272. These recorded stories are accompanied by a book.

Africa: Shona Mbira Music recorded in Mondoro and Highfields, Rhodesia [Zimbabwe]. Nonesuch Explorer Series H-72077-A. A good sound source of mbira music of the *Shona* people from Zimbabwe.

Drame, Adam-Adama Drame (traditional, new, and improvised rhythms on the *Djembe* drum). Auvdis A-6126. Outstanding drummer from the Ivory Coast.

Drums of West Africa: Ritual Music of Ghana. Lyrichord LLCT 7307. The *Anlo Ewe* are found on the Guinea Coast from Anloga to Aflao. The recording features dances of a more recreational character and includes the *axatse* (beaded gourd rattle).

Espi-Sanchis, Pedro. The Children's Carnival: An African Musical Story. African musical instruments are introduced by means of Pedro's musical story, narrated by Gay Morris. *Another Lion on the Path* and *Cowbells and Tortoise Shells* are recommended for primary schools. Write to Pedro Espi-Sanchis at 36 Dartmouth Road, Muizenberg 7945 or phone/fax 021 788 7001.

Ghana: Music of the Northern Tribes. Lyrichord LLRCD (LLCT) 7321. The first example is of the hourglass-shaped pressure drum known in Ghana as the *donno.*

Jobartah, Malamini and Dambo Donte—Jaliya (Kora duets). Rounder 5021 (C 5021).

Music from Mozambique: Chopi Timbila. Ethnic Folkways Records FE 4318. A fine example of *Chopi* xylophone music.

Music from Mozambique: Chordophone Music. Folkways 4319.

Master Drummer of Ghana, Mustapha Tettey Addy. Lyrichord LLCT 7250. Drid Williams, social anthropologist at Oxford University, writes: "Addy presents us with a rare combination, to be found in all of the truly great drummers of Africa—fine traditional rhythms which he respects and which are expertly played, together with creative innovative drumming which will add to and enrich that tradition."

Nettl, Bruno et al. *Excursions in World Music.* Cassette 2, Side c. Silverdisc SCA 510. These recordings are available from Prentice-Hall, Englewood Cliffs, NJ 07632.

*22 Traditional mbira piece: *Karigamombe.* Mr. T. Chigamba, first mbira; Garadziva Chigamba, second mbira; recorded in Zimbabwe.

*23 Traditional mbira piece: *Shumba.* Mr. T. Chigamba, first mbira; Garadziva Chigamba, second mbira; Henry Chigamba, *hosho* (shaker); recorded in Zimbabwe.

*25 Traditional *Atsiagbekor* dance piece of the Ewe: *If It Comes to Fight with Guns.* Instruments: five drums, one double bell, three–six rattles; recorded in Ghana.

Pete Seeger: *"Wimoweh" and other Freedom Songs.* Folkways Recordings FTS 31018. "Wimoweh" was written by Solomon Lindo of Johannesburg as "an instrument number for voices." The original words mean: "The lion is sleeping, the lion, the lion."

Soul of Mbira. Nonesuch Explorer Series. H-72054. Can be used in conjunction with the book of the same title by Paul Berliner. It features *Shona* musicians from Zimbabwe.

*Sounds of West Africa: The Kora and the Xylophone. Lyrichord LLRCD (LLST) 7308. This recording illustrates one of Africa's most striking harp-like instruments, the *kora* from the Gambia, and the Lobi-Dagarti xylophone (or *balophon*) of Northern Ghana.

*Zulu Songs from South Africa. Lyrichord LLCT 7401. This album features three types of musical bows, one being the *umakhweyana*.

Note. Entries with an asterisk can be used in Lesson Eight.

FILMOGRAPHY

African Drumming: Babatunde Olatunji. VHS, 60 minutes. Available from Multicultural Media, RR3 Box 6655, Granger Road, Barre, VT 05641. African master drummer Olantunji covers techniques for playing drums. Traditional and original rhythms.

Atumpan. 16 mm and VHS, 43 minutes, color. The University of California at Los Angeles. This outstanding film deals with the geographical location, construction, performance, and social context of the *atumpan*, a Ghanaian drum.

Bitter Melons. 16 mm, 32 minutes, color. Documentary Educational Resources. This is a well-known film about the people who live in the Kalahari Desert. Filmed in Botswana, the sound track includes the singing of an old man, who accompanies himself on a musical bow. There are also some games with accompanying songs. It is a very realistic and impressive film. Preview the film before showing it in class. This film can be obtained from Audio-Visual Services, Main Library, Kent State University, Kent, OH 44242.

Black African Heritage. Four films, 60 minutes each, color. Distributed by Westinghouse Film Division and the University of California at Los Angeles. These four films are narrated by Julian Bond, Ossie Davis, Maya Angelou, and Gordon Parks. A great deal of Western and African music is included. Information is provided from many parts of the continent, although West Africa is emphasized. Connections are made with the music in the West.

Discovering the Music of Africa. VHS, 19 minutes, color. Available from Dove Music, PO Box 08286, Milwaukee, WI 53208 or West Music Co., 1208 Fifth Street, PO Box 5521, Coralville, IA 52241. This film shows UCLA students working with a Ghanaian master drummer. Drums are demonstrated, and the different patterns and parts of a percussion ensemble are played alone and together.

Jumpstreet: The West African Heritage. 30 minutes, color. Available from the New York State Education Department, Center for Learning Technologies, Media Distribution Network, Room C-7, Concourse Level, Cultural Education Center, Albany, NY 12230; phone: 516-474-3168. This program is from a series of thirteen 30-minute television programs of the same nature. It is useful in providing an African cultural perspective.

Music of Africa. This videotape explains how to make your own African instruments. Write to CEFT Video, P/Bag X460, Pretoria, 0001, South Africa.

Repercussions: A Celebration of African American Music. Seven videocassettes, 60 minutes each, color. Distributed by RM Arts Home Vision, PO Box 800, Concord, MA 01742; phone: 800-262-8600. Especially interesting are Program One—"Born Musicians: Traditional Music from Gambia"—a 60-minute videotape available in VHS or Beta formats that focuses on the music of the *jalis*, the professional musicians of the *Mandinka* people; Program Five—"The Drums of Dagbon"—which examines the relationships between traditional music and popular dance music, or *high-life*, featuring drummers of northern Ghana; and Program 7—"Africa Comeback—The Popular Music of West Africa"—which focuses on *Juju* performer King Sunny Ade with Fela Ankulapo-Kuti and Segun Adewale from the world of Ghanaian popular music.

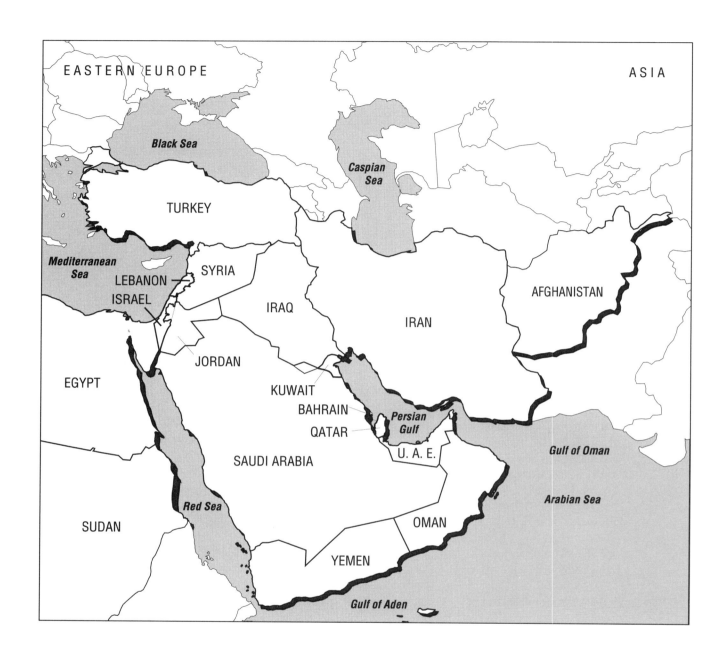

Map of the Middle East

CHAPTER 8

THE MIDDLE EAST

THE ARAB MIDDLE EAST

by George D. Sawa

The area known as the Middle East includes many cultures and varying geography. It is important to know the different parts that make up the whole to better understand the area. The Arabian Peninsula is surrounded by the Red Sea on the west, the Persian (or Arabian) Gulf and Gulf of Oman on the east, and the Arabian Sea to the south. Kuwait, Saudi Arabia, Bahrain, Qatar, and the United Arab Emirates are on the eastern side of the peninsula. Oman is on the southeast side, Yemen is on the southwest, and Saudi Arabia, the area's largest country, occupies most of the west coast, part of the east coast, and most of the center of the peninsula. The Levant is made up of Syria, Lebanon, Israel, and Jordan. The Nile Valley consists of Egypt and the Sudan. Considered by some Middle Eastern specialists to be part of the Middle East, North Africa includes Libya, Tunisia, Algeria, and Morocco, all of which are on the southern Mediterranean coast. Turkey, which is north of Syria, is surrounded by the Black Sea to the north, the Aegean Sea to the west, and the Mediterranean to the south. Iraq, which is east of Syria, includes the Tigris-Euphrates Valley. Afghanistan is the easternmost country in the Middle East. It is landlocked and bordered by Iran, the former Soviet Union, China, and Pakistan. Iran has the Caspian Sea on its north and the Persian Gulf and the Gulf of Oman on its south.

Taken as a whole, the topography and climate of the Middle East vary a great deal. There are coastal plains, oases, large fertile areas, arid deserts, plateaus, and mountainous regions. This wide variety has led, since ancient times, to a diversity in economic production and brought about a need for market centers, which explains the precocious growth of Middle Eastern cities.[1] Cities were also crucial because the Middle East occupies a unique geographical position: it serves as the land connection between the continents of Europe, Asia, and Africa. This geographical position has historically given Middle Easterners the role of an intermediary in trade, commerce, and culture.[2]

The outstanding Middle Eastern achievements in the sciences, arts, architecture, literature, philosophy, and religion are the reasons the area has been dubbed the "Cradle of Civilizations."[3] Three of the great religions (Judaism, Christianity, and Islam) developed in the Middle East. King Hammurabi of Babylon (fl. 1792–1750 B.C.) produced one of the greatest ancient codes of law, and the area's temples, paintings, and engravings are testaments to Middle Eastern artistry.

Middle Easterners speak a variety of languages. Arabic is spoken from Morocco to the Arabian Peninsula. Turkish is spoken in Turkey, Cyprus, and parts of Iran. Persian is spoken in Iran, and variations of Persian are spoken in Afghanistan. Hebrew, Yiddish, and Arabic are spoken in Israel. In addition, there is a multitude of other languages currently in use, including Aramaic (the language of Palestine during Jesus Christ's lifetime), Kurdish (a language related to Persian and spoken in many parts of the Middle East), Armenian (spoken in many parts of the Middle East), Greek (spoken in Cyprus), and Berber (spoken in parts of Morocco, Algeria, and Tunisia).

The Arabic-Islamic invasions, which started in the seventh century, resulted in the creation of an empire that extended from Spain to North Africa, the Middle East, and the borders of India and China. The empire was heir to the cultural legacies of the ancient Near East, Greece, Rome, Spain, India, and Persia. These legacies were received, developed, and expanded, and new ideas were brought in. The result is what Western scholars term "Islamic civilization." Arabs, Persians, Turks, Berbers, and Europeans (peoples that practiced creeds including Islam, Christianity, Judaism, and Zoroastrianism) were among the contributors to this civilization.

This multicultural input is evident in the architecture of the Dome of the Rock in Jerusalem, the Alhambra Palace in Granada, Spain, and the Great Mosque at Yazd in Iran. Andalusian music (the music of *al-Andalus*, the Arabic word for Spain) thrived in the western part of the empire, in Granada and Cordoba; it was a product of cultural interchange among Arabs, Berbers, and Spaniards. Musicians of the eastern part of the empire flourished in cities such as Damascus, Baghdad, and al-Madina.

The Caliph al-Ma'mūn (d. 833) created an important center for music theory and many other fields of learning when he established the *Bayt al-Hikma* (House of Wisdom) in Baghdad. It served as a library, research facility, and center for the translation of Greek, Persian, and Hindu books. Translations of Persian works inspired a great deal of historical and belles lettres writing. An important music example of this tradition is al-Isbāhanī's

Grand Book of Songs, which contains ten thousand pages that cover, in anecdotal form, musical and poetical life of Arabia, Syria, Persia, and Iraq from the sixth to the tenth centuries A.D.

Baghdad was also a center for the preservation of works on Greek music theory by translation into Syriac and Arabic, and scholars studied the Greek music concepts of the tetrachord as well as Greek theories on modes and rhythm. These ideas were then expanded and developed in Arabic writings and combined with new methods and ideas to evolve a theory that reflected the musical practices of the era. The greatest theorist of this period was al-Fārabī (d. 950). His writings have had, and continue to exert, a continuous influence on music theory.

After attaining its maximum military strength in the early eighth century, the empire began to disintegrate into petty dynasties. Art thrived in this period because rulers competed with one another to attract the best talents to their courts. Successive invasions brought vitality and renewal to the arts and the rebuilding of a vast empire, the Ottoman Empire, which dominated the Middle East for the four centuries ending in 1917. Music at the Ottoman court was again the product of many cultures. The most serious impact on the music of the Middle East in this period was that of the West, starting with Napoleon's expedition into Egypt in 1798 and continuing to the present time with the importation of such stylistic traits as triadic harmonies and arpeggios.

The musical styles found in the Middle East vary greatly from country to country and even from region to region. The following sections concentrate on (a) the secular music of Egypt and parts of the Levant and (b) Jewish music in Israel.

Music of the Middle East

Middle Eastern music is essentially melodic in the sense that it does not use the harmonic and contrapuntal devices of Western music. Instrumental or vocal soloists or ensembles perform highly ornamental melodies. Musical ornamentation, whether melodic, rhythmic, or timbral, embellishes and supports the melody. In ensemble music, melodies are performed in unison or in octaves. Each performer ornaments the melody according to his or her own taste and according to idiosyncratic capabilities of the instruments at hand. This approach results in a rich, heterophonic texture.

Melodies are built according to a complex modal system known in Iran as *dastgāh*, in Turkey as *makām*, and in the Arab world as *maqām*. This system includes the concepts of melodic mode—its motifs, cadences, ranges, and the concepts of tetrachords, tonics, and tonal centers. At their most basic level, modes are identified by scales of various intervallic structures using these approximate sizes: 1, 1/2, 3/4, 5/4, and 1 1/2. Middle Eastern modes vary widely in the size of their intervals (for example, the 3/4 tones of Egypt, Iran, and Turkey are all different) and their melodic movements, motifs, and cadences.

A tone system foreign to American students is sure to present a challenge. A study of the multitude of these Middle Eastern systems would surely frustrate and confuse students. This chapter, therefore, concentrates on only one system found in Egypt and the Levant. Once your students learn this system, they will be equipped with the basics to study other Middle Eastern traditions.

Modes in scalar representations are made up of eight or more notes. Modes are usually built on tetrachords, less often on trichords and pentachords. Some of the most important types are shown in figures 1 through 5.

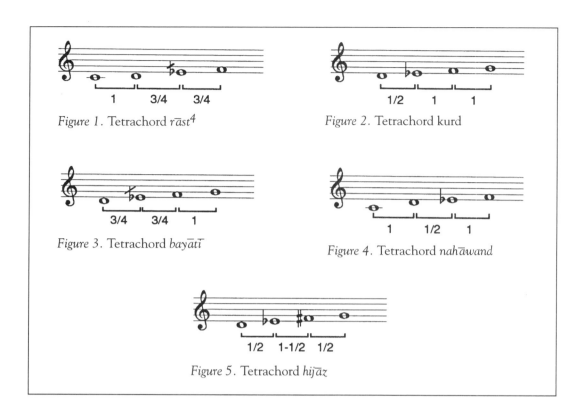

Figure 1. Tetrachord *rāst*[4]

Figure 2. Tetrachord kurd

Figure 3. Tetrachord *bayātī*

Figure 4. Tetrachord *nahāwand*

Figure 5. Tetrachord *hijāz*

When tetrachords are strung together, they produce modal scales. It is the way in which they are strung together that determines the tonal centers and principles of modulation. Usually the *maqām* is named according to its lower tetrachord. Figures 6 through 11 show some of the most important modes.

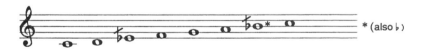

Figure 6. Maqām *rāst*

Figure 7. Maqām kurd

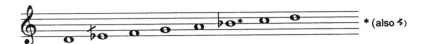

Figure 8. Maqām bayātī

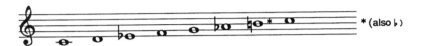

Figure 9. Maqām nahāwand

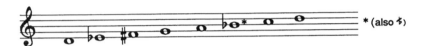

Figure 10. Maqām hijāz

Figure 11. Maqām hijāzkār

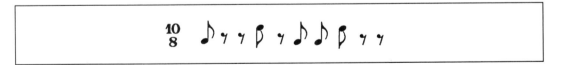

Figure 12. Īqāᶜ pattern

Figure 13. Dumm and takk

The notated examples provided in the lessons that follow illustrate some of these modes. Some examples use all eight notes; some use fewer.

Iqāᶜ is the Arabic term for rhythm. Its definition includes the concepts of meter, rhythmic mode, rhythm, dynamics, timbre, and tempo, and it is especially used to denote a pattern of attacks performed on percussion instruments. These attacks are separated by rests of unequal durations, leading to a pattern such as that shown in figure 12.

Patterns could be as short as 2/8 and as long as the Ottoman Turkish 176/4. The attacks performed on percussion instruments carry both dynamic and timbral characteristics. In theory, there are two types of attacks: *dumm*, a low resounding sound represented by a note with a stem up, and *takk*, a short crisp sound of a higher pitch, represented by a note with a stem down (see figure 13).

The basic rhythmic patterns are highly ornamented in performance (however, ornamentation should not obscure or alter the nature of the pattern). Rhythmic ornamentations consist of filling in rests with attacks, removing attacks (resulting in syncopation), altering the timbre (a low *dumm* replacing a crisp *takk*, and vice versa), and creatively expanding the timbre and dynamic quality by performing an infinite variety of *dumms* and *takks*.

The role of percussion instruments—besides playing solos for dancers—is to control the tempo for a melody instrument or ensemble, to give punctuation and phrasing to a melody, and to support the rhythm by means of attacks with duration and accents (dynamics and timbre). The percussionist also acts as a conductor, tying together the members of the ensemble. Some *Iqāᶜ* patterns are notated in Lesson One. Instructions on how to play the finger cymbals and the tambourines in order to obtain the dynamics and timbres are given in Lessons Two and Three.

Most Middle Eastern music is performed mezzo forte with little change in dynamics (except for the percussion instruments). With the impact of Western music, dynamic contrasts have been used in some musical styles.

A kaleidoscopic effect of timbres is always present in Middle Eastern ensemble music. Each instrument has its own timbre, and a good instrumentalist has at his command a vast array of tone colors idiosyncratic to the instrument. Singers also have a variety of timbres at their disposal. (One often hears about vocal timbre as being pure, rough, smooth, soft, metallic, nasal, humid, or dry.) Some vocal timbres are specific to certain regions—the Iranians, for instance, are famous for their *tahrīr*, a vocal trill akin to sobbing.

Middle Eastern ensemble music has a rich, heterophonic texture that is caused by the interaction of percussion and melody instruments, a vocalist, and often a chorus. Melody instruments accompany a highly ornamented vocal melody in unison or in octaves; each instrumentalist then ornaments the melody according to his own taste and the capabilities of the instrument. Performers on melody instruments use rhythmic and timbral ornamentations as well as a rich array of ornaments consisting of notes added to the original melody, the removal of notes (resulting in syncopation), the replacement of notes, turns, tremolo, and drones. The vocalist uses similar melodic and rhythmic ornamentation techniques.

One can often hear a thinner texture and a contrast when a dialogue occurs between instruments, between a vocalist and chorus, or between a vocalist and instruments. The heterophonic texture is most dense when the number of performers is large and when each performer ornaments the melody differently. Today, the trend is toward large ensembles that maintain little heterophony.

The most important form in Middle Eastern urban music was a compound form similar to a suite. It contained instrumental and vocal pieces, composed and improvised, which lasted for at least one hour. Often more than one suite was performed in an evening, and was called *nawbah* in North Africa, *waslah* in Egypt, and *fāsil* in the Levant and in Turkey. The suite underwent changes in the twentieth century and is now extinct in Egypt, although long multisectioned songs still exhibit many features of the suite.

The component parts of a suite are fashioned in one melodic mode with occasional brief modulations, although a variety of meters and some free rhythm sections are found. Thus, an essential feature of the Middle Eastern suite is modal unity and rhythmic diversity.

The suite often starts with an instrumental prelude followed by improvisations. A series of precomposed songs (often featuring an improvised dialogue between vocalist and chorus and interspersed with improvisations) then follows. The suite ends with a lively vocal or instrumental postlude. Today, the component parts of the suites are often played outside the context of the traditional form as self-contained pieces. Strophic, ABA, rondo, reverse rondo [known as *samāᶜī* or *bashraf* and has the form A (Refrain), B (Refrain), C (Refrain), D (Refrain)], and multisection are some of the forms of a Middle Eastern suite's component parts.

The following are common Middle Eastern improvisatory musical genres:

- *Taqsīm:* This is an unmeasured improvisation on a solo instrument in free rhythm with no regular pulse. This genre features the characteristics of a mode: tonal centers, cadential formulas, and melodic motives. Performers often modulate to neighboring modes. The *taqsīm*, usually unmeasured but occasionally measured, is often performed over an ostinato bass on a percussion or melody instrument.
- *Mawwāl, gazel, āvaz:* These are the Arabic, Turkish, and Persian vocal equivalents to instrumental improvisation. The vocalist improvises music to a poem and is accompanied by a melody instrument that closely follows the vocal melodic line. Between the vocal sections, the instrumentalist improvises interludes based on the preceding vocal cadence.
- *Layālī:* This is the Arabic equivalent to a *mawwāl* except that the vocalist improvises music to the simple words *Yā lēlī, yā ēnī* ("O my night, O my eye").

LESSON 1

■ Objectives

Students will:
1. Tap on a table or desk an assortment of rhythm patterns commonly heard in Middle Eastern music (a skill taught to classical singers to enable them to rhythmically guide their performance).
2. Produce particular timbres known as *dumm* (low) and *takk* (crisp).

■ Materials

1. Student's hand and table (or his or her own thigh)

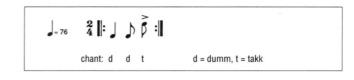

Figure 14. Īqāᶜ of Ayyūb el-Masrī

Figure 15. Iqāᶜ Saᶜīdī

Figure 16. Īqāᶜ Wahdah w Noss

Figure 17. Īqāᶜ Samāᶜī Thaqīl

■ Procedures

1. Explain the concept of rhythmic patterns and the role of percussion instruments as outlined in the beginning of this chapter. The low *dumm* and the crisp *takk* sounds are produced by the hand in the following manner: The *dumm* (the low resounding sound represented by a note with its stem up) is performed by striking a table, desk, or thigh with the palm and fingers extended flat in one plane. The *takk* is performed with the hand closed into a fist and by striking the table, desk, or thigh with the wrist, the first or second knuckles of the index, middle, ring, and little fingers, and all of the thumb. Students should follow the teacher, who may demonstrate the pattern first on his or her lap and then on a drum. The chanting of *"dumm"* and *"takk"* may enhance the learning and can later be said silently. Have the students try these rhythms:

    a. *Īqāᶜ of Ayyūb el-Masrī*—a pattern known as "Job the Egyptian," used in music to accompany therapeutic dances of women who are believed to be possessed (see figure 14).

    b. *Iqāᶜ Saᶜīdī*—used in the folk songs and dances of Upper (southern) Egypt (see figure 15).

    c. *Iqāᶜ Wahdah w Noss*—a very popular rhythmic pattern used in rural and urban music, songs, and dances (see figure 16).

    d. *Iqāᶜ Samāᶜī Thaqīl.* This is a rhythmic pattern used to accompany instrumental music known as *samāᶜī* and to accompany some *muwashshahāt* songs (see figure 17).

    Once students have maintained ease and facility in tapping these rhythms on desks, tables, or laps, they can transfer the rhythms to a drum.

L E S S O N   2

■ **Objectives**

Students will:

1. Perform the finger cymbal techniques and sounds that are often used by Middle Eastern dancers, folk ensemble instrumentalists, and urban music groups. The three basic sounds are derivatives of the two basic *dumm* and *takk* sounds explained in Lesson One. They increase students' awareness of the concepts of timbre and dynamics.

■ **Materials**

1. Provide two pairs of finger cymbals for each student. Use elastic to tie the cymbals to the thumb and middle fingers. Cut a piece 1 1/2" to 2" long (depending on finger size and student's comfort). Let the middle of the elastic go through the lower cymbal hole, and tie the two ends of the elastic on the inside of the cymbal.

■ **Procedures**

1. Students should wear one finger cymbal on the left-hand thumb, one on the right-hand thumb, one on the left-hand middle finger, and one on the right-hand middle finger. Adjust these so that the bottom of the thumb cymbal faces the bottom of the middle finger cymbal. Practice the following sounds separately with each hand:

    a. *Dumm.* With the bottoms of the thumb and middle finger cymbals in a parallel position, hit the thumb and the middle finger cymbals together. Release the cymbals immediately after striking (see figure 18). The sound should be bright and resounding.

    b. *Takk.* With the bottoms of the thumbs and middle finger cymbals in a parallel position, hit the thumb and middle finger cymbals together and *do not* release cymbals after striking (see figure 19).

    c. *Sakkah.* Two actions are required to obtain this sound: (1) placing the edge of the middle finger cymbals over the center of the thumb cymbal at a forty-five degree angle and (2) sliding the middle finger cymbal down over the thumb cymbal and toward the palm. Stop sliding when the two bottom flat surfaces meet, and do not release them (see figure 20). This sound is halfway between a *dumm* and a *takk* and is equivalent to the *sakkah* sound on a tambourine. It is represented by a note, stem down, and an arrow crossing through it (see figure 21).

2. After the students have practiced each sound and each hand separately, have the class play eighth- and sixteenth-note patterns, with alternative left-hand and right-hand strokes. Students should play each pattern, using only one type of sound—*dumm, takk,* or *sakkah.*

3. Using the finger cymbals, students perform the rhythms in Lesson One and experiment with the *dumm, takk,* and *sakkah* sounds.

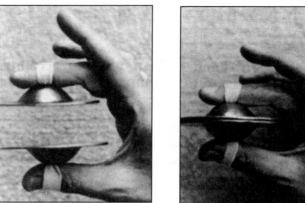

Figure 18. *Dumm*   Figure 19. *Takk*   Figure 20. *Sakkah*

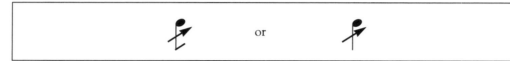

or

Figure 21. *Sakkah* note

LESSON 3

■ Objectives
Students will:
1. Hold the tambourine in a Middle Eastern fashion and produce particular sounds.

■ Materials
1. Large and small tambourines (avoid those with an inner wooden handle)

■ Procedures
1. Explain the role of percussion instruments in the Middle East. Stress that tambourine playing is a great art; in the case of the classical *riqq*, a bachelor's degree can be obtained in tambourine playing. Give students the following background information: Middle Eastern tambourines come in a large variety of sizes and are constructed of different materials. The *riqq*, the chief percussion instrument used in urban nineteenth- and twentieth-century music, has five sets of four brass jingles, and transparent Nile fish skin is used for its head. Its diameter is approximately eight inches. Large tambourines with jingles are made of goat or donkey skin and are known as *mazhar*. Tambourines without jingles are called *duff* or *tār*. Some *tār* have two buzzing metallic wires that are attached to the frame and buzz over the skin. Some tambourines also have small bells attached to the inside of the instrument. Large tambourines are used

in folk music and are now used increasingly in urban music. Conversely, the small tambourine is also used today in folk and urban music.

2. Divide the class into two groups; the first group plays the small tambourines, and the second group plays the large tambourines. After the techniques are well learned, switch the groups.

3. Using the following instructions, teach the following ways to play small and large tambourines:

Small tambourines (*riqq*)

Initial position. (See figures 22 and 23.)

Dumm sound. With a brisk wrist motion, strike the head of the tambourine just above the rim with the first knuckle of the right-hand index finger. Release immediately (see figure 24).

Takk sound. Strike one set of jingles with the ring finger of the right hand (see figure 25).

Sakkah sound. Keep the left hand in its initial position and strike the center of the tambourine with the first knuckles of both the right-hand thumb and index finger in a brisk wrist motion. Rest the fingers on the head after striking it (see figure 26).

Tremolo sound. Keeping the left hand in its initial position, place the middle and ring fingers of the right hand on the rim of the tambourine. With the left hand motionless, shake the tambourine with the right hand without removing it from its rim-resting position (see figure 27).

Large tambourines without jingles (*tār or duff*)

Initial position. (See figures 28 and 29.)

Dumm sound. Keeping the four fingers of the right hand close together, strike the rim of the tambourine and the head next to the rim with the first two or three knuckles. Release immediately (see figure 30).

Takk sound. Gently tap the head of the tambourine with the four protruding fingers of the left hand while keeping the fingers pressed on the head. The left-hand thumb is holding the instrument, so the *takk* sound will be faint (see figure 31). For a right-hand *takk*, hit the rim of the tambourine with the first knuckles of the middle and ring fingers. Stay on the rim or release immediately, depending on the desired sound.

Sakkah sound. The wrist of the right hand should be positioned above the head, halfway between the center and the rim. First, hit the tambourine with the wrist of the right hand, and then snap the head with all five fingers outstretched. Rest the fingers on the head after striking it (see figure 32).

4. Using the tambourines, have the class perform the rhythms of Lesson One. Ask the students to experiment with the *dumm, takk,* and *sakkah* sounds and to create their own rhythms.

Figure 22. Small tambourine:
initial position (front view)

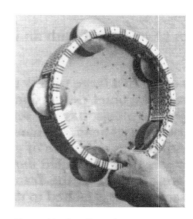

Figure 23. Small tambourine:
initial position (back view)

Figure 24. Dumm

Figure 25. Takk

Figure 26. Sakkah

Figure 27. Tremolo

Figure 28. Large tambourine: initial position (front view)

Figure 29. Large tambourine: initial position (back view)

Figure 30. Dumm

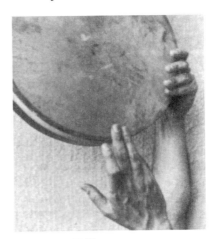

Figure 31. Takk

Figure 32. Sakkah

L E S S O N   4

■ **Objectives**

Students will:

1. Sing or play a short instrumental prelude written in the basic mode, *nahāwand*, and become familiar with the 1/2 tone, whole tone, and 1 1/2 tone.
2. Tap the rhythmic pattern as they hum the prelude.
3. Listen to the heterophonic layers of sound.

■ **Materials**

1. Any melody instrument can be used to perform the plain and ornamented melodies in this lesson. Students can use violins, recorders, piano, xylophones, or other available instruments, along with small tambourines, to mark the rhythmic pattern. Students may find singing on the vocable "ah" easier than playing on instruments, and they may internalize the sound more quickly.

■ **Procedures**

1. This music selection, which functions as a prelude to be performed at the beginning of a concert, is transcribed in two versions: plain and ornamented. Performing the ornamented version in figure 33 will depend on the students' ability to sing or to play the instruments and should be left to the discretion of the teacher. The ornamented version is only one of an infinite number of possible ornamentations, and it is given here to illustrate performance practice.
2. After students feel comfortable performing the melodies on their respective instruments, the teacher should use what he or she thinks is the easier selection and have the students hum it as they tap the rhythm pattern. Figure 34 shows older and more contemporary patterns.
3. If time permits:

   a. Select a few students to perform either rhythmic pattern on small tambourines.
   b. If the students are able to perform the prelude in its ornamented form, divide the class into three groups: (1) one performing the melody plain, (2) one performing the melody ornamented, and (3) one performing the rhythmic pattern on tambourines. Thus, students will be able to experience the heterophonic effect that is so prevalent in Middle Eastern ensemble music.
   c. The teacher can explain that these preludes were performed and repeated many times before the beginning of the vocal or instrumental suite.

4. For another project, choose a Western folk song. Ornament and perform it in Middle Eastern style.

Figure 33. Dūlāb in mode *nahāwand*

Figure 34. Older (left) and more contemporary (right) rhythm patterns

L E S S O N   5

■ Objectives

Students will:
1. Become familiar with a song composed in an unusual meter.
2. Develop skill in singing and tapping a rhythm pattern at the same time.
3. Learn the flowery language of a classical love song.
4. Experience one of the *muwashashah* song forms.

■ Materials

1. Any melody instrument such as a flute, recorder, guitar, violin, or piano
2. Tambourine (preferably small) with jingles

■ Procedures

1. Figure 35 is a *muwashashah*, a love song that is part of a suite. The text is flowery, and it combines the ideas of nature and the singer's beloved; he compares the lady to the stem of a flower. Students should read the Arabic text and the translation. Discuss the context of the song and emphasize the theme of love, the flowery language, and the comparison of nature and the singer's beloved.

   A translation of "Lammā Badā Yatathannà" ("When My Love Appeared Walking with a Swinging Gait") follows. The word *amān* in the text means "safety" or "protection." It is often used in love songs by the lover to ask for mercy and protection from the torments of love. The word "stem" refers to the stem of a flower, or in this context, to the beloved's body.

   Verse 1
   When my love appeared walking with a swinging gait (*Amān*)
   Her beauty infatuated me (*Amān*).

   Verse 2 [not sung]
   Her look and glance made me prisoner of love (*Amān*)
   Her stem bent when she leaned during the walk (*Amān*).

   Verse 3 [not sung]
   I am bewildered at an unfulfilled promise.
   Who can respond to my complaints
   About love and its torments
   Except my beautiful queen (*Amān*).

2. Have the students hum the melody.
3. Hum the melody and tap the rhythmic pattern in figure 36 together.
4. Sing the song, adding the words and continuing to tap the rhythm.
5. Add the rhythmic pattern on tambourines and the melody (in unison or octaves, played by any students who have melody instruments and sung by the remainder of the class).

Figure 35. "Lammā Badā Yatathannà"

Figure 36. "Lammā Badā Yatathannà" rhythm pattern

L E S S O N 6

■ **Objectives**

Students will:
1. Listen to the sounds of some Middle Eastern instruments.
2. Identify some Middle Eastern genres.

■ **Materials**

1. Film:
   Discovering the Music of the Middle East (see Filmography)
2. Publications:
   Refer to the articles by Pacholczyk, Racy, Feldman, and Zonis, along with Jenkins and Olsen's *Music and Musical Instruments in the World of Islam,* for photographs and descriptions of the instruments studied in this lesson (see Bibliography)
3. Recordings:
   Arab Music, Volume 1 (Lyrichord LLST 7186)
   Arab Music, Volume 2 (Lyrichord LLST 7198)
   Classical Music of Iran: Dastagh Systems, Volumes 1 & 2 (Folkways FW 8831 and FW 8832)
   Music in the World of Islam (Tangent TGS 131–136)
   Taqāsīm and Layālī: Cairo Tradition. Modal Music and Improvisations, VI-5, Unesco Collection, Musical Sources (Philips 6586010)
   Taqāsīm: Improvisations in Arab Music (Lyrichord LLST 7374)
   Tunisia. Volume I. The Classical Arab-Andalusian Music of Tunisia (Folkways FW 8861)
   Songs and Dances of Turkey (Folkways FW 8801)

■ **Procedures**

The instruments of Middle Eastern music are far too numerous to be covered in one class period. The teacher may choose to concentrate on one small geographical area and limit the instruments to one musical category (for example, urban or folk).

The following is an outline of such an approach, taking the *takht* ensemble as an example. The urban *takht* ensemble used in the nineteenth and early twentieth centuries consisted of a *qānūn,* ᶜ*ud, nāy, riqq,* and *kamanjah* (a spike fiddle that has been replaced by the Western violin). The *takht* later developed into a larger ensemble, with violins, cellos, accordions, electric organs, and guitars added to the Middle Eastern instruments. The *takht* in its nineteenth-century format survives in some Arab countries such as Syria and in conservatory-type concerts in Egypt.

The *qānūn* is a trapezoidal zither with twenty-six sets of triple strings; the three strings in each set are tuned in unison. The strings are made of nylon, metal, copper, or silver-wound silk. On the right-hand side, a nonmovable bridge rests on five rectangular pieces of Nile fish skin, giving the instrument its characteristic brilliant sound. On the left-hand side, six or more copper levers, built for each set of three strings, are raised or lowered to supply intervals ranging from a quarter tone to a full tone. The performer plucks each set of three strings simultaneously with water buffalo-horn picks attached to the two index fingers by means of silver or gold rings (see figure 37). The instrument has a range of three octaves plus a fifth. Play a recording of this instrument, using any of the examples from *Arab Music, Volume 1; Arab Music, Volume 2;* or *Taqāsīm and Layālī,* and show the class figure 38.

The ʿūd is a fretless lute that has five double strings tuned in fourths. The strings are made of gut, nylon, copper, or silver-wound silk. They are plucked with a water buffalo-horn pick. Play examples from *Arab Music, Volumes 1 and 2; Taqāsīm and Layālī;* or *Taqāsīm: Improvisations in Arab Music,* and show figure 39 to the class.

The *nāy* is a reed flute with seven holes that is obliquely end-blown. It has a range of almost three octaves. Play one of the examples from *Arab Music, Volumes 1 and 2* or *Taqāsīm and Layālī,* and show figure 40 to the class.

The *riqq* is a fish-skin tambourine with brass jingles. Play one of the examples from *Arab Music, Volume 2* or *Taqāsīm and Layālī.*

The *darabukkah,* not part of the *takht,* is occasionally used together with the *riqq.* It is a clay drum that has a Nile fish-skin head. Play the last selection on *Taqāsīm and Layālī,* and show figure 41.

Instruments of the *takht* are often used together with folk music instruments; for example, the ʿūd and the violin are used with *duff* and *salamiyyah* (folk flute, shown in figure 42). Play an example from *Arab Music, Volume 1.*

Examples of several important genres of Middle Eastern music (*taqāsīm, layālī,* and *mawwāl*) can be found in *Taqāsīm and Layālī.* Descriptions of these forms are found in the first section of this chapter. The measured *taqāsīm* can be found in *Arab Music, Volume 2* (side one, band three). Examples of a free rhythm *taqāsīm* can be found in *Taqāsīm: Improvisations in Arab Music.* Many *samāʿis* are recorded on *Arab Music, Volumes 1 and 2* and *Taqāsīm and Layālī.*

Integrating music with other subjects

Musical events in the Middle East are not abstract, fossilized activities; they are vibrant and functional, and they are used in specific contexts. Music accompanies every step of the human life cycle: birth, love, marriage, sickness, and death, to name a few. Each step of the life cycle has its repertoire of songs and often its own rhythmic pattern.

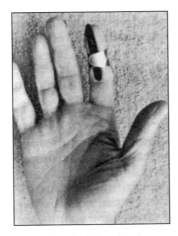

Figure 37. Pick for *qānūn*

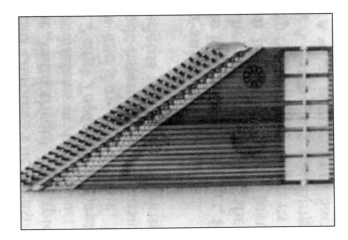

Figure 38. Qānūn

A person not watching an event can immediately tell from the rhythmic pattern what is going on. Sacred chants and hymns are essential to the prayers, services, and festivals of Judaism, Christianity, and Islam. These chants and hymns vary according to ethnicity as well as denomination. Work songs accompany and facilitate the activities of fishermen, farmers, bricklayers, and other workers. Urban concert-type music functions as entertainment and as an aesthetic and emotional expression that often leads to a state of trance. Songs effectively function as vehicles for protest against social and political oppression. On the other hand, rulers often use songs to enhance their status and validate their institutions.

Middle Eastern music and the visual arts are intimately related. Al-Fārabī (d. 950), a philosopher and music theorist, related plain melody and ornaments in music to similar constituents in the arts of textiles and architecture:

> Every melody consists of two types of notes [those that form the main melody and orna-mental tones. The first plays the role of the warp and woof in a cloth, the mud, bricks, and wood in buildings. The second plays the role of the carving, the engraving, the facili-ties, and the exteriors in buildings, and the dyes, smoothing, ornaments and fringes in the cloth.[5]

Illustrate ornamentation techniques by studying and performing the examples in Lesson Four. There is a strong connection between the concept of ornamentation in music and that in Arabic, Persian, and Ottoman Turkish calligraphy and paintings; in rugs, furniture, and objets d'art; and in jewelry and cosmetics (the word "mascara" is derived from Arabic).

Musical instruments are themselves works of art. They are ornamented with inlaid ivory and mother-of-pearl, as well as carved wood in floral, animal, and geometric designs not unlike the patterns used in Persian carpets and Islamic architecture.[6] The visual orna-ments on instruments have an obvious aesthetic function—to make the instrument look beautiful. They also function as a visual counterpart to the musical ornamentation, satis-

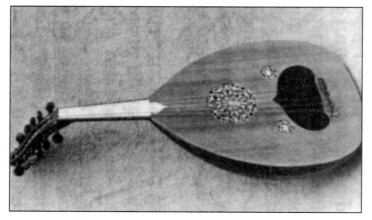

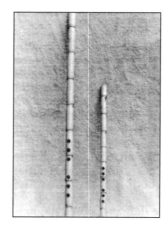

Figure 39. ᶜŪd

Figure 40. Nāy

fying both the aural and the visual senses.

Musical events, both sacred and secular, often include dancing. The type best known is what Westerners (not Easterners) have termed the "belly dance." This dance has been greatly popularized and grossly misrepresented (with coarse sexual connotations) in Hollywood movies, and is now extremely popular in North America, where schools have sprung up all over the continent. The music often borrows popular folk and urban melodies, adding to its own specific repertoire. In the Middle East, the so-called belly dance is not confined to night clubs, but is performed by men and women, youngsters, adults, and the aged, in urban as well as rural settings. In the words of the famous Egyptian dancer Suhayr Zakī, "Dancing is the body's way to smile."

NOTES

1. W. B. Fisher, "The Middle East and North Africa: An Introduction," in *The Middle East and North Africa 1987*, 33d ed. (London: Europa Publications, 1986), 12.
2. Fisher, 12.
3. See J. R. Hayes, ed., *The Genius of Arab Civilization: Source of the Renaissance*, 2d ed. (Cambridge, MA: MIT Press), 1983.
4. A flat sign with a slash through the stem, as shown in figure 1, indicates a note that is lowered by approximately 1/4 tone. A sharp sign with only one vertical line is used to indicate a note that is raised by 1/4 tone.
5. George D. Sawa, "The Survival of Some Aspects of Medieval Arabic Performance Practice," *Ethnomusicology* 25, no. 1 (1981): 80.
6. See Jean Jenkins and Poul Rovsing Olsen, *Music and Musical Instruments in the World of Islam* (London: World of Islam Festival Publishing, 1976), 34–35, 48, 81, and 84. Photographs are found on pages 84 and 85.

Figure 41. Darabukkah

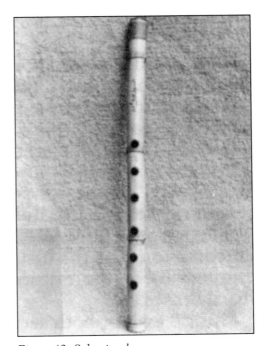

Figure 42. Salamiyyah

JEWISH MUSIC IN ISRAEL

by Rita Klinger

In 1948, the tiny mass of land extending 260 miles from the southern port city of Eilat on the Gulf of Aqaba to the northern town of Kiryat Shmona became the State of Israel. Including the occupied West Bank, the inland territory is a mere sixty miles wide. Israel has a varied geography for such a country that is only slightly larger than the state of New Jersey. From the desert of the southern part of the country, it is a brief drive north to the mountains. The Dead Sea, the world's lowest elevation, is only an hour away from the beaches of the Mediterranean.

Jerusalem is the capital and largest city in Israel, closely followed in size by Tel Aviv and Haifa.[1] Over 90 percent of the population live in urban centers. Rural settlers often farm cooperatively on communal settlements called kibbutzim.

Of the almost 5.5 million residents of the tiny country known as Israel, almost 4.5 million are Jews with ethnic roots from all over the world. Jews immigrate to Israel each year by the thousands. In 1994, eighty thousand Jews immigrated to Israel, mostly from the countries of the former Soviet Union. In addition to Soviet Jews, the past several decades have also seen newcomers to Israel from countries as diverse as Ethiopia, Yemen, Iran, Iraq, Morocco, and Tunisia as well as European nations such as Germany, Poland, Hungary, Romania, and the former Yugoslavia. There are so many ethnic groups in Israel that there is not a single ethnic group that makes up more than one-seventh of the total Jewish population of the country. This makes Israel one of the most rapidly formed multicultural societies in the world today. Of the recent immigrants to Israel, Jews from the former Soviet Union represent the single largest wave. Russian Jews are likely to soon become the largest ethnic grouping in the country. The Jewish population of Israel is often categorized in one of the three groups shown in figure 43.

Each immigrant group to Israel brought with it a distinct musical culture consisting of songs of the motherland as well as regional Jewish folk and liturgical music. The Jews of Europe primarily brought Russian, German, Hungarian, and Polish folk melodies along with liturgical songs of the Ashkenazim (European Jewry) and Yiddish (a language combining Middle German, Slavic, and Hebrew, written in Hebrew characters) folk melodies. European Jewry also brought Western European art music to Israel. Symphony musicians, primarily string players, and their instruments arrived along with opera singers, conductors, and composers. North African Jews also brought a variety of musical styles, including the highly ornamented wedding songs from Yemen and traditional music of Morocco and Tunisia. Large numbers of Persian, Iraqi, and Kurdistani Jews also brought both the religious and secular music of their regions. The Jews of Sephardic (Spanish-Jewish) descent add yet another musical flavor to the pot with romances and folk songs sung in Ladino (a Spanish-Jewish language, written in Hebrew characters).

The music of Oriental and Sephardic Jewish immigrants, while reflecting a variety of cultural characteristics, shared several common features: the traditional music was primarily transmitted orally through immersion in the culture, a religious repertoire existed with Hebrew texts in common, and there was a predominance of vocal music over instrumental music. The sacred and traditional music of the European Jewish communities also shared common Hebrew texts and was learned primarily through oral transmission, but there was one important distinction: Western notation was common and readily accessible for preservation and study of songs.

Musical diversity is a reflection of the diversity of ethnicities in Israel. The Jews of Israel can be categorized as belonging to one of the following three groups:

Ashkenazim (Eastern European ancestry)

Poland, Romania, Hungary, Germany, Austria, sections of the former Soviet Union

Sephardim (Spanish-Portuguese ancestry)

Spain, Morocco, Tunisia, Egypt, Turkey, Greece, Italy, and the Balkan countries

Oriental

Yemen, Iraq, Persia (Iran), Kurdistan, Central Asia (Bukhara), and Ethiopia

Immigrants to Israel from the United States, England, and South Africa are usually Ashkenazim, while immigrants from South American countries such as Brazil and Argentina are often either Ashkenazim or Sephardim.

Figure 43. Jewish population groups in Israel

Although there is much crossover between sacred and secular melodies, melodies that are intended to be liturgical are more likely to be somewhat improvised and highly embellished. This practice can be traced back to biblical times when the Levites (musicians of the ancient Temple, circa 955 to 586 B.C.E.) were responsible for teaching the congregation both responsorial prayers and biblical cantillations (tropes). This was accomplished by rote with the aid of hand signs that corresponded to musical patterns. This system, called Chirnomy, was later put to parchment in an iconic fashion, becoming the basis for Western notation as it is known today. These trope symbols, standardized between 500 and 800 C.E., also evolved to a form of notation called *te'amim*, which indicates the agogic accents (those constructed by duration) of words and melodies to which a biblical phrase is sung. Since the *te'amim* serves mainly as reminders, the element of oral transmission through rote learning is still predominant. The use of *te'amim* provides for and encourages embellishment and improvisation. Many changes have necessarily occurred in musical cantillations due to environmental changes and migration patterns of the Jews. Yet this form of notation is unique not to a specific geographic region but rather to the Jewish people, because it is used only with Hebrew text.

Song is the essence of all traditional Jewish music, be it Ashkenazic, Oriental, or Sephardic. In Ashkenazic and Oriental households alike, birth, circumcision, bar mitzvah, marriage, and death are celebrated through song. The Sabbath is welcomed, celebrated, and ushered out in song. There are songs to celebrate every holiday of the year, both sacred and secular. The songs of different communities may sound different, but the underlying spiritual associations with each event are the same, as is the Hebrew text.

Musical characteristics

The multicultural nature of Israel makes it difficult to delineate the country's musical characteristics. "Israeli music" is no easier to define than "American music." It is important to note, however, that it was the official position of the European founding fathers of Israel to discard their ethnic roots as quickly as possible in order to create a new, unified Israeli society. A history of religious persecution and the scars of the Holocaust greatly influenced this attitude. A new cultural identity was almost imposed on early immigrants to Israel, regardless of their country of origin. To this end, it was a policy of the government to promote the ideals of the new state by setting familiar tunes to newly composed Hebrew texts. Early song collections included Russian, German, Yiddish, and Yemenite melodies with the words of famous poets or Biblical passages serving as texts. The practice of setting new texts to familiar melodies is still widespread in Israel and involves a mixture of many elements. Secular words are often set to previously designated liturgical melodies; liturgical texts are commonly sung to secular melodies; and children's singing games, songs, and chants are sung to the tunes of parents and grandparents.

In the early days of the state of Israel, singing and dancing became popular forms of recreation in both the cities and on the communal farming settlements (kibbutzim). The Balkan folk dance, called the "hora," was brought to Israel by these early settlers and became the national symbol of dance. Lively accordion accompaniments full of rich harmonies made this style somewhat different than that of the melancholic melodies of Eastern European Jewry.

Sacred and secular vocal music and instrumental music from each ethnic group that immigrated to Israel exist side by side with preexisting regional music, new folk music that has evolved over a relatively short period of time, and contemporary art music of native composers. These various cultural components have mingled and, in many cases, have merged to form the music that is distinctly Israeli. Some popular performers today, like Ofra Haza and Ethnix, intentionally use musical elements of their ancestry to form contemporary Israeli sounds. (See figure 44 for the names of popular performing artists representing a variety of ethnic styles.)

Although music in Israel varies widely, there are some common musical characteristics (see figure 45). Melodically, Israeli music may be major, minor, or modal. Liturgical music tends to have more use of melisma than secular music. Most music is in either duple or triple meter with a simple, repetitive form. While there is very little use of metrical asymmetry in secular music, much nonmetered sacred music exists. Syncopation and dotted rhythms are common, particularly in folk dance. While sacred music is usually unaccompanied, secular music may be accompanied by instruments such as the accordion, guitar, drums, or flute. Although vocal timbres vary depending on the ethnic influence, there tends to be a preference for guttural, throaty tones. This natural reflection of the Hebrew language is most pronounced in children's music. Like most music of the region, dynamics are important primarily in composed music.

NOTE

1. Israel proclaimed Jerusalem its capital in 1950, but the United States, like nearly all nations, does not recognize this status and maintains its embassy in Tel Aviv.

Pop/Rock/Ethnic	Ethnix, Ofra Haza, Aric Einstein, Halonot G'vohot, Shlomo Artzi
Folk/Folk-pop	Ester Ofarim, Yehoram Gaon, Ilanit, Shlomo Artzi, Chava Alberstien, Naomi Shemer
Ladino/Sephardic	The Parvarim, Flory Jagoda, Judy Frankel, Nico Castel
Klezmor	Brave New World, Giora Friedman, Klezmorim
Ashkenazic Cantorial	Jan Peerce, Richard Tucker
Yiddish	Ruth Rubin, Theodore Bikel, Barry Sisters, Deborah Eisenstein
Children's Songs	Ester Ofarim, Chava Alberstien, and American artists such as Fran Avni and Debbie Friedman

Figure 44. Popular performing artists

Rhythm	simple/syncopated/accented
Meter	mainly simple/duple
Melody	diatonic/modal melisma (liturgical music)
Timbre/Vocal Production	nasal/guttural/chest
Texture	mainly monophonic
Instruments	*tof* (drum), accordion, and *halil* (flute); and all Western orchestral instruments
Influences	Eastern Europe, Middle East, North Africa

Figure 45. Characteristics of Israeli music

L E S S O N   1

■ **Objectives**

Students will:
1. Clap rhythm patterns containing sixteenth notes.
2. Sing the song "Hava Netse Bemachōl."
3. Learn an accompanying folk dance (hora).

■ **Materials**

1. Space for movement
2. Recording: "Hava Netse Bemachōl," from *Songs of the Sabras* (Vanguard Classics VRS 9069)
3. "Hava Netse Bemachōl"

■ **Procedures**

1. This lesson is intended for children in grades 4 through 8. Have the children echo clap (or read from the chalkboard, if they are able) four-beat patterns of rhythm that include sixteenth notes such as those found in figure 46. End by having the children clap the predominant rhythm in "Hava Netse Bemachōl," as shown in figure 47.
2. Sing "Hava Netse Bemachōl" for the children (see figure 48). (The song is pronounced *hah-vah neh-tsay beh-mah-chohl*. The "ch" represents a guttural sound, similar to the correct pronunciation of "ch" in Bach's name.) The song title means "Let Us Go Out and Dance." Ask the students to listen for this dotted rhythm at the beginning of each four-beat pattern. Have them listen for the number of times the rhythm pattern is repeated in the song, and then sing it again. Ask the children if the words are the same for each of the patterns (the words are basically the same for each four-beat pattern; the word *machōlōt* is the plural form of *machōl*). Point out the subtle differences. Have the children repeat the words after you and then sing each phrase of the song.
3. Teach the basic four-beat "grapevine" step of the dance:

Moving to the left
Beat one: Cross the right foot in front of the left.
Beat two: Bring the left foot out from behind.
Beat three: Cross the right foot behind the left.
Beat four: Bring the left foot back to the side.

Moving to the right
Beat one: Cross the left foot in front of the right.
Beat two: Bring the right foot out from behind.
Beat three: Cross the left foot behind the right.
Beat four: Bring the right foot back to the side.

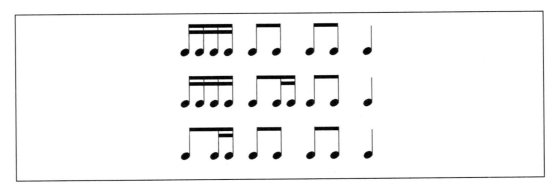

Figure 46. Four-beat pattern with sixteenth notes

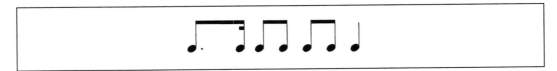

Figure 47. Predominant rhythm in "Hava Netse Bemachōl"

Figure 48. "Hava Netse Bemachōl"

4. Teach the dance:
   - Join hands in a circle and move to the left for four patterns of grapevine steps (sixteen beats).
   - Move to the right by reversing the grapevine for the next sixteen beats.
   - Walk to the center of the circle with arms extending upward for eight beats; then walk back with arms down for eight beats. Repeat this.
5. Listen to the recording and perform the dance. When the words are secure, have the children sing while they dance.

Extension of Lesson One (for older children)

1. Play an ear training game with the class: Have the students identify half steps or whole steps that you play or sing for them. Then have the children listen to and identify major and minor scale forms and identify where the half steps fall in each case. Play or sing the notes found in "Hava Netse Bemachōl" from lowest to highest, noting that this scale begins with a half step. Finally, notate and have the children find the half steps to the corresponding mode, the *maqām hijāz* (see figure 10).

L E S S O N   2

■ **Objectives**

Students will:
1. Sing and play an Israeli song and an American song about a snail.
2. Clap rhythmic patterns of quarter notes and eighth notes contained in both songs.

■ **Materials**

1. Recording: *The Sounds of Jerusalem* (Folkways FW 8552) (side 1, band 3)
2. "Bereleh" and "Snail"
3. Chalkboard

Figure 49. "Snail"

■ Procedures

1. This lesson is intended for students in grades 1–3. Play and sing "Snail" (see figure 49) with the children. Lead the children in winding up "like a snail" as they sing (you and the children wind up into a tight spiral).
2. Have the children clap the rhythm notation (see figure 50) written on the chalkboard while they sing the song.
3. Clap the first eight beats of "Bereleh" (see figure 51) while the children look at the rhythmic notation for "Snail." Have the children identify and mark the changed rhythms (see figure 52).
4. Dictate the next eight beats to complete the song, as shown in figure 53.
5. Sing the new song this rhythm creates for the children ("Bereleh").
6. Have the children each extend one hand, palm up. Walk around the room as you sing the song to the children and "draw" a snail (circular motion on the palm) on some of the children's palms. This "tickle" is the action of the game as it is used in Israel. Repeat this so that the children have several opportunities to hear the song.
7. Have the children say, then sing, the words after you:

   Pronunciation: Beh-reh-leh, Beh-reh-leh, tsay ah-choo-tsah
                            Ah-bah veh-ee-mah eek-noo leh-chah oo-gah.

   Translation: Little Snail, Little Snail, come outside
                            Daddy and Mommy will buy you cake.

8. Have the children find partners and take turns drawing the snail on each other's palms while they sing.

Extensions of Lesson Two

1. Have the children note that the rhythm notation for "Bereleh" is twice that for "Snail."
2. Play the wind-up game while alternately singing "Snail" and "Bereleh." Have the children decide on tempo changes.
3. For children who are learning notation, discuss or discover the range and/or number of different notes in each of the snail songs.
4. Have the children listen to the chant "Shirley Temple" on the recording *Sounds of Jerusalem*. Can they recognize the same melody as "Bereleh" with different words? To the children in Israel, this is the basic chant of childhood.

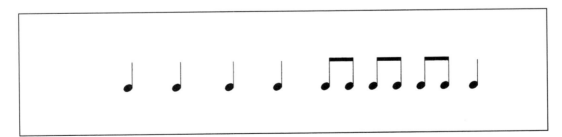

Figure 50. Rhythm notation for "Snail"

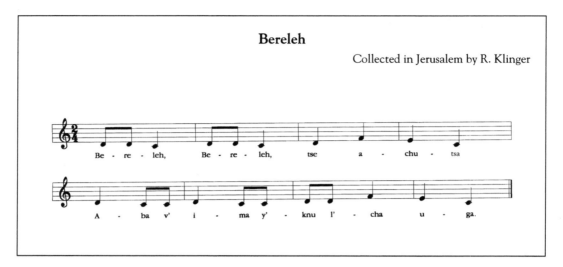

Figure 51. "Bereleh"

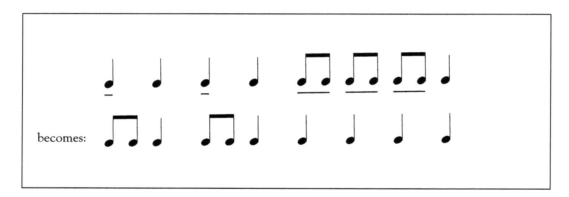

Figure 52. Changed rhythms

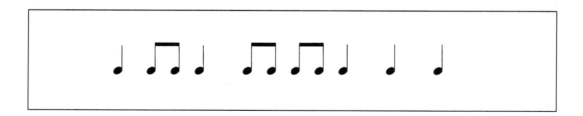

Figure 53. Beats that complete the song "Bereleh"

LESSON 3

■ **Objectives**

Students will:
1. Sing the song "Ha Rakevet."
2. Play the singing game.

■ **Materials**

1. Space for movement
2. "Ha Rakevet"

■ **Procedures**

1. This lesson is intended for children in grades K–3. Tell the children that the Hebrew word for train is "rakevet" (pronounced rah-keh-vet). Sing "Ha Rakevet" to the children (see figure 54), asking them to raise their hands when they hear the word. Repeat the song, asking the class to listen for the Hebrew word for "children" (yeh-leh-deem):

   Pronunciation:

   Ben hah-reem oo-ben slah-eem
   Tah-sah hah-rah-keh-vet
   Oo-mee-chohl hah-yeh-leh-deem
   Oh-tach ah-nee oh-heh-vet

   Translation:

   Between mountains and rocks
   Travels the train
   And of all the children,
   You are the one I love!

2. Tell the children that this is a game about a train that Israeli children play. In the game, a train travels between mountains and rocks and finally chooses someone to be the next train.

3. Have the children sing after you, one four-beat phrase at a time. Repeat each phrase as necessary. Although this may take several repetitions, don't worry if the children don't catch all of the words this time. Try not to perfect the pronunciation. It is more appropriate for them to enjoy the action of the game.

4. Have the children join hands in a circle. Sing the song again for the children, demonstrating the game by being the first "train." The children raise their arms to form "mountains" through which the train will weave during the first half of the song. On the words "otach ani ohevet," the train must choose someone. During the refrain, the train dances with his or her partner in the middle of the circle, while the rest of the children clap to the beat. The children raise their arms again for the new "train" to pass through for each repetition of the game.

Extensions of Lesson Three

1. Younger children can compare the Israel train songs to other songs about trains, such as "Little Red Caboose" or "Train Is a Comin'."
2. Older children can find the syncopated rhythm in the refrain.

Figure 54. "Ha Rakevet"

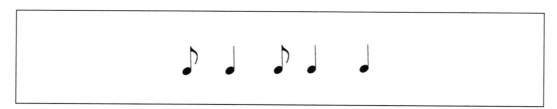

Figure 55. Pattern 1

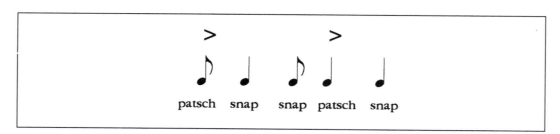

Figure 56. Pattern 2

L E S S O N   4

■ Objectives
Students will:
1. Sing the song "Et Dodim."
2. Sing the song while performing a rhythmic ostinato.

■ Materials
1. Hand drums, tambourines, and finger cymbals
2. "Et Dodim"
3. Overhead projector and transparency

■ Procedures
1. This lesson is intended for students in grades 4–6. Have the children echo clap or compose a variety of four-beat patterns containing syncopations.
2. Have the children perform the ostinato pattern found in figure 55. Practice playing the pattern by placing an accent on different notes. End by accenting the first eighth note and second quarter note of the pattern. The children may play the pattern the way it appears in figure 56.
3. Sing "Et Dodim" (see figure 57) for the children while they softly repeat the ostinato pattern.
4. Have the children repeat the words and then sing the song after you (it may be helpful to show this song on an overhead projector):

Pronunciation:	*Translation:*
Eht doh-deem kah-lah	Now is the time for love, my bride;
Boh-ee leh-gah-nee	Come to my garden,
Pah-reh-chah hah-geh-fen	The vine is blooming,
Heh-neh-tsoo ree-moh-neem.	The pomegranate budding.

5. Transfer the pattern to hand drum and finger cymbals (students may want to compare it to the *Iqāᶜ Wahdah w Noss* shown in figure 16). Invite a student to play the accented rhythms on a tambourine, while another student plays the unaccented rhythms on the finger cymbal. A third student may keep a steady beat on the hand drum.
6. Have the children sing the song as they take turns playing the ostinato on these or other classroom instruments.

Extension of Lesson Four
1. Have the children compose a variety of four-beat patterns that may be used to accompany this song. Let the children take turns using a hand drum, finger cymbals, tambourine, or other classroom instruments to play the patterns they create while singing the song.

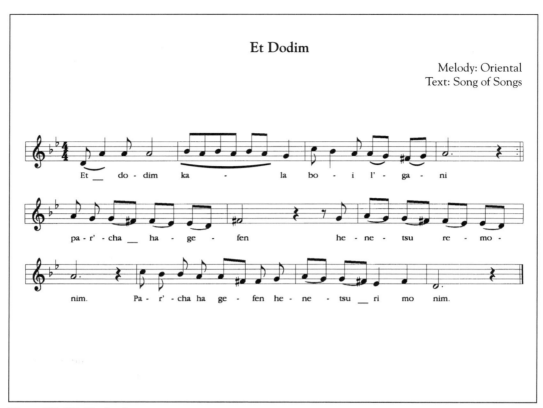

Figure 57. "Et Dodim"

THE ARAB MIDDLE EAST

BIBLIOGRAPHY

Browning, Robert H. *Maqām: Music of the Islamic World and Its Influences.* New York: Athens Printing Company, 1984. This book contains concise articles on the music of the Arab world, Morocco, Iran, Turkey, Central Asia, Kashmir, and Judaic Spain. It also includes a useful bibliography and discography and a useful section on musical instruments.

Feldman, Walter Z. "Ottoman Turkish Music." In *Maqām: Music of the Islamic World and Its Influences,* edited by R. H. Browning, 21–24. New York: Athens Printing Company, 1984. This article provides the cultural background of Ottoman Turkish music, its theory and practice, forms, and instruments.

Hayes, J. R., ed. *The Genius of Arab Civilization: Source of the Renaissance.* 2d ed. Cambridge, MA: MIT Press, 1983. This book contains an excellent collection of essays in which the authors describe the achievements of the Middle Eastern people in literature, philosophy and history, architecture and art, music, the exact sciences, the life sciences, mechanical technology, and trade and commerce. It is a useful introduction as well as a guide to the film *The Gift of Islam* (see Filmography).

Jenkins, Jean, and Poul Rovsing Olsen. *Music and Musical Instruments in the World of Islam.* London: World of Islam Festival Publishing, 1976. This book contains excellent drawings and photographs of instruments, as well as photographs of instrumentalists in the playing positions used in the world of Islam (Middle East and beyond to Islamic Africa and Southeast Asia). It also contains a section on Islamic influences on the music of the world. This is an excellent handbook that should be used in conjunction with its six albums (see Discography, *Music in the World of Islam*).

Pacholczyk, Josef M. "Secular Classical Music in the Arabic Near East." In *Musics of Many Cultures: An Introduction,* edited by Elizabeth May, 253–68. Berkeley: University of California Press, 1980. This article is a brief sketch of the history of the Middle East (as well as North Africa) from the rise of Islam. It provides a profile of current artistic music as a descendant of the court music traditions in the Islamic empire. The article also provides a discussion of the history of music theory (including the legacy of ancient Greek theory), musical forms, and instruments. It contains a glossary, a bibliography, a discography, and a filmography.

Racy, Ali Jihad. "Music." In *The Genius of Arab Civilization: Source of the Renaissance.* 2d ed., edited by J. R. Hayes, 121–45. Cambridge, MA: MIT Press, 1983. The author emphasizes both the unity and diversity of Arabic music, from the Atlas mountains in Morocco to the Arabian Gulf, and explains the five processes that have shaped Arabic music, from the rise of Islam in the seventh century until the modern era. The article includes a list of the most important modes (rhythmic and melodic), genres, and forms, as well as a useful section on musical instruments.

Sawa, George Dimitri. "The Survival of Some Aspects of Medieval Arabic Performance Practice." *Ethnomusicology* 25, no. 1 (1981): 73–86. The author traces some rhythmic and melodic ornamental techniques used in contemporary Arabic music (shown in transcriptions in this chapter) to a tenth-century source on musical practices in Middle Eastern courts.

Zonis, Ella. "Classical Iranian Music." In *Musics of Many Cultures: An Introduction.* Edited by Elizabeth May, 269–83. Berkeley: University of California Press, 1980. This article includes a discussion of the context of performance of classical Iranian music, its theory, and its improvisation principles. The article contains excellent photographs that show instrumentalists in playing positions, a glossary, a bibliography, and a discography. There are minor inaccuracies in the medieval sections; for example, Islamic medieval treatises are not solely modeled after the Greeks, and Islamic disapproval of the practice of music is in fact theoretical.

DISCOGRAPHY

Arab Music, Vol. 1. Lyrichord LLST 7186. Side one, bands one to four are Upper Egyptian folk songs sung by a female soloist and a chorus. The accompanying ensemble has folk instruments such as the *duff* and *salamiyyah* (folk flute) as well as urban instruments (ᶜ*ud* and violins). These selections are interesting because they show the breakdown of the categories of folk instruments and urban instruments and illustrate the role of instrumental music. In addition, side one, band two illustrates an improvised dialogue between the vocalist and the ensemble. Side one, band five contains a *samāᶜī* in the major mode, played on the *qānūn*, and shows the Western influence of harmonies in thirds. Side two contains some important instrumental genres, namely one *samāᶜī* and improvisations. Side two, bands three and four contain superb *taqsīm* on the *nāy* (*maqām bayātī, sabā*) and ᶜ*ud* (*maqām bayātī*). Side two, band two is a *taqsīm* on the *qānūn* in *maqām hijāzkār* that shows the Western influence of triads and arpeggios. The information on the record jacket is, however, unreliable.

Arab Music, Vol. 2. Lyrichord LLST 7198. Side one, bands one, two, and four are *samāᶜi*. Band one, an Ottoman selection played on the *qānūn*, is in the *maqām shadd-Caraban* (a transposition of *hijāzkār*). Band two, played by a classical ensemble (ᶜ*ud, qānūn, nāy, riqq*) is in *maqam* *bayati* and is incomplete. Band four, played by the ᶜ*ud*, is in *maqām nahawand*; the last section before the refrain is in 3/8 meter. Band three is in an instrumental genre in which instruments perform measured improvisations on rhythmic patterns played by a *riqq*. Side two, bands one and two are Western-influenced examples of the *qānūn*, in the major and minor modes respectively. Side two, band three is in *maqām saba*, played on the ᶜ*ud*, *nāy*, *qānūn*, *and riqq*, and contains a folk song and *nāy* improvisations. Side two, band four contains improvisations for *qānūn* (in a modern style) and *nāy*. The information on the record jacket is unreliable.

Classical Music of Iran: Dastagh Systems, Vols. 1 and 2. Folkways FW 8831 and FW 8832. This useful set illustrates the modal system of classical Persian music. Because of space limitations, the *dastgahs* are short. The two records include classical instruments and vocal renditions of classical Persian poems.

Music in the World of Islam. Tangent Records TGS 131–136. This set of six records is a good representation of music from Morocco in the West to Indonesia in the East. The records are divided into six areas: the voice, lutes, strings, flutes and trumpets, reeds and bagpipes, and drums and rhythms. The set should be used with its accompanying handbook, *Music and Musical Instruments in the World of Islam.* The records and the handbook are an excellent pedagogical tool.

Songs and Dances of Turkey. Folkways FW 8801. The record includes a variety of folk instruments and folk styles from many regions of Turkey. There is also military music, and side two, bands one and two are excellent examples of the highly refined art of Turkish music.

Taqāsīm and Lāyalī, Cairo Tradition: Modal Music and Improvisations, V1–5. Unesco Collection. Musical Sources. Phillips 6586010. Side one, band one illustrates two widespread and related vocal genres, the *lāyalī* and *mawwal*. The vocalist is closely followed by the *qānūn* accompanist and improvises in *maqām bayati* and related modes. Side one, band two illustrates both free rhythm and measured *taqāsīm* on the *nāy*, and side one, band three is an excellent example of a *samaᶜi* performed by a *takht* (an instrumental ensemble made up of *qānūn*, ᶜ*ud*, *nāy*, *riqq*). Side two includes two *taqāsīm* and an out-of-context though very useful *darabukkah* (drum) solo that demonstrates variations of the following meters: 10/8, 3/4, 7/8, 9/8, 13/4, and 16/8, as well as an improvisation.

Taqāsīm: Improvisation in Arab Music. Lyrichord LLST 7374. This record contains three *taqāsīms* in *kurd*, *nahawand*, and *bayati* with artful modulations to related *maqāms*. The record features Simon Shaheen on the ᶜ*ud* and Ali Jihad Racy on the *buzuq*, both acknowledged virtuosos on their instruments. The record jacket notes are excellent.

Tunisia, Vol. 1, The Classical Arab-Andalusian Music of Tunisia. Folkways FW 8861. Side one contains instrumental genres known as *bashraf* and *taqāsīm*. (The *nāy taqāsīm* is recorded at the wrong speed; it should be slower.) Side two contains *taqāsīm*, as well as a very important (though short) example of a *nawba*, the North African-type suite.

FILMOGRAPHY

Editor's note: The information about the films listed below is derived from data presented in *The World of Islam, Images and Echoes: A Critical Guide to Films and Recordings*, general editor, Ellen Fairbanks-Bodman. Islamic Teaching Materials Project, Unit #7. New York: American Council of Learned Societies, 1980. This book is highly recommended for follow-up and long-term activities requiring additional films and recordings. The publisher's address is American Council of Learned Societies, 228 East Forty-Fifth Street, Sixteenth Floor, New York, NY 10017.

Afghanistan. 15 minutes. ACI Films, 1972. This film offers a panorama of daily life in the villages and in the capital (Kabul), for example, bazaars, cooking, weaving, farms, mosques, and monuments. There is also a musical performance. It can be obtained from AIMS, 626 Justin Street, Glendale, CA 91201; phone: 213-240-9300.

Arabesque. 7 minutes. John Whitney. 1976. In this film, a computer program uses the notes C, D, and E to produce color image graphics that evolve from random arabesques to patterns reminiscent of formal Persian designs. It could be used to show the connection between music and Middle Eastern art and architecture. Contact Pyramid Films, PO Box 1048, Santa Monica, CA 90406; phone: 213-828-7577.

Discovering the Music of the Middle East. 21 minutes. Bernard Wilets. In *Discovering Music Series*, 1968. Although the studio-produced demonstrations of traditional instruments and dances are out of context, this film is a useful tool that enables the student to watch the instruments being performed and to acquire further understanding of the concept of music ornamentation. It can be obtained from West Music, 1208 Fifth Street, Coralville, IA 52241; phone: 800-397-9378.

An Egyptian Village—Gueziret Eldahab. 18 minutes. Goudsou Films, 1960. Stressing the theme of the unchanging nature of peasants in rural Egypt, this short film portrays aspects of life in an Egyptian village, for example, streets, mosques, irrigation, harvest, brickmaking, wedding rites, and rituals. It can be obtained from BFA Educational Media, 2211 Michigan Avenue, Dept. 7002-A, PO Box 1795, Santa Monica, CA 90406; phone: 213-829-2901.

The Gift of Islam. 28 minutes. Ray Graham, n.d. This cinematographic gem introduces the great cultural achievements of the Islamic world to the West in the fields of architecture, engineering, navigation, geography, mathematics, astronomy, medicine, horticulture, crafts, metallurgy, calligraphy, literature, music, and philosophy. This film can be used as a companion to *The Genius of Arab Civilization: Source of Renaissance*, edited by J. R. Hayes (see Bibliography). It can be obtained from Graham Associates, 1899 L Street NW, Washington, DC 20036; phone: 202-833-9657.

In Arab Lands: An Age of Change. 28 minutes. Sunset Films, 1979. The theme is the challenge of and response to change in the traditionalist societies of the Arab Gulf States. With the coming of oil and modern technology, people now subjugate the land and plan their future. The film addresses modern problems such as the status of women as well as the role of television. Contact Bechtel Power Corporation, Public Relations, 50 Beale Street, San Francisco, CA 94105; phone: 415-768-4596.

Journey to the West (Rihlah ila Gharb). 30 minutes. Don Dixon, Middle East Education Trust, 1978. This film is about Muslim and Christian Arabs, those who are newly arrived as well as those well established in the United States. It shows scenes of intercultural studies, maintenance of Arab cultural traditions, and the diversity of occupations and worship in localities such as Brooklyn, Detroit, Houston, and Washington, D.C. It is an adequate production with an overall emphasis on Arab participation in the fulfillment of the American dream. It can be obtained from James D. Johnstone, Route 4, Box 169, Charlottesville, VA 22901; phone: 703-973-5726.

Mideast: Land and the People. 20 minutes. Vocational and Industrial Films, 1977. The film emphasizes regional diversity. Arabs, Iranians, and Turks are presented as the three main peoples with a careful explanation of their linguistic, ethnic, and cultural differences. It juxtaposes the traditional and the modern in various settings—urban, villages, and nomad; barren mountain plateaus; lush farmlands; and arid deserts. The film, however, ignores the multitude of ethnic minorities. The film can be obtained from BFA Educational Media, 2211 Michigan Avenue, Department 7002-A, PO Box 1795, Santa Monica, CA 90406; phone: 213-829-2901.

Rivers of Time. 25 minutes. Contemporary Films, 1962. Artifacts, paintings, sculptures, and models of ancient cities from museums in Baghdad (and other cities) are used to illustrate aspects of Sumerian, Chaldean, and Babylonian life. Current use of ancient ways (for example, methods of irrigation) is shown in contemporary scenes. The film also focuses on ideas and techniques that were introduced by the Arabs and spread throughout the Mediterranean. The film is a good didactic mixture of artifacts and film footage of the Tigris and Euphrates valleys of Iraq. It can be obtained from McGraw-Hill Films, 1221 Avenue of the Americas, New York, NY 10020; phone: 212-997-1221, or from CRM, 110 Fifteenth Street, Del Mar, CA 92014; phone: 714-453-5000.

JEWISH MUSIC IN ISRAEL

BIBLIOGRAPHY

Binder, Abraham Wolf. *Studies in Jewish Music: Collected Writings of A.W. Binder*. New York: Bloch Publishing Co., 1971.

Bohlman, Philip. *"The Land Where Two Streams Flowed": Music in the German Jewish Community of Israel*. Urbana and Chicago: University of Illinois Press, 1989.

Bohlman, Philip V. and Slobin, Mark, eds. "Music in the Ethnic Communities of Israel." Special issue of *Asian Music* 17, no. 2 (1986).

Collin, Rachel. *New Music in Israel, 1983–1985*. Tel Aviv, Israel: Israel Composers' League, 1985. This twenty-page English booklet indexes music by Israeli composers over the two–year period.

Eisenstein, Judith Kaplan, and Irene Heskes. *Israeli Music: A Program Aid*. New York: Jewish Music Council of the Jewish Welfare Board, 1978. This document includes bibliographies, discographies, concert programs, and directories relating to Israeli music.

Gradenwitz, Peter. *The Music of Israel: Its Rise and Growth through 5000 Years*. New York: W.W. Norton, 1949. This classic work traces the musical development of Israel from biblical times to the present.

Keren, Zvi. *Contemporary Israeli Music: Its Sources and Stylistic Development*. Ramat Gan, Israel: Bar Ilan University Press, 1980. This book contains musical examples and bibliographical references and indexes.

Musleah, Rahel. *Songs of the Jews of Calcutta*. New York: Tara Publications, 1991. For those interested in the diversity of Jewish life, this song book is a must. The unaccompanied song transcriptions are introduced with an account of the Syrian and Bagdadi roots of the Jewish community in Calcutta. This hardcover book also contains the Hebrew and English translations for each song and photographs of Jewish life in Calcutta. An audiotape is available separately from Tara.

Pasternak, Velvel. *Israel in Song*. New York: Tara Publications, 1973. This is one of a collection of over twenty song books containing folk and popular songs of Israel and the Jewish people compiled and arranged by Pasternak. Each book includes texts in both Hebrew and transliterated Roman characters, translations as well as guitar chords. For a complete catalogue, write to: Tara Publications, 29 Derby Avenue, Cedarhurst, NY 11516.

Pasternak, Velvel. *The Sephardic-Oriental Songbook*. New York: Tara Publications, 1989. This unique collection contains folk and liturgical melodies from Jews of such Sephardic and Oriental communities as Spain, Portugal, the former Yugoslavia, Bulgaria, and Yemen. It includes a brief discography cross-referenced to contents of the book.

Rubin, Ruth. *Jewish Folk Songs*. New York: Oak Publications, 1965. This collection contains Yiddish folk songs with singable English translations and guitar chords. Illustrations selected by Moses Asch add meaningful context.

Schwadron, Abraham A. "On Jewish Music." In *Musics of Many Cultures: An Introduction*, edited by Elizabeth May, 284–306. Berkeley: University of California Press, 1980. This article contains a useful, concise overview of the diversity of Jewish music in relation to Jewish history and religion. It also contains a glossary, a bibliography, a discography, and a filmography.

Sendrey, Alfred. *Music in Ancient Israel*. New York: Philosophical Library, Inc., 1969. This is the definitive book for those interested in music and instruments mentioned in the Bible. Sendrey systematically discusses all aspects of music and musicians of ancient Israel in historical, spiritual, and sociological contexts.

Tischler, Alice. *A Descriptive Bibliography of Art Music by Israeli Composers*. Warren, MI: Harmonie Park Press, 1988. This is part of the Detroit studies in music bibliography.

Vinkovetzky, Aharon, Abba Kovner, and Sinai Leichter. *Anthology of Yiddish Folksongs*. Jerusalem,

Israel: Mount Scopus Publications by the MagnesPress, Hebrew University, 1983. This collection contains notation and texts in both English and Hebrew with song lyrics in Yiddish, romanized Yiddish, and English. Songs range from children's songs and wedding and festival songs to religious and nationalistic songs.

DISCOGRAPHY

Authentic Israeli Folk Songs and Dances. Legacy CD 324. 1988. This CD contains one hour of traditional songs accompanied by flutes, guitar, accordion, and drums. "Hava Netse Bemachōl" (see Lesson One) is the fourth song on this recording.

The Beautiful Songs of Naomi Shemer. MC 35414 Acum. 1991. This audiocassette contains songs composed and sung by Naomi Shemer. Shemer remains among the most popular of Israeli composers of popular music in the folk style.

Bridges of Song: Music of the Spanish Jews of Morocco. Titanic Ti 189. 1990. This is one of a series of CDs by the Boston-based group, Voice of the Turtle. The group specializes in Sephardic-Jewish music. Each collection includes a booklet with program notes and texts in Ladino with translations.

Cante Judeo-Español. CBS 22070. 1980. These two historical records contain the sacred and secular Sephardic songs collected by Isaac Levy. They are sung in Ladino (the Spanish-Jewish language of Sephardic Jews) and Hebrew, with various instrumental accompaniments.

From the Flory Jagoda Collection of Sephardic Songs. Altarasa Records SF FJA 20-C. 1982. This cassette tape contains songs performed in Ladino by Flory Jagoda. For printed music with guitar chords, see also *The Flory Jagoda Songbook: Memories of Sarajevo* (Cedarhurst, NY: Tara Publications, 1993).

Israeli Songs for Children. Smithsonian Folkways FC 7226. Performed by Miriam Ben-Ezra. 1991. Originally issued in 1958 as Folkways FC 7226, this cassette contains program notes and texts with transliteration and English translations.

Judische Lebenswelten: Patterns of Jewish Life. Wergo SM 281604-2. 1993. This two-CD collection highlights performances from the 1992 Berlin concert series, "Traditional and Popular Jewish Music." The first CD contains two Klezmer groups (Brave New World and the Epstein Brothers) and a twenty–minute excerpt from the *Golden Age of Yiddish Theatre.* The second CD contains Sephardic and Askenazic liturgical music and Ladino folk songs. It also contains a seventy-five page booklet with texts and translations.

Les Juifs d'Ethiopie (The Jews of Ethiopia). Ocora 558.670. Recorded in Israel and distributed by Harmonia Mundi in 1986. This record contains sacred and secular vocal music of Ethiopian Jews in Israel. The songs are performed by various artists. Two languages are used: Ge'ez for sacred music and Amharic for popular. The recording includes program notes in French and English.

The Most Famous Israeli Folk Songs. Hataklit CD 111/2. 1992. Distributed by Hed-Arzi Ltd. This two-CD collection contains performances of fifty well-known folk songs by various artists. It also includes two booklets with song lyrics in Hebrew.

Nigun: A Recital of Jewish Music. Musique Internationale CM 545. 1992. Performed by Yehuda Hanani. This audiocassette contains arrangements for solo cello of well-known Jewish/Israeli melodies by composers such as Paul ben Chaim and Ernst Bloch.

Shaday. Teldec Record Service MCB 626841. 1988. This is the tape in which Ofra Haza blends the sacred and secular sounds of her native Yemen with contemporary Israeli rock.

Shashmaqam. Smithsonian Folkways CD SF4 40054. 1991. This cassette contains Jewish music from central Asia performed by the Bukharan Jewish Ensemble.

Songs of Israel. CBS S63576. 1970. Various artists and ensembles perform a variety of popular Israeli songs. The record contains a twenty-four page illustrated booklet in English.

Songs of the Sabras. Vanguard Classics VRS 9069. 1993. This CD contains a new collection of previously released Israeli classics performed in Hebrew by the Karmon Singers and Dancers with folk instrument accompaniment. The fourth cut is a performance of "Hava Netse Bemachōl" (see Lesson One).

The Sounds of Jerusalem. Folkways FW 8552. 1959. Edited by Yehuda Lev. This early field recording contains cuts such as street cries and classroom, synagogue, and mosque sounds that give a taste of the ethnic and linguistic variety in Israel. There is also a brief excerpt of children jumping rope while singing "Shirley Temple" to the same tune as "Bereleh" (see Lesson Two).

Theodore Bikel Sings More Jewish Folksongs. Bainbridge BCD 2508. 1993. This CD was originally released in 1959 by Elektra Records. It includes an illustrated sixteen-page booklet with songs and translations.

The Very Best of Israel. NMC Music. 1990. This cassette recording contains a variety of popular Israeli songs composed in the folk style and often performed by the Israeli artists who originally recorded each song. "Yerushalayim Shel Zahav," "Tzena," "Hava Nagila," and the "Hatikvah" (Israeli national anthem) are among the songs on this recording.

FILMOGRAPHY

Behind My Glasses, with Arik Einstein. 1990. New York: Sisu Home Entertainment, Inc. This film, primarily an interview with the popular Israeli singer, Arik Einstein, presents the state of popular music in Israel. The fifty-one minute cassette is in Hebrew with English subtitles.

Heritage, Civilization and the Jews with Abba Eban. 1984. Wilmette, IL: Films Incorporated (distributor); New York: This series of nine videocassettes was produced by WNET Television. This series chronicles over three thousand years of Jewish history in eighteen countries. The ninth cassette features Jewish life post WWII.

Jerusalem: Center of Many Worlds. 29 minutes. Hagopian, 1969. The historical, economic, geographic, and religious significance of Jerusalem to three major religions—Judaism, Christianity, and Islam—is illustrated by contemporary scenes: shrines, the Wailing Wall, churches, and mosques. The film shows scenes of everyday life in the Arab and Jewish sectors, for example, markets, modern stores, and religious life (e.g., services of the three religions). It can be obtained from Atlantis Productions, 1252 La Granada Drive, Thousand Oaks, CA 91360; phone: 805-495-2790.

New Immigrants. Culver City, CA: Ariella Films, Inc., circa 1985. This twelve-minute videocassette contains immigrants from various countries talking about their new life in Israel.

Ofra Haza From Sunset Till Dawn. 1988. Teaneck, NJ: Ergo Media, Inc. This forty-eight minute videocassette captures various performances of Israeli-Yemenite singer Ofra Haza.

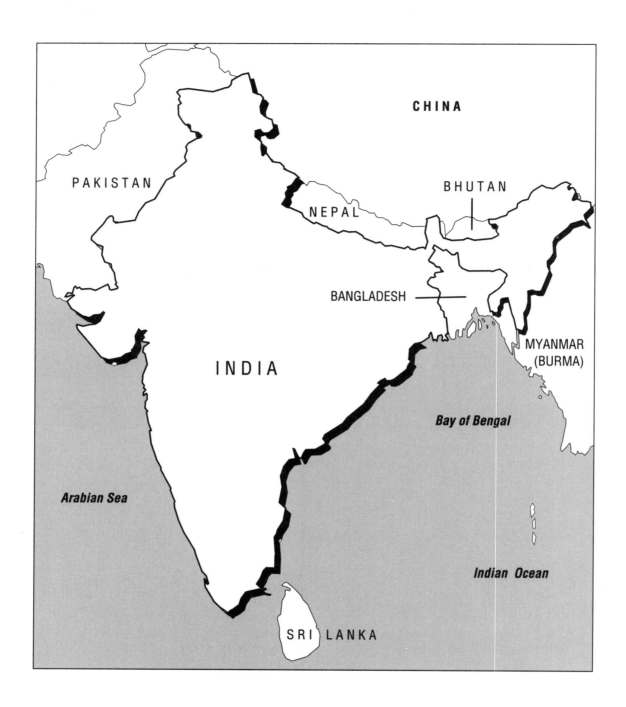

CHINA

PAKISTAN

NEPAL

BHUTAN

BANGLADESH

MYANMAR
(BURMA)

INDIA

Bay of Bengal

Arabian Sea

Indian Ocean

SRI LANKA

Map of South Asia

CHAPTER 9

SOUTH ASIA: INDIA

by William M. Anderson

Sweeping southward from the world's highest peaks in the Himalayan mountains is the nation of India, the second largest country in Asia. Triangular in shape and often referred to as the subcontinent of Asia, India extends approximately two thousand miles from central Asia to the tropical waters of the Indian Ocean surrounding Cape Comorin and approximately seventeen hundred miles latitudinally from the state of Rajasthan to the eastern border with Myanmar (Burma).

Although positioned just north of the equator, South Asia experiences great variety in weather and climate. The snow-capped peaks in the north provide a welcome coolness from the warmth of much of the subcontinent and at the same time function as the source of the life-giving rivers—the Indus, the Ganges, and the Brahmaputra—that sustain much of the country. As one follows these rivers into the Indo-Gangetic plain of northern India, a huge, fertile river valley area emerges. The rich soil and the warm, humid climate that results from the lower elevation support some of the best agriculture in the country. To the west of this region, in stark contrast, lie the parched desert areas of Rajasthan. Moving farther south and toward the center of the country, one finds a large and relatively high plateau region known as the Deccan, where the weather is integrally related to the monsoons, or prevailing winds. Stretching southward from the Deccan, the land forms a temperate coastal plain leading to tropical, palm tree-dotted beaches bordering the sea.

Because more than 70 percent of the people living in the subcontinent make their living from agriculture, the weather is an important factor in many lives. Although it lies near the equator, India experiences seasonal changes principally through the action of the monsoons. In April, May, and June, extremely hot weather grips most of the country until the onslaught of the west winds, which bring quenching rains to many parched areas from late June through September. In the winter, the winds reverse, providing a cool, easterly flow of air that may actually make it necessary for those living in the capital city of New Delhi to wear light coats.

India has often been described as a dozen countries in one, a democratic republic that seems to exemplify the doctrine of "unity through diversity." Its twenty-five states and seven union territories form a mosaic of different ethnic groups who have learned to coexist separately. Millions of negrito tribal peoples, who are ethnically related to the aboriginals of Malaysia, the Philippines, and Australia, live in remote jungle areas. In the southern regions of the country are dark-skinned peoples who are descendants of some of the most ancient people on the subcontinent, the Dravidians. Farther north, innumerable invasions from Central Asia, the Near East, and Europe have today made the majority of Indians primarily of Caucasian stock. It is interesting and somewhat overwhelming to realize that India today has a burgeoning population of over 900 million inhabitants, the second largest in the world (exceeded only by China). Certainly this large and ethnically diverse population has made India one of the most fascinating countries in Asia, and nowhere is this more apparent than in languages and religions.

The linguistic diversity of the subcontinent is almost beyond comprehension. Although India is less than half the size of the United States, its inhabitants speak 845 languages and dialects. From this group, fourteen major languages emerge, each being spoken by millions of people. The news on All-India Radio, for example, is broadcast in Hindi, English, Bengali, Oriya, Tamil, Telugu, Kannada, Malayalam, Punjabi, Marathi, Gujarati, Assamese, Urdu, and Kasmiri. Hindi has been made the official language of the country, but English remains the language of the government and of the educated. It is interesting to note that while the British promoted the English language in this area of the world, many Indian words were adopted by Westerners, including such familiar ones as "bungalow," "dungarees," "punch," "shampoo," and "pajamas."

One of the strongest binding agents in the enormously diverse population has been religion. At least 85 percent of the population is Hindu, with the remainder practicing the Muslim, Jain, Buddhist, Sikh, Parsi, and Christian faiths. The lives of millions of people are closely intertwined with the sanctions and mores of Hinduism. A host of gods and goddesses oversee almost every facet of existence, often providing a common basis for uniting the lives of millions of ethnically diverse peoples. The arts have also thrived under Hinduism, with many striking architectural examples of temples flourishing throughout the country around which sculptors, painters, writers, and musicians have found inspiration.[1] Saraswati, the goddess of music and learning, is usually depicted holding the *vina* (a stringed instrument), and Krishna is typically shown playing the flute. These are two visible symbols of music's close relationship with religion.

In addition to Hinduism, the cultural traditions of India have been enormously influenced by the Islamic religion, which was brought to India by the Muslims over a thousand years ago. Great Muslim courts were established throughout northern India, and spectacular buildings, such as the Taj Mahal in the city of Agra, are vivid examples of Indo-Islamic art.

At about the same time that Columbus was sailing to the New World, the Portuguese explorer Vasco da Gama arrived in India with hopes of establishing trading posts. India was rich in silk, gems, indigo, and spices, which were much in demand in the West. The Portuguese were soon followed by Dutch, Danish, French, and British traders, who were also attracted to this Eastern paradise. The British gradually took control of the country, bringing about great changes through the development of cities, industries, and transportation.

In 1947, India became an independent nation with many aspirations as the world's largest democracy. Since that time, Indians have become leaders not only in their own country but also throughout the world. Today, India is listed among the world's top ten industrial nations. Indians have made outstanding achievements in all areas of human endeavor, including the sciences, humanities, and arts.

Music has become part of the curriculum of many primary and secondary schools and universities, and such distinguished Indian musicians as Ravi Shankar and Ali Akbar Khan have traveled to Europe and the United States to make Westerners increasingly aware of the sophistication and brilliance of the Indian musical tradition. Interestingly, both Shankar and Khan established music schools in California, where many Americans have studied Indian vocal and instrumental music.

Characteristics

India has one of the world's oldest and most sophisticated musical traditions. Its history may be traced back at least thirty-five hundred years. Since that time, a great variety of vocal and instrumental music has developed, along with two principal stylistic traditions—the *Hindustani* system of North India and the *Carnatic* system of South India. This chapter will focus on music in North India; some general characteristics of this music follow.

Melody

- Melodies are derived from a prescribed series of notes known as ragas.
- There are hundreds of ragas, and each has a particular name and a distinctive structure (see figure 1).

Figure 1. Raga *bhupali*

- Ragas provide the pitches to be used in musical compositions.
- Ragas often indicate the contours (shapes) of melodies. Thus, the notes of ragas do not move straight up and down but in "crooked" melodic fashion.
- The pitches of ragas are often ornamented with subtle "slides" and "shakes." This ornamentation often involves microtonal intervals; that is, intervals that are smaller than a half step.
- Ragas express feelings or emotions.
- To evoke particular emotions most effectively, ragas are designated to be performed at specific times of the day or night or at certain times of the year.

Rhythm

- Rhythm in Indian music may be free/flexible or strictly organized.
- Strict rhythm is organized in a system known as tala; a tala is a cycle of beats. Talas have names and distinctive characteristics, which include overall length and division into subsections. For example, *tintala* is a rhythmic cycle of sixteen beats that is divided into four sections of four beats each (4 + 4 + 4 + 4), while *jhaptal* is a rhythmic cycle of ten beats that is divided into four sections: a group of two beats, followed by a group of three beats, followed by a group of two beats, followed by a group of three beats (2 + 3 + 2 + 3).

Texture

- Some Indian music is monophonic (one melodic line).
- Most music, however, makes use of "drone harmony"; that is, one or more drone pitches sound constantly, over top of which other melodic lines are sung or played.
- The technique of imitation is often used.

Timbre

- A great variety of timbres or tone colors are present in Indian music. In general, singers tend to produce a more nasalized tone color with less vibrato than that which occurs in Western classical singing.
- Sympathetic vibrating strings on many instruments also help to create distinctive timbres.

Dynamics

- Much Indian music is meant for small groups, with soft and medium dynamic levels occurring frequently.

Form

- Many compositions begin with the *alap*, an improvised section in free/flexible rhythm. This section is followed by a precomposed piece of music—known as *chiz* in vocal music and *gat* in instrumental music—that is cast in strict rhythm in a particular tala. The precomposed section is not improvised but rather has been thought out prior to the performance; it is followed by another section featuring improvisation.

Alap	**Chiz/Gat**	**Improvisation**
Improvised	Precomposed	
	Strict rhythm with tala	

Sometimes the form is enlarged to include several precomposed and improvised sections, the first in a slow tempo followed by one or more in faster tempos.

Alap	Chiz/Gat	Improvisation	Chiz/Gat	Improvisation
	Slow Tempo		Fast Tempo	

NOTE

1. For good pictures of architecture, sculpture, and painting, see Mario Bussagli and Calembus Sivaramaurti, *Five Thousand Years of the Art of India* (see Bibliography); Marguerite-Maria Deneck, *Indian Art*. London: Paul Hamlyn, 1967; Sherman E. Lee, *Far Eastern Art* (see Bibliography); Eleanor C. Munro, *The Encyclopedia of Art* (see Bibliography); Stuart C. Welch, *India: Art and Culture, 1300–1900* (see Bibliography).

L E S S O N   1

■ Objectives

Students will:
1. Sing the short Indian composition "Namane Kare Chature" in raga *bhupali*.
2. Add a tambura drone accompaniment to "Namane Kare Chature."
3. Keep track of the tala rhythmic cycle in "Namane Kare Chature."

■ Materials

1. Pictures of musical instruments can be found in Ravi Shankar's *My Music, My Life* (New York: Simon and Schuster, 1968) and Bonnie Wade's *Music in India: The Classical Traditions* (Englewood Cliffs, NJ: Prentice-Hall, 1979; reprinted 1987) (see Bibliography)
2. Indian tambura (or makeshift drone played either on a guitar or on a piano)
3. Sixteen-beat tala cycle displayed on a chalkboard or transparency

■ Procedures

1. This lesson is for upper-elementary school students. Have the students design a bulletin board or a chalkboard with information about the music of India. Include pictures of musical instruments. Organize categories of melody, rhythm, texture, timbre, dynamics, and form.
2. Sing the Indian composition "Namane Kare Chature" (see figure 2). First, pronounce the Hindi words with the class. The text is as follows: Namane kare chature shiri guru charana (pronounced *nah-mah-nuh kah-ruh cha-too-ruh shee-ree goo-roo chah-rah-nah*)/ tane mane niremale kare bhave taraha (pronounced *tah-nuh mah-nuh nee-ruh-mah-luh kah-ruh bhah-vuh tah-rah-nah*).

    Translation: Respect your teachers and
    keep a clean body and mind.

    Some students will probably know the word "guru" (teacher). Comment on the text, which focuses on one's guru. You may wish to read and paraphrase for the class

Namane Kare Chature

Na-ma-ne Ka - re Cha-tu-re   Shi - ri Gu-ru   Cha-ra - na

Ta - ne Ma-ne   Ni - re - ma-le   Ka - re Bha-ve   Ta - ra - na

Na-ma - ne Ka - re Cha-tu - re   Shi - ri Gu-ru   Cha-ra - na

Figure 2. "Namane Kare Chature," a song about one's guru

some of the remarks about the importance of the guru from pages 11–13 of Ravi Shankar's book *My Music, My Life* (see Bibliography). Second, sing the song for the class. Call attention to the repeated phrases (the first line repeats, and the last line is the same as the first). Teach the song phrase by phrase, singing slowly with the students so they can grasp the pitches and the pronunciation of the words. Third, tell the students that singing in India is often accompanied by a stringed instrument known as the tambura, and show the class a picture of a tambura (see figure 3).

Explain that the instrument has a large base made from either wood or a hollowed-out gourd. Extending from this base is a long neck with pegs at the top. Four strings run across the base of the instrument and along the neck to the pegs. The instrument is held in an upright fashion, and the middle and index fingers of the right hand pluck the strings from left to right.

The strings of the tambura are normally tuned to the pitches G3, C4, C4, and C3, and are plucked over and over in a flexible rhythmic style to produce a steady drone. The distinctive tone color of this instrument is produced by small threadlike strings inserted between the main strings and the flat bridge (see figure 4). The effect of this arrangement is to lift the main strings just slightly above the flat bridge. Then, as the strings are plucked, they vibrate against the bridge, producing a distinctive buzzing timbre.

Try to obtain an actual tambura for your students to use. A tambura may be purchased from The House of Musical Traditions or from the Ali Akbar College Music Store (see Discography), or there might be someone in your community who would

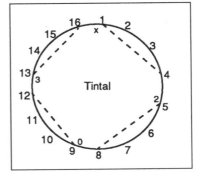

Tintal

Figure 3. Woman playing the tambura

Figure 4. (above) Base of tambura

Figure 5. (below) Tintala

lend the school an instrument. If you are unable to acquire the instrument, you may wish to devise a makeshift tambura by tuning the four highest-pitched strings of a guitar to G3, C4, C4, and C3. Position the guitar with the base on the floor and the neck pointing upward.

Have a student pluck the strings one at a time in a repetitive cycle to produce the drone sound. If a guitar is not available, have a student play the tambura pitches over and over on a piano with the damper pedal depressed, which will produce the continuous drone effect.

3. Have the students sing "Namane Kare Chature" with tambura accompaniment. For a follow-up discussion, ask the students if they can think of other types of music that make use of drone harmony. You might start the discussion by using examples such as the bagpipe or Kentucky mountain dulcimer music.

4. Introduce students to talas. Explain that talas are cycles of beats that repeat over and over in a musical composition. Tell them that there are many talas, and that each has a particular name and structure. One of the most common North Indian talas is known as *tintala*. It has sixteen beats, divided into four sections (see figure 5).

Indians have devised a number of ways to count the beats in talas. A common way to follow *tintala* is to clap lightly on the strong beats (one, five, and thirteen), wave the right hand outward on the weak beat (nine), and count the intervening

1	2	3	4	5	6	7	8
clap	(Count 2, 3, and 4 by placing right thumb on little, fourth, and middle fingers.)			clap	(Count 6, 7, and 8 by placing right thumb on little, fourth, and middle fingers.)		
9	10	11	12	13	14	15	16
wave	(Count as 2, 3, and 4 above.)			clap	(Count as 6, 7, and 8 above.)		

Figure 6. A common way of counting the beats in *tintala*

beats by touching the right-hand fingers against the thumb, beginning with the little finger and moving toward the middle finger. Emphasis is placed on the first beat, which is marked with an "X." Count and clap the tala over and over (see figure 6). Have the class count the sixteen beats of the tala over and over and follow the beats by clapping, waving, and counting the intervening beats on the fingers. Start the cycle on another beat, such as nine (the cycle will, in this case, continue through sixteen to finish with counts one to eight). Continue practicing with the class until keeping track of the cycle of beats becomes fairly easy.

5. Divide the class, having half sing the song "Namane Kare Chature" (with tambura accompaniment) while the other half keeps track of the tala, which in this piece is the sixteen-beat *tintala*, as previously outlined. Note that "Namane Kare Chature" begins on beat nine of the tala. After the students have learned to sing the song and keep track of the tala easily, switch the groups so that all members of the class have a chance to follow the tala.

6. Summarize the lesson by having the students place comments on the board (under the appropriate categories) about what they have learned in this lesson: rhythm (cycles of beats known as the tala), texture (drone harmony through use of the tambura), timbre ("buzzing" tone color on the tambura achieved by the use of small threads placed between the main strings and the flat bridge).

L E S S O N   2

■ Objectives

Students will:
1. Recite rhythmic syllables and then play them either on the tabla (drums) or on a substitute such as the bongo drums.
2. Play the rhythmic syllables for *tintala* on either tabla or bongos.
3. Add a tabla accompaniment to "Namane Kare Chature."

■ Materials

1. Tabla or substitute such as bongo drums

2. The composition "Namane Kare Chature," shown on a transparency
3. Overhead projector

■ Procedures

This lesson is for upper-elementary school students. Explain that the tabla (see figure 7) are the most important drums of North India. Tabla actually consist of two drums: a large, somewhat low-pitched drum made from metal and a higher-pitched drum most often constructed of wood. Both drums have membrane heads with black, circular patches made from a paste of iron filings, flour, and water. Tabla are traditionally played from a sitting position. Sounds are made by striking various parts of the drum heads with the fingers and hands. Memory syllables known as *bols* are learned in order to facilitate the playing of rhythms on the drums. For example, striking the left drum with the third and fourth fingers is identified with the *bol* "dhe"; striking the right drum on the edge with the index finger produces the *bol* "na" or near the center, the *bol* "tin" (see figure 8). If "dhe" and "na" are combined into a single stroke (both left- and right-hand fingers striking at the same time), the *bol* is known as "dha." If "dhe" and "tin" are combined into a single stroke, the *bol* "dhin" is produced.

1. Have the students try to produce the *bols* "dhe, "na," "tin," "dha," and "dhin" either on the tabla or on a substitute such as the bongo drums. Those without drums can practice on desk tops or laps.
2. Have the students play several rhythmic patterns on the drums after reciting the syllables in each line from memory.

Figure 7. Man playing tabla

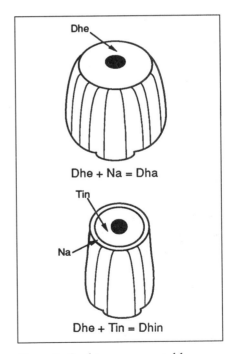

Figure 8. Striking areas on tabla

Dhe Na/Dhe Na/Dhe Dhe Na   (repeat)
Dhe Tin/Dhe Tin/Dhe Dhe Tin   (repeat)
Dha Dha Na/Dha Dha Na   (repeat)
Dhin Dhin Na/Dhin Dhin Na   (repeat)
Dha Dhin Dhin Na/Dha Dhin Dhin Na   (repeat)
Tin Tin Na/Tin Na/Tin Na   (repeat)

Have the class learn the tabla rhythmic syllables for the sixteen-beat tintala. Explain that for each tala there is a standard rhythmic pattern played on the drums. For example, the rhythmic pattern for tintala is as follows:

Dha	Dhin	Dhin	Dha	Dha	Dhin	Dhin	Dha
1	2	3	4	5	6	7	8

Dha	Tin	Tin	Na	Na	Dhin	Dhin	Dha
9	10	11	12	13	14	15	16

   a. Have the class learn to pronounce the syllables from memory, chanting rhythmically and with vocal inflection. (Note that there are four groups, each with four syllables; call attention to the similarity of groups one, two, and four.)

   b. Have one or two students play the rhythmic syllables on a tabla or bongo drums while the rest of the class recites the syllables. Practice until the rhythmic syllables can be played on the drums with ease.

   c. Divide the class into three groups: (1) one or two students who play the tabla (or bongos), (2) a large group that recites the drum syllables (Dha, Dhin, Dhin, Dha, and so on), and (3) a large group that keeps track of the sixteen-beat *tintala* by means of hand claps, waving the right hand outward, and counting the intervening beats on the fingers (as outlined in Lesson One).

3. Divide the class into three groups with the first singing the song "Namane Kare Chature," the second keeping track of the tala (*tintala*, beginning on beat nine), and the third comprised of several students playing the rhythm on the tabla or bongos.

4. Summarize the lesson by having the students discuss and add comments to the music section of their Indian bulletin board regarding the following items: Indian drums known as tabla, rhythmic syllables known as *bols*, and the specific *bols* for *tintala*.

L E S S O N   3

■ Objectives

Students will:

1. Explore Indian ragas by singing the Western major scale and two Indian ragas (*bhairavi* and *purvi*) on a neutral syllable. Students will identify differences in whole- and half-step patterns between an Indian raga and the Western scale. They will learn that ragas have distinctive names and structures.

2. Sing the familiar song "America," first in the Western major scale and then in the ragas *bhairavi* and *purvi*.

3. Create a short, improvised composition on the *jaltarang* in raga *bhupali*.

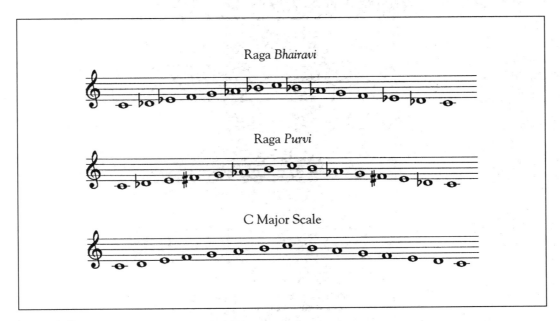

Raga *Bhairavi*

Raga *Purvi*

C Major Scale

Figure 9. Ragas

■ **Materials**

1. Two ragas (*bhairavi* and *purvi*), and the C major scale on a transparency or on the chalkboard
2. "America" on transparency—first in a major scale and then in the ragas *bhairavi* and *purvi*
3. Overhead projector
4. Seven glass soup or cereal bowls

■ **Procedures**

1. This lesson is for upper-elementary or middle school students. Compare several Indian ragas to the Western major scale. Explain that one of the major reasons why melodies in Indian music sound so different to us is that they are developed from ragas, which are an organized series of pitches from which musical compositions are developed. There are hundreds of ragas, and each has a particular name and structure.
2. Figure 9 shows several ragas. Have the class sing each one on a neutral syllable such as "ah" or "loo." Then sing the Western major scale on a neutral syllable. What differences do you see and hear?
3. Write or project transcriptions of "America" as sung in the Western major scale system and the Indian ragas, *bhairavi* and *purvi* (see figure 10). Have the class sing and compare the sound of each example.
4. Improvise short compositions in the ragas *bhairavi* and *purvi* on the *jaltarang* (see figure 11).
    a. The *jaltarang* is an interesting musical instrument consisting of a series of tuned bowls arranged in a semicircle around the performer. The bowls are of different sizes and are tuned precisely to the pitches of various ragas by adding appropriate

Figure 10. Transcriptions of "America"

Figure 11. Student playing *jaltarang*

amounts of water. The instrument is played by striking the inside edge of the bowls with two small wooden sticks, one held in each hand.

   b. Collect seven glass soup or cereal bowls and devise a *jaltarang*. Tune the various bowls to the pitches in raga *purvi* by filling them with appropriate amounts of water. Using a pair of chopsticks as mallets, create an improvised piece of music in flexible or free rhythm.

     (1) Change the pitches of the bowls to raga *bhairavi* and create another improvised piece of music in flexible or free rhythm.

     (2) Compare the sounds produced by ragas *purvi* and *bhairavi* and the Western scale by creating an improvised composition on the *jaltarang* in the C major scale.

  5. Add to the bulletin board chart those things that you have learned in this lesson: the ragas *purvi* and *bhairavi* and the *jaltarang*.

L E S S O N   4

■ **Objectives**

Students will:
1. Follow the seven-beat tala known as *rupak* by clapping hands, waving, and counting on their fingers. Learn about the asymmetrical subdivisions of the tala (3 + 2 + 2). Draw parallels to compositions such as Paul Desmond's "Take Five," in which the beats are grouped asymmetrically (3 + 2).
2. Learn to speak the drum (tabla) syllables for *rupak* (tin-tin-na, dhin-na, dhin-na). Keep track of the tala while speaking the syllables.
3. Play the pattern indicated by the drum syllables on tabla or bongo drums.
4. Learn the composition "Ha-Nan-De," which is cast in the seven-beat *rupak* tala. Keep track of the tala and add a tabla accompaniment.
5. Keep track of *rupak* tala in a composition played by a sitar with accompaniment by tabla and tambura.

South Asia: India   295

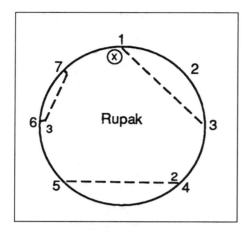

Figure 12. *Rupak* tala

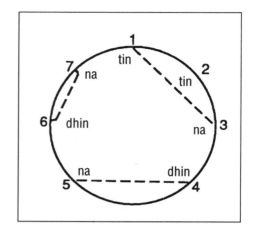

Figure 13. *Bols* for *rupak*

Ha-Nan-De

Ha   Nan-de   La - le   A - ti   Hi - ra   Sa - le
Hah   Nahn-duh Lah-luh   Ah-tee   Hee-ray   Sah-luh

Ni - re - tet - te   Sun - ge   Goo - pi
Nee - ruh Teht - tuh   Soon - guh   Goo - pee

Gwa - le   Ha   Nan - de   La - le
Gwah - luh   Hah   Nahn-duh   Lah - luh

Figure 14. "Ha-Nan-De," a song about the Hindu god, Krishna

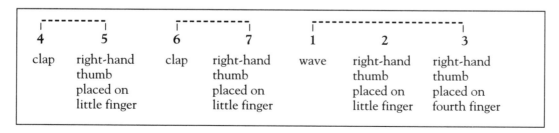

4	5	6	7	1	2	3
clap	right-hand thumb placed on little finger	clap	right-hand thumb placed on little finger	wave	right-hand thumb placed on little finger	right-hand thumb placed on fourth finger

Figure 15. A common way of counting *rupak* tala

■ Materials

1. Tabla or a pair of bongo drums
2. Sitar composition in *rupak* tala (*Music Resources for Multicultural Perspectives*, side C, No. 20. Reston, VA: Music Educators National Conference, 1995)
3. "Take Five," from *Time Out: The Dave Brubeck Quartet* (Columbia CK 40585)

■ Procedures

1. This lesson is for middle or junior high school students. Review with the class the rhythmic cycle known as *tintala*, introduced in Lesson One. Have the students follow the beats by clapping and waving their hands on the principal beats and counting the intervening beats on their fingers. Draw particular attention to the four even sections.

2. Explain that in some talas the internal sections are not equally divided. Have the students follow the unequal groupings of beats found in the seven-beat rupak tala. The children should speak the numbers and clap lightly on the beginning of each subdivision (1–2–3, 4–5, 6–7) (see figure 12). Notice the asymmetrical rhythmic feeling of the group of three beats followed by the two groups of two beats (3 + 2 + 2). You may wish to draw parallels to other Western compositions such as Desmond's "Take Five" (referring to 5/4 meter), in which the meter comprises asymmetrical groups of beats (1–2–3, 4–5).

3. Have the students recite the tabla (drum) rhythmic syllables (*bols*) for *rupak* tala:

tin	–	tin	–	na,	dhin	–	na	dhin	–	na.
1		2		3	4		5	6		7

   Then have half the class recite the syllables over and over while the other half counts the numbers.

4. Have several students play the rhythmic syllables on tabla or bongo drums (see figure 13). Sing the song "Ha-Nan-De" (see figure 14).
   a. Pronounce the words with the students. Explain that this song is about the Hindu god Krishna. Show a picture of Krishna.
   b. Point out that the first line of the song is sung twice, the second line is sung once, and then there is a return to a short portion of line one.
   c. To assist the students, provide a tambura accompaniment with either the actual instrument or one of the substitutes suggested in Lesson One.

5. Divide the class in half, with some students singing "Ha-Nan-De" and the others keeping track of the tala. Note that this piece begins on beat four of *rupak* tala, so that the pattern from the beginning is 4 5 / 6 7 / 1 2 3, which is usually kept track of by clapping on beats four and six, waving outward on beat one (an idiosyncracy of this tala), and counting the intervening beats on the fingers. See figure 15.

6. Divide the class in thirds, with some singing "Ha-Nan-De," others keeping track of the tala, and still others providing a tabla accompaniment.

7a. Show a picture of the sitar (see figure 16), and explain that it is one of the principal stringed instruments of India. The sitar has a large base fashioned from a hollowed-out gourd. A long neck supporting a number of curved, movable frets extends from the base. Seven strings run over the top of these frets and are attached to pegs at the upper end of the neck. Some of these strings are used to play melodies and are plucked by a wire plectrum attached to the right-hand index finger. To produce

 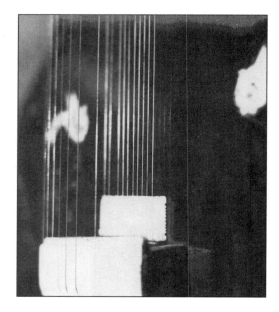

Figure 16. Student playing the sitar   *Figure 17.* Sympathetic vibrating strings on sitar

Figure 18. North Indian ensemble; from left: tabla, sitar, and tambura

different pitches, the performer presses the strings against the frets at various points. Several of the strings running over the frets are not used to play melodies but rather are tuned to the drone and are plucked by the performer to provide rhythmic accentuation. An additional group of small metal strings, known as the sympathetic vibrators, are stretched along the neck of the instrument under the frets. As their name suggests, these strings are not plucked but rather oscillate in sympathy when the strings running over the frets are activated (see figure 17).

7b. A common instrumental ensemble of North India features the sitar accompanied by the tabla and tambura (see figure 18). Listen to this ensemble, keeping track of *rupak* tala.

8. Summarize on the board what you have learned in this lesson: *rupak* tala with its unequal subdivisions, drum syllables *(bols)* for *rupak*, vocal and instrumental compositions in *rupak* tala, and instruments (sitar, tabla, and tambura).

L E S S O N 5

■ Objectives

Students will:
1. Sing the raga *bhupali* and study some characteristics of ragas.
2. Identify the form in a North Indian vocal composition (accompanied by the tambura and tabla) in raga *bhupali* by performing a short, improvised introduction (*alap*) in flexible rhythm, a precomposed segment (*chiz*) in the sixteen-beat cycle *tintala*, and improvised phrases.
3. Follow the form in an Indian instrumental composition (featuring the sitar with tabla and tambura accompaniment) in raga *maru bihag* by listening to an improvised introduction (*alap*) followed by a precomposed piece (*gat*) in the ten-beat *jhaptal* tala and improvised phrases.
4. Listen to the rock composition "Love You Too" by the Beatles, which features both Indian instruments (the sitar and tabla) and Western instruments; follow the "Indian form" in the piece.

■ Materials

1. Transparency with transcriptions of raga *bhupali*, an *alap*, a *chiz*, and improvised phrases
2. Tambura and tabla or appropriate substitutes
3. Pictures (slides) of a sitar, tabla, and tambura
4. Recordings:
   Ravi Shankar, *The Sounds of India* (Columbia CK 09296)
   "Love You Too" from The Beatles, *Revolver* (Capitol Records C41H-90452)

■ Procedures

1. This lesson is for middle or junior high school students. Indian musical compositions are created from prescribed series of notes known as ragas. Have the students study the raga known as *bhupali* as follows: First, sing the raga using the Indian note names:

sa (*sah*), re (*ray*), ga (*gah*), pa (*pah*), and dha (*dhah*) (see figure 19). Explain that ragas have many characteristics. List some of the following characteristics on the chalkboard or bulletin board for discussion:

a. Each raga has a particular name, such as *bhupali*.

b. Ragas provide pitches (notes) that are used in creating musical compositions.

c. Ragas often have a "crooked" movement with different ascending and descending forms, thus indicating some of the shapes of melodies created from the raga.

d. Ragas often have specific ornamentation such as the "slide" in pitch from pa (G) to ga (E), indicated by a straight line in figures 19 and 20.

e. Ragas convey specific moods or feelings; for example, *bhupali* conveys the mood of majesty or grandeur.

f. Ragas are often assigned particular performance times throughout the day and night when it is felt that their mood can best be achieved. *Bhupali*, for example, is an evening raga.

2. Background information: Most Indian musical compositions begin with an improvised section of music known as the *alap*. In the *alap*, the performer uses the notes of a selected raga to create a segment of music in free, flexible rhythmic style.

3. Figure 20 provides a transcription of a short *alap* in raga *bhupali*. The music is improvised and therefore usually not written down, but notation is used here so that the *alap* can be easily followed.

a. Have the students sing the *alap* in free, flexible rhythm using either the Indian scale degree syllables—sa (*sah*), re (*ray*), ga (*gah*), pa (*pah*), and dha (*dhah*)—or a neutral syllable such as "ah." Assist the class by singing or playing the notes on the piano or melody bells.

b. The *alap* is generally accompanied by the tambura (as discussed in Lesson One), which produces a drone accompaniment. Try performing the *alap* with accompaniment by a tambura or a substitute instrument on which a drone can be played, such as a guitar or piano.

4. The *alap* is followed by a segment of precomposed music (thought-out beforehand rather than improvised) known in vocal music as the *chiz*. The *chiz* is organized in a tala rhythmic cycle with accompaniment by tabla. The tambura continues throughout this segment.

Have the class perform the *chiz* (see figure 21). Divide the class in half so that one group sings while another group keeps track of the tala (*tintala*) through hand claps, hand waving, and counting on the fingers. Add a drum accompaniment on either tabla or bongos (see Lessons One and Two).

5. Following the precomposed section, the performer begins to improvise again. The improvisation is often accomplished by taking a portion of the precomposed music (for example, "Namane Kare Chature," transcribed in figure 22) and adding improvised phrases. Encourage the students to try singing, with a neutral syllable such as "ah," the improvised phrases shown in figure 22. Have the students make up some short, improvised phrases by using the first section of "Namane Kare Chature" to create several eight-beat improvised phrases.

6. Follow the form in an Indian instrumental composition in raga *maru-bihag* (pronounced mah-roo-bee-hahg), featuring the sitar (stringed instrument) accompanied by the tabla (drums) and tambura (stringed instrument) (see *The Sounds of India*).

a. Show a picture of the sitar (see figure 16, Lesson Four). Explain that the sitar is

SA RE GA PA GA DHA PA GA SA DHA PA GA GA RE SA DHA SA

Figure 19. Raga *bhupali*

GA RE SA DHA SA RE GA PA DHA PA GA

RE GA RE SA SA RE GA RE GA PA GA

DHA PA GA SA DHA PA GA GA RE SA

Figure 20. Alap in raga *bhupali*

NA-MA-NE KA -RE CHA-TU-RE   SHI- RI GU-RU CHA-RA-NA

TA-NE MA-NE   NI - RE-MA - LE   KA-RE BHA-VE TA-RA-NA

NA-MA-NE KA - RE CHA-TU - RE   SHI - RI GU-RU CHA-RA-NA

Figure 21. Chiz in raga *bhupali*

one of the principal stringed instruments of India. It has a large base fashioned from a hollowed-out gourd. Extending from the base is a long neck along which are positioned a number of curved, movable frets. Seven strings run over the top of these frets and are attached to pegs at the upper end of the neck. Some of these strings are used to play melodies and are plucked by a wire plectrum attached to the right-hand index finger. To produce different pitches, the performer presses the strings against the frets at various points. Several of the strings running over the frets are not used to play melodies, but are instead tuned to the drone and are plucked so that they provide rhythmic accentuation. The sitar has an additional group of strings known as the sympathetic vibrators. These small metal strings are stretched along the neck of the instrument under the frets. As their name suggests, these strings are not plucked but rather oscillate in sympathy when the strings running over the frets are activated (see figure 17, Lesson Four).

b. Show a picture of the sitar, tabla, and tambura, a common instrumental ensemble of North India (see figure 18, Lesson Four).

c. On the recording, Ravi Shankar illustrates the ascending and descending forms of the raga *maru-bihag*. Listen to the raga and discuss some of its distinctive characteristics: different ascending and descending patterns of notes with "crooked" melodic movement, its ornamentation of particular notes (indicated in figure 23 by a wavy line), and the fact that it is an evening raga, conveying a feeling of melancholy or loneliness.

d. Place a diagram (illustrated in figure 24) on the board for the students to follow as they listen to the music.

(1) In the opening section of the *alap*, the sitar improvises in the raga. Notice the free, flexible rhythmic style. The sitar is accompanied by the tambura, which provides a soft drone background.

(2) The *alap* is followed by a precomposed section of music known in instrumental music as the *gat*. The *gat* is cast in strict rhythm, and is shown here in figure 25 in a tala known as *jhaptal*. *Jhaptal* has ten beats that are divided into four subsections (2 + 3 + 2 + 3). Make sure that the class understands the asymmetrical quality of this tala. Have the class follow the tala by speaking the numbers and clapping lightly on beats one, three, and eight; waving the right hand outward on beat six; and counting the intervening beats on their fingers (see figure 26).

(3) The sitar player begins to improvise again. Listen for the increasingly elaborate melodic phrases and the faster tempo.

7. Listen to "Love You Too" from the album *Revolver* by The Beatles.

a. Listen for the combination of Indian and Western instruments and the "Indian" form:

Free/flexible rhythm introduction	*Strict rhythm, main segment*
Slow tempo	Medium tempo
Sitar playing main melody	Singers accompanied by sitar, tabla, and Western guitars

8. Summarize on the board what you have learned in this lesson. List some characteris-

Figure 22. "Namane Kare Chature" with improvisation

Figure 23. Raga *maru-bihag*

Alap Section	**Gat** Section	Improvisation
Sitar plays melody ————————————		⟶
Tambura plays drone accompaniment ————————————		⟶
Flexible, free rhythm ⟶	Change to steady beat of tala *jhaptal* ————————	⟶
	Tabla enters ————————————	⟶

Figure 24. A diagram and listening guide for raga *bhupali*

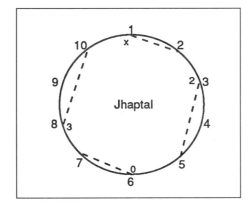

Figure 25. Jhaptal

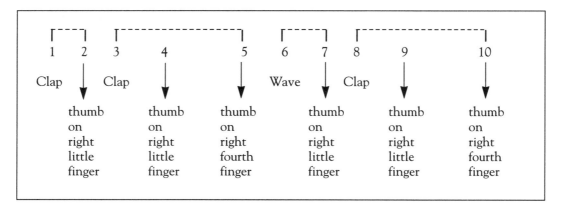

Figure 26. Counting the beats of *jhaptal*

tics of ragas, including distinctive ascending and descending forms, ornamentation, moods, and performance times. Describe the form in Indian compositions, beginning with *alap,* followed by *chiz* (in vocal music) and *gat* (in instrumental music), in turn followed by increasingly elaborate improvised phrases. Also discuss *jhaptal* with ten beats subdivided into unequal groups of (2 + 3 + 2 + 3) and Western popular music that combines Indian and Western musical traits.

Integrating music with other studies

Developing the proper cultural context is an important part of any program of teaching Indian music. Students tremendously enjoy learning about other peoples and their customs and crafts, their architecture, sculpture, painting, literature, dance, and music. Through an interrelated study of many aspects of a culture, they develop new and important understandings of other peoples. They also begin to realize the integral place of the arts in many aspects of a society.

The following are some suggestions to assist teachers in placing the study of music in a broader cultural context:

1. Plan a study of Indian geography. Using a globe, have the students locate India. Compare its size to that of the United States. Develop a bulletin board with a map of India in the center. Have the students draw (or trace) the map and identify with stick-pin flags some of the most important cities. Study the various kinds of terrain found throughout the country, including the gigantic mountains in the North (the Himalayas), the fertile river valley areas such as the Ganges, the parched desert areas such as those in Rajasthan, and the balmy seacoast areas such as those found in Kerala. Look for pictures of different geographical areas. *National Geographic* magazine provides good sources for pictures (see the Bibliography).

2. Look for pictures of Indian architecture, sculpture, and painting. These should include Hindu and Muslim temples, the Taj Mahal, sculptures of Hindu gods and goddesses, and the intricately designed, multicolored "miniature" paintings. Place these on the bulletin board.

3. Encourage students to visit the library and find books about India. They will read

about the country's various cultural groups. Encyclopedia articles, such as those found in the *World Book Encyclopedia,* are good sources of information.

4. Invite Indians living in the community to come and speak to your students. If possible, have them bring native dress and musical instruments.

5. Have the students study the two largest Indian religions—Hinduism and Islam—and discuss with them some of the most important beliefs of these religions. Children are particularly fascinated to learn why certain animals, such as cows, are held in such high regard. As a good introduction to this subject, teachers may enjoy reading Veronica Ions's *Indian Mythology* (see Bibliography). Since Hindu temples and Muslim mosques are now found in the United States, it might be possible to arrange a visit to one of these centers.

6. A number of Indians now living in the United States have had training in their native dance. Search your Indian community for someone who might perform for your students. Also view some of the videotapes on dance listed at the end of this chapter.

7. Show videotapes or films on Indian music (an annotated list appears in the Filmography). India also has one of the largest movie industries in the world, and many Indian films are now shown in the United States, particularly in metropolitan areas. Students may enjoy attending these.

BIBLIOGRAPHY

Arden, Harvey, and Raghubir Singh. "Searching for India: Along the Grand Trunk Road," *National Geographic* 177, no. 5, May 1990, 118–38. This article provides a description and pictures of the famous Grand Trunk Road extending from Calcutta in eastern India to Amritsar in northwest India.

Bussagli, Mario, and Calembus Sivaramurti. *Five Thousand Years of the Art of India.* New York: Harry N. Abrams, 1971. This book includes pictures and information about India.

Capwell, Charles. "The Music of India." In *Excursions in World Musics,* edited by Bruno Nettl et al. Englewood Cliffs, NJ: Prentice-Hall, 1992, 14–42. This provides an excellent brief introduction to Indian music.

Edwards, Mike, and Roland Michaud. "Paradise on Earth: When the Moguls Ruled India," *National Geographic* 167, no. 4, April 1985, 463–93. This article contains photographs and information about India.

Heiderer, Tony. "Sacred Space, Sacred Time: India's Maha Kumbh Mela," *National Geographic* 177, no. 5, May 1990, 106–117. This article offers a description, with pictures, of India's largest religious festival, the Hindu Maha Kumbh Mela.

Hodgson, Bryan, and Steve Taymer. "Mirror of India: New Delhi," *National Geographic* 167, no. 4, April 1985, 506–33. This article contains photographs and information about present-day India.

Holroyde, Peggy. *The Music of India.* New York: Praeger Publishers, 1972. This interesting book, about many facets of Indian music, is written for the general reader.

Ions, Veronica. *Indian Mythology.* New York: P. Bedrick Books, 1984. This is a good introduction to Indian religions: Hinduism, Buddhism, and Jainism.

Jairazbhoy, N. A. *The Rags of North Indian Music.* Middletown, CT: Wesleyan University Press, 1971. This book contains a detailed discussion of rags [ragas] in North India. Chapter One on present-day classical music is particularly recommended for the novice. A record is included with Vilayat Khan playing the sitar; he illustrates the characteristics of eight rags.

Kaufmann, Walter. *The Ragas of North India.* Bloomington, IN: Indiana University Press, 1968. This paperback contains a detailed discussion of the ragas of North Indian music. It is useful for the teacher who is looking for information on the characteristics of various ragas.

Lee, Sherman E. *Far Eastern Art,* 5th ed. New York: Prentice-Hall and Harry N. Abrams, 1994.

This book contains information about Indian art.

Munro, Eleanor C. *The Encyclopedia of Art*. New York: Golden Press, 1961. This book contains photographs of Indian architecture, sculpture, and painting.

Neuman, Daniel M. *The Life of Music in North India*. Chicago: University of Chicago Press, 1990. This is a well-written study of music in the culture of North India.

Putman, John J. "Focus on India: Festivals across the U. S. Celebrate a Diverse Culture," *National Geographic* 167, no. 4, April 1985, 460–61. This article contains photographs and information about India.

Rai, Raghu. "India: Life on the Edge," *National Geographic* 174, no. 6, December 1988, 930–34. This article contains excellent pictures with some commentary.

Sadie, Stanley, ed. *The New Grove Dictionary of Music and Musicians*. New York: Grove's Dictionaries of Music, 1994. An outstanding section on the music of India is included in Volume 9.

Satow, Michael G. "India's Railway Lifeline," *National Geographic* 165, no. 6, June 1984, 744–49. This article contains both information and excellent photographs.

Scofield, John, and Raghubir Singh. "Bombay, the Other India," *National Geographic* 160, no. 1, July 1981, 105–29. This article contains information about and excellent photographs of Bombay.

Shankar, Ravi. *My Music, My Life*. New York: Simon and Schuster, 1968. This paperback contains one of the best short descriptions of North Indian music. Pictures of musical instruments are provided, as is a section on learning to play the sitar.

Sivaramurti, Calembus. *5000 Years of the Art of India*. New York: Harry N. Abrams, 1971. This is a good source of art reproductions.

Van Dyk, Jere, Raghubir Singh, and Galen Rowell. "Long Journey on the Brahmaputra," *National Geographic* 174, no. 5, November 1988, 672–711. This article contains a description and pictures of a trip along the Brahmaputra, one of India's longest rivers extending eighteen hundred miles from western Tibet to the Indian Ocean.

Wade, Bonnie C. *Music in India: The Classical Traditions*. Englewood Cliffs, NJ: Prentice-Hall, 1979; reprinted 1987. This book provides a concise introduction to both the North Indian (Hindustani) and South Indian (Karnatak) musical traditions. It includes an annotated bibliography, discography, and filmography, as well as a glossary.

Wade, Bonnie C. "Some Principles of Indian Classical Music." In *Musics of Many Cultures*, edited by Elizabeth May. Berkeley, CA: University of California Press, 1980, 83–110. This article serves as an excellent introduction to Indian music. It includes a selected bibliography, discography, and filmography.

Welch, Stuart C. *India: Art and Culture, 1300–1900*. New York: Metropolitan Museum of Art and Holt, Rinehart, and Winston, 1985. This book contains good photographs of Indian architecture, sculpture, and painting.

DISCOGRAPHY

Festival of India: A Hindustani Sampler. Music of the World (MOW) CDT-121. An excellent CD featuring a number of North Indian musical compositions.

Hariprasad Chaurasia, Flute Concert. Bainbridge RSC-22. This recording features two of India's most outstanding contemporary performers: Hariprasad Chaurasia, flute, accompanied by Zakir Hussain, tabla, performing in raga *madhuvanti*.

Zakir Hussain–Super Percussion of India. World Music Library CD 5113. This is a recording by one of India's most distinguished tabla performers.

Improvisations, featuring Ravi Shankar (sitar) and Paul Horn and Bud Shank (flutes). Bainbridge RSC-6. This recording combines Indian melodic and rhythmic modes and jazz to produce an exciting contemporary musical ensemble.

Percussion of India. World Music Library CD 5168. This is an excellent compact disc featuring a variety of India's percussion performers.

G. S. Sachdev—*Flights of Improvisation.* Lyrichord LYRCD 7416. This recording features two of India's most outstanding artists, G. S. Sachdev, flute, with accompaniment by Zakir Hussain, tabla.

Shivkumar Sharma and Zakir Hussain—Music for Santur and Tabla. Nimbus NI 5110. This recording features Shivkumar Sharma on the *santur* (struck zither) accompanied by Zakir Hussain on tabla.

The Sounds of India: Ravi Shankar. Columbia CK 09296. This recording contains four North Indian instrumental compositions performed by Ravi Shankar; an explanation of the raga and tala used is given before each performance.

Editor's note: *Schwann/Spectrum Recordings* (published quarterly by Stereophile, Inc., 208 Delgado Street, Santa Fe, New Mexico 87501) lists, among other things, the currently available recordings of Indian music. In addition, an excellent selection of compact discs, audiocassettes, and videotapes is provided by the World Music Institute, 49 West 27th Street, Suite 810, New York, NY 10001, and the Ali Akbar College Store, 215 West End Avenue, San Rafael, CA 94901.

FILMOGRAPHY

Classical Music of North India. 33 minutes, color. Available from the University of Washington, Educational Media Collection, 35 Kane Hall, Seattle, WA 98195; phone: 206-543-9909. This film features the distinguished *sarod* performer Ali Akbar Khan.

Discovering the Music of India. Videocassette. 22 minutes, color. Available from West Music Company, 1208 Fifth Street, PO Box 5521, Coralville, IA 52241. This film contains excellent examples of both North and South Indian music. South Indian examples include the flute (*venu*), the drum (*mridangam*), the violin, and the tambura. Featured instruments from North India are the sitar and tabla. A short example of Indian dance is also included.

The JVC Video Anthology of World Music and Dance. Available from Rounder Records, 61 Prospect Street, Montpelier, VT 05602. This video anthology contains three tapes (11, 12, and 13) devoted to Indian music and dance, along with an accompanying book.

Kathak: North Indian Dance. Videocassette. Available from The Asia Society, Performing Arts Department, 725 Park Avenue, New York, NY 10021. Birju Maharaj and Company appear in this presentation, which includes *vandana* (prayer dance), a *kathak* solo demonstration of pure dance movement and intricate rhythms, and *Geetopadesh,* the gambling scene between the Pandava and the Kaurava princes as depicted in a story from the Mahabharata.

Kathakali: South Indian Dance-Drama from the Kerala Kalamandalam. Videocassette. Available from The Asia Society, Performing Arts Department, 725 Park Avenue, New York, NY 10021. Dating from the sixteenth century, *Kathakali* dance-drama is India's most dynamic epic theater form. *Kathakali* performance technique stems in part from a vigorous martial arts tradition. The form is a fascinating combination of music, a sung text, mime, and dance with rich costume and elaborate makeup.

Sitara. Videocassette. Available from The Asia Society, Performing Arts Department, 725 Park Avenue, New York, NY 10021. India's most celebrated *Kathak* dancer, Sitara, performs an invocation to the elephant god Ganesha, as well as *Tora Tukra,* a pure dance form emphasizing time measure and different rhythmic patterns; *Mayur Nritya,* the dance of the peacock; and *Tatkar,* in which the intricate footwork displays *Kathak*'s complicated and varied rhythms.

Yamini Krishnamurti: South Indian Dance. Videocassette. Available from The Asia Society, Performing Arts Department, 725 Park Avenue, New York, NY 10021. A virtuoso of South Indian dance, Yamini Krishnamurthi performs in two classical styles. In the *bharata natyam* style, she presents "Navarasa Slokam" ("The Nine Classical Sentiments"), and in the romantic, ebullient style of *Kuchipudi,* she dances "Manduka Sabdam" ("The Frog Who Became a Queen"). The program ends with "Tillana," a pure, abstract, *bharata natyam* dance.

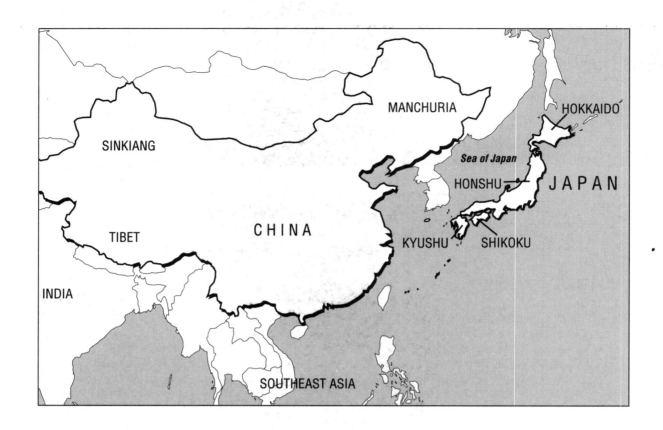

SINKIANG

MANCHURIA

HOKKAIDO

TIBET

CHINA

Sea of Japan

HONSHU

JAPAN

INDIA

KYUSHU   SHIKOKU

SOUTHEAST ASIA

Map of East Asia

CHAPTER 10

MUSIC OF EAST ASIA

by Han Kuo-Huang, Ricardo D. Trimillos, William M. Anderson, and Tatsuko Takizawa

The term East Asia (used interchangeably with "the Far East" and "the Orient") can be defined in three ways: geographically, racially, and culturally. Geographically, it includes the area from the Mongolian Plateau in the north to the monsoon coastline of southeastern China and the western Tibetan mountains to the eastern volcanic Japanese islands. Before the modern industrial age, geographical barriers kept this vast area fairly independent from the rest of the world, resulting in a unique culture.

The majority of East Asian people belong to the Mongoloid race, one of the three major racial classifications of humanity. Mongoloid people are characterized by yellowish skin, brown eyes, and straight, black hair. Numerous subgroups of different languages, dialects, customs, and habits exist throughout this region. The largest linguistic division is the Sino-Tibetan family of languages; Tibetan, Mandarin, and many Chinese dialects belong to this family. The second largest group is the Altaic languages; the Mongolian, Korean, and Japanese languages belong to this classification.[1] The majority of people who speak these languages practice various forms of Buddhism, while a minority practice Islam and Christianity.

East Asia was ruled for hundreds of years by the highly developed civilization of China and was sometimes referred to as the "Chinese culture area." Despite the close association with China, each country or region also developed its own unique culture. The major cultural divisions of East Asia are China (mainland China and Taiwan), Japan, Korea, Mongolia, and Tibet (an autonomous region of China). In a sense, Vietnam, though a country in Southeast Asia, is also culturally related to East Asia (see Chapter 11). This chapter focuses on China and Japan.

This introduction was contributed by Han Kuo-Huang.

CHINA

by Han Kuo-Huang

The immense land mass of China, which stretches across more than three million square miles, is slightly smaller than continental Europe and slightly larger than the continental United States. Only Canada exceeds China in size. The country is enclosed by high plateaus or towering mountains on three sides and is sheltered by the Pacific Ocean on the east and southeast. The country can be broadly divided into five principal regions: Northeast (Manchuria), North (Yellow River area), South (Yangzi River area and southeastern coast), Tibet, and Northwest.[2]

Since about four-fifths of the land is composed of mountains and plateaus, the eastern plains are heavily cultivated and densely populated. The majority of Chinese people who live in the plains are farmers. This eastern portion (with the exception of the northeast) has served as the heartland of Chinese culture. Two great rivers, the Yellow and the Yangzi, pass from west to east and play key roles in the lives of Chinese people. Each river also represents one of the two conventional north-south divisions of Chinese culture: the Yellow River is the cradle of Chinese civilization, and the Yangzi River is the Chinese equivalent of the Mississippi.

China's population is close to one billion—the largest in the world. One of every four persons on earth is Chinese. The majority of the Chinese people belong to the Han people, who were named for the great Han Dynasty. They make up 94 percent of the total population, so the Chinese culture we know is essentially the Han culture. The remaining 6 percent of the population is composed of fifty-five national minorities, scattered over 50 to 60 percent of the country. They live mostly in mountainous hinterlands or border areas. Their languages and customs may be totally assimilated in the dominant culture or completely foreign. For instance, the Manchu in the Northeast are highly Sinicized, but the Uygur in Xinjiang (northwest region) are Turkic people whose religion is Islam and whose culture is Central Asian.

The Han Chinese are further divided into various subgroups, each of which has its own dialect and customs. A northerner would not understand a southern dialect and vice versa. For thousands of years, the unifying element of the people has been a common written language. The language is based on single characters; many characters have been formed from a representative picture of a word.

Since the early twentieth century, the Beijing dialect (Mandarin) has been adopted as the national language. Like many African languages, Mandarin is a tonal language with four levels of intonation for each phoneme. This means that a phonetic can have four meanings depending on the tonal level at which it is pronounced, and the written character for each one of the four is different. For instance, "ma" can mean "mother" (with *ping*, or even intonation), "hemp" (with *shang*, or rising intonation), "horse" (with *qu*, or falling intonation), or "to curse" (with *ru*, or entering intonation, an abrupt downward pitch glide). Its monosyllabic nature and changing tones distinguish Mandarin from Western languages, which are written with combinations of letters in an alphabet.

Many Westerners believe that Chinese people subscribe to three major religions: Confucianism (native), Daoism (native), and Buddhism (imported from India). To the Chinese, however, Confucianism is a code of ethics rather than a religion. Its philosophical principles permeate many aspects of their lives and merge with Daoism, Buddhism, and Christianity. The Chinese are able to embrace two or more philosophical and religious beliefs without contradiction. The following anecdote reflects this: "When a man is in a position of authority, he is a Confucianist because that doctrine supports the status quo. Out of power or office, a man becomes a Daoist because Daoism deprecates both worldly authority and individual responsibility. As death approaches, a man turns to Buddhism because that faith offers hope of salvation."[3] No matter what religion a Chinese person embraces, the most fundamental principle in his or her life is the filial piety that is realized in the practice of ancestor worship.

The Chinese refer to their country as *Zhongguo*, which is literally translated as "The Middle Country." In ancient times, the Chinese considered their locality to be the center of the world and their culture far superior to those of surrounding peoples. In a historical and cultural sense, *Zhongguo* is more appropriately translated by Western authors as "The Middle Kingdom." The Han Chinese have lived and worked in this Middle Kingdom for more than four thousand years.

The legendary history of China begins with the Five Emperors Period (2250–2140 B.C.). The Zhou Dynasty succeeded the Five Emperors Period and set up a system of feudal lords. By the end of the Zhou Dynasty, the feudal lords were in constant battle, and a powerful lord was needed to unite the country. Qin Shi Huang became the First Emperor of China in 221 B.C. (the Qin Dynasty). Under his rule, the Chinese built the famous Great Wall and created thousands of terracotta warriors and horses. Imperial China lasted for two thousand years, and in 1912, the last emperor was dethroned and a republic was founded. Some of the important dynasties include the Zhou (1122–221 B.C.), Han (206 B.C.–220 A.D.), Tang (618–907), Sung (960–1127), Yuan or Mongolian (1278–1368), Ming (1368–1644), and Qing, the Manchu (1644–1912).

Unlike many ancient civilizations that have risen and fallen, Chinese culture has continued uninterrupted for thousands of years. The numerous contributions the Chinese offer to the world are not limited to philosophy and applied science, but include the arts. Chinese bronze casting, jade carving, ceramic making, sculpture, painting, calligraphy, and music are highly valued throughout the world.

Chinese music

When discussing Han Chinese music, it is common to distinguish two major styles: northern and southern. The styles correspond to the two major geographical and cultural areas where most Han people live. Although both styles emanate from the general Han Chinese culture, they differ in detail because of environmental conditions. The north is cold, dry, and windy. The hardships of life are reflected in the high-pitched, tense, and agitated style of folk song. The south, on the other hand, has mild weather and much rain. Life seems to be easier, and the folk songs of the south are generally lyrical and gentle in nature. Chinese music today is also influenced by Western musical concepts, which is an inevitable consequence of historical and social change.

The common belief that the Chinese scale is a pentatonic scale (without half steps) is only partly correct. The Han Chinese have at least three forms of a seven-tone scale (see figure 1). They also use various forms of a five-tone pentatonic scale (see figure 2).

Southern Chinese folk songs tend to progress in more conjunct motion and smoother lines and emphasize the intervals of thirds and fifths. Northern melodies tend to progress in more disjunct, angular motion, and emphasize intervals of a fourth. These tendencies in the use of melodies are related to the tonal characteristics of the contrasting dialects of the two areas.

Except in special cases (such as free-rhythm introductions), most Chinese music is in duple rhythm. This fondness for duple rhythm (the Western equivalent of 2/4 and 4/4) can be attributed to the belief in the principle of natural duality (such as the female-male or yin-yang relationship). Chinese rhythm patterns may also reflect the Confucian *Zhongyong* concept: a "doctrine of the mean" that stresses moderation and balance. However, the weak beat to strong beat stresses in Western music are not necessarily used. Triple meter is rare, even in modern folk compositions. Syncopation, on the other hand, is the norm rather than the exception.

Chinese instrumental music is traditionally heterophonic if it is performed on more than one instrument or for an instrument and voice. Although Chinese music does not use the triadic, four-part harmonic progressions of Western music, harmony may occur occasionally. In fact, the *sheng* mouth organ (see figure 3) produces fourths and fifths when played in the traditional manner, and some *qin* and *zheng* zither (see figure 4) pas-

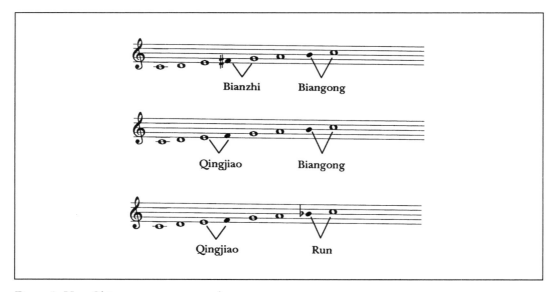

Figure 1. Han Chinese seven-tone scales

sages have two or more pitches sounding together when the musicians pluck two or more strings simultaneously. The Chinese people's fondness for clarity may have prevented them from developing a heavy musical texture.

Perhaps the most intricate aspect of traditional Chinese music, and of much East Asian music, is the use of nuance in instrumental and vocal timbre. Even when playing one instrument, there are minute differences in timbre production of a single tone. Much attention is placed on the production and control of single tones; each tone is regarded as a musical entity. The best example of this is heard in *qin* zither music.

Vocal music is also complicated because of complex tonal inflections and the intricacies of the Chinese language. For example, even though Chinese words are monosyllabic, a singer takes great care in enunciating the "head" (beginning), "belly" (middle), and "tail" (end) of each word in Kun opera and Nanguan music. Therefore, timbre in Chinese music has a deeper meaning than simply tone color as an end in itself.

Chinese vocal quality is often described as being high-pitched and nasal. This is generally true, but there are regional differences. The northern style of singing (such as Peking opera) tends to be higher and more shrill than the southern style of singing (such as Kun opera or Nanguan). This north-south contrast in vocal quality can even be heard in the local Baiguan (northern-style theater) and Nanquan (southern-style theater or lyric song) on the island of Taiwan.

Thousands of indigenous and Sinicized musical instruments exist in China, but the Chinese seem to favor chordophones and aerophones. The famous term "silk and bamboo" refers to the ancient use of stringed instruments with silk strings and wind instruments made of bamboo. Of all the chordophones, the *qin* zither is by far the most venerated. It is depicted in many paintings and mentioned in classic literature. Next in importance to the *qin* zither is the *zheng* zither. In the past, solos and small ensembles were more characteristic of traditional Chinese music making; the large Chinese orchestra with a baton-waving conductor is a product of the twentieth century.

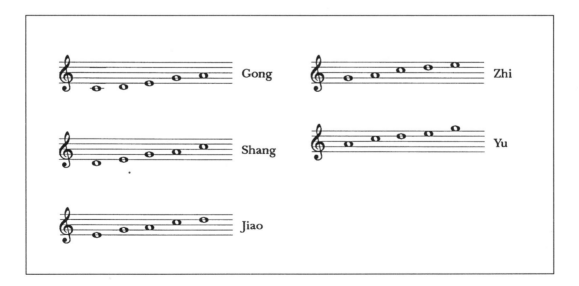

Figure 2. Han Chinese pentatonic scales

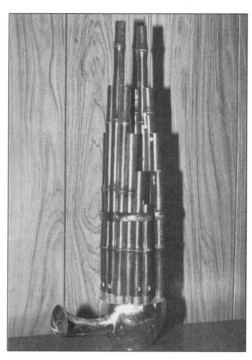

Figure 3. Sheng (mouth organ)

Figure 4. Professor Liang Tsai-Ping playing the *zheng* (zither)

314   *Multicultural Perspectives in Music Education*

Figure 5. *Pipa* (lute)

Figure 6. *Erhu* (a two-stringed fiddle)

Figure 7. *Di or dizi* (side-blown flute)

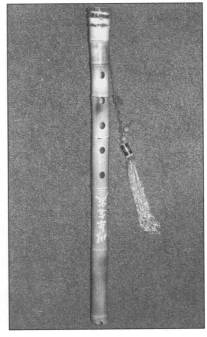

Figure 8. *Xiao* (end-blown flute)

The *pipa* lute (see figure 5) originated in Central Asia and is an instrument of great virtuosic possibilities. It is the subject of many paintings and poems and has held a societal position similar to that of the guitar in Western culture. Currently, the *erhu*, or two-stringed fiddle (see figure 6), is the most popular instrument in China. It originated in the northern tribes and is available in many sizes and variations. This fiddle is the "violin" of the modern Chinese orchestra. The *sanxian* lute is a banjo-like instrument that is used to accompany narrative singing. The *yangqin* is a many-stringed hammer dulcimer that originated in Persia. Its function is somewhat like that of the piano: it serves as either a solo instrument or an accompanying instrument.

In the aerophone category, *di* or *dizi* side-blown flutes (see figure 7) are the most numerous. The *xiao* end-blown flute (see figure 8) is also a popular instrument. Perhaps the most exotic wind instrument is the *sheng*, a mouth organ that can produce many notes simultaneously. A popular folk wind instrument is the *suona*, a double-reed instrument that evolved from the Middle Eastern *zurna*. Because of recent archaeological discoveries, Chinese musicians have had a revived interest in the ancient *bianzhong* (bronze bell chimes) and *bianqing* (stone chimes). Variations of many Chinese musical instruments can be found in Japan, Korea, Vietnam, Tibet, and Mongolia.

Westerners sometimes describe Chinese music as "loud." The Chinese themselves consider the northern style more dynamic and energetic and the southern style softer and more graceful. All of these characterizations are oversimplified, as the dynamics in Chinese music actually vary according to the nature of the musical genres and instruments. The classical music of Confucian scholars, such as *qin* zither music and lyric songs, is naturally soft. Players of *pipa* lute music are capable of expressing a full range of dynamics. Music for the *suona* is loud and piercing because of the instrument's construction and its function as an outdoor instrument. Theater orchestra music is loud because it was originally played outdoors in a festive atmosphere. Because of the many factors affecting dynamics in Chinese music, there is no one concept that can adequately describe them.

With the exception of work songs and *shange* (mountain songs), most Han Chinese folk songs, like most songs in Western folk music, are constructed in strophic form. Chinese folk music, however, uses fewer refrains. Typically, a folk song consists of two or four phrases of equal length; each phrase contains a new musical idea. Two-phrase songs are called "question-answer" songs, and four-phrase songs are "open" (*qi*), "inheriting" (*cheng*), "turned" (*zhuan*), and "closed" (*he*) songs, all of which are terms borrowed from literary writing techniques. Much of Chinese opera music is based on a more complex melodic and rhythmic motivic system called *Banqian*.[4]

Of all the instrumental forms of Chinese music, the most popular are suites and variations. These forms are not, however, entirely equivalent to their Western counterparts. A Chinese suite is a series of musical movements that are loosely connected. These movements may be independent selections that do not have an apparent melodic or rhythmic relationship, or they may be related for programmatic reasons.

A major characteristic of Chinese instrumental variations is the use of identification motives called the *hetou* (refrain head) or *hewei* (refrain tail) that appear in the beginning and end of each movement. Again, except for these refrain motives, there might be no other relationship between the variations and the refrains or among the variations themselves. Sometimes, a movement appears several times among the other movements in a suite; this is considered a variation technique. Due to Western influence, ABA form has become extremely popular in modern instrumental folk music.

The Chinese have traditionally shown a fondness for extramusical connotations, so program music, poetic titles, and descriptions of compositions are popular. The existence of a sophisticated literary class is responsible for shaping this tradition, which is found not only in old music but also in modern socialist and so-called revolutionary works.

LESSON 1

■ **Objectives**

Students will:
1. Sing the songs "The Eldest Daughter of the Jiang Family" and "Jasmine Flowers of the Sixth Moon."
2. Identify the pentatonic scales in each song.
3. Identify the use of duple (quadruple) meter and syncopation.
4. Identify strophic form.

■ **Materials**

1. Photos of the Great Wall of China from *Journey into China* by Kenneth C. Danforth, ed. (Washington, DC: National Geographic Society, 1982)
2. Chalkboard

■ **Procedures**

1. Sing "The Eldest Daughter of the Jiang Family" (see figure 9) and "Jasmine Flowers of the Sixth Moon" (see figure 10). The first song, "The Eldest Daughter of the Jiang Family," is about a woman who thinks of her husband, who has gone off to build the Great Wall. Students should look for good photos of the Great Wall to place on the bulletin board. The second song, "Jasmine Flowers of the Sixth Moon," is from Taiwan and is about a girl who compares herself to jasmine flowers. "Sixth moon" means the sixth month of the lunar calendar, which is in the spring.
2. Have the students write the five pitches of the pentatonic melodies for each song on the chalkboard. These pitches are G, A, B, D, and E for "The Eldest Daughter of the Jiang Family" and G, A, C, D, and E for "Jasmine Flowers of the Sixth Moon."
3. Have the students conduct the duple (or quadruple) meter as they sing the songs.
4. Have the class clap the syncopated rhythms found in the first measure of "The Eldest Daughter of the Jiang Family" and the sixth measure of "Jasmine Flowers of the Sixth Moon."
5. Have the students outline the phrases of the songs by moving their right arms alternately right and left in time with the four-measure phrases in "The Eldest Daughter of the Jiang Family" and the two-measure phrases in "Jasmine Flowers of the Sixth Moon."
6. As the class sings the various verses of text to the same melodies, call attention to the strophic form of each song.

This lesson was contributed by Han Kuo-Huang and William M. Anderson.

The Eldest Daughter of the Jiang Family

Jiangsu

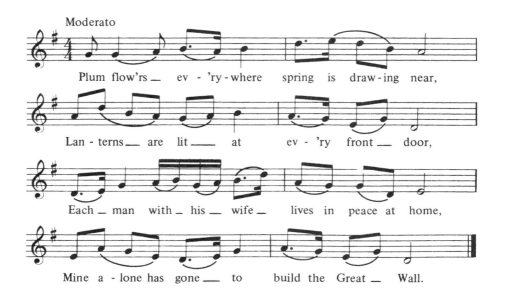

Moderato

Plum flow'rs ev-'ry-where spring is draw-ing near,

Lan-terns are lit at ev-'ry front door,

Each man with his wife lives in peace at home,

Mine a-lone has gone to build the Great Wall.

2. The lotus trembles in the summer heat,
    Flying insects fill the evening air,
    Let them feast on my limbs tender and frail,
    Lest they should torment my love Xi Liang.

3. Autumn flowers gild the Ninth Moon,
    Wine cups pass round where the asters bloom,
    My cup untouched, brimming like my tears,
    Since my love is away, I cannot drink wine.

4. Winter ushers in ice and snow,
    Meng Jiang Nü toils a thousand miles through,
    I trudge alone, for I hear the call,
    Of my love dying by the Great Wall.

Figure 9. "The Eldest Daughter of the Jiang Family"

Jasmine Flowers of the Sixth Moon
(Liuyue Moli)

Taiwan
Text adapted by Rebecca Schwan

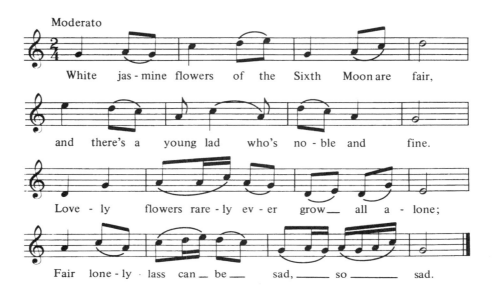

White jas - mine flowers of the Sixth Moon are fair,

and there's a young lad who's no - ble and fine.

Love - ly flowers rare - ly ev - er grow__ all a - lone;

Fair lone - ly · lass can __ be __ sad, ____ so _____ sad.

2.   White jasmine flowers of the Sixth Moon are fair,
     Lovely lass has never been found.
     Flowers and lasses should never be alone;
     Sad is the lovely lass who's never, never found.

3.   White jasmine flowers of the Sixth Moon are fair,
     Lasses alone are sorry and sad.
     Lovely flowers should be blooming side by side,
     When will the lass be found and never be alone?

Figure 10. "Jasmine Flowers of the Sixth Moon"

LESSON 2

■ **Objectives**

Students will:
1. Play in a Chinese percussion ensemble.
2. Perform several compositions with percussion instruments.

■ **Materials**

1. Cymbals
2. Small gongs played with a thin wooden mallet
3. Large gongs played with a padded mallet
4. Large drums played with two thick sticks

■ **Procedures**

1. Give the students the following background information: The Chinese call their percussion ensemble *luogu,* which means "gongs and drums" (see figure 11). It may range in size from two to a small group of players. Percussion ensembles are used in a variety of settings: in theaters, parades, and folk music groups. The four major instruments used in Chinese percussion music are the *bo* cymbals, the *xiaoluo* (small gong), the *daluo* (large gong), and the *dagu* (large skin-headed drum). If Chinese instruments are not available, use Western substitutes, such as drums, tam-tam, and small cymbals.

Figure 11. Luogu ensemble

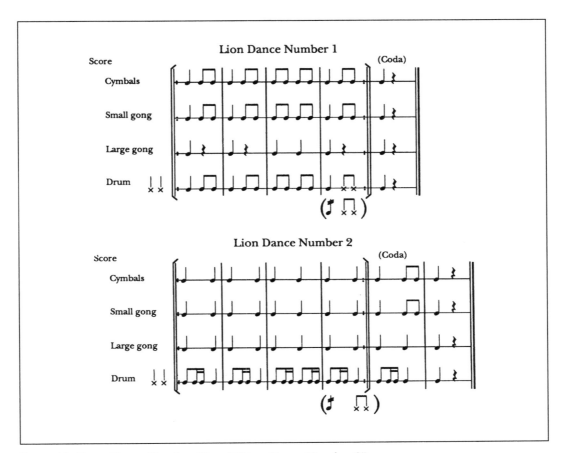

Figure 12. "Lion Dance Number 1" and "Lion Dance Number 2"

Figure 13. "Dragon Dance"

2. Perform the "Lion Dance Number 1" and the "Lion Dance Number 2" (see figure 12), and then perform the "Dragon Dance" (see figure 13). Read the following performance instructions before proceeding:

   a. The drummer is the leader of the ensemble and sets the tempo (each quarter note equals approximately 100–112) by striking the drum twice on the rim before each selection (indicated in the score by the x-shaped note heads). Each composition repeats in ostinato fashion. To end the performance, the drummer should play the ending signal, which is a drum roll followed by two eighth notes, shown just below the appropriate measure of the score. This signal leads the group to the conclusion.

   b. Perform each composition alone. When the students have mastered the performances, play all the compositions together as a suite, repeating the individual segments as many times as you wish. When played as a suite, only the introductory signal for the first piece is used; the ending measures of the first and second pieces are omitted. The "ending signals" in the first and second pieces become "changing signals" for the next section.

This lesson was contributed by Han Kuo-Huang.

L E S S O N   3

■ Objectives

Students will:
1. Sing the song "Fuhng Yang Wa Gu" ("Flower Drum Song") and identify the pentatonic scale and the quadruple meter.
2. Accompany the song with percussion instruments.

■ Materials

1. Cymbals
2. Small gongs played with a thin wooden mallet
3. Large gongs played with a padded mallet
4. Large drums played with two thick sticks

■ Procedures

1. Have the class sing "Fuhng Yang Wa Gu" ("Flower Drum Song") (see figure 14).[5] Explain that this is one of the most famous Chinese folk songs. It even became the title of a Broadway musical. Traditionally, the song is sung by a girl who dances and plays a small, flower-decorated drum attached to her waist. Another person, usually a man, plays an accompaniment on a small gong. The words *Drr ling dang piao e piao* mimic the sounds produced by the drum. The students can imitate the drum rolls by rolling their tongues on the syllable *drr*. Notice the pentatonic scale and the quadruple meter.
2. Add a percussion accompaniment as a prelude to the song. As accompaniment to the

Figure 14. "Fuhng Yang Wha Gu"

Figure 15. Accompaniment to the refrain of "Fuhng Yang Wha Gu"

refrain, use *bo* (cymbals), *xiaoluo* (small gong), *daluo* (large gong), and *dagu* (large skin-headed drum) (see figure 15). You may substitute Western drums, tam-tam, and small cymbals.

This lesson was contributed by Han Kuo-Huang.

L E S S O N   4

■ **Objectives**

Students will:

1. Listen to the *zheng* and *xiao* in the composition "Winter Birds Flying over the Water." Students should be able to identify the duple meter, heterophonic texture, and the programmatic character of the music.
2. Listen to the last two minutes of the programmatic composition "The Hero's Defeat." This work is played on the *pipa*, a plucked, stringed instrument.
3. Listen to the composition "Old Monk Sweeping the Buddhist Temple," played on the *sheng*.

■ **Materials**

Recording: "Winter Birds Flying over the Water," "Hero's Defeat," and "Old Monk Sweeping the Buddhist Temple," from *Music Resources for Multicultural Perspectives* (Reston, VA: Music Educators National Conference, 1995)

■ **Procedures**

1. Place a picture of the *zheng* on the bulletin board (see figure 4). Explain that the *zheng* is a zither with strings that run parallel across the instrument (an Autoharp is also a zither). The number of strings on the *zheng* varies from sixteen to twenty-one. Originally, the strings were made of silk, but today they are brass. The instrument is tuned by moving the small bridges under each string, and the instrument is often tuned pentatonically. The *zheng* is traditionally played by plucking the strings with the right hand; in modern playing, performers also use the left hand. A great variety of subtle ornamentations are possible on this instrument.
2. Place a picture of a *xiao* on the bulletin board (see figure 8). The *xiao* is a vertically played flute constructed from bamboo. A notch is fashioned at the upper end of the instrument, and air is directed across it to produce sounds. The air moving across the notched area produces a distinctive, somewhat breathy tone. Different pitches are made possible by the six tone holes, five on top and one on the underside of the instrument.
3. Listen to the composition "Winter Birds Flying over the Water" (on *Music Resources for Multicultural Perspectives*, side D, no. 21) and point out how the title is depicted programmatically in the music (particularly in the sweeping, decorative quality of the melodic lines that capture the sense of birds flying over the water). Also note the distinctive heterophonic texture created by the use of two instruments that are basically

playing the same melody with simultaneous variations. (Heterophonic texture is sometimes present in Western musical genres such as Dixieland.)

4. Write the following list on the board and circle the appropriate items as you listen to the music:

    (1)   (Stringed and wind instruments)   or   Stringed and percussion instruments

    (2)   (Duple meter)   or   Triple meter

    (3)   Major scale   or   (Pentatonic scale)

    (4)   (Soft dynamic level)   or   Loud dynamic level

    (5)   Chordal harmony   or   (Heterophony)

5. Place a picture of the *pipa* on the bulletin board (see figure 5). Explain that the *pipa* is a plucked stringed instrument similar to the Western guitar. Unlike our guitar, however, the *pipa* is held with the base end of the instrument resting on the lap with the neck standing more or less straight up. Sounds are produced by plucking the four strings of the instrument. Since the sounds of the vibrating strings die away quickly, *pipa* players pluck the strings repetitively, rolling the fingers in a tremolo technique like that used on the flamenco guitar so that a nearly continuous sound is produced.

6. Explain that many of the compositions for the *pipa* are programmatic; that is, a program or story is depicted through music. In "Hero's Defeat," the *pipa* is used to depict a battle between the kingdoms of Han and Chu. The marching of the armies and the clashing of swords are vividly portrayed in the music.

7. As you listen to the last two minutes of the "Hero's Defeat" on *Music Resources for Multicultural Perspectives*, side D, no. 23, circle the appropriate items listed below:

    (1)   Bowed stringed instrument   or   (Plucked stringed instrument)

    (2)   Very slow tempo   or   (Moderate tempo)

    (3)   (Duple meter)   or   Triple meter

    (4)   (Program music)   or   ABA form

8. Listen to the composition "Old Monk Sweeping the Buddhist Temple" (on *Music Resources for Multicultural Perspectives*, side D, no. 22) played on the *sheng* (see figure 3). Explain that the Chinese *sheng* is one of the most unusual wind instruments in the world. It is constructed with a rounded, bowl-shaped base from which extend many vertical bamboo pipes of different lengths. Each of these contains a small, "free" reed that is activated when air passes through the pipe. A mouthpiece is joined to the base of the instrument and the performer both exhales and inhales air into the instrument. To produce different pitches, the performer covers small holes located at the bottom of each bamboo pipe, making the air move through the pipe and activate a reed. One of the distinctive features of *sheng* music is produced by uninterrupted exhaling and inhaling, making a continuous sound on the instrument. Another feature is that a *sheng* player can play several notes at once—a kind of harmony—by covering the holes in several bamboo pipes at the same time. The harmonica is a distant relative of

the *sheng*. Bring a harmonica to class and demonstrate how "continuous" sound is produced by exhaling and inhaling air through the instrument. Demonstrate how harmony is created by several different reeds being activated at the same time. Carefully remove the outer covering of the instrument and show the students the "free" reeds that are activated to produce the sound.

9. Have the students listen to "Old Monk Sweeping the Buddhist Temple" again, this time circling the appropriate items in the following list as they listen:

(1) Stringed instrument or (Wind instrument)

(2) (Music is loud) or Music is soft

(3) (Music has harmony) or Music has no harmony

(4) (Music moves in twos (duple meter)) or Music moves in threes (triple meter)

10. Summarize the lesson by having the students discuss similarities and differences between Chinese instruments and instruments with which they are more familiar.

This lesson was contributed by William M. Anderson.

L E S S O N   5

■ Objectives

Students will:
1. Study Chinese opera by sketching pictures of Chinese opera characters and musical instruments.
2. Watch the film *A Night at the Peking Opera,* noting the elaborate costuming, the sparse staging, and the highly developed use of mime.
3. Listen to a brief segment of spoken dialogue and an aria from Peking opera, particularly noticing the tense, nasalized vocal quality.

■ Materials

1. Illustrations of Chinese opera characters and instruments—one source is *Peking Opera: A Short Guide* by Elizabeth Halson (Hong Kong: Oxford University Press, 1966)
2. Film: *A Night at the Peking Opera*
3. Recording: "The Chinese Opera," from *Music Resources for Multicultural Perspectives* (Reston, VA: Music Educators National Conference, 1995)
4. Bulletin board

■ Procedures

1. Explain that Chinese opera is a brilliant art form in which musical dramas are executed

Figure 16. Chinese opera character

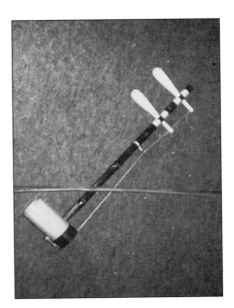

Figure 17. Jinghu (bowed-string instrument)

by elaborately attired actors who speak the dialogue and sing songs (arias). Among the interesting visual features of the opera are the beautiful costumes and the ornate make-up used by the characters (see figure 16). Each character is dressed in a distinctive costume to highlight his or her position in the drama.

2. Have the students sketch pictures of Chinese opera characters and musical instruments (using models from *Peking Opera: A Short Guide*) and place them on the bulletin board.

3. Watch the film *A Night at the Peking Opera*. This film contains several segments from different operas. Notice the elaborate costuming of the characters, the great attention placed on mime (specifically how the characters are able to create powerful effects through imaginative suggestion), and the distinctive spoken dialogue and singing style.

4. Listen to an aria from *The Chinese Opera*. This aria contains brief segments of dialogue and is sung by two characters who are accompanied by *jinghu* (see figure 17) and *erhu* (see figure 6), *dizi* (see figure 5), and percussion (see figure 11). Have the students pay particular attention to the singers' nasalized tone quality and lack of wide vibrato, the elongated speech patterns of the dialogue, the heterophonic nature of the accompanying stringed and wind instruments, and the punctuating and concluding percussion sounds. As the students listen, have them circle the appropriate items from the following list:

(1)	Voices only	or	(Voices and instruments)
(2)	(Loud dynamic level)	or	Soft dynamic level
(3)	(Nasalized tone colors)	or	Open, full sounds
(4)	Brass instruments	or	(Percussion instruments)
(5)	Chordal harmony	or	(Heterophony)

5. Summarize the lesson by having the class review some of the distinctive features of Chinese opera.

This lesson was contributed by William M. Anderson.

NOTES

1. John K. Eairbank, Edwin O. Reischauer, and Albert M. Craig, *East Asia: Tradition and Transformation* (Boston: Houghton Mifflin, 1973), 6–8.
2. Philip A. True, "Geography," in *The People's Republic of China: A Handbook,* ed. Harold C. Hinton (Boulder, CO: Westview Press, 1979), 9–10.
3. Loren Fessler, *China* (New York: Time-Life International, 1968), 78.
4. For more information, see Mingyue Liang, *Music of the Billion: An Introduction to Chinese Music Culture* (New York: Heinrichshofen Edition, 1985), 143–254.
5. "Fuhng Yang Wa Gu" is the title of this song in the older (Wade-Giles) system of romanization. It may also be spelled "Feng Yang Hua Gu."

JAPAN

by Ricardo D. Trimillos

Japan forms the eastern boundary of northeast Asia and the Chinese culture area (the area in which Chinese cultural influence is dominant). Japanese culture is the East Asian culture most familiar to Americans and serves as a summary of the northeast Asian experience. It has drawn in the past on the civilizations of China, Korea, and Okinawa. In a sense, it is a living museum of some traditions of these other cultures.

The Japanese archipelago forms the northern part of an island chain that extends through Taiwan and the Philippines to the south. Okinawa (the Ryukyu Islands) was formerly an independent kingdom situated between Japan and the Philippines. It is now politically part of Japan but maintains a distinct culture. The central island of Honshu, where the capital city of Tokyo and the historical capitals of Kyoto and Nara are located, is the focal point for traditional Japanese culture as well as for many economic, religious, and political developments important to present-day Japan.

The islands are volcanic in origin, with dramatic, mountainous landscapes. The topography, climate, and geography of the islands have helped shape a cultural attitude of great respect and closeness to nature. The Japanese have survived in a harsh natural environment, featuring limited arable land, typhoons, earthquakes, and tidal waves. An aesthetic counterpoint is provided to this harshness by hot springs, mountains, whirlpools, and lakes. The changes in the seasons are extreme. Most of Japan experiences seasons similar to the northeastern United States: cold, snowy winters and hot, humid summers. Spring and fall are transitions between these two extremes, times for celebrations such as cherry blossom viewing in the spring and rice festivals in the fall. Southern Japan is semi-tropical, which contrasts with the rest of the country. In Okinawa, tropical fruit such as pineapple and papaya can be found.

As an island nation, Japan's relation to the sea is a very special one. Rather than functioning as a barrier, the ocean serves as an important means for international contact and trade. Japanese merchant and military fleets have traveled throughout Asia and the Pacific. The Japanese have used this seagoing mobility to enrich their own culture as well as to influence other cultures. The sea is also the basis for such disparate industries as growing cultured pearls and oil supertanker construction. The sea is also the source of the fish and seaweed that form a major part of Japanese cuisine. The staple food, rice, dominates the Japanese diet so much that the word for rice (*gohan*) also means "meal." The important cycle of planting, growing, and harvesting rice is marked by a number of folk and court ceremonies. Rice is also the source of *sake*, the distinctive wine used for rituals such as marriages or the dedication of a shrine, as well as for general celebrations.

The ritual life of traditional Japan is greatly enriched by the presence of two belief systems: Shinto, an indigenous veneration of ancestors, and Buddhism, a religion taken from China. Many Japanese families observe both Shinto and Buddhist rites, exhibiting a talent for accommodation that has served the Japanese well in both the cultural and economic spheres. Shinto has a rich repertoire of music and dance used for its rituals and observances. Buddhism has had far-reaching effects on philosophy, aesthetics, and literature and has also had a profound impact on the secular performing arts, particularly theater and music. Japan today is a fairly homogeneous society and is one of the few modern Asian nations that has had a single language throughout most of its history. The elite or "artistic" cultural traditions, in particular, encapsulate the Japanese cultural identity. It is therefore these formal traditions, rather than the regionally distinct folk traditions, that are discussed here.

History

In its first historical phase (Nara Period, 553–794 A.D.), Japan was greatly influenced by Chinese civilization and subsequently absorbed cultural streams from Korea and India as well. Buddhism was introduced from India via China, and court life borrowed much from the Qin and Tang courts. Buddhist chant and the ritual music of Shinto developed in this early era. The first Golden Age followed (Heian Period, 794–1185), in which foreign elements were assimilated, forming the basis for many Japanese traditions. The emperor unified political power, his divine right rule reinforced by Shinto principles. During this period, traditions of Buddhist music and *gagaku* court music were prevalent. In the fourteenth century, political unity disintegrated, the emperors lost their power, and a rising merchant class led to the development of popular theater and other entertainment traditions.

In the seventeenth century, Japan enjoyed a second Golden Age, politically unified by the military rule of the shogunate with its samurai warrior class. During this remarkable two centuries of conscious isolation from the rest of the world (Tokugawa Period, 1615–1868), the traditional arts as we know them reached their zenith: *kabuki* theater, lyric, and narrative song traditions; the chamber music of *koto*, *shakuhachi*, and *shamisen*;

and the renewed sixth century *gagaku* court music, to name a few. In the last few decades of the nineteenth century (Meiji Restoration), Japan opened itself to the rest of the world, accepting and actively importing Western products and culture, including technology, public education systems, and music. This was a second era of internationalism, this time absorbing European and American sources rather than Chinese and Korean ones. The Western-influenced folk song, such as "Sakura" ("Cherry Blossoms"), was a creation of this time (see Lesson Five).

The mercantile economy of the second Golden Age was joined by industrialization and colonial efforts, a combination that led to World War II. At the conclusion of this war in 1945, familiarity with and interest in things Japanese increased, especially in the United States. The musical traditions of eighteenth- and nineteenth-century Tokugawa Japan were particularly appealing. At the same time, post-war Japan developed a cultural pluralism in which traditional music, European concert music, and a variety of international commercial musics all thrived.

Throughout its history, Japanese culture can be characterized as innovative rather than inventive. It is successful in borrowing items from other cultures and then changing, improving, and incorporating them into the cultural mainstream. This process of innovation is found in many parts of Japanese society. For example, it can be seen in musical instruments (the three-stringed *shamisen* was developed from the Chinese *sanxian*), cuisine (*tonkatsu* is a Japanese version of the Austrian wiener schnitzel), and manufacturing (lenses and cameras were originally made by German industries).

A grasp of Japanese values is helpful in understanding cultural attitudes toward music and the arts. First, great value is placed on preservation. Old artifacts, including musical instruments, are highly regarded and often revered. A particularly old musical instrument might be given a proper name. Second, there is a focus on form or design. For example, an often used compositional form in music is *danmono*, a set of strict variations. Similarly, the triangle is popular in design; it provides the basic structure for *ikebana* (flower arrangement). Finally, the Japanese give great attention to formalism, the way in which tasks are accomplished. This attention is reflected by the prescribed order of brush strokes in writing *kanji* (Chinese ideographs), in the steps for folding a square piece of paper to produce an origami (folded paper) crane, and through the codified gestures and movements of *cha-no-yu* (the tea ceremony).

Music

Pentatonic melodies are quite common in Japanese music. However, the generalization that all Japanese music is pentatonic is not entirely true. There are often five main pitches in Japanese melodies (giving a pentatonic orientation), but secondary pitches are also used, raising the total number of pitches to seven or ten. Indigenous folk melodies often use a pentatonic scale with two half-steps. There are also pentatonic melodies without half steps. These melodies are based on scales that are derived from Chinese models.

Although there is some music that is in free meter, such as Buddhist chant or solo *shakuhachi* flute music (see figure 18), the majority of Japanese music is set in duple meter, usually in groups of four beats or multiples of four. The metric pulse may be reinforced by instrumental or body percussion (drums, gongs, or hand clapping).

Characteristics of rhythm include offbeat (or more accurately, between beat) syncopations, common in singing with the *koto* (thirteen-stringed zither—see figure 19), and

Figure 18. Shakuhachi (flute)

Figure 19. Koto (zither)

rhythmic ostinatos such as the percussion patterns in *gagaku*. Another characteristic is a composite rhythm formed by two interlocking parts superimposed on one another. Such composite rhythm phrasing results from the interlocking *otsuzumi* hip drum and the *kotsuzumi* shoulder drum in *noh* and *kabuki* theater.

The most notable texture in Japanese music is heterophony, in which a single melody is sung or played and simultaneously varied in one or more independent lines. In Japanese heterophony, each line is rhythmically displaced from the others (this may be done in a number of ways), although the lines (as a sequence of pitches) are essentially the same. For example, in *koto*-accompanied song, the melody line of the *koto* and that of the voice are heterophonic. In addition, monophony occurs, such as the chorus in *noh* theater or in *kagura* Shinto dance-song.

Polyphony also exists, although it is not as common. A second part, called *kaede* in the *koto* repertoire and *uwajoshi* in *nagauta shamisen* tradition, may be added (often by another composer) to composed pieces. Finally, there are instances in *kabuki* theater in which a number of unrelated pieces are played at the same time to musically represent different aspects of the scene, yielding a texture that William P. Malm terms "multiphony."[1]

The timbres of Japanese music are generally heterogeneous rather than homogeneous; that is, each instrument has a unique tone color or timbre. Even the two indigenous bamboo flutes, the *shakuhachi* and the *nohkan*, have very different timbres within the constraints of the hollow sound produced by all flutes. Ensemble music makes use of the distinctive timbre of each instrument; the *sankyoku* chamber ensemble consists of *koto* (a zither), *shamisen* (a plucked lute), *shakuhachi* (an end-blown flute), and voice. The *shakuhachi* itself illustrates how a number of different tone colors are produced by one instrument—its tone quality runs the gamut from a breathy, airy sound to a tightly focused one that sounds almost electronic.

Vocal performance also exploits a number of tone qualities. In theater traditions like *kabuki* and *bunraku*, there is a wide range of vocal sound that includes speech-like and shouted sounds as well as those more similar to our concept of singing. Most Japanese vocal production centers in the throat, with little head resonance or vibrato. The quality, therefore, is direct and penetrating, closer to rock than to opera.

Attention to form is characteristic of Japanese tradition in general, and music is no exception. Music structure often follows an overall design of three parts, called *jo ha kyu*. The *jo* is the introduction, the *ha* presents the principal material, and the *kyu* is the drive toward the conclusion. In a single *gagaku* work, for example, the *jo ha kyu* design is expressed through tempo—the first part of the work (*jo*) is in flexible meter, the bulk of the piece (*ha*) maintains a slow and steady tempo, and the final part (*kyu*) increases both the tempo and the rhythmic density as it drives toward conclusion. This tripartite form is hierarchical. It governs multimovement works; for example, the piece "Goshoraku" has three movements, called *jo*, *ha*, and *kyu*, respectively. On an even broader level, it guides the arrangement of items in a program. For example, dance pieces (*bugaku*) constitute the *kyu* of a *gagaku* presentation and are placed at the end. The *jo ha kyu* design is also applied to *noh* drama and *shamisen* song traditions.

There are also specific composition forms. In *koto* music, there are two principal forms—one for *koto* compositions with song and one for purely instrumental compositions. The form for *koto* with song is *tegotomono*. It consists of three principal sections: the opening song (*maeuta*), the instrumental interlude (*tegoto*), and the closing song (*atouta*).

The melodies of the opening and closing songs are not necessarily related, so the form (in terms of melodic material) can be described as ABC, or progressive. However, the form still has the flavor of an ABA or closed form, since both the first and third sections are *koto* with song, while the second section is purely instrumental, a strong contrast in performing medium.

The second form is a set of variations, called *danmono*. Each variation must be 104 beats long, a limitation similar to the syllable count of the haiku. The best-known *danmono* includes one with six sections ("Rokudan") and one with eight sections ("Hachidan"). Interestingly, for these instrumental pieces, the tempo increases toward the end, similar to the *jo ha kyu* treatment in *gagaku*.

LESSON 1

■ Objectives
Students will:
1. Sing the song "Kokiriko-bushi."
2. Accompany the song with bamboo sticks (*kokiriko*) or a substitute such as pencils or other types of wooden sticks.
3. Discover musical characteristics of the song (pentatonic melody, duple meter).

■ Materials
1. "Kokiriko-bushi"
2. Bamboo sticks (or pencils or other type of wooden sticks)
3. Map or globe of Japan
4. Chalkboard

■ Procedures
1. Have the students locate Japan on a map or globe. Identify the main islands (Hokkaido, Honshu, Shikoku, Kyushu) and cities (Tokyo, Kyoto, Nara, Hiroshima). Also find the prefecture (district) of Toyama, which is along the western coast of Japan.
2. Sing the song "Kokiriko-bushi," which is from Toyama (see figure 20). *Kokiriko* is a folk song (*bushi*) about bamboo sticks that are used to accompany a dance. Work slowly phrase by phrase until everyone can comfortably sing the melody with the Japanese words. Notice that the last two phrases are the same.
3. Have a student place the five tones of the pentatonic scale on the board (see figure 21). Sing the tones on a neutral syllable, listening to the distinctive pentatonic quality.
4. Outline the duple meter of the song by having the class accompany "Kokiriko-bushi" with bamboo sticks (or pencils or other wooden sticks). Bamboo, a type of grass, is very common in Japan. Carefully notice the stick placement in the photo (see figure 22).
5. Summarize with the students some of the things they have learned in the lesson.

This lesson was contributed by Tatsuko Takizawa.

Figure 20. "Kokiriko-bushi"

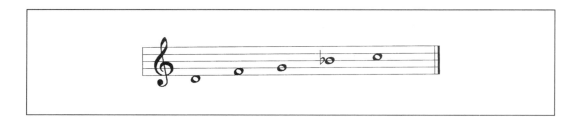

Figure 21. Pentatonic scale

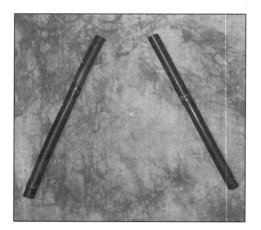

Figure 22. Bamboo sticks (kokiriko)

334   Multicultural Perspectives in Music Education

LESSON 2

■ Objectives
Students will:
1. View and identify instruments of the Japanese *gagaku* orchestra.
2. Listen to the composition "Etenraku" played by a *gagaku* ensemble.
3. Identify the sound of the instruments.

■ Materials
1. Photos of *gagaku* instruments from *Japanese Music and Musical Instruments* by William P. Malm (Rutland, VT: Charles E. Tuttle, 1959); *Performing Arts of Japan, V: Gagaku—Court Music and Dance* by Masataro Togi (New York: Weatherhill, 1971); and *The Traditional Music of Japan*, 2d ed. by Shigeo Kishibe (Tokyo: Ongaku no Tomo sha, 1984)
2. Recording: "Etenraku," from *Gagaku: The Imperial Court Music of Japan, Music Resources for Multicultural Perspectives* (Reston, VA: Music Educators National Conference, 1995)

■ Procedures
1. Show photos of the Japanese *gagaku* court orchestra. Explain that the *gagaku* ensemble consists of three types of melody instruments (*ryuteki* flute, *hichiriki* oboe, and *sho* mouth organ); two instruments that play set melodic formulas that relate to structural aspects of a specific piece (*koto* zither and *biwa* lute); and three percussion instruments (*kakko* small drum, *taiko* big drum, and *shoko* gong). You may wish to have your audiovisual department place pictures of the instruments onto slides. As part of the class presentation, you can lead the students in a discussion of the designs and shapes of the instruments and their animal symbolism as discussed in *Japanese Music and Musical Instruments*.
2. Listen to "Etenraku." Explain that the melody is played by the *ryuteki*, a transverse bamboo flute. Ask the students to pick out the flute melody (it begins the selection). Play the recording several times, asking the students to hum along. Have the students keep the beat. They will notice that the duration between beat four and beat one of the next measure is slightly elongated, a technique that is referred to as "breath rhythm." The elongation is particularly noticeable in the first two phrases. This breath rhythm is a style characteristic of *gagaku* performance that provides some of its suspense, as the listener must wait for the first beat. Also notice the distinctive quality created by the entrance of the *sho* mouth organ, the *koto* zither, the *biwa* plucked lute, and percussion.
3. Review the pictures and names of the *gagaku* instruments. In what ways is the *gagaku* orchestra like the Western orchestra? (Both have wind, stringed, and percussion instruments.) In what ways does it differ from the Western orchestra? (There is no conductor in the *gagaku* orchestra, the *gagaku* orchestra does not have brass instruments, and the dynamic level of *gagaku* music is softer and slower than much Western orchestral music.)

This lesson was contributed by William M. Anderson.

L E S S O N   3

■ **Objectives**

Students will:
1. Look at pictures of the *noh* theater.
2. Perform a short segment of *noh* music.
3. Listen to a segment of *noh* theater.
4. Watch the film *Noh Drama*.

■ **Materials**

1. *Japanese Music and Musical Instruments* by William P. Malm (Rutland, VT: Charles E. Tuttle, 1959) and *Performing Arts of Japan, IV: Noh—The Classical Theatre* by Yusuo Nakamura (New York: Walker-Weatherhill, 1971)
2. Recording: *UNESCO Collection—A Musical Anthology of the Orient: Japan III* (Barenreiter Musicaphon BM L 2014)
3. Film: *Noh Drama*
4. Bulletin board

■ **Procedures**

1. Prepare a bulletin board of photos from *noh* theater, including musical instruments, from the sources listed in the Materials section.
2. Explain that *noh* is one of the oldest forms of theater drama in Japan. It began approximately six hundred years ago but is still a popular form of theater in modern Japan; it is said to have at least one million enthusiastic followers. *Noh* drama features a story that is told by actors who sing their parts. A small chorus sometimes performs in the plays. There is also dancing in the plays. The instruments of *noh* drama include:
   - *taiko*—a round floor drum; played with sticks
   - *otsuzumi*—an hourglass-shaped drum held at the left side and played by striking it with the right hand
   - *kotsuzumi*—an hourglass drum held on the right shoulder and played by striking it with the right hand
   - *nokan*—a horizontally played flute
3. Perform a short segment of music from a *noh* drama (see figure 23). Follow these steps:
   a. Sing the melody.
   b. Clap the rhythm of the voice line.
   c. Explain that in order for instruments, such as the *otsuzumi* and *kotsuzumi*, to play in correct rhythm, the Japanese use *kakegoe* (calls; for example, "Yo" and "Ho") to coordinate the drumming. Following the diagram in figure 23, have half of the class count the beats in the selection (one through eight) while the other half of the class gives the calls "Yo" and "Ho." Have the students play drums at the appropriate times to simulate the *otsuzumi* and the *kotsuzumi*. Repeat the example several times.
   d. Have some students sing the melody while others speak the "Yo" and "Ho" syllables and others perform on the drums. Repeat the example several times.
   e. Call attention to the *jo-ha-kyu* (*jo*, introduction; *ha*, principal material; and *kyu*,

drive toward the end) form of the selection.

4. Listen to an example of music from the *noh* drama *Hagoromo* ("The Robe of Feathers," the first two minutes of side one on the *UNESCO Collection—A Musical Anthology of the Orient: Japan III)*. As the students are listening, have them circle the appropriate items from the following list:

(1) (Woodwind and percussion instruments)   or   Brass and percussion instruments

(2) (Performers recite rhythmic syllables)   or   Performers count (1, 2, 3, etc.) out loud

(3) (Male singing)   or   Female singing

(4) Loud dynamics   or   (Soft dynamics)

5. Watch the film *Noh Drama*. Observe the staging, costumes, placement of musicians, the extremely sustained movement of the actors, and the singing style. Discuss the concept of "less is more" as it is reflected in the musical and dramatic elements of this art form.

This lesson was contributed by William M. Anderson.

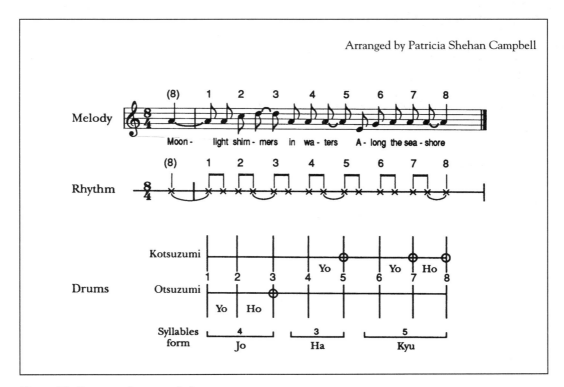

Figure 23. Segment from a *noh* drama

L E S S O N   4

■ **Objectives**

Students will:
1. Look at pictures of *kabuki* drama.
2. Listen to a segment of music from the *kabuki* theater.
3. Watch a film about *kabuki*.

■ **Materials**

1. *Japanese Music and Musical Instruments* by William P. Malm (Rutland, VT: Charles E. Tuttle, 1959) and *Performing Arts of Japan, II: Kabuki, The Popular Theater* by Yasuji Toita (New York: Walker-Weatherhill, 1970)
2. Recording: *Japan: Kabuki and Other Traditional Music* (Electra/Nonesuch H-72084) (the last two minutes of side one)
3. Film: *Kabuki: Classic Theater of Japan*

■ **Procedures**

1. Look for photos of *kabuki* theater in the books listed in the Materials section or in other sources and place them on the bulletin board. Explain that *kabuki* is perhaps the most flamboyant of the musical dramas of Japan. Established approximately four hundred years ago, it involves elaborate scenery, costuming, acting, dance, and music.
2. Both singing and instrumental music are found in *kabuki*. Some of the most prominent instruments include the *nokan* (flute), the *otsuzumi* and *kotsuzumi* (hourglass shaped drums), the *taiko* (floor drum), and the *shamisen* (a three-stringed plucked lute).
3. Listen to a short selection of music from the *kabuki* theater while circling the appropriate items from the following list:

   (1) Brass and percussion instruments   or   (Strings, flute, and percussion instruments)

   (2) Slow tempo   or   (Fast tempo)

   (3) (Duple meter)   or   Triple meter

   (4) Female singing   or   (Male singing)

4. Watch the film *Kabuki: Classic Theater of Japan*. Call attention to the on-stage instruments and the extremely flamboyant costumes of the actors. Compare *kabuki* to the more subtle *noh*.

This lesson was contributed by William M. Anderson.

L E S S O N   5

■ Objectives

Students will:

1. Listen to the *shakuhachi* composition "Deer Calling to Each Other in the Distance."
2. Identify the programmatic nature of the music (use of imitation to indicate the calling of two deer). The students will discover that the composition exemplifies the Japanese ideal of "less is more" through free rhythm (the absence of a steady beat), a slow pace, a soft dynamic level, and a thin texture created by only two instruments.
3. Compare the music to Japanese visual and literary art.
4. Sing the Japanese song "Sakura." Identify the pentatonic scale and the duple meter of the song.
5. Listen to the composition "Variations on 'Sakura'" played on the *koto* and identify the use of the variation form.
6. View the *koto* and *shakuhachi* in the film *Discovering the Music of Japan*.

■ Materials

1. Books:
   Cricket Songs by Harry Behn (New York: Harry N. Abrams, n.d.) (This is a book of haiku.)
   A History of Far Eastern Art, 5th ed. by Sherman E. Lee (New York: Harry N. Abrams, 1994)
2. Pictures of *shakuhachi* and *koto* in *Japanese Music and Musical Instruments* by William P. Malm (Rutland, VT: Charles E. Tuttle, 1959) and the October 1972 issue of the *Music Educators Journal*
3. Recordings:
   "Deer Calling to Each Other in the Distance," from *UNESCO Collection—A Musical Anthology of the Orient: Japan III* (Barenreiter Musicaphon BM 30 L 2014)
   "Variations on 'Sakura'" from *Art of the Koto: The Music of Japan Played by Kimio Eto* (Elektra Records, CD 70234) (also available on records accompanying Holt, Rinehart, and Winston's *Exploring Music*, Book 4)
4. Film: *Discovering the Music of Japan*

■ Procedures

1. Place a photo of the *shakuhachi* (see figure 18) on the bulletin board. Explain that the instrument is made from bamboo, which is plentiful in Japan. Bring a small piece of bamboo to class and let the students see and feel the material. Notice the "joints" between the segments. To make a *shakuhachi*, a notch is cut at the upper end of the bamboo. (The sound is produced by blowing across the notch as you would on a soda

bottle.) Five holes are cut along the bamboo: one on the back and four on the front. The back hole is covered by the thumb of the left hand; the other four holes are covered by the second and fourth fingers of both hands. The *shakuhachi* was derived from the Chinese *xiao*.

2. Listen to the composition "Deer Calling to Each Other in the Distance," which is played on two *shakuhachis*. This composition, like much Japanese music, is programmatic; that is, the music depicts a theme or story. In this composition, the two *shakuhachis* answer each other in imitation, thus portraying two deer calling to each other. As you listen to the music, circle the appropriate items from the following list:

    (1)   Stringed instrument   or   (Wind instrument)

    (2)   (Soft dynamics)   or   Loud dynamics

    (3)   Fast tempo   or   (Slow tempo)

    (4)   (Monophonic texture)   or   Harmonic texture

3. You will notice that this piece seems understated (this is achieved primarily through the soft dynamics, slow tempo, and monophonic texture). Much Japanese art seems to be understated. Read selections of haiku poetry, which is based on minimal materials (three lines, seventeen syllables, organized into groups of five, seven, and five syllables). Look at traditional Japanese paintings that are delicately executed with just a few lines and the use of muted colors.

4. Look for photos of Japanese cherry trees in blossom, perhaps those surrounding the Jefferson Memorial in Washington, D.C. These trees were given to the United States by Japan—you can find photos of these trees in the Spring 1984 issue of *National Geographic Traveler*. Have the students include these pictures on a bulletin board devoted to Japan. Also, look for examples of Japanese art and haiku that focus on nature.

5. Sing the song "Sakura" (Sah-koo-rah) (see figure 24), both in Japanese and in English. Notice the references to nature (cherry blossoms, mist, clouds). Write the pentatonic scale of the song (E, F, A, B, C) on the chalkboard and have the students sing it on a neutral syllable such as "loo" or play it on classroom instruments. Have the students conduct the duple meter as they sing the song.

6. Listen to the composition "Variations on 'Sakura'," band one of *Art of the Koto*. Place a picture of the *koto* (see figure 19) on the bulletin board and explain that the instrument is made of paulownia wood, a soft wood of the acacia family that grows only in Japan and Korea. The *koto* is approximately six feet long and ten inches wide. There are thirteen silk strings that are stretched parallel across the body of the instrument. Bridges hold the strings above the body of the instrument. These bridges are movable to allow the player to adjust the tuning of the instrument, which is commonly tuned to any one of several pentatonic scales. The *koto* is played by plucking the strings with three plectra attached to the thumb, index, and middle fingers of the right hand. As the class listens to the selection, have them circle the appropriate items in the following list:

    Variation 1:   slow tempo   or   (fast tempo)

                       (theme with added melodic figures)   or   unadorned theme

340   *Multicultural Perspectives in Music Education*

<table>
<tr><td>Variation 2:</td><td>fast tempo</td><td>or</td><td>(slow tempo)</td></tr>
<tr><td></td><td>(soft dynamics)</td><td>or</td><td>loud dynamics</td></tr>
<tr><td>Variation 3:</td><td>slow tempo</td><td>or</td><td>(fast tempo)</td></tr>
<tr><td></td><td>unadorned theme</td><td>or</td><td>(decorated theme)</td></tr>
</table>

7. View the *shakuhachi* being played in the film *Discovering the Music of Japan*. Make sure that the class notices the emphasis on nature and the Japanese ideal of "less is more."

This lesson was contributed by William M. Anderson.

Sakura (Cherry Blossoms)

Sa - ku - ra! Sa - ku - ra! Ya - yo - i no so - ra _ wa,
Sa - ku - ra! Sa - ku - ra! Cher-ry blos-soms, mist and_ clouds,

Mi - wa - ta - su Ka - gi - ri Ka - su - mi ka ku - mo _ ka,
Gent-ly float-ing in the_ sky, As _ far as one can _ see,

Ni _ o - i zo i - zu _ ru. I - za - ya,
The_ fra - grance is ev-'ry - where. Come,_____

i - za - ya, Mi _____ ni yu _ ka - n.
come, _____ Let____ us go _ and see!

Figure 24. "Sakura"

Integrating music with other studies

The following are some suggestions for integrating the study of Chinese and Japanese music with other classroom learning experiences:

1. Make a bulletin board composed of pictures from many different aspects of Chinese and Japanese culture, such as architecture, music, painting, sculpture, and other forms.
2. Invite Chinese and Japanese guests to speak to your students. Encourage the visitors to bring authentic items such as textiles.
3. Show films of Chinese and Japanese cultures. Excellent film rental catalogs are available from university film libraries (for example, the Universities of Michigan, Washington, and Wisconsin).
4. Combine songs with social studies. For example, along with singing the Chinese song "The Eldest Daughter of the Jiang Family" (see figure 9), plan a geography and history lesson based on the Great Wall of China.
5. Have your class plan a Chinese New Year celebration (it falls on the second moon after the winter solstice, sometime between January 21 and February 19 on the Western calendar). Lion and dragon dances are often performed. Collaborate with art and physical education teachers in designing costumes and performing lion or dragon dances. The percussion pieces given in figures 12 and 13 can be used as accompaniment.
6. Study the relationships between music and other arts; for example, the texture of heterophony can be related to the Japanese aesthetic of clarity for all aspects of an art expression. Just as all the elements of a formal Japanese garden are clearly presented (for example, the rocks and the pine tree), each musical part is made clear through heterophony and by the difference in timbres of each instrument ensemble.

The **Integrating music with other studies** section was contributed by William M. Anderson.

NOTE

1. William P. Malm, "Ethnomusicology: The World of Music Cultures," in *Research News* (Ann Arbor: University of Michigan, 1970), 11.

CHINA

BIBLIOGRAPHY

Blunder, Caroline, and Mark Elvin. *Cultural Atlas of China.* New York: Facts on File, 1983. This is a very useful book for quick reference. In addition to maps for many purposes and fine photographs, there are also short articles on all aspects of Chinese culture (including the arts).

Chen, Chin-hsin, and Shin-hsing Chen. *"The Flower Drum" and Other Chinese Songs.* New York: John Day, 1942. This book contains seventeen songs arranged with piano parts and grouped by geographical divisions and subjects; texts in Chinese and English.

Chen, Lan-ku. *Development of a Chinese Music Listening Program.* Ann Arbor, MI: University Microfilms, 1983. (University Microfilms number DA 8322188). Using multiple media, the author outlines and develops a listening program for teaching Chinese music in elementary schools in this Ed.D. dissertation from Columbia University Teachers College.

Craig, Dale A. *The Chinese Orchestra: An Alternative Instrumental Group for School*. Queensland, Australia: Global Music, 1984. This is a practical pamphlet for teachers who wish to organize a Chinese orchestra.

Danforth, Kenneth C., ed. *Journey into China*. Washington, DC: National Geographic Society, 1982. This is a good source for photographs of the Great Wall of China.

Eberhard, Wolfram, ed. *Folktales of China*. Chicago: University of Chicago Press, 1965.

Halson, Elizabeth. *Peking Opera: A Short Guide*. Hong Kong: Oxford University Press, 1966. Based on the author's personal observations, this book explores all aspects of Peking opera in nontechnical language. The illustrations are hand drawings; no photographs. Fourteen stories of famous operas are given. A handy book for the subject.

Han Kuo-huang. "Folk Songs of the Han Chinese: Characteristics and Classifications." *Asian Music*, Vol. 20, No. 2 (1989): 107–128. The article follows the Chinese method in classifying Han folk songs into categories and regions. Many musical examples are included.

Han, Kuo-huang. "The Modern Chinese Orchestra." *Asian Music* 9, no. 1, 1979, 1–40. This article traces the rise of the type of orchestra that is currently popular in all Chinese communities.

Han, Kuo-huang. "Titles and Program Notes in Chinese Musical Repertoires." *The World of Music*, no. 1, 1985, 68–78. This is an exploration of the nature of the Chinese people and their fondness of program music.

Han Kuo-huang and Patricia Shehan Campbell. *The Lion's Roar: Chinese Luogu Percussion Ensemble*. Danbury, CT: The World Music Press, 1992. This book for teachers includes history, instrumentation, scores, and methods; a cassette accompanies the book.

Liang, Minguye. *Music of the Billion: An Introduction to Chinese Music Culture*. New York: Heinrichshofen Edition, 1985. This is the best and only comprehensive book on Chinese music in a Western language. Though it is labeled as an introduction, it covers all aspects of Chinese music. There is a useful general description of musical instruments for quick reference. A discography, classified by musical genre and instrument, is given along with many music examples.

Lieberman, Fredric. *Chinese Music: An Annotated Bibliography*. 2d ed. New York: Garland Publishing, 1979. This is the standard research tool for anyone working with Chinese music in Western languages. Included are more than two thousand items ranging from popular concert reviews to scholarly research.

Mai, Ding. *Chinese Folk Songs: An Anthology of 25 Favorites with Piano Accompaniment*. Beijing: New World Press, 1984. This anthology includes some newer folk songs and songs of national minorities.

Malm, William P. *Music of the Near East, Pacific, and Asia*. 3d ed. Englewood Cliffs, NJ: Prentice-Hall, 1996. This is a concise introduction to major musical constructs, genres, and instruments from these regions. Cassette tapes accompany the book.

Myers, John. *The Way of the Pipa: Structure and Imagery in Chinese Lute Music*. Kent, Ohio: The Kent State University Press, 1992. This is the first book on this important instrument in English.

Perris, Arnold. *Music as Propaganda: Art to Pursue, Art to Control*. Westport, CT: Greenwood Press, 1985. Chapter five gives information on the control of the arts in China, a practice partly learned from the Russians and partly inherited from ancient Chinese ideas.

Scott, Adolphe Clarence. *The Classical Theatre of China*. London: Allen and Unwin, 1957. Still a classic for the general reader, this book investigates all aspects of Peking opera. It includes a glossary of technical terms.

Thrasher, Alan R. "The Role of Music in Chinese Culture." *The World of Music*, no. 1, 1985, 3–17. Much Western writing on Chinese music has been concerned with ancient music and historical documents. This article explores music in a modern social setting.

Thrasher, Alan R. "The Sociology of Chinese Music: An Introduction." *Asian Music* 12, no. 2, 1981, 17–53.

Wiant, Bliss. *Chinese Lyrics*. New York: J. Fischer and Brothers, 1947. A collection of twenty-seven songs arranged with piano accompaniment.

Note: China Books and Periodicals has a large stock of English books (including children's books) related to Chinese culture. Catalogs are available. Their addresses and telephone numbers are 136 West Eighteenth Street, New York, NY 10011, 212-627-4044; 2929 24th St., San Francisco, CA 94110, 415-282-2994.

General articles on Chinese and Japanese music and musical instruments can be found in standard dictionaries such as *The New Grove Dictionary of Music and Musicians*, edited by Stanley Sadie (New York: Macmillan, 1980), *The New Grove Dictionary of Musical Instruments*, edited by Stanley Sadie (New York: Macmillan, 1984), and *The New Harvard Dictionary of Music*, edited by Don Michael Randel (Cambridge, MA: Belknap, 1986).

DISCOGRAPHY

Ancient Art Music of China. Lyrichord LYRCD 7409. Lily Yuan's virtuoso performance on the *yangqin* (hammered zither). This is the first Western recording on this important Chinese instrument, which originated from the Middle East (a *santur* type of instrument). However, the title is misleading because most of the pieces are modern or newly arranged.

China I. Anthology AST 4000. A collection of fine performances by masters on *qin*, *zheng*, *yangqin*, and *sanxian*. Good annotation by Frederic Lieberman.

China: Chuida Wind and Percussive Instrumental Ensembles. UNESCO/Auvidis D 8209. Opposite to the famous *Sizhu* (silk and bamboo) music, *Chuida* (blowing and striking; i.e. winds and percussion) music represents a different kind of Chinese sound. Most of this kind of loud music is for festivals. Selections come from Quanzhou, Shanghai, and the eastern part of the Zhejiang Province. Recorded by François Picard.

China: Music from the People's Republic of China. Rounder Records CD 4008, 1976. Taped live in Hubei, this is an interesting album containing short examples of instrumental and vocal performances by professionals and children. Instruments featured are *suona*, *zheng*, *erhu*, *pipa*, and *sheng*.

China: Shantung Folk Music and Traditional Instrumental Pieces. Nonesuch 72051-4. The Lu-Sheng Ensemble gives a fine performance of a repertoire of Shantung (northern Chinese) music.

China's Instrumental Heritage. Lyrichord LYRCD 792. Performed by the *zheng* master, Liang Tsaiping, and his group, this album features *zheng*, *xiao*, *sheng*, *erhu* (called *nanhu*), and a rare example of the *xun* ocarina.

Chine Populaire: Musique Classique. Ocora 558519. Reproduced from Chinese recordings, this album features good examples of *qin*, *zheng*, *erhu*, *di*, and *pipa*. The annotation is not very complete.

Chinese Classical Masterpieces. Everest 3212. The two works featured in this album are not classical, but contemporary. They represent a fusion of Western and Chinese musical idioms.

Chinese Classical Masterpieces, Lyrichord LLST 7182. This album consists of standard solo compositions for the *pipa* lute and *qin* zither. The *pipa* piece, "The Hero's Defeat," is included. The master who performs these two instruments, Lui Tsun-yuen, taught at UCLA.

Chinese Masterpieces for the Erhu. Lyrichord LLST 7231. Performed by Lui Man-sing and his group, this album features the *erhu* and small ensemble pieces in heterophonic style.

The Chinese Opera. Lyrichord LLST 7212. Children trained in the Fu Hsin Opera School in Taiwan perform works; their vocal quality is not typical of the genre.

Chinese Opera: Songs and Music. Folkways FW8880. Includes excerpts from Cantonese (*Guangdong*) local opera. Included are good examples of instrumental works performed in heterophonic style.

Exotic Music of Ancient China. Lyrichord LLST 7122. This album includes the famous *pipa* piece, "Ambush from Ten Sides" (The Great Ambush).

Floating Petals, Wild Geese, The Moon on High: Music of the Chinese Pipa. Nonesuch 72085-2. This album contains seven masterpieces for *pipa*, and the modern work "Dance of the Yi Tribe" is included.

Hong Kong. UNESCO/EMI C 064-17968. Musical Atlas. The instruments featured are the *qin, zheng, pipa, yangqin, sheng, erhu,* and *xiao.*

Music Resources for Multicultural Perspectives. 1995. Music Educators National Conference, 1806 Robert Fulton Drive, Reston, VA 22091-4348; phone 800-336-3768 or 703-860-4000.

Musik für Ch'in—China. Museum Collection Berlin MC 7. *Qin* master Liang Mingyue provides commentary. Fine photos show the finger and hand positions for playing the instrument.

Nan-Kouan, Vol. 1: Musique et chant courtois de la Chine du Sud. Ocora C559004. The first good recording in the West of this refined and courtly genre (Nanguan). The singer (Cai Xiaoyue) and the instrumentalists are the very best in Taiwan.

Orchestral Music of China. Orion PGM 6903. Side A contains works written in the 1950s and 1960s for the modern Chinese orchestra. The famous composition "Dance of the Yao" is included.

Peking Opera. Seraphim 60201. Only three compositions are actual Peking opera excerpts. The rest are works for the *pipa, zheng,* and *gaohu.*

Phases of the Moon: Traditional Chinese Music. CBS M 36705. Recordings produced by the China Record Company for the CBS Masterworks Album. A fine album of works performed by the modern Chinese orchestra.

Shantung: Music of Confucian Homeland. Lyrichord LLST 7112. This album features *sheng, di, erhu* (*nanhu*), and the special effect of *suona* (imitating human voice).

Sizhu: Chamber Music of South China. Pan Records Ethnic Series 2030 CD. *Sizhu* (silk and bamboo; i.e., strings and soft winds) is the ideal chamber music sound for the Chinese. This album includes the most famous *Sizhu* music, the Jiangnan (Shanghai area) *Sizhu* as well as examples from Hakka, Chouzhou, Minnan, and Canton, all from southern China. Recorded by Alan R. Thrasher.

The Song of the Phoenix: Sheng Music from China. Lyrichord LLST 7369. Ten traditional and modern compositions for the *sheng.*

Taiwan: Music from the Ethnic Minorities of Taiwan. Arion ARN 64109. Good examples of the aborigines (non-Han people) in Taiwan. Some of the music is polyphonic, but there are selections of the Hakka, the Han minority group in Taiwan. Recorded by Cheng Shuicheng.

Vocal Music of Contemporary China. Vol. 1: The Han People. Folkways FE4091. The album contains folk songs and contemporary songs; some are accompanied by traditional ensemble and others by piano.

Xian Conservatory of Music: Ancient Music of Chang'an. Inedit W 260036. The first Western recording of a genre rarely heard outside of Xian (ancient capitol: Chang'an). The music is believed to be very old. The performance was recorded at a festival held in Paris in 1991.

Note: Records and audiocassettes produced in Mainland China, Hong Kong, and Taiwan can be obtained through World Music Enterprises, 717 Avondale Street, Kent, OH 44240.

Chinese musical instruments are available from Exelsis Music, 816 Sacramento Street, San Francisco, CA 94018, 415-986-7038. Additional contacts include The Asia Society, 725 Park Avenue, New York, NY 10021, 212-288-6400; and the Chinese Music Society of North America, 2329 Charmingfare, Woodridge, IL 60517.

FILMOGRAPHY

Asian Dance and Drama, Vol. 3: East Asia. The Asia Society. This is a collection of three hundred slides with an illustrated annotated guide. The cultures represented in this volume include Korea, Japan, and China.

Chinese Music and Musical Instruments, 16 mm, 24 minutes, color. Chinese Information Service

(Taiwan). This film can be obtained from Audio-Visual Services, Northern Illinois University, DeKalb, IL 60115, or the Chinese Coordination Council for North American Affairs Office in the United States, 5061 River Road, Washington, DC 20016. This movie, which was filmed in Taiwan, depicts the social and educational aspects of Chinese music and introduces all types of musical instruments. Scenes of Confucian ceremony and imaginary court dance are included. It concludes with a performance of a modern Chinese orchestra. The lengthy and somewhat monotonous section in which each instrument is shown but not played is a drawback.

Chinese Musical Instruments: An Introduction, VHS videocassette, 30 minutes, color. The Yale-China Association. Available from Erlham College, East Asian Studies Program, Richmond, IN 47374. This film features four Chinese musicians performing six compositions. The instruments used are the *zheng, pipa, erhu, sanxian, yangqin, sheng, di,* and *xiao.*

Chinese Shadow Plays, Wango Wen, 16 mm, 11 minutes. China Film Enterprise of America, 1947. Available from Erlham College, East Asian studies program, Richmond, IN 47374. After a brief introduction, this film presents episodes from the famous story, "White Snake Lady." The back-stage is shown at the end.

Chinese Shadow Plays, VHS videocassette, 30 minutes, black and white. The Asia Society, 725 Park Avenue, New York, NY 10021. This film, directed by Wango Wen, features the shadow puppet troupe from Taiwan performing scenes from the famous story, "The Monkey King." A demonstration is included.

The Fujan Hand Puppets from the People's Republic of China, VHS videocassette, 30 minutes, color. The Asia Society. This film features the three-dimensional hand puppets performing a story that has a slight socialist overtone. A short demonstration is included at the end of this skillful performance.

The Heritage of Chinese Opera, 16 mm, 32 minutes, color. Chinese Information Service (Taiwan). This film can be obtained from the Chinese Coordination Council for North American Affairs Office in the United States of America, 5061 River Road, Washington, DC 20016. It introduces the various aspects (pantomime, acrobatics, singing, and dancing) of Peking opera and shows the training of an opera school (Fu Hsin Opera School). The excerpts that follow are "The Jade Bracelet," "The Monkey King," "The Cross Road," "Two Loyal Officials," and "Yueh Fei."

Hu Hung-yen: Aspects of Peking Opera, videocassette, 30 minutes, color. The Asia Society. Hu, a famous actress of Peking Opera, demonstrates the make-up and performs two excerpts.

An Introduction to Traditional Chinese Music: Instrumental Music, VHS videocassette, 60 minutes, color. Ministry of Education and the National Taiwan Normal University. This videotape was made in Taiwan at the request of MENC. Most of the performers are high school or college students. It includes an explanation of the classification of instruments, demonstrations of six solo instruments and percussion instruments, and five ensemble compositions performed by a high school Chinese orchestra and a primary school chorus.

A Night at the Peking Opera, 16 mm, 20 minutes, color. Film Images. This resource can be obtained from Audio-Visual Services, University of Michigan, Ann Arbor, MI 48015, or Northern Illinois University, DeKalb, IL 60115. It is a classic film that shows excellent performances of four excerpts performed at the Paris International Festival of Dramatic Art in 1955. The excerpts are "The White Snake Lady," "The Monkey King," "The Cross Road," and "The Autumn River."

Shantung: Traditional Music, Videocassette, 30 minutes, black and white. The Asia Society. Performances by the Lu-Sheng Ensemble from Taiwan. The *suona,* the *di,* and the *sheng* are the instruments featured.

Tai Ai-lien in Chinese Folk Dance, 16 mm, 12 minutes, color. Fictura Films, 1972. This film can be obtained from Audio-Visual Services, University of Illinois, Urbana, IL 61801. Tai, the leading dancer and dance teacher in China for forty years, performs a drum dance and a southwest Chinese folk tale allowing her to play both parts simultaneously.

JAPAN

BIBLIOGRAPHY

Araki, Nancy, and Jane M. Mori. *Matsuri: Festival, Japanese American Celebrations and Activities*. San Francisco: Heian International, 1978. This is an informative manual of specific activities that can be done in the classroom, including recipes, paper folding, and one Bon dance, "Tankobushi."

Behn, Harry. *Cricket Songs*. New York: Harry N. Abrams, n.d. This is a collection of haiku.

Kelly, John M., Jr. *Folk Music Festival in Hawaii*. Rutland, VT: Charles E. Tuttle, 1963. This is a compendium of songs from Hawaii, the Pacific, and Asia, most with piano accompaniment. Translations are included for all songs. Japanese songs include "Sakura," "On-koto," "Kisobushi," "Hiraita," and "Kutsu ga naru."

Kishibe, Shigeo. *The Traditional Music of Japan*, 2d ed. Tokyo: Ongaku no Tomo sha, 1984. This book contains a detailed introduction to the major genres of Japanese art music, including history, description of instrument tuning systems, and musical features. Many black-and-white illustrations of instruments and performers are included.

Lee, Sherman E. *A History of Far Eastern Art*. 5th ed. New York: Harry N. Abrams, 1994. This is an excellent general survey of Asian art.

Malm, William P. *Japanese Music and Musical Instruments*. Rutland, VT: Charles E. Tuttle, 1959. An informative and thorough account of music in Japan, this text is very readable, with many illustrations in both color and black and white. The most comprehensive treatment of Japanese music by a non-Japanese.

Nakamura, Yusuo. *Performing Arts of Japan, IV: Noh—The Classical Theatre*. New York: Walker-Weatherhill, 1971. This is an excellent introduction, with good illustrations, to *Noh* drama.

Togi, Masatoro. *Performing Arts of Japan, V: Gagaku—Court Music and Dance*. New York: Weatherhill, 1971. This book gives an engaging description of *gagaku* by a court musician in his own words. There are many pictures of actual court performances and some good plates of instrument construction.

Toita, Yasuji. *Performing Arts of Japan: 11—Kabuki, The Popular Theater*. New York: Walker-Weatherhill, 1970. This is a good, well-illustrated introduction to *kabuki* theater.

Yamaguchi, Osamu. "Musics of Northeast Asia." *Music Educators Journal*, 59 no. 2, Oct. 1972, 31–34. An overview of Northeast Asia with other pictures useful for instruction. This special issue of *MEJ* is useful for the teacher interested in world music; it contains a useful bibliography and discography.

Note: General articles on Chinese and Japanese music and musical instruments can be found in standard dictionaries such as *The New Grove Dictionary of Music and Musicians*, edited by Stanley Sadie (New York: Macmillan, 1980), *The New Grove Dictionary of Musical Instruments*, edited by Stanley Sadie (New York: Macmillan, 1984), and *The New Harvard Dictionary of Music*, edited by Don Michael Randel (Cambridge, MA: Belknap, 1986).

DISCOGRAPHY

Art of the Koto: The Music of Japan Played by Kimia Eto. Elektra Records, CD 70234. This record includes an example of *tegotomono* ("Yachiojishi"), *danmono* ("Hachidan"), and an arrangement of "Sakura" (Cherry Blossoms).

Gagaku: The Imperial Court Music of Japan. Lyrichord LYRCD 7126. This is a recording of a shortened version of "Etenraku" performed by the Kyoto Imperial Court Music Orchestra.

Japanese Traditional Music for Two Shakuhachi. Lyrichord LLST 7386. This record includes solos and duets for *shakuhachi* by two American performers with detailed liner notes. It illustrates the different timbres of *shakuhachi* and the concept of free meter.

Japan: Kabuki and Other Traditional Music. Nonesuch H-72084. This is a collection of traditional music, performed by the famed ensemble Nipponia.

Kyomono Series, Vol. 1: Works of Matsuura Kengyo. Hogaku Society HS-101. This is a recording of performances of *sankyoku* (*koto, shamisen, shakuhachi,* and voice) by American and Japanese performers with translations and notes. It illustrates the *tegotomono* genre of *koto* music and heterophony.

UNESCO Collection—A Musical Anthology of the Orient: Japan III. Barenreiter Musicaphon BM 30 L 2014. This is an anthology (part of a six-volume set of traditional Japanese music) that includes the *shamisen*-song traditions, *danmono* form ("Rokudan"), and *shakuhachi* duets ("Shika no tone").

Traditional Folk Songs of Japan. Ryutaro Hattori, collector. Folkways FE 4534. "Kuroda-bushi" is sung, accompanied by *shamisen*, bamboo flute, and drum. Also includes "Tanko Bushi" ("Coal Miner's Song" in *Kyushu*).

FILMOGRAPHY

The Awaji Puppet Theater of Japan, 16 mm, 20 minutes, color. Available from The Asia Society. Scenes from classic Japanese tales: Keisei Awa Naruto, The Miracle of Tsubosaka Temple, and Ebisu-Mai, as well as a demonstration of how the puppets are manipulated.

Bugaku: The Traditional Court, Temple and Shrine Dances from Japan, 3/4" videocassette, 30 minutes. Available from The Asia Society. For more than a thousand years, Bugaku has been the ceremonial dance of the Japanese Imperial household, temples, and shrines. The ancient music of drums, flutes, strings, and gongs accompanies the elegant and austere movements of the dance.

Discovering the Music of Japan, 16 mm, 22 minutes, color, Bernard Wilets, Film Associates, 1967. This is an introduction to three Japanese instruments—*shakuhachi, koto,* and *shamisen*. It's available from West Music Co., 1208 Fifth Street, PO Box 5521, Coralville, IA 52241.

Edo Festival Music and Pantomime, 16 mm, 50 minutes, color. Available from The Asia Society. This three-part film recreates the Lincoln Center performance of the famed Taneo Wakayama troupe. The film consists of three dance-pantomimes: "Destroying the Giant Serpent" (*Orochi Taiji*), "Homage to the Gods and Love for the Homeland" (*Keishin Aikoku*), and "The Felicitous Lion" (*Kotobuki Jishi*). All three features are available on separate reels.

Kabuki: Classic Theater of Japan, 16 mm, 30 minutes. Available from Japan Information Service, Consulate General of Japan, Water Tower Place, Suite 950 E, 845 North Michigan Avenue, Chicago, IL 60611.

Martial Arts of Kabuki from the National Theater Institute of Japan, 3/4" videocassette, 30 minutes. Available from The Asia Society. Dancers from the National Theater Institute of Japan demonstrate stage fighting based on the martial arts and perform two excerpts from the *kabuki* repertory: "Hama Matsukaze" (a major battle between a man and a woman using makeshift weapons including an oar and a piece of rope) and "Kujira no Danmari" (in which a samurai is swallowed by a whale and eventually fights off a swarm of reptilian creatures).

Noh Drama, 16 mm, 29 minutes. Available from Japan Information Service, Consulate General of Japan, Water Tower Place, Suite 950 E, 845 North Michigan Avenue, Chicago, IL 60611.

The Soloists of the Ensemble Nipponia, 3/4" videocassette, 30 minutes. Available from The Asia Society. This is a performance by the soloists of the Ensemble *Nipponia of Tsuru no Sugomori* (the Tenderness of the Crane on the *shakuhachi*, a bamboo flute, *Makuai Sanju* (Kabuki interlude) on the *shamisen*, *Oji-no-Nato* (the Folding Fan as a target) on the *biwa*, and *Tatsuta no Kyoku* (the Venus in Autumn) on the *koto*, as well as *Wa* (a composition for ensemble).

Note: The address of The Asia Society, a supplier for many of the films listed here, is The Asia Society, Performing Arts Department, 725 Park Avenue, New York, NY 10021.

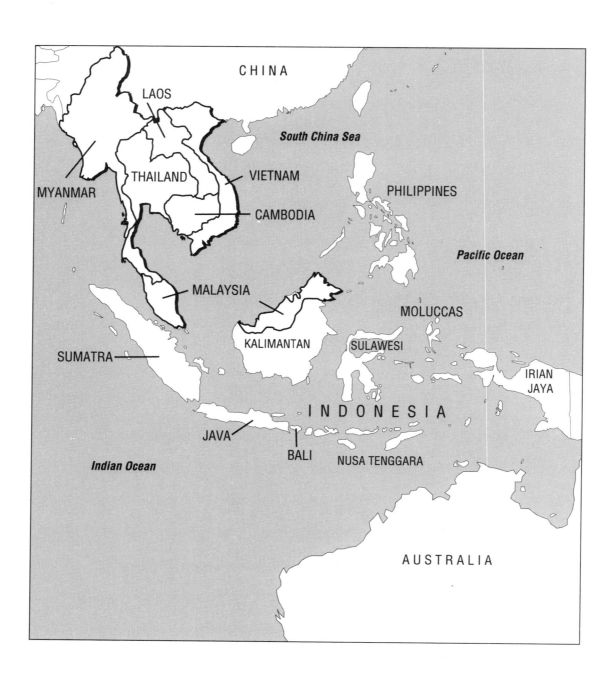

CHINA

LAOS

South China Sea

MYANMAR

THAILAND

VIETNAM

PHILIPPINES

CAMBODIA

Pacific Ocean

MALAYSIA

MOLUCCAS

KALIMANTAN

SULAWESI

SUMATRA

IRIAN
JAYA

I N D O N E S I A

JAVA

BALI

NUSA TENGGARA

Indian Ocean

AUSTRALIA

Map of Southeast Asia

CHAPTER 11

MUSIC OF
SOUTHEAST ASIA

by Patricia Shehan Campbell, William M. Anderson,
and Michael B. Bakan

CAMBODIA, LAOS, THAILAND, AND VIETNAM

by Patricia Shehan Campbell

Mainland Southeast Asia is located south of China and east of India and includes the countries of Vietnam, Laos, Cambodia, Thailand, Burma (Myanmar), and Malaysia. Its geographical setting between powerful neighbors has always been of prime importance in the development of its philosophy, architecture, legends, dance, drama, and music.

The influence of Indian and Chinese cultures has been considerable, despite the partial isolation imposed on the region by mountains and flooding river valleys. Many Indian artists and scholars enjoyed high status in the courts of Southeast Asia as they introduced aspects of Hindu and Buddhist traditions. Young men frequently traveled to India for training in literature, art, and culture. China annexed Vietnam in the first century B.C., and during this period Vietnamese culture was strongly influenced by its northern neighbor.

Ethnic groups from southern China, including the Mons, Lao, Shan, Siamese, Karen, and Khmer, followed the Mekong and Irrawaddy rivers to settlements in Southeast Asia. The Hmong people migrated from China as recently as two thousand years ago. The growth of nationalism led to the adoption of an official language by each country, but the large number of languages still in use today is evidence of the mainland's multicultural society.

With the arrival of missionaries in the sixteenth century and merchants and statesmen in the seventeenth, Southeast Asia was introduced to Western culture. From the late nineteenth century through World War II, France was the area's principal colonial power, but the unique, millennium-old cultural identities of Vietnam, Laos, and Cambodia were maintained throughout this period. The kingdom of Siam remained independent during the colonial period, and, in 1939, it took the name of Thailand ("land of the free") to reflect its status. Compared to other Southeast Asian countries, Thailand today is relatively prosperous. The capital city of Bangkok seems Western in its fashion, media, music, and cuisine, whereas the ethnic minorities in rural areas of the north and northeast retain traditional customs from the past.

While the French whittled away at Indochina, the British annexed portions of Burma and slowly built a political state during the nineteenth century. The states at the southern end of the Malay Peninsula became British protectorates in the late nineteenth century. Burma gained its independence in 1948, and Malaysia attained independence fifteen years later, in 1963.

In the mid-1970s, the condition of the war-torn countries of Vietnam, Laos, and Cambodia brought about a massive influx of refugees to the United States. As their governments disintegrated, the South Vietnamese, Cambodians (Khmer), Lao, and ethnic groups such as the Hmong were transported to camps in Thailand, Hong Kong, Guam, and Indonesia before they finally settled not only in America, but throughout the world. Life in the New World held promise for these Southeast Asians, but the memory of their homeland remained an important influence in their lives.

The traditional sounds of ancient civilizations can be heard in Southeast Asian communities in cities such as Los Angeles, San Francisco, Seattle, and Dallas. Refugees brought folk and classical instruments and a repertoire of songs and melodies that had been transmitted through many generations. These musical traditions also survive in those areas of Southeast Asia where the governments give permission and support.

This guide to Vietnamese, Thai, Lao, and Cambodian traditional music styles is organized by elements of melody, rhythm, texture, form and genre, and timbre. Unfortunately, there is little information available on the music of Burma and Malaysia, but students can learn that Burmese music shows strong Indian characteristics and that Malaysian music resembles the Islamic-influenced styles of the two populous Indonesian islands of Java and Sumatra.

Vietnamese music

Pentatonic melodies, with the addition of two auxiliary pitches used primarily for ornamentation, are common in Vietnamese music. These melodies are seldom plain; they are distinguished by the use of decorative techniques similar to tremolos and trills.

Almost all metered Vietnamese music is in duple meter. Except for the recitative-style music of certain religious chants and opera, rhythmic cycles of eight or sixteen beats are standard. Vietnamese vocal and instrumental music frequently uses unaccompanied solos and simultaneous melodic variations called heterophony.

The most common formal device is strophic form, in which the melody repeats as the verses change. Some traditional pieces have an introductory section called a *rao*, similar to the Indian *alap* (see Chapter 9). Theme and variation, as well as programmatic devices such as the portrayal of bird calls and falling water, are typical in instrumental works. Opera is particularly prominent in the south.

In folk and classical music, vocal quality may be strident and rather nasal. Among the traditional instruments are the indigenous *dan bau* (monochord) and Chinese-influenced stringed instruments, such as the *dan tranh* (a sixteen-stringed zither), the *dan co* (a two-stringed fiddle), and the *dan ty ba* (a four-stringed, long-necked lute). Folk instruments include flutes, oboes, mouth organs, bells, gongs, coin clappers, and barrel drums.

Thai, Lao, and Cambodian music

Folk music in these countries is derived from pentatonic scales, and art music is based on seven-tone scales. The pitches of the heptatonic scales are each separated from the next by an equal interval slightly larger than the Western semitone (100 cents) yet slightly smaller, at about 171 cents, than the whole step (200 cents). Duple meter is the standard, with most music set in two-beat groupings. In classical forms, a rhythmic cycle of beats can be heard, throughout which various drums, gongs, and hand cymbals punctuate phrases (see figure 1).

Heterophonic texture is common in the classical orchestras, with instruments giving impetus to the music by having individual lines rather than providing a unified, harmonic approach. Certain folk instruments, including the free-reed mouth organ (*kaen*), produce drone-like harmonic accompaniments.

Strophic form is found in many vocal pieces. Orchestral music is frequently organized in a three-part form, in which the melody is reduced by half or enlarged to twice its original length by adding or subtracting melodic detail. In the reduced melody, the ornamentation is removed and only the chief structural pitches are retained. The expanded version features greater ornamentation than in the original melody. Improvisational styles exist in Lao folk music in the *mawlum* form for voice and *kaen*.

Singers typically have a nasal quality. The instruments of the *pi phat* (also called the *pin peat*) orchestra include the *ranat* (wooden xylophones) shown in figure 2, the *kong wong* (a circle of knobbed gongs) shown in figure 3, the *pi nai* (oboe), several percussion instruments, and drums. There are also string ensembles that feature two-stringed fiddles, lutes, and zithers. The *ching* (finger cymbals) serve as the beat keepers for all classical ensembles. Mouth organs of the Lao (*kaen*) and Hmong (*gaeng*) produce an open timbre and tuning that is Western-sounding and immediately pleasing, even to the uninitiated.

Figure 1. Students playing in a Thai classical orchestra at Kent State University

Figure 2. Ranat

Figure 3. Kong wong

354   Multicultural Perspectives in Music Education

LESSON 1

■ **Objectives**

Students will:
1. Watch films that show the land, the people, and the costumes and customs of Southeast Asia.
2. Discuss recent political events and their effects on arts and lifestyles.
3. List instruments and musical elements evident in a first hearing of brief selections.
4. Locate Southeast Asia on a map.

■ **Materials**

1. Books:
   Angel Child, Dragon Child by Michele Maria Surat (New York: Scholastic, Inc., 1983)
   Voices from Southeast Asia by John Tenula (New York: Holmes and Meier, 1991)
2. Recordings:
   Eternal Voices: Traditional Vietnamese Music in the U.S. (New Alliance Nar CD 053)
   From Rice Paddies and Temple Yards: Traditional Music of Vietnam (this cassette accompanies the book, which is listed in the Bibliography)
   Silent Temples, Songful Hearts: Traditional Music of Cambodia (this cassette accompanies the book, which is listed in the Bibliography)
3. Videotapes:
   Ao Dai. 1991, 13 minutes, color
   Thailand—An Exotic Paradise. 1993, 56 minutes, color
   Rebuilding the Temple: Cambodians in America. 1993, 58 minutes, color
4. Map of Southeast Asia

■ **Procedures**

1. Show *Ao Dai* or *Thailand—An Exotic Paradise* as an introduction to Southeast Asia and its people. Note cultural features such as clothing, modes of transportation, and the role that religion plays in these cultures. Refer to the map of Southeast Asia and note its position in relation to India and China (countries that have been important historical influences in the region).
2. Read selections from *Voices from Southeast Asia*, a collection of personal stories of Vietnamese, Lao, Cambodian, Hmong, and other Southeast Asians who fled their homelands during the war years of the 1960s and 1970s. Discuss the sentiments expressed by people uprooted from their first culture and note the challenges they faced in making new homes in the United States, France, Australia, New Zealand, Canada, and elsewhere in the world. Show *Rebuilding the Temple* to illustrate the challenges of the Cambodian people in their period of adjustment; discuss the challenges of resettlement for Cambodians and other Southeast Asian refugees. *Angel Child, Dragon Child* similarly illustrates the difficulties of fitting into a new community and can be read and discussed by primary-age children. (Note that most Southeast Asians who came to the U.S. to escape war are no longer classified as refugees, but are non-U.S. citizens—as indeed are their offspring, who were born and raised in this country.)

3. Have students listen to selections of traditional musics from Southeast Asia. Play brief 20–30-second excerpts, guiding students in their attention to the musical instruments and voices heard. Ask students to name or describe the timbres they hear. Vietnamese music is generally string oriented, while much of the traditional music of Cambodia, Thailand, and Laos tends to feature percussion instruments, including xylophones, gongs, and drums.
4. Play each musical excerpt again. This time, discuss the role, intention, or meaning of the music. Use liner notes, companion books or brochures, and selection titles as description.

L E S S O N 2

■ **Objectives**
Students will:
1. Listen and identify instruments of the *pi phat* ensemble.
2. Discover aspects of rhythm, melody, and texture by performing "Courtly Evening."

■ **Materials**
1. Wooden xylophones, small hand (finger) cymbals, drums
2. Recording: "Lao," from *Sounds of the World: Music of Southeast Asia* (Reston, VA: Music Educators National Conference, 1986)

■ **Procedures**
1. Have the students listen to the recording of a court music ensemble from *Sounds of the World*, tape 1, example 1. The ensemble in the recording is comprised of Lao refugees; they are playing in a style that is derived from the Thai *pi phat* ensemble also found in Cambodian culture. Describe the instrumentation: It includes melody instruments such as the *ranat* (wooden xylophone), the *kong wong* (circle of knobbed gongs with a characteristic mellow timbre), and the *pi nai* (oboe). It also includes the rhythm instruments *chap* (cymbals), *ching* (small cymbals), and *taphon* (double-headed drum).
2. Direct the students' attention to the steady duple meter and lead them in patting the first beat of each measure (listen to the *chap* cymbals as a guide). Note the continuous melodies of xylophones and knobbed gongs, which are derived from a pentatonic scale. Emphasize the heterophonic texture, in which many layers of melodies occur simultaneously. Have the students tap the rhythmic ostinato of the *taphon* drum, as shown in figure 4.

Figure 4. Rhythmic ostinato of the *taphon*

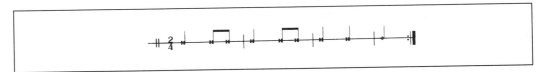

Figure 5. Four-measure ostinato

Figure 6. "Courtly Evening"

3. Play a traditional *pi phat* orchestra composition, "Courtly Evening," using classroom instruments.

> Melody 1: *ranat* (or wooden xylophone)
> Melody 2: *pi nai* (use recorder substitute or wooden xylophone)
> Rhythm: *ching* (or small cymbals): In the notation, "o" = "chop" (strike cymbals flat and hold together to prevent ringing) and "+" = "ching" (let cymbals ring). Play the finger cymbals every measure, alternating between "ching" and "chop."
> *chap* (hand cymbals): Play one stroke on beat 7 of every 8 beats, letting the hand cymbals ring.
> *taphon* (drum): Play a four-measure ostinato (as shown in figure 5)

   a. Begin by asking the entire class to sing "Courtly Evening" (see figure 6), on "nah" or another neutral syllable. The text printed in the example is a liberal translation of the nineteenth-century romantic song. Students may wish to clap lightly on the first beat of each measure.

   b. Demonstrate the role of the *ching* finger cymbals, the true conductor of the court orchestra, by dividing the class into singers and "chingers." The second group will chant "chop" as they muffle a clap with the cupped hands and will chant "ching" as they brush their fingers together in a quick clap. Switch groups; select a student to play the *ching* while the others chant.

   c. Double the melody on the xylophone. Add the second melody on recorder or on a second xylophone, calling attention to the independent lines that converge on the same pitch every four measures. If enough instruments are available, divide the class into groups and have everyone play a part.

   d. Add the drum ostinato and the hand cymbal part.

L E S S O N 3

■ Objectives

Students will:

1. Listen to examples of *kaen* music.
2. Demonstrate an understanding of texture by singing several versions of "Frère Jacques" in unison, in canon, and as a melody with chordal accompaniment on piano or Autoharp.
3. Discover the principle of free-reed performance on the harmonica.
4. Play a *kaen* piece arranged for classroom instruments.

■ Materials

1. Recordings:
   Thailand: Lao Music of the Northeast (Lyrichord LLST 7357)
   "Lao," from *Sounds of the World: Music of Southeast Asia* (Reston, VA: Music Educators National Conference, 1986)
2. Piano
3. Xylophones

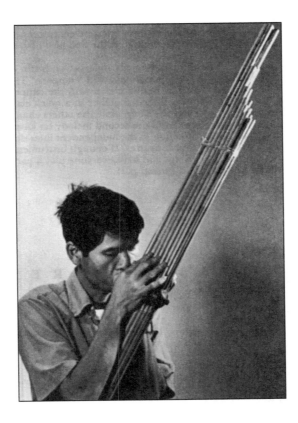

Figure 7. Kaen

Procedures

1. Listen to the national instrument of Laos, the *kaen*, a free-reed mouth organ (both recordings listed under "Materials" have appropriate excerpts). The *kaen* is shaped like a raft and is made from sixteen bamboo tubes and a wooden central wind chest (see figure 7). There are holes in the bamboo tubes just above the wind chest. Players select pitches by stopping the holes with their fingers or produce drones by blocking the holes with beeswax. *Kaen* music is highly virtuosic and improvisatory.

2. Listen to the continual sound of the *kaen*. Explain that the player produces sound on the instrument both by inhaling and exhaling. Demonstrate this principle on the harmonica.

3. Note the homophonic texture with the use of cluster chords (chords built with a combination of intervals such as seconds and thirds, such as d-e-g-b) and drones in the solo *kaen* selections. Contrast the homophony of the *kaen* with the heterophony of the classical *pi phat* orchestra. Demonstrate these textures vocally by singing "Frère Jacques" as a single melody (monophonic texture), a melody with chordal accompaniment (homophonic texture), and simultaneous melodies (heterophonic texture). Demonstrate heterophonic texture by asking the class to sing "Frère Jacques" while you sing a simultaneous variation on the melody (see figure 8).

4. Play the example of *kaen* music in figure 9 on the piano or divide it among students on xylophones in order to sample the homophonic texture of simultaneously sounding pitches in "cluster chords."

Figure 8. Heterophonic version of "Frère Jacques"

Figure 9. Kaen music example

LESSON 4

■ **Objectives**

Students will:
1. Sing the song "Bac Kim Thang."
2. Learn and be able to describe the meaning of the text.
3. Play a variety of ostinati patterns as drum accompaniment.

■ **Materials**

1. "Bac Kim Thang"
2. Drums (conga drums or bongo drums with mallets, if possible)
3. "Voice of Trong," from *From Rice Paddies and Temple Yards: Traditional Music of Vietnam* by Phong T. Nguyen and Patricia Shehan Campbell (Danbury, CT: World Music Press, 1991)

■ **Procedures**

1. Introduce "Bac Kim Thang" ("Setting Up a Golden Ladder") as a children's song from southern Vietnam (see figure 10). One of the book's authors, Phong T. Nguyen, learned it as a child growing up in a small Vietnamese village in the 1950s. Share the song's translation:

   > Let's set up a golden ladder, "kah lahng" [not translatable].
   > It's the color of a pumpkin!
   > We can climb from the pole to the beam on top of the houses
   > Hey! Look! See the oil vendor falling from the bridge,
   > And now the frog vendor is afraid of the bridge.
   > The "le le" bird is playing his drum.
   > The "bim bip" bird is playing his trumpet: "Taw tee lair taw lair."

   The "le le" bird is commonly found in the rice paddies, and the "bim bop" bird sings rhythmically a "bim bop" phrase (see figure 11) when the river tide is up.
2. Sing the song. Ask students to listen carefully to the mention of the "le le" bird and to the sound of the "bim bop" bird, who "trumpets" his sound at the close of the melody.
3. Sing the song again, directing students to pat a steady pulse, accenting every other note as shown in figure 12.
4. Practice singing the first and last phrases of the song, which are "Bac kim thang ca lang bí ro" and "Con bìm bip thôi tò tí le tò le."
5. Play the steady, duple meter pattern on drums. Direct students to sing the first and last phrases and to join you on the middle phrases if they can.
6. Play variations of accompaniment pattern on the drums, as shown in figure 13.
7. Assign the pulse to a woodblock and the three rhythm patterns to three drums. These instruments should be played with mallets while the class sings the song.
8. Compare the percussion patterns to the sound of a Vietnamese percussion ensemble in the "Voice of Trong" excerpt. Notice the use of wood and "skin" (drum) instruments in this traditional ensemble. The match of timbres and playing style between "Voice of Trong" and "Bac Kim Thang" should be obvious—and inspiring.

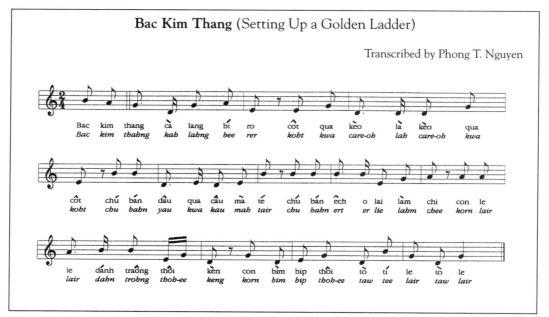

Figure 10. "Bac Kim Thang"

Figure 11. "Bim bop" phrase

Figure 12. "Bac Kim Thang" pattern

Figure 13. Variations of accompaniment pattern

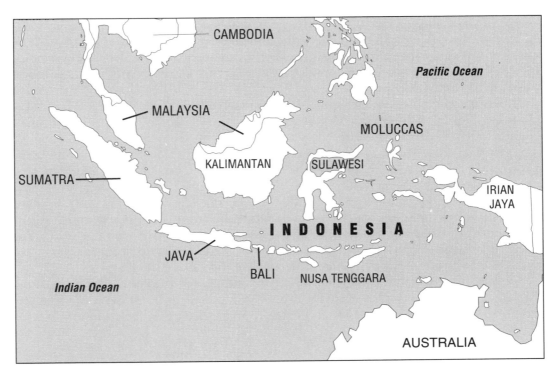

Figure 14. Map of Indonesia

INDONESIA

by William M. Anderson

Indonesia, the largest country in Southeast Asia, is composed of more than thirteen thousand islands stretching between mainland Southeast Asia and Australia (see figure 14). The islands that form Indonesia stretch nearly three thousand miles (the approximate distance from San Francisco to Boston) but contain only twice the land area of Texas. The principal islands or island groups include Java, Bali, Sumatra, Kalimantan (the Indonesian section of Borneo), Sulawesi (Celebes), the Moluccas, Nusa Tenggara (The Lesser Sundas), and Irian Jaya (West New Guinea).

In the relatively small land area of Indonesia live approximately 198 million people, making it the fifth most populous nation in the world. More than two-thirds of the inhabitants reside on the island of Java, which contains Jakarta, the capital of the republic.

The people of Indonesia are generally short and slender with light brown skin and straight black hair. Ethnic diversity abounds in the islands, however, and several million Chinese constitute an important minority in the society. Most Indonesians are Moslem, but their beliefs often consist of a mixture of Islam, Hinduism, and animism. The people of the island of Bali, just off the east coast of Java, are predominantly Hindu.

Large numbers of Indonesians earn their living from farming and fishing. The islands of Indonesia are intersected by the equator, which makes the climate warm and humid except in the cooler regions of the volcanic mountains. The warm temperatures, combined with the rich, volcanic soil, allow the growth of various agricultural crops, including rice, tobacco, rubber, spices, and tea. Early explorers called Indonesia "the Spice Islands," and it was a western route to these islands that Christopher Columbus sought when he discovered America.

Many diverse influences have shaped Indonesian culture. As early as 2500 B.C., people from southern China were migrating to the islands. At the time of the Roman Empire, Indian traders traveled to Indonesia, bringing with them the Hindu and Buddhist religions. The many Hindu and Buddhist monuments found throughout the islands today attest to their brilliant artistic accomplishments. In the fourteenth and fifteenth centuries, Moslem traders brought Islam to the islands, particularly to Java. The nearby island of Bali, however, became a haven for Hindus, who nurtured one of the most brilliant artistic traditions in the islands. European traders began arriving in the sixteenth century. The Dutch exerted the greatest influence on the islands, which they called the "Netherlands East Indies." Growing nationalism in the twentieth century eventually led to the establishment of the independent Republic of Indonesia in 1949.

Today, the traditional arts of music, dance, and puppet theater continue to thrive throughout Indonesia as they have for centuries. Further, in recent decades these arts have spread beyond the borders of Indonesia to many countries, including the United States.

General characteristics

One of the most sophisticated types of music found in Indonesia is played by ensembles known as gamelan (often translated as "orchestra") (see figure 15). While gamelan traditions exist on several Indonesian islands, the best known are those of the islands of Java and Bali. A Javanese gamelan is comprised primarily of xylophone-like instruments and knobbed gongs. The gongs and the keys of the xylophone-type instruments are usually made of bronze. The orchestra may also contain flutes, several stringed instruments, and drums. Vocalists are also important members of the orchestra.

For many centuries, gamelans have been an integral part of Indonesian life, accompanying puppet plays and dance-dramas and being featured at temple festivals, weddings, birthdays, visits of guests and heads of state, and numerous other occasions. Thousands of gamelans are present throughout the islands today, and their performances are an important artistic and recreational activity for many people. Performances by the most distinguished ensembles are often broadcast on the radio. Conservatories of music have also been established so students can study this orchestral tradition. There are a great many forms and styles of gamelan music in Indonesia. While there are similarities among the styles, the following musical characteristics are specifically related to the court tradition of central Java.

Melodies use two principal scale or tuning systems: the five-toned *slendro* and the seven-toned *pelog*, as shown in figure 16. The scale intervals used in Java are quite different from those used in Western music, so the Western notation can give only an approximation of the actual pitches. Indonesian musicians often use numbered notation like that printed above the notes shown in figure 16. Melodies have considerable stepwise motion in ascending, descending, and undulating contours. Hocket or resultant melodies (those made when several different players add notes at appropriate

Figure 15. Javanese gamelan

times) are sometimes used.

The musical texture is polyphonic with melodies organized in strata or levels. Musicians often play simultaneous variations of a core melodic line. Javanese music commonly employs duple meter with beats grouped into cycles that are marked off by the sounding of various sizes of gongs. Musical forms in gamelan music often involve the repetition of melodies and rhythms.

Gamelan compositions are cast in both loud and soft playing styles. The loud style features gongs, metallophones, and drums, while the soft style emphasizes the flute, several stringed instruments, and voices. The nasalized timbre of female singing is quite different from most Western music.

The lessons in this section are designed to introduce students to some of the principal characteristics of Indonesian gamelan music through performance on instruments that are commonly found in most schools. The lessons include instructions for fashioning a makeshift gamelan using xylophones, melody bells, glockenspiels, and so on. Students will learn the principal characteristics of Indonesian music more quickly through a hands-on approach than from just listening to a lecture (see figure 17).

Along with performing in an American gamelan, have students listen to several examples of gamelan music from Indonesia. It is especially important for students to listen to these authentic examples carefully since they are the actual musical sounds of the Indonesian gamelan.

Figure 16. *Slendro* and *pelog*

Figure 17. American children playing *gamelan* music

Figure 18. Core melody for "Ricik-Ricik"

LESSON 1

■ **Objectives**

Students will:
1. Perform the Javanese gamelan composition "Ricik-Ricik" ("Sound of Flowing Water").

■ **Materials**

1. Xylophones, glockenspiels, and melody bells of different sizes
2. Gongs of different sizes (which can be fashioned from pie pans or other kitchen utensils)
3. A small, barrel-shaped drum (although a drum of any size may be used)

■ **Procedures**

1. At its simplest, Javanese gamelan music is based on a core melody that is played over and over in ostinato fashion (see figure 18). In "Ricik-Ricik," the melody is in the *pelog* scale system. The numbers under the notes in figure 18 refer to specific pitches. Write the numbers on melody bells (ensuring that the numbers do not leave permanent marks) so the students can easily see and play the pitches. Make certain that the students notice the repetition in the melody.

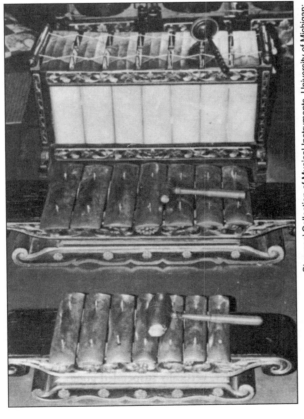

Stearnes' Collection of Musical Instruments, University of Michigan; photo by William M. Anderson.

Figure 19. Saron barun, saron demung, and slentum (front to back)

2. Traditionally, the core melody is generally played on the *saron barung, saron demung,* and *slentum* (see figure 19). In the classroom, you can use glockenspiels, melody bells, or xylophones (see figure 20). Have several students play the melody while the rest of the class sings on a neutral syllable, such as "loo" (see figure 21).

3. In a gamelan composition, the core melody is punctuated at various points by a series of gongs (see figure 22). The largest gong, called gong *ageng* (marked "G" in the score), is sounded at the ends of the longest melodic phrases; in "Ricik-Ricik," this occurs on every eighth beat. The *kempul* (marked as "P" in the score), which are smaller, vertically suspended gongs, sound on beats three, five, and seven of each melodic phrase. The *kenong* (marked as "N" in the score), which are pot gongs placed horizontally on wooden-frame supports, are played on beats two, four, six, and eight (see figure 23). The *ketuk* (marked as "T" in the score), which is a set of small, horizontally placed gongs, is played on the off beats (the eighth note following each beat: counted "1 and 2 and"). In effect, the sounding of the gongs at various points in the melody forms a cycle of beats, as shown in figure 24.

4. Have the students devise some gong-like instruments analogous to the Indonesian gongs and play them at the appropriate places in the core melody. Create gongs by using pots and pans. Select some that produce a pleasant sound when struck in the middle with a soft-headed mallet, made from a stick that is covered with heavy cloth on one end.

Figure 20. Students playing a *gamelan* melody on Orff instruments

Figure 21. Students playing a melody on *saron*

Figure 22. Foreground: *ketuk* (right) and *kenong* (left); background: gong *ageng* (right) and *kempul* (left)

Figure 23. Student playing the *kenong*

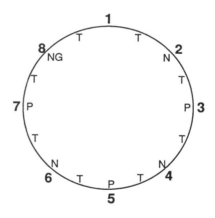

Figure 24. Cycle of beats

Figure 25. Core melody with gong *ageng* on beat eight

Figure 26. Core melody with *kenong* added

Figure 27. Core melody with *kempul* added

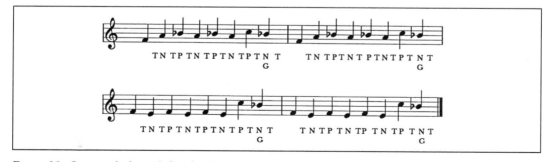

Figure 28. Core melody with *ketuk* added

Figure 29. Embellishing instruments: *Peking, gender, gambang,* and *bonang* (foreground to background)

Play the core melody and add the *gong ageng* ("G") on beat 8, as shown in figure 25. Play the core melody and *gong ageng* and add the *kenong* ("N") on beats two, four, six, and eight, as shown in figure 26. Play the core melody, *gong ageng,* and *kenong,* and add the *kempul* ("P") on beats on three, five, and seven, as shown in figure 27. Play the core melody and *gong ageng, kenong,* and *kempul,* and add the *ketuk* ("T") on the off-beats, as shown in figure 28.

5. The core melody, with its underlying framework of gongs, is embellished or elaborated upon by a series of instruments (see figures 29 and 30). The embellishing parts in a gamelan composition range from simple to highly complex. Some require years to learn well. One of the simplest embellishing techniques consists of reiterating each tone of the core melody, as shown in figure 31. Have several students play the core melody while other students embellish it by playing a "doubling part" on xylophones, glocken-spiels, or melody bells.

6. Perform the entire piece. Divide the class so that some students are playing the core melody, others are adding gongs, and still others are playing embellishing parts. Play the piece through several times at a moderate tempo (quarter note = 88).

7. There are two basic musical styles in gamelan compositions: a loud/fast style featuring gongs, metallophones, and drums, and a softer/slower style emphasizing the flute, several stringed instruments, and voices. To approximate these two styles, play "Ricik-Ricik" several times, first with a moderate tempo and loud dynamic level. Then continue by repeating the melody several times but with a slower tempo and softer dynamic level; if possible, add a flute (or recorder) embellishing part (by doubling the melody). Then conclude by returning to the louder tempo and faster dynamic level, repeating the melody several times. You or a student should keep the beat on a drum (*kendang*) (see figure 32) and should lead the group in making changes in tempo (see figure 33).

8. Have the students summarize on the board some of the things they have learned in this lesson: *pelog* scale, ostinato, duple meter with cycle of beats outlined by the sounding of gongs, loud and soft sections, and the emphasis on percussion instruments/timbres.

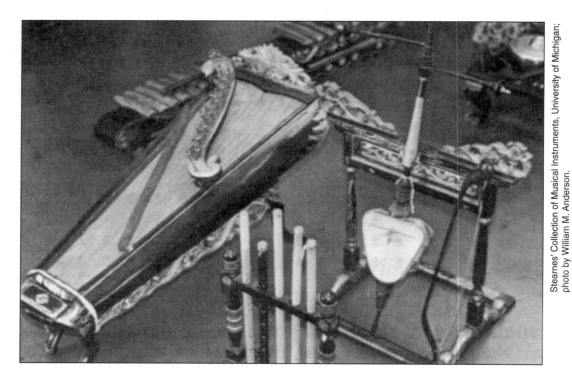

Figure 30. Embellishing instruments: *celempung, suling,* and *rebab* (left to right)

Figure 31. Core melody and embellishing instrument part

Figure 32. Student playing the *kendang*

Loud/Fast	Soft/Slow	Loud/Fast
3 5 6 5 6 5 7 6	3 5 6 5 6 5 7 6	3 5 6 5 6 5 7 6
3 5 6 5 6 5 7 6	3 5 6 5 6 5 7 6	3 5 6 5 6 5 7 6
3 2 3 2 3 2 7 6	3 2 3 2 3 2 7 6	3 2 3 2 3 2 7 6
3 2 3 2 3 2 7 6	3 2 3 2 3 2 7 6	3 2 3 2 3 2 7 6

Figure 33. Music styles and tempo changes in gamelan compositions

L E S S O N   2

■ **Objectives**

Students will:
1. Perform the Javanese gamelan composition "Udan Angin" ("The Monsoon").
2. Identify the use of ostinato, duple meter with cycle of beats outlined by the sounding of gongs, embellishment of the core melody, and the timbre of percussion instruments.
3. Listen to a selection of Javanese gamelan music and correctly identify musical events.
4. View a section of a student puppet play from Java.

■ **Materials**

1. Several Orff metallophones to simulate the *sarong barung, saron demung,* and *slentum* and embellishing instruments
2. Four sizes of gongs made from pots and pans (Select those that produce a pleasant sound when struck in the middle with a soft-headed mallet, made from a stick that is covered with a heavy cloth on one end.)
3. Recording: "Puspawarna" (which means "Kinds of Flowers"), from *Javanese Court Gamelan* (Elektra/Nonesuch 72044)
4. Videotape: "Wayang-Shadow Puppet Play," from the *JVC Video Anthology of World Music and Dance* (tape 10, item 2)

■ **Procedures**

1. Play the Javanese gamelan composition "Udan Angin," which is in the *slendro* scale system.
   a. Using several sizes of Orff metallophones (which simulate the *saron barung, saron demung,* and *slentum*), have students play the melody shown in figure 34. (Notice that phrase 1 is the same as phrase 2, and phrase 3 is the same as phrase 4.) As students play the core melody, have other members of the class sing along on a neutral syllable, such as "loo." Repeat the melody over and over until everyone has learned it. Take turns with other class members playing the melody.
   b. Have the students fashion four sizes of gongs (large to small) from pots and pans (simulating *gong ageng, kempul, kenong,* and *ketuk*). Attempt to make gongs that produce a pleasant sound when struck in the middle with a soft-headed mallet (the mallets may be made from sticks with heavy cloth covering on one end). In the gamelan composition "Udan Angin," gongs are sounded at various points in the core melody given in figure 34.
2. A large vertical gong (called *gong ageng,* abbreviated "G") should be struck on the last note of each phrase of the core melody of "Udan Angin." Have the students play and sing the core melody with the large *gong ageng* sounding on the last beat, as shown in figure 35.
3. Somewhat smaller horizontally struck gongs (called *kenong,* abbreviated "N") should sound on beats 2, 4, 6, and 8 of the core melody (see figure 36). Have the class fashion *kenongs* and play them when appropriate. The sounds of the *kenongs* should blend with the pitches on which they sound.

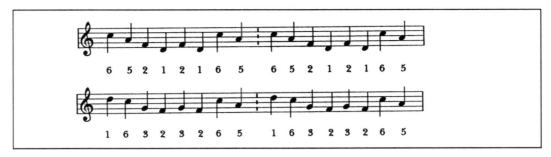

Figure 34. Core melody of "Udan Angin"

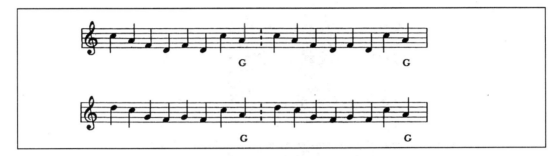

Figure 35. Core melody with gong *ageng*

Figure 36. Core melody with *kenong*

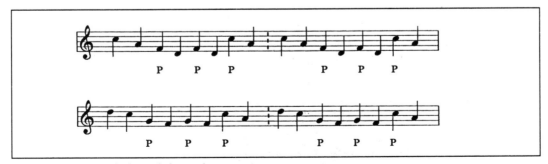

Figure 37. Core melody with *kempul*

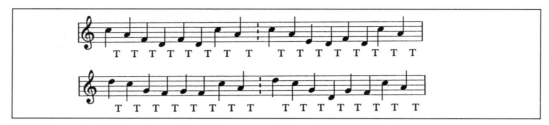

Figure 38. Core meldoy with *ketuk*

Figure 39. Doubling the core melody

Figure 40. Doubling and anticipating the core melody

4. Medium-sized vertically struck gongs (called *kempul*, abbreviated "P") should sound on beats 3, 5, and 7 (see figure 37). Have the class fashion *kempul* and play them when appropriate. (Again, the sounds of the *kempul* should blend with the pitches on which they sound.)

5. A small horizontally struck gong (called *ketuk*, abbreviated "T") should sound on the offbeats (see figure 38).

6. Practice "Udan Angin" with some members of the class playing and singing the core melody while other members of the class add the gong parts. Repeat the composition over and over in ostinato fashion.

7. Add simple embellishing parts to the core melody and gongs. Choose several small metallophones and have students double the core melody, as shown in figure 39.

8. Once the students feel comfortable doubling the melody, ask several of them to also double and anticipate the core melody, as shown in figure 40.

9. Have the students practice "Udan Angin" by playing the core melody, with gongs and embellishing parts, over and over for as many times as they wish. Have one student keep a steady beat on a small drum (quarter note = 88). When the students wish to end the composition, the drummer should gradually increase the tempo to a close on the final note of the core melody.

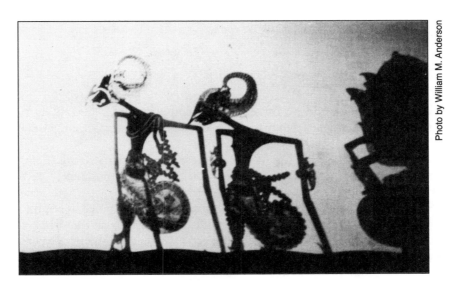

Figure 41. Javanese shadow puppet theater

10. Have the students listen to the selection from *Javanese Court Gamelan*. This piece is played for the entrance of the Prince into the Pendopo (the reception hall at a royal palace). Place the following items on either the chalkboard or a handout for the students, and have them circle the appropriate musical events as they listen to the composition:

   (1)   Instruments only   or   (Instruments and voices)

   (2)   (Tempo moderate)   or   Tempo very fast

   (3)   One line of music   or   (Many lines of music)

   (4)   Rapid changes in   or   (Dynamic levels stay
          dynamic levels   at about the same level)

   (5)   (Orchestra composed   or   Orchestra composed
          mainly of percussion   mainly of wind
          instruments)   instruments

   (6)   (Music generally   or   Music generally active/
          reserved/restrained)   spirited

11. Show the students a short segment of the puppet theater (*wayang*) from Java (see figure 41), which is accompanied by the gamelan. Explain that puppet theater is very popular in Java, and the plays often run all night. Families come with their children, and as they watch the play, they will also eat and converse. As the night proceeds, children sometimes doze off but awaken for the more exciting segments. The plays are most often drawn from the great epics, the Ramayana and the Mahabharata. As you view the videotape, particularly notice both the puppets and the accompaniment provided by the gamelan.

L E S S O N   3

■ Objectives

Students will:

1. Compare Balinese and Javanese gamelan compositions, especially noting in Balinese music the different instruments, faster tempos, and interlocking parts played by pairs of instruments.

2. Perform a simplified version of the Balinese dance-drama *Kecak* (*Cak*), the so-called "Monkey Chant" or "Monkey Dance," which features music executed vocally in the style of a Balinese *gamelan suara* ("orchestra of voices").

   a. Develop a new concept of the potential uses of the voice as a musical instrument. Learn basic techniques of rhythmic interlocking, call-and-response, and onomatopoeic vocalizing using vocables to create a performance experience.

   b. Combine music making, dancing, acting, and imaginative visualization within a single group performance.

■ Materials

1. Book (for photographs and supplemental information):
   Balinese Music by Michael Tenzer (Berkeley/Singapore: Periplus Editions, 1991)

2. Recordings:
   "Golden Rain" ("Hudjan Mas") and "Ketjak: The Ramayana Monkey Chant," from *Music from the Morning of the World* (Elektra/Nonesuch Explorer Series 9 79196-2)
   "Hudjan Mas" ("Golden Rain") in *Music Resources for Multicultural Perspectives* (Reston, VA: Music Educators National Conference, 1995)
   "Ketawang Puspawarna," from *Javanese Court Gamelan* (Elektra/Nonesuch 72044)

3. Videotapes:
   "Sekar Jupun," from the *JVC Video Anthology of World Music and Dance* (Southeast Asia IV: Tape 9, Indonesia 1, selection 1) and "Kekak," from the *JVC Video Anthology of World Music and Dance* (Southeast Asia V: Tape 10, Indonesia 2, selection 1)
   Bali: Masterpiece of the Gods (National Geographic)

4. Map of Indonesia/Southeast Asia

■ Procedures

1. Introduce the island of Bali, Indonesia. Point out Bali on a map and explain that it is a very small island (about the size of Rhode Island) on the other side of the world. It is so far away that it takes about twenty-four hours to get there by airplane. Show photographs of Bali (*Balinese Music* is a good source). If time permits, show an excerpt of National Geographic's excellent documentary film, *Bali: Masterpiece of the Gods*.

2. Discuss the central importance of the arts in Balinese culture. Explain that in Bali, the arts are an integral part of daily life and that almost every Balinese actively participates in artistic life, whether as a musician, dancer, painter, sculptor, or actor. The artistic traditions of Bali are admired throughout the world, and the famous anthropologist Clifford Geertz has gone so far as to claim that Bali's "most famous cultural attribute is her artistic genius."[1]

3. Discuss the Balinese gamelan tradition in comparison with its Javanese counterpart (see figure 42). As in Java, the main types of instrumental ensembles in Bali are gamelans. Bali is home to over twenty distinct types of gamelans, each with its own name, instrumental configuration, and specific associations to certain kinds of rituals, ceremonies, and other performance contexts. The most well-known type is the gamelan *gong kebyar*, which features bronze metallophones, gongs, and gong-chimes. The word "kebyar" means "to burst open" or "to flare up like a match," and the "kebyar style" of music is indeed very flashy and energetic. The ensemble is led by a pair of drums (*kendang*) and may also include bamboo flutes (*sulingp*), fiddle (*rebab*), and small and large cymbals (*cengceng*). (A good color picture of a Balinese gamelan is found on pages 8 and 9 of Tenzer's *Balinese Music*.) Both musically and in terms of instrumentation, Balinese and Javanese gamelan traditions are notably different, radically so in some respects. In general, compared with Javanese gamelan music, Balinese gamelan music (at least in the twentieth century) tends to be faster in tempo, more fiery in spirit, and more dependent for its structure upon the precise execution of complementary interlocking parts (*kotekan*) between pairs of instruments within the ensemble.

Play recorded music and/or video examples to demonstrate the sound of Balinese gamelan music. If possible, show a short excerpt from "Sekar Jupun," the first selection on tape 9 of the *JVC Video Anthology of World Music and Dance*. This is a modern-style piece for gamelan *gong kebyar*. If the JVC video is not an option, play an excerpt of a Balinese gamelan *gong kebyar* piece, such as "Hudjan Mas" ("Golden Rain" in *Music Resources for Multicultural Perspectives*, side d, no. 27). Compare this with a recording of the central Javanese gamelan piece "Ketawang Puspawarna" to illustrate differences between Balinese and Javanese musical styles, in particular,

Figure 42. The Balinese Gamelan of Florida State University, directed by Michael Bakan

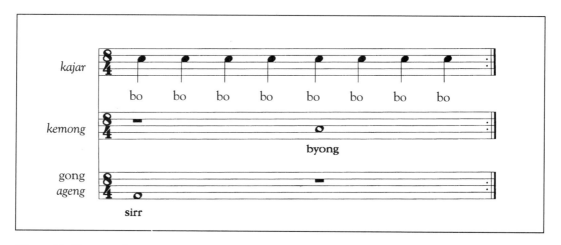

Figure 43. Gong cycle pattern

instruments, tempo, and interlocking parts played by pairs of instruments.

4. Discuss the concept of "interlocking" in Balinese music as it relates to Balinese social life. An "interlocking concept" (*kotekan*) is fundamental to Balinese musical practice, as it is to most aspects of Balinese social life. Whether engaged in work, play, or the performance of rituals, Balinese individuals are expected to work in close cooperation with each other and to structure their lives around a philosophy of *gotong royong*, that is, mutual dependence and cooperative effort. The complex and tightly integrated structures of Balinese gamelan music seem to reflect and model this cooperative ideal of mutual dependency in social life.

5. A great variety of gamelans are found in Bali. In certain types, one finds iron- or bamboo-keyed instruments in place of bronze instruments. While the sound, look, construction, and function of each type of Balinese gamelan distinguishes it from all other types, there is one kind of gamelan that truly stands apart from all the rest, the gamelan *suara*, or "gamelan of voices." In the gamelan *suara*, all the sounds are produced vocally, and the vocal sounds onomatopoeically represent the sounds of particular instruments. Thus, the large gong (gong *ageng*) is represented by the vocable "sirr," the tiny gong *kemong* by "byong," and the tempo-keeping kettle gong *kajar* (from "ajar," meaning "to teach," since this instrument provides the basic pulse that "teaches" the others how to relate their parts) by a short, sharply articulated sound of "bo" (sometimes "pung"). The gamelan *suara* may consist of two hundred or more members (traditionally all male) and is characteristically associated with the *Kecak* dance-drama, a play with music and dance featuring a large "monkey army" and a host of colorful mythological characters in which an episode from the Hindu epic Ramayana is enacted.

6. Learn "Monkey Chant."

   a. Perform vocal gamelan sounds in call and response. Have the children imitate your call-and-response style as you produce the onomatopoeic "sirr," "byong," and "bo" sounds of gong *ageng*, *kemong*, and *kajar*.

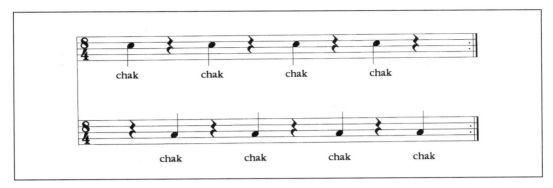

Figure 44. Quarter-note interlock

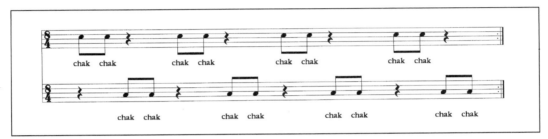

Figure 45. Alteration of doubled eighth notes

b. Next, divide the class up into three groups: the "sirrr" group, the "byong" group, and the "bo" group. Starting with the "bo's," help them establish a steady four-beat (quarter-note) pulse, and then add in the interlocking "sirrr's" and "byong's." The resultant "gong cycle" pattern is represented in figure 43.

c. Introduce *Kecak* and "monkey" sounds and rhythms.

(1) Once the class can perform the gong cycle pattern, tell them: "Now we have to add in the monkeys. Yes, the monkeys! Because in a little while we're going to perform our own version of a Balinese *kecak* play in which you get to play monkey soldiers in a big monkey army, and in this play, the monkeys get to be musicians, too!" Ask the class, "Do you want to be monkey soldiers?" (They usually say yes.) "Okay, then. This is the sound that Balinese monkey soldiers like to make: 'CAK!!' " (pronounced "chak"). Have the children shout it back. Repeat this call-and-response "chak shout" a few times.

(2) Now divide the class in half. Instruct each half of the class to shout "chak" every time you point to them. Get a steady quarter-note interlock going between the two groups (see figure 44) at a tempo of quarter note = 96–132. If establishing a steady pulse proves difficult, use the analogy of a clock going "tick-tock-tick-tock" but making the sound "chak-chak-chak-chak." This will help inculcate the concept of a steady-pulsed interlocking rhythm.

(3) Next, have each of the two groups double up its rhythm so that the resultant rhythm becomes an alternation of doubled eighth notes instead of alternating quarter notes, as shown in figure 45.

Figure 46. Continuous stream of interlocked, overlapping eighth notes

(4) Have each group add a third eighth note to its pattern, which will result in a continuous stream of interlocked, overlapping eighth notes (see figure 46).

(5) Keeping the eighth-note rhythm going without pause, now reintegrate the gong cycle parts learned earlier. First, point to a small group of children within the class and model the steady "bo" pulse of the *kajar*, indicating gesturally for them to imitate you. Next, isolate another subgroup and have them pick up the gong *ageng* part on the syllable "sirrr," and finally, do the same for the *kemong* part (on "byong"). The rest of the class continues with their interlocking "cak" patterns. At this point, a five-part interlocking rhythmic polyphony of voices will have been produced (see figure 47). Let the music continue for a while, reinforcing any of the rhythms that may begin to fall out of sync and, if possible, improvising some "cak" rhythms of your own over the top.

(6) Next, select another subgroup within the class to add in the *pokok*, or core melody. This is an eight-beat-long ostinato tune in quarter notes with an ornamental turn preceding every other main beat (see figure 48).

(7) If you are working with older children, or if some members of the class are rhythmically gifted, you can add a further interlocking layer to the texture by incorporating the set of two interlocking "cak" rhythms notated in figure 49. These complex rhythms move at twice the speed (i.e., in sixteenth-notes) of the other "cak" parts and are quite difficult to execute.

(8) Figure 50 is a complete score of all of the parts discussed so far, including the challenging optional rhythms of figure 49.

(9) Congratulate the class for having successfully transformed themselves into a "gamelan of voices" (gamelan *suara*) and a monkey chorus at the same time, and for having mastered the "Monkey Chant" music. Tell them to remember their individual parts since they will have to perform them again later when they put on the "Monkey Chant" play.

Figure 47. Five-part polyphony of voices

Figure 48. Pokok melody

Figure 49. Incorporation of two interlocking "cak" rhythms

Figure 50. Complete score for a "gamelan of voices"

Extension of Lesson Three

1. Preparing for the *Kecak* performance

Now the class is ready to begin to prepare the *Kecak* drama performance. Explain that in Bali, the kind of vocal music they have just learned is used to accompany the *Kecak*, a special play otherwise known as the "Monkey Chant" or "Monkey Dance" because it features a big army of monkey soldiers who chant and dance. Tell them that now that they have mastered the "monkey chant" music, they are ready to produce their own *Kecak* play, but first, they need to hear the story on which the play is based. Begin with a line like: "It's a really good story about heroes and villains and kings and queens and monkeys and magic and all kinds of other neat stuff. Here's how it goes." Proceed to tell the story of "The Abduction of Sita" from the Ramayana. (The version that follows is a greatly abridged and liberal adaptation of the original that has worked well for the author in his *Kecak* classes and workshops for school children. See *Myths of the Hindus and Buddhists* by Amanda K. Coomaraswamy and Sister Nivedita (New York: Dover Publications, 1967),

56–94, for a more complete version of the story.)

2. The Abduction of Sita

Once upon a time in a land far, far away, there lived a great king and queen named Rama and Sita and an evil demon-king named Rawana. One day, Rawana decided to kidnap Queen Sita and steal her away from King Rama. Rawana used his magic powers to create a Golden Deer, which was the most beautiful animal in the whole world, and sent the deer out running in Queen Sita's enchanted garden while she and Rama were taking their daily stroll. Sita spotted the Golden Deer grazing near the forest. "Look, look, Rama," she said excitedly as she pointed toward the deer. "I think that deer must be the most beautiful animal in the whole world! Please go fetch him and bring him back so I can pet him."

At first Rama resisted because he did not want to leave Sita alone and unprotected. But Sita was persistent, and eventually Rama broke down and went chasing after the deer. The deer ran deep into the forest, and Rama followed in hot pursuit, leaving Sita all by herself.

Seizing the opportunity, Rawana, who had been hiding behind a tree, now approached Sita. She didn't recognize him as the evil king because he had magically disguised himself as a poor, old wise man. Since he seemed kindly and wise, Sita was not afraid, and she invited him to come sit with her while she awaited Rama's return. Then, suddenly, Rawana transformed himself into a huge monster with ten heads and twenty arms and great bulging red eyes. He grabbed the beautiful Sita. "Ha ha," he cackled. "Now you will be mine!" Sita screamed and cried out to Rama, but Rama was too far away to hear. Rawana threw Sita over his shoulder and flew away with her to Lanka, his kingdom on the other side of the world.

A bird sitting in a treetop witnessed the kidnapping and was alarmed. She flew to the home of the white monkey Hanuman, King Rama's chief messenger. "The queen has been kidnapped! The queen has been kidnapped," sang the bird, and then told Hanuman the whole sordid tale. Taking advantage of his great speed and keen sense of smell, Hanuman ran into the forest after King Rama, who was still tracking the Golden Deer. The king was startled by Hanuman and drew his bow, but luckily recognized his monkey friend just in time. "Something terrible has happened," shrieked Hanuman as he came bouncing toward the king. "The Queen has been kidnapped by Rawana!" The king was alarmed and angered by this awful news, but he quickly pulled himself together and came up with a plan. "I should never have left her alone," he said, "but what's done is done. Now Hanuman, make haste. Call General Sugriwa and have him bring together the entire monkey army. We must do battle with Rawana and save the queen!"

Sugriwa assembled the troops and off they went: Rama, Sugriwa, Hanuman, and the entire monkey brigade. As they marched heroically from the palace chanting their famous "Monkey Chant," crowds of people and monkeys lined the streets and cheered them on. Once outside the town, they entered the Great Forest. Marching through the forest, they had to be very quiet and very careful because of all the lions and tigers and bears. Oh my! After traveling day in and day out for a long, long time, they finally got tired—even the great Sugriwa himself—and had to sleep. Finding a clearing in the forest, the army pitched tents and set up camp for the night. While they slept, they snored loudly, as monkey soldiers tend to do.

After a good night's sleep, it was time for breakfast. What do you think monkeys eat for breakfast? Well, bananas, of course! After breakfast, Sugriwa led the morning monkey exercises and then the troops were on their way again, chanting the "Monkey Chant" as they marched. Day in and day out, they traveled on toward the other side of the world, and as tired as they became, Sugriwa would not let them rest. Then, finally, they reached their destination: the royal palace of the evil King Rawana. When Sugriwa saw the palace, he quickly silenced the troops, who had kept up their "Monkey Chant" the whole way. The soldiers huddled around Sugriwa and he reviewed the battle plan. They would ambush at sundown, catching Rawana's imperial guard by surprise, and then storm the palace gates and rescue Queen Sita.

Sundown came and Sugriwa gave the signal to attack. The monkey army swarmed the palace. Rawana's troops put up a good fight but were no match for Sugriwa's superior warriors. The evil king's army was quickly defeated and Rawana himself was slain by a magic arrow from Rama's bow. Sugriwa, Rama, and Hanuman then led the charge as the soldiers stormed the palace gates. They found Queen Sita imprisoned in a small garden, surrounded on all sides by hundred-foot-high walls. She was crying when the troops arrived, but soon her tears of sadness and despair turned to tears of joy. She saw her beloved Rama and immediately knew that all was well once again. Her nightmare was over. Rama whisked Sita up and led the brigade out of the palace.

The long journey home to Rama's kingdom on the other side of the world did not seem long at all, since now, with good having triumphed over evil and Rama and Sita reunited, everyone was very happy. As the soldiers marched toward home, they performed their "Monkey Chant" with great joy and exuberance. Rama, Sita, Sugriwa, Hanuman, and the entire monkey army received heroes' welcomes when they finally returned home, and everyone lived happily ever after (or at least until the next crisis!).

3. Organize and rehearse for the *Kecak* performance

    a. Once you have finished telling the story, immediately begin preparing the *Kecak* performance, explaining to the class that it is now time to transform themselves into a monkey army and to turn the story about the kidnap and rescue of the queen into their own play featuring their own "monkey chant" music. Explain that you will play the role of General Sugriwa, chief commander of Rama's monkey army. Solicit volunteers to play the roles of King Rama, Queen Sita, Evil King Rawana, the Golden Deer, the Bird, and Hanuman. Everyone else is cast as a monkey soldier.

    b. In general, it is best to direct and create the play as you perform it, without explaining or rehearsing scenes or dialogue ahead of time. Simply instruct the children on what to say and what to do as the drama unfolds. There is one part of the play, however, that should be rehearsed prior to the "performance" in order to avoid the possibility of children hurting each other. This is the "battle scene" between Rama's and Rawana's monkey armies just before the end of the play. To rehearse it, organize the class into two lines with equal numbers of children. Through the entire first part of the play, both lines will be made up of soldiers of Rama's "good" army, but in the battle scene, one line is suddenly "transformed" into Rawana's "evil" army as the two lines split apart and face off against each other. Explain emphatically that when monkey armies battle, they do not actually touch each other. The enemy soldiers simply sway forward and back, moving toward and away from each other while shaking their hands in front of their bodies and making hissing sounds. They never make physical contact.

4. Performing the *Kecak* drama

   a. Direct and lead the performance, using the following scene scheme for guidance.

Scene 1: The kidnapping of Queen Sita

Have the children sit side by side in two equal-sized rows and ask the principal actors to come out front onto the stage in front of the rest of the class. The stage can be any cleared space in a classroom, lunchroom, or auditorium, or an outdoor field. Direct the actors through the kidnapping scene as they perform it, feeding them lines of dialogue as necessary.

Breakdown of scene 1: Queen Sita and Rama are together, center stage, walking in the enchanted garden. Sita sees the Golden Deer, points at the animal, and exclaims to Rama, "Look, look, Rama. I think that deer must be the most beautiful animal in the whole world! Please go fetch him and bring him back so I can pet him." Have Sita coax Rama into running after the deer. As Rama chases the deer into "the forest," he and the deer exit, stage left, leaving Sita alone at center stage. At this point, evil King Rawana, disguised as an old man, enters from stage right. He sits and converses briefly with Sita, then transforms himself into the hideous ten-headed monster. Cackling "Ha ha. Now you will be mine!" he ushers the screaming Sita off stage right. (Avoid having Rawana throw Sita over his shoulder to avoid injury.)

At this point, the Bird, who has been watching from the wings, "flies" over to the white monkey Hanuman, who is now at center stage. The Bird hurriedly tells Hanuman the terrible story of the kidnapping. Hanuman runs directly to Rama (located stage left) and frantically explains what has happened. Rama, after briefly berating himself for having left Sita unprotected, regains his composure and orders Hanuman to find the Monkey General Sugriwa and have him call together the entire monkey army in preparation for the battle against Rawana.

Scene 2: Assembly and mobilization of the monkey army

Begin the journey to Rawana's kingdom in Lanka, on "the other side of the world." Assuming the role of Sugriwa, command the two rows of monkey soldiers to stand up, turn 90 degrees, and stand "at attention." At this point, the entire army should be facing you back-to-front in two long rows. Place Hanuman at the front of one row and Rama at the front of the other. The children playing the roles of Rawana, Sita, the Golden Deer, and the Bird should now be "transformed" into monkey soldiers so they can participate in the next part of the production.

Begin with vocal and movement warm-ups using call-and-response vocables like "chak," "chi-o-ak," "sirrr," "bo," and "mong." Hissing, hooting, and other vocal sounds are also fair game. Be imaginative in creating sounds and movements for the class to imitate. Segue directly from the warm-ups into the multipart "monkey chant" learned earlier in the lesson, beginning with the *kajar* pulse ("bo"), and then adding in the other parts one by one ("sirrr's," "mong's," the various "cak" parts, and the core melody). Use the model-

Figure 51. The troops follow Monkey General Sugriwa (Michael Bakan) through the Great Forest

and-copy method to remind the children of their various parts.

Once the "monkey chant" is going strong, turn around 180 degrees so that you are facing away from the children at the front of the procession (i.e., rather than standing backwards, facing them). Begin a "monkey march" in time to the music as you lead the troops away from the imaginary palace, waving at the imaginary crowd lining the streets as you go and encouraging the children to do the same. Directly model the "monkey march" for the children to imitate as they follow you around the perimeter of the room, stage, or field on your way to Rawana's palace on "the other side of the world." You can make up your own "monkey march" step, or use the traditional basic movement pattern, which is as follows: alternating steps (RLRL, etc.) at a rate of one step per *kajar* pulse ("quarter note"), with knees slightly bent and feet turned slightly outward. Arms are raised above the shoulders, with elbows bent, and the hands "shake" constantly as the wrists rotate quickly back and forth.

Scene 3: The journey through the forest, part I

After a minute or two of loud chanting and marching, announce to the soldiers that they have now reached the forest and must proceed very quietly and with caution because of the lions and tigers who dwell there. Continue the "monkey chant," but at a very low dynamic level. Similarly, continue the "monkey march," but with smaller motions and a bit more crouch to the basic stance. Intersperse lion and tiger sounds and bird calls and encourage the children to add their own animal and bird sounds (see figure 51).

Figure 52. Morning exercises for the Monkey Army

Scene 4: Camping out

After a minute or two in the "forest," announce to the troops that it is time to set up camp and get some sleep. Pitch imaginary tents and lie down, beginning to snore as you "fall asleep." The children will generally join in with the snoring.

Scene 5: Breakfast and morning exercises

Suddenly awake from your snoring slumber and command the soldiers to get up immediately, form into their two rows, and sit cross-legged facing you. Hand out imaginary bananas for breakfast and pantomime the peeling and eating of a banana, gesturing for the children to peel and eat theirs in the same manner.

After breakfast, conduct an exercise session. Call-and-response style, have the children imitate whatever sounds (rhythmic vocalizations, hand claps, thigh slaps, and so on) or movements (swaying side to side, stretches, waving of hands back and forth over your head) you model. Eventually, get a steady rhythm going and use the established tempo to segue back to the standard "monkey chant" music, again building up the parts one by one, beginning from the *kajar* pulse (see figure 52).

Scene 6: The journey through the forest, part II

Once the "monkey chant" is going again, have the children continue chanting as they stand up and take their positions in the standard two row formation. Proceed onward with the "monkey march" toward "the other side of the world," again circling the perimeter of the performance area.

Scene 7: Arrival at Rawana's palace

After a minute or so of marching, stop suddenly and "shush" the troops. Rawana's palace is now finally in view. Everyone must be completely silent and still in order to ensure the success of a surprise attack. Take this opportunity to set the staging for the upcoming battle scene. As was practiced in the rehearsal prior to the performance, the two rows of soldiers now separate into the "good" and "evil" armies. The "evil" army soldiers are positioned outside of Rawana's palace as guards. Meanwhile, Sita takes her place in the palace "prison garden" and Rawana in his palace sleeping chambers. Once the staging is set, proceed to the battle scene.

Scene 8: The battle

Before giving the command to charge into battle, remind the children once again that *no physical contact of any kind* can occur during the battle and demonstrate one more time the noncontact monkey combat technique described earlier (i.e., swaying forward and back toward and away from the "enemy soldier" while hissing). Once the battle gets underway, instruct Rawana's soldiers to fall to the ground gently as they are defeated by Rama's superior forces. Once all of Rawana's soldiers have fallen, have Rama "shoot" Rawana with his magic arrow, bringing the battle to a climactic end as Rawana tumbles dramatically to the ground.

Scene 9: The rescue

Lead the troops as they storm the palace, find and rescue Sita, reunite her with Rama, and depart the palace quickly after the victory. Rawana and the "slain" soldiers of his army can now be "transformed" back into members of Rama's army and join the triumphant procession back to Rama's palace.

Scene 10: Triumphant return to Rama's palace

Lead the entire entourage back home. As Rama, Sita, and their charges approach Rama's palace, the "monkey chant" music and "monkey march" should be performed with unprecedented vigor and intensity, leading up to a rousing climax and a sudden blatantly directed cut-off to end the performance.

5. Listen to or watch a Balinese *Kecak* performance

    a. If possible, conclude the session by showing a videotaped performance of a Balinese *Kecak*. If no video is available, conclude with the playing of a *Kecak* sound recording.
    b. The *Kecak* performance found at the beginning of tape 10 ("Southeast Asia V: Indonesia 2") of the *JVC Video Anthology of World Music and Dance* is highly recommended. Fast forward to the middle of the selection, about eight or nine minutes in, for the best short "sound bite" example.
    c. There are several good commercial audio-recordings of *Kecak* available, including the "Ketjak" selection on the CD *Music from the Morning of the World* (Elektra/Nonesuch Explorer Series 9 79196-2). A photograph of a *Kecak* performance is also available on page 96 of Tenzer's *Balinese Music*.

This lesson was contributed by Michael B. Bakan.

Integrating music with other studies

Whenever possible, teachers will want to integrate the study of Southeast Asian music with other subject areas, thus helping students begin to develop a broader cultural context for their musical study. Teachers may wish to consider the following suggestions:

1. Develop a bulletin board focusing on Southeast Asia. Have the students look for maps and good pictures of the people and their arts and crafts (*National Geographic* magazines are a good source of both information and pictures). Color code the areas whose artistic traditions have been influenced by Chinese, Indian, and Islamic cultures. Emphasize, however, that although some regions are influenced by other cultures, there are indigenous elements that produce unique interpretations of musics from beyond the borders. In mainland Southeast Asia, these unique elements include instruments such as the wooden xylophones; the knobbed gongs (in particular the circle of gongs); the *ching* (finger cymbals) of the Thai, Lao, and Cambodian cultures; and the Vietnamese monochord. Copy illustrations of these native musical instruments from the illustrations in this chapter, and attach them to the map of Southeast Asia.

2. Invite a Southeast Asian person to visit the class and share his or her stories, arts and crafts, songs, and descriptions of lifestyles. A university community or international center may be able to suggest people who represent mainland Southeast Asian countries, or your students may have friends or family members who would be willing to volunteer. Encourage them to wear native dress and to bring artifacts, including art works and musical instruments, from their culture.

3. Ask the students to imagine that they are French missionaries in 1700, traveling by boat up the Mekong River, which runs through Cambodia, Laos, and Thailand. What would be their first impressions of the people and their music? Teach the class a French folk song (for example, "Sur le pont d'Avignon"). How might the Southeast Asian peoples react to it? What are the similarities and differences between a French folk song and "Courtly Evening"? List the students' responses on the board.

4. Tell the Thai story of "Why the Parrot Repeats Man's Words," the Lao tale of "Mister Lazybones," or the Vietnamese fable of "The Little Lizard's Sorrow" in *Best-Loved Folk Tales* (see Bibliography). Read aloud, or have primary grade children read, *Tuan and Toad Is the Uncle of Heaven*. Guide the students to an understanding of the moral of each story as it might be applied to American life. Point out that these morals are easily grasped in any culture. Images such as the parrot, the lizard, and jungle flowers, on the other hand, are not easily transferable to life in North America but are characteristic of Southeast Asia.

5. If you live near a college, university, or an embassy having a gamelan, a Thai or Vietnamese ensemble, plan a field trip to see and perhaps play the real instruments.

6. Link the study of music with science by getting children interested in "monkeys" in a participatory context, which can segue into a study of "famous" Indonesian primates such as the orangutan. "Orang" is Indonesian for "person" and "utan" [hutan] means "forest." Thus, the "orangutan" is a "person of the forest," a rather nice connection with the *Kecak* play. More broadly, the study of Balinese *Kecak* can be used to inspire interest in indigenous animals of Indonesia (Sumatran tiger, etc.) or primates of the world. The "humanizing" of monkeys that the *Kecak* play achieves can also be

employed to engender compassion and sensitivity toward animals in general.

7. For social studies, it is interesting to study the "interlocking" structures that largely define Indonesian musics (gamelan and *Kecak*) and provide a good reference point for discussion of social systems in Indonesia, where the concept of *gotong royong* ("community self-help, mutual cooperation") is central to the ideal of social existence. The *kotekan* (interlocking patterns of Balinese music), for example, symbolically models a world in which the successful execution of any single task requires the cooperative effort of two or more individuals.

8. For linkages to astronomy/cosmology, study the Indonesian concept of "cosmological symbolism" (see *Traditional Music in Modern Java* by Judith Becker) where the gamelan actually serves as a handy analogy for teaching about the solar system. Just as planets revolve around the sun in different-length time cycles depending upon proximity, the instruments of gamelan "revolve" around the central gong *ageng* (the largest gong in a gamelan) at varying rates of speed; every stroke of the gong *ageng* represents the point from which all things emanate and to which all will ultimately return.

9. Discuss contemporary films and plays that illustrate the American experience in Southeast Asia from the 1950s to the present: *Apocalypse Now; The Deer Hunter; Platoon; Good Morning, Vietnam; The Killing Fields; Vietnam: A Television History; Indochine;* and *Miss Saigon.* Which parts of these films or plays can be interpreted as strictly Hollywood interpretations and which parts are authentic renderings of the historical situations? Assign readings from newspapers and magazines of that period as a comparison.

NOTE

1. Clifford Geertz, *The Interpretation of Cultures* (New York: Basic Books, 1973), 400.

CAMBODIA, LAOS, THAILAND, AND VIETNAM

BIBLIOGRAPHY

Boholm-Olsson, Eva, and Pham Van Don. *Tuan.* Stockholm: R&S Books, 1986. This is a beautifully illustrated book of the life of children and their families in a traditional Vietnamese village (for K–3 students).

Campbell, Patricia Shehan. *Sounds of the World: Music of Southeast Asia: Lao, Hmong, and Vietnamese.* Reston, VA: Music Educators National Conference, 1986. The three tapes include performances of refugee musicians residing in the United States and interviews with them. A teaching guide is included with transcriptions of some of the recorded music.

Chandler, David. *A History of Cambodia.* Boulder: Westview Press, 1983. This is a concise history of the Khmer people, and of the streams of ethnic, social, and political influences of the modern state of Cambodia.

Cole, Joanna. *Best-Loved Folk Tales.* Garden City, NY: Doubleday, Anchor Press, 1983. This book contains some Southeast Asian folk tales.

Crew, Linda. *Children of the River.* New York: Delacorte Press, 1990. For younger readers, grades five and up, this book is about a young high school girl from a Khmer (Cambodian) family in the U.S. who falls in love with a non-Cambodian boy, and the challenges of living in two "worlds."

De Roin, N. *Jataka Tales.* New York: Dell Yearling, 1975. This book includes stories about the virtues and adventures of Buddha in his former lives. An important source of Southeast Asian education and folklore.

Lee, Jeanne M. *Toad Is the Uncle of Heaven*. New York: Henry Holt and Company, 1985. This is a picture book of a well-known folk tale from Vietnam, which can easily be dramatized, and for which music can be composed (for K–3 students).

Miller, Terry E. *The Traditional Music of the Lao*. Westport, CT: Greenwood Press, 1985. This is a scholarly description of the music and culture of the lowland Lao people, with particular emphasis of *kaen* playing and *mawlum* singing in the northeastern region of Thailand (called "Isan").

Nguyen, Phong T., and Patricia Shehan Campbell. *From Rice Paddies and Temple Yards: Traditional Music of Vietnam*. Danbury, CT: World Music Press, 1991. This is the first English-language description of traditional music of the Vietnamese, including children's songs, instrumental pieces for zithers, lutes, and percussion instruments. With tape and lessons.

Rutledge, Paul J. *The Vietnamese Experience*. Bloomington, IN: Indiana University Press, 1992. This is an account of the resettlement and adjustment of Vietnamese refugees, and their reflections on the challenges of making new lives in the U.S. while retaining links to their homeland and heritage.

Sam, Sam-Ang, and Patricia Shehan Campbell. *Silent Temples, Songful Hearts: Traditional Music of Cambodia*. Danbury, CT: World Music Press, 1991. This is a collection of children's songs, instrumental pieces for zithers, lutes, and percussion instruments, poems, and dances from the Khmer people in Cambodia and in Khmer (Cambodian) communities in the U.S. With tape and lessons.

Tenula, John. *Voices from Southeast Asia*. New York: Holmes & Meier, 1991. Interviews and personal stories of refugees from Southeast Asia, including Vietnamese, Lao, Khmer (Cambodian), and Hmong, offer more personal perspectives of life in their old and new worlds.

DISCOGRAPHY

Eternal Voices: Traditional Vietnamese Music in the U.S. New Alliance Nar CD 053. A magnificent recording of Vietnamese traditional musical forms, instruments, and vocal styles. Included is "Vong Co," the well-known Vietnamese suite that conveys "longing for the past."

Hi Neighbor! CMS UNICEF, 8 vols. Vol. 3: *pi phat* orchestra from Thailand, music accompaniment for a classical play, and folk dance music. Vol. 8: *pi phat* orchestra from Cambodia, music accompaniment to the classical ballet, and Buddhist chant-song.

Music of Southeast Asia. Folkways FE 4428. Selections from Burma, Malaya, Thailand, Laos, and Vietnam.

Musiques de l'Asie traditionnelle. 17 vols. Available from International Book and Record distributors, 40–11 Twenty-fourth Street, Long Island City, NY 11101. Examples of folk and classical styles are included, with representative vocal and instrumental selections from urban and rural areas. Four of the volumes deal with Southeast Asia: Volume 1, Cambodia. PS 33501; Volume 2, Laos. PS 33502; Volume 10, Vietnam. PS 33514; Volume 8, Thailand. PS 33512.

Music of Vietnam. Lyrichord LLST 7337. Includes music for classical zither and lute, monochord, and such folk instruments as coin clappers.

Thailand, Its Music and Its People. Desto D–502. Songs, stories, description of people, instruments.

Thailand: Lao Music of the Northeast. Lyrichord LLST 7357. Features the *kaen* mouth organ and the oil-can fiddle.

Vietnamese Dan Tranh. Available from World Music Enterprises, 707 Avondale Drive, Kent, OH 44242. This record includes seven improvisations, representing six modes, played on the seventeen-stringed zither by Phong Nguyen.

FILMOGRAPHY

Ao Dai. 1991, 13 minutes, color. The *ao dai*, the traditional Vietnamese *tuni* dress, is offered as a gauge of Vietnam's prosperity; its reappearance since the war is indicative of a cultural rebirth. One high school student named Trinh is the focus of this delightful documentary.

City Streets and Silk Sarongs. 29 minutes, color. St. Louis: St. Louis International Center, 1986. Appropriate for junior high school. A video shows a day in the life of a young Lao refugee girl who adjusts to American life but learns the traditional dance of her ancestors.

From Angkor to America. 1991, 60 minutes, color. Narrated by a teenage Cambodian-American girl, this video chronicles the history of a community-based arts project striving to preserve Cambodian classical dance and music. There are performances of twelve dance pieces; many are led by Cambodian dance expert Chan Moly Sam, with music by Sam-Ang Sam.

Rebuilding the Temple: Cambodians in America. 1993, 58 minutes, color. The life of Cambodians in the U.S. is conveyed through interviews and glances at daily life, religious functions, and cultural celebrations. Musicians and dancers perform on several occasions.

Thailand—An Exotic Paradise. 1993, 56 minutes, color. This is a travel video. It shows Bangkok's floating market, an orchid farm in Chiang Mai, village life, and Buddhist monasteries, temples, and statues.

INDONESIA

BIBLIOGRAPHY

Balungan is a publication of the American Gamelan Institute, a non-profit organization that sponsors courses, workshops, and concerts in the United States. *Balungan* is published three times a year and contains a variety of articles and sources of materials on gamelan. Write to the American Gamelan Institute, Box 5036, Hanover, NH 03755.

Becker, Judith. *Traditional Music in Modern Java.* Honolulu: University Press of Hawaii, 1980. This is an outstanding book on Javanese gamelan music by a prominent ethnomusicologist.

Coomaraswamy, Amanda K., and Sister Nivedita. *Myths of the Hindus and Buddhists.* New York: Dover Publications, 1967, 56–94. This book provides the original version of "The Abduction of Sita" (see Lesson Three). It is a concise, accessible, and engaging introduction to the Ramayana, as well as to the Mahabarata and other important Asian epics.

Geertz, Clifford. *The Interpretation of Cultures.* New York: Basic Books, 1973. This is an excellent reference for the teacher and includes several of this leading anthropologist's classic essays on Indonesia.

MacLeish, Kenneth, and Dean Conger. "Java-Eden in Transition," *National Geographic* (January 1971): 1–43. This is a good introduction to Indonesia's largest island—text and pictures.

Miller, Peter, Fred Miller, and Margaret Eiseman. "Bali Celebrates a Festival of Faith," *National Geographic,* 157, (March 1980): 41–427. This article contains pictures and commentary on Bali's largest and most important religious celebration, Eka Dasa Rudra.

McPhee, Colin. *Music in Bali.* New Haven, CT: Yale University Press, 1966. This is a classic study of Balinese music. It's detailed and comprehensive, and contains many good black-and-white pictures.

Morton, W. Brown, and Dean Conger. "Indonesia Rescues Ancient Borobudur," *National Geographic* 163 (January 1983): 126–142. This article provides a fine description, with color pictures, of Java's Buddhist stupa, Borobudur.

Oey, Eric (ed.). *Insight Guides: Indonesia.* 3d ed. Hong Kong: APA Publications, 1992. (Distributed by Houghton Miffin Co., 222 Berkeley St., Boston, MA 02116.) This is a travel introduction to Indonesia. The book contains good summary articles on many phases of Indonesian culture, along with outstanding color photographs (e.g., Balinese *Kecak,* pp. 8–9).

Hutton, Peter, and Jeremy Allan. *Insight Guides: Java.* Hong Kong: APA Publications, 1993. (Distributed by Houghton Mifflin Co., 222 Berkeley St., Boston, MA 02116.) This is a travel introduction to Java with many excellent color photographs.

Plage, Dieter, and Mary Dieter. "Return of Java's Wildlife," *National Geographic* 167 (June 1985): 750–771. This article has good pictures, with commentary, of Indonesian wildlife.

Sadie, Stanley (ed.). *The New Grove Dictionary of Music and Musicians*. London: MacMillan Publishers, Ltd., 1980. This dictionary contains a good overview of the music of Indonesia (see "Indonesia" entry, Vol. 9, pp. 167–220).

Sorrell, Neil. *A Guide to the Gamelan*. Portland, OR: Amadeus Press, 1990. This is a concise and informative 142-page introduction to Javanese gamelan.

Sprague, Sean. *Bali: Island of Light*. Palo Alto, CA: Kodansha International Ltd., 1970. This is a beautiful pictorial introduction to Bali. Many outstanding color pictures are included in this paperback, including several of Balinese dances.

Sumarsam. *Gamelan: Cultural Interaction and Musical Development in Central Java*. Chicago: University of Chicago Press, 1995. This is a recent ethnomusicological study written by one of Java's most distinguished musicians and scholars.

Sutton, Richard Anderson. *Traditions of Gamelan Music in Java: Musical Pluralism and Regional Identity*. Cambridge and New York: Cambridge University Press, 1991. This is a fascinating scholarly study of gamelan music in Java by a leading ethnomusicologist. Includes bibliographical references and discography.

Sutton, Richard Anderson. *Variation in Central Javanese Gamelan Music: Dynamics of a Steady State*. DeKalb, IL: Northern Illinois University, 1993. This is a scholarly monograph on central Javanese gamelan music.

Tenzer, Michael. *Balinese Music*. Berkeley: Periplus Editions, 1991. This is an outstanding introduction (143 pp.) to Balinese music. Includes a number of excellent color pictures.

Vitale, Wayne. "*Kotekan*: The Technique of Interlocking Parts in Balinese Music," *Balungan* 4, no. 2 (Fall 1990): 2–15. This is a great article on how interlocking parts are composed in Balinese music.

Zich, Arthur, and Charles O'Rear. "Two Worlds, Time Apart—Indonesia," *National Geographic* 175 (January 1989): 96–127. This is a good introduction to Indonesia with a map and a number of excellent color pictures.

DISCOGRAPHY

Bali: Gamelan and Kecak, Elektra/Nonesuch 79204. Excellent recordings of Balinese gamelan music and "Kecak, the Ramayana monkey chant."

Gamelan Music of Bali, Lyrichord cassette LLCT-7179. A fine recording featuring seven Balinese gamelan selections.

Gamelan Semar Pegulingan from the Village of Ketewel, Lyrichord LYRCD 7408. A well-produced recent digital recording of performances by one of the most outstanding Balinese gamelan ensembles, featuring an ancient and historically important set of musical instruments.

Java: Music of Mystical Enchantment, Lyrichord cassette, LLCT-7301. Recording of Javanese gamelan music from Yogyakarta, one of the principal musical cities of Indonesia.

Javanese Court Gamelan, Elektra/Nonesuch 72044-4. An outstanding recording of the court gamelan tradition of central Java.

Music from the Morning of the World, Elektra/Nonesuch (Elektra/Nonesuch Explorer Series 9 79196-2). This compact disc features a variety of Balinese music, including "Golden Rain" ("Hudjan Mas"), "Bumblebee" ("Tambulilingan"), and "Ketjak, the Ramayana Monkey Chant."

FILMOGRAPHY

The *JVC Video Anthology of World Music and Dance*, "Indonesia," Tapes 9 and 10 (distributed by Rounder Records, 61 Prospect Street, Montpelier, VT 05602). Tape 9 includes examples of Balinese gamelan, gong *kebyar*, the Baris (warrior) dance, Legong Keraton (court dance), and Kebyar Trompong (seated dance with gong-chime). Tape 10 includes *Kecak* ("monkey chant") and a segment of Javanese *wayang* (shadow puppet theater).

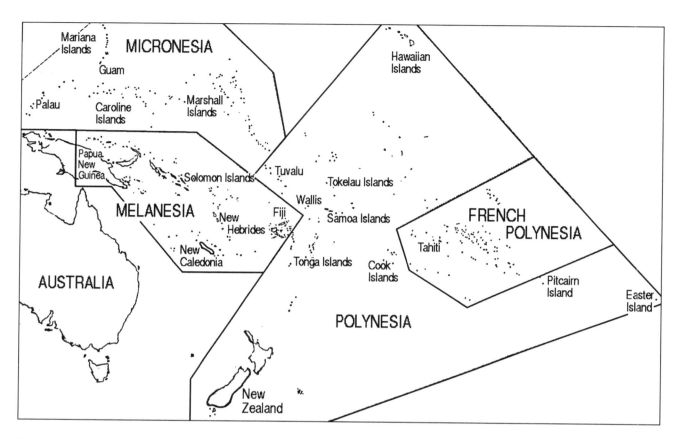

Figure 1. Map of the Pacific Islands showing Micronesia, Melanesia, and Polynesia

South Pacific Islands

CHAPTER 12

OCEANIA

by Robert Engle

As a result of tourist promotions and the media, the popular image of life in the Pacific islands is generally portrayed as simple and easy, in an environment of extreme beauty and abundance. The history of this area, by contrast, points to complex, highly diversified cultures, organized to respond to numerous natural hazards and hostile environments. The violence and cruelty present in historic Polynesian cultures included ritual sacrifice and cannibalism. Intertribal warfare generally resulted from the pressures of population growth and limited resources.

Even though the Pacific Ocean covers nearly one-third of the earth's surface, the total land area of the Pacific islands adds up to an area the size of Alaska. New Guinea and New Zealand represent 90 percent of this total, with the remaining fifty thousand square miles (an area the size of North Carolina) divided among more than ten thousand islands (see figure 1). The Pacific islands, sometimes referred to as Oceania, include all the islands of three distinct cultural groupings: Melanesia (dark persons' islands), Micronesia (tiny islands), and Polynesia (many islands).

These groups include the following:

Melanesia: Fiji, New Caledonia (France), New Hebrides, Papua New Guinea, Solomon Islands, Vanuatu.

Micronesia: Guam (U.S.), Kiribati, Marshall Islands (U.S.), Federated States of Micronesia (U.S.), Northern Mariannas Islands (U.S.), Palau (U.S.), Pohnpei.

Polynesia: American Samoa (U.S.), Cook Islands (New Zealand), Easter Island (Chile), French Polynesia (France), Hawaii (U.S.), Nauru, New Zealand, Niue (New Zealand), Pitcairn (U.K.), Tokelau (New Zealand), Tonga, Tuvalu, Wallis and Futuna (France), Western Samoa.

The races of indigenous Pacific peoples are a composite of Mongoloid, Caucasoid, and Negroid elements. Present-day Oceania, however, differs greatly from the past. Inhabitants of the Northern Marianna Islands or Easter Island, for example, are more often Spanish and Chilean, respectively, than they are Micronesian or Polynesian. Some islands include substantial populations of East Indian, Chinese, Japanese, or European/North American origin, as in countries such as Fiji, where the native population is in the minority. More than 1,350 languages are spoken in the Pacific, with over half of these spoken in Papua New Guinea.

With the notable exception of Tonga, which has remained an independent kingdom under British protection since 1900, nearly all of the Pacific passed under the control of European or American power between 1842 and the end of the century. Today, with the exception of some French, American, and Chilean territories, most of the Pacific islands have achieved independence.

Hawaii

Hawaii, first settled in about the third century A.D. by explorers from the Tahitian island group, had a flourishing Polynesian culture when discovered by Captain James Cook in 1778. The islands were first united under monarchy rule by Kamehameha the Great, beginning in 1790. The period of missionary influence dates from 1820, and in 1959, Hawaii became the fiftieth state of the United States. Its present population of 1.2 million, although heavily influenced by America, is known for its cultural pluralism.

Samoa

The Samoan way of life, in contrast, is communal. Extended families are arranged in villages, which are grouped into districts. This pattern was consistent from the first settling of the islands in approximately 1000 B.C. Even after decades of American and British influence, most Samoans live according to Samoan custom, and nearly all of them are fluent in the Samoan language. American Samoa is an unincorporated, unorganized territory, and its inhabitants are classified as U.S. nationals. In 1962, Western Samoa became the first independent Polynesian state, with a constitution that provides for parliamentary government but blends Samoan and English traditions. While education in American Samoa is compulsory between the ages of six and eighteen, it is optional in Western Samoa; most Western Samoan children, however, attend private church-related schools.

New Zealand

New Zealand was first inhabited by the Maoris who are believed to have first arrived in the ninth century A.D. The indigenous Maori name for these islands is Aotearoa (Land of the Long White Cloud). Captain James Cook brought these islands to the attention of Europe when he first visited them in 1769, and British missionary influence dates from 1814. Maori chiefs, acting under duress, signed over their tribal lands to Queen Victoria via the Treaty of Waitangi (1842) in exchange for her protection. In 1846, New Zealand took its first steps toward independence from Great Britain, and, in 1876, free primary education was made compulsory for both Maori and white children. Though relatively uninvolved in foreign affairs, New Zealand has been active in the past administration of other Pacific islands, notably Western Samoa and Niue. Today, Auckland is the world's largest Polynesian city, with over 40 percent of its one million people connected to Polynesian cultures.

Characteristics of Pacific island music

The importance of dance to Pacific islanders cannot be overstated. High schools in Tahiti, for example, offer classes in Tahitian dance but do not offer any of the choral or instrumental performing groups so common in America and Europe. Dance drew the wide attention of most explorers, missionaries, travelers, and anthropologists who wrote about Pacific island music in past years. Comments by foreigners more often concentrated on the writer's attitude toward the dance, whether favorable or critical, than it did with objective description. With the exception of Kaeppler's work on Tongan dance, little attention has been given to the structure of dance and its meaning to Pacific islanders.

The importance of music in the Pacific has often been tied to its utility in accompanying the dance, although there are also incidences of chant and other music tied to pageantry and formal custom. In general, Pacific music has been predominantly vocal, with strong evidence of part-singing and polyphony predating European contact. Prominent in the area are a variety of percussion instruments, the conch shell, and the use of body percussion.

Previous attempts have been made to analyze the music of the Pacific islands in the context of European theoretical constructs. This process resulted in highlighting some aspects regarded insignificant by islanders, while overlooking some of the features of greatest importance to them. In Hawaiian chant, for example, precise melodic intervals are far less important than are the short glissandos that precede or follow particular notes. Tone production and the primacy of text are also considered more important than melodic development, but neither of these features was analyzed by early writers. The emphasis on text over melody and rhythm in the traditional repertoire has often resulted in poetry of very intricate design coupled with rather monotonous, lackluster melodic lines. Rhythm is generally structured around the natural flow of the text, often resulting in irregular meter.

HAWAII (Chant)

Melody   Generally limited range; usually pentatonic
Rhythm   Ostinato patterns; duple meter predominant, occasional asymmetric patterns
Texture   Monophonic (accompanied by ostinato drum patterns)

Form	Free form; call and response; strophic
Genres	Entrance and exit chants; chants honoring significant events, places, and Hawaiian royalty
Timbre	Body percussion, *pahu* (drums), other percussion instruments

SAMOA

Melody	Very limited range, many strings of repeated tones; considered far less important than the text
Rhythm	Follows the flow of the text; often asymmetric
Texture	Homophonic (melody accompaniment), chordal or parallel harmonies
Form	Free form, strophic
Genres	Songs celebrating places, events, affairs of the heart, religion
Timbre	Body percussion, *pate* (drum), guitar, bass

NEW ZEALAND (MAORI)

Melody	Built around chordal outlines
Rhythm	Frequent use of triple meter; duple meter
Texture	Homophonic (melody accompaniment), chordal and parallel harmonies
Form	AB (binary), strophic, and ABA
Genres	Farewell songs; songs celebrating the culture and composer's own locality; songs of war
Timbre	Guitar, bass, poi balls, spears used as percussion instruments

L E S S O N   1

■ **Objectives**

Students will:
1. Understand the importance of the entrance dance to the performance of Hawaiian hula.
2. Learn the *kaholo* step, a basic hula foot pattern, and accompanying hand motions.
3. Perform the dance "Ho'opuka e ka Lā" in a call-and-response format.
4. Perform the dance "Ho'opuka e ka Lā" while chanting, accompanied by a basic ostinato drum beat.

■ **Materials**

1. Hawaiian *pahu* drum or other available drum
2. "Ho'opuka e ka Lā"

■ **Procedures**

1. The entrance onto and exit from the stage is an important aspect of Hawaiian hula performance. It is not considered proper for a dance troupe simply to walk onto the stage and find their places. The chant *Ho'opuka e ka Lā* is commonly used both as an entrance and an exit chant.
2. The only foot pattern necessary to perform this hula is the *kaholo*. With feet together:

Ho'opuka e ka Lā

Traditional Hawaiian chant

Figure 2. "Ho'opuka e ka Lā" (continued on next page)

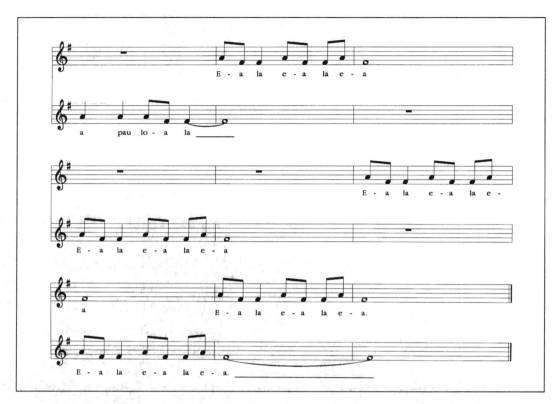

Figure 2, continued

Figure 3. Hawaiian students displaying the *'uli'uli* (feathered gourd) and the *ipu* (hollowed gourd)

(1) step right with the right foot; (2) step right with the left foot, bringing the feet together again; and (3) repeat this process once again: right foot right, left foot right. This is called a *kaholo* right. A *kaholo* left simply reverses the process: (1) step left with the left foot; (2) step left with the right foot, bringing the feet together again; and (3) repeat this process. The foot pattern for the entire chant is an ongoing alternating series of *kaholo* right (two times) and *kaholo* left (two times).

   When the feet are moving in *kaholo* right, the right arm is extended straight out from the shoulder, and the left arm is high and even with the right arm, bent at the elbow, with a stiff hand fronting the left shoulder. When the feet are moving in a *kaholo* left, the arms are reversed. The hands and arms for the entire chant alternate in the same manner as do the feet.

3. The chant *Ho'opuka e ka La* is shown in notation in figure 2. The pronunciation and translation are as follows:

   Ho'opuka e ka la ma ka hikina.
   HO-oh-POO-kuh AYE kuh LUH, MUH KUH hee-KEE-nuh
   (Just as) the sun (consistently) appears in the East

   E ola mau a pau loa la
   AYE OH-luh *MOW UH POW LOW-uh LUH (*"mow" rhymes with cow)
   May all things live forever.

4. The chanter (teacher) should establish the drum beat for two measures and then begin the chant. The drum beat is consistent throughout. As soon as the chanter begins chanting, the dancers (students) should begin to *kaholo* right with the accompanying hand motions. Dancers should dance in singular file to the formation they wish to use for the first dance on the program. Generally, this means the dancers will form rows before the chant is completed. If there is not enough chant to get the dancers onstage, the chant may be repeated. Figure 3 shows a student group that performs these dances and uses Hawaiian instruments.

L E S S O N   2

■ Objectives
Students will:
1. Recognize the importance of chant in the history of Hawaiian music.
2. Understand the basic features of Hawaiian chant.
3. Chant and dance a hula *noho*.

■ Materials
1. "A Hilo Au"

■ Procedures
1. In recent years, there has been a resurgence of interest in the pre-European contact music of Hawaiians. This interest, which began about 1972, has been called the

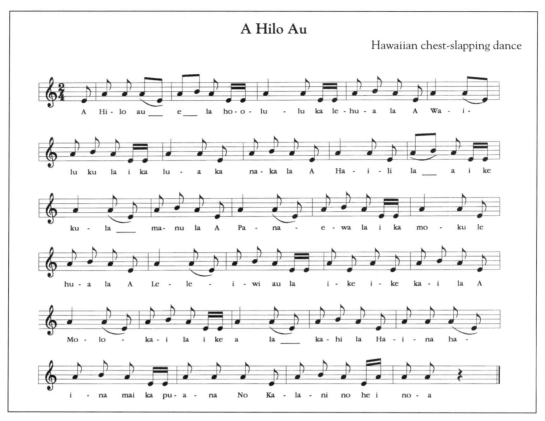

A Hilo Au

Hawaiian chest-slapping dance

A - Hi - lo au___ e___ la ho-o-lu - lu ka le-hu - a la A Wa - i -

lu ku la i ka lu - a ka na-ka la A Ha - i - li la ___ a i ke

ku - la ___ ma-nu la A Pa - na - e - wa la i ka mo - ku le

hu - a la A Le - le - i - wi au la i - ke i - ke ka - i la A

Mo - lo - ka - i la i ke a la ka - hi la Ha - i - na ha -

i - na mai ka pu - a - na No Ka - la - ni no he i no - a

Figure 4. "A Hilo Au"

Hawaiian Renaissance. Traditional Hawaiian chant was a mixture of poetry, rhythm, melody, and movement that accompanied functions ranging from prayer to entertainment. The most important chant element was the text. This poetry often told a story, relating its hidden meanings through metaphor and allusion. Dancers' hand and foot movements aided the storytelling process.

2. The basic text of Hawaiian chant (see figure 4) was composed in the context of a rhythmic scheme, but the melody attached to the text was not necessarily consistent. The association of one chant with a variety of melodic possibilities was as natural to the Hawaiian in his own culture as is the Euro-American idea that one melody can support a variety of texts. Definite pitch was also a foreign concept to the Hawaiian; beginning pitches were chosen on the basis of comfort.

   Hawaiian chant generally features a short recurring melodic framework that supports a number of related verses. These verses are often separated by a four-beat percussive interlude, commonly referred to as a vamp. Dancers will *kahea* (call out the first few words) of the upcoming verse to ensure that the chanter(s) and dancers are all presenting the same verse. The last verse is nearly always some variation on *Ha'ina mai ka puana*, meaning "this ends the telling of my story."

3. Hawaiian dance (hula) can be subdivided into several categories. One of the least complicated is the hula *noho*, or sitting hula. Motions are simplified by the lack of foot movements. "A Hilo Au," the subject of this lesson, is a sitting hula. Dancers should sit

either cross-legged or with their lower legs tucked under their thighs.

4. There is basically only one motion to remember for each verse of this hula, and that motion is related to the key activity the composer talked about on his journey to that particular place. The text, a pronunciation guide, and a translation of "A Hilo Au" follow, with the hula motion word italicized.

Verse 1.　*A Hilo au e la, ho'olulu ka lehua la.*
　　　　 uh HEE-loh AH-oo aye luh, ho-oh-LOO-LOO kuh leh-HOO-uh luh.
　　　　 At Hilo, I appreciated the *lehua* blossoms.

Verse 2.　*A Wailuku la, i ka lua kanaka la.*
　　　　 uh VYE-ee-loo-koo luh, ee kuh LOO-wuh kuh-NUH-kuh luh.
　　　　 At Wailuku, there was a *pool* where men often *fall in.*

Verse 3.　*A Haili la, i ke kula manu la.*
　　　　 uh huh-EE-lee luh, ee kay KOO-luh MUH-noo luh.
　　　　 At Haili, I saw a field full of *birds.*

Verse 4.　*A Pana'ewa la, i ka moku lehua la.*
　　　　 uh puh-nuh-EH-vuh luh, ee kuh MOH-koo leh-HOO-wuh luh.
　　　　 At Panaewa, I saw lehua *trees* growing out of *lava.*

Verse 5.　*A Leleiwi au la, 'au'au i ke kai la.*
　　　　 uh leh-leh-EE-vee Ah-oo luh, OW-OW EE-kay KUH-ee luh.
　　　　 At Leleiwi, I swam in the *sea.*

Verse 6.　*At Moloka'i la, i ke ala kahi la.*
　　　　 uh moh-loh-KUH-ee luh, ee kay UH-luh KUH-hee luh.
　　　　 At Moloka'i, I saw the *narrow pathway.*

Verse 7.　*Ha'ina, ha'ina mai ka puana no Kalani no, he inoa.*
　　　　 huh-EE-nuh, huh-EE-nuh MY kuh poo-UH-nuh noh kuh-LUH-nee noh,
　　　　 hey ee-NOH-uh.
　　　　 This ends the *telling* of my story, dedicated to David Kalakaua.

5. The unique hand motions (see figure 5) for each verse are as follows:

Verse 1.	pick flower	Verse 5.	swimming motion
Verse 2.	pool/fall in	Verse 6.	narrow pathway
Verse 3.	birds	Verse 7.	tell the story
Verse 4.	lehua trees, lava		

6. The remainder of the motions are done the same way in every verse:

Measure 1:
Hi-	**lo**	**a-**	**u**
slap	slap	slap	rest
thighs	thighs	thighs	

Measure 2:
e-	**la**	**ho'o**
RH	LH	
ext*	ext*	
LH	RH	
slap	slap	
chest	chest	

ext = extended away from body

Measure 3:	**lu**		**lu**	**ka le**
	slap	slap	slap	rest
	thighs	thighs	thighs	
Measure 4:	**hu-**	**a**	**la**	
	pick		flower*	

*or whatever unique motions accompany the particular verse

The introduction and vamp, if used, can be done without text by using the motions described (see figure 6) for measures 1 and 2, twice (i.e., slap-slap-slap-rest, extend and reach, extend and reach).

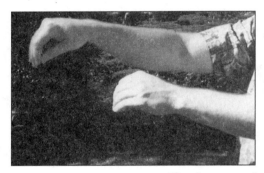 

Hand motions for Verse 1 (pick flower)

Hand motions for Verse 2 (pool/fall in)

Hand motions for Verse 3 (birds)

Figure 5. Hand motions for "A Hilo Au"

Hand motions for Verse 4 (lehua trees, lava)

Hand motions for Verse 5 (swimming motion)

Hand motions for Verse 6 (narrow pathway)

Hand motions for Verse 7 (tell the story)

Figure 5. Hand motions for "A Hilo Au" (continued from previous page)

Figure 6. Students performing "A Hilo Au"

LESSON 3

■ Objectives
Students will:
1. Locate the islands of American Samoa and Western Samoa on a map.
2. Introduce the Samoan language and vocabulary used in this song.
3. Create hand and/or body motions for each phrase.
4. Accompany the song on guitar and/or Autoharp with F, C₇, and B♭ chords.

■ Materials
1. World map or map of the Pacific
2. "Savalivali Means 'Go for a Walk'"
3. Guitar and/or Autoharp

■ Procedures
1. There are two Samoas on the map (see figure 1): American Samoa, a territory of the United States, and Western Samoa, an independent country. Although the two are only about a fifteen-minute plane ride apart, a passport is required to travel between them. The islands are located approximately halfway between Hawaii and New Zealand.
2. Discuss the pronunciation of the Samoan (SUH-moh-uhn) language. All vowels are pure, as they are in Spanish, Italian, and Japanese. The accent is on the penultimate syllable, with some exceptions. "G" is pronounced as *ng*. The four word-phrases in

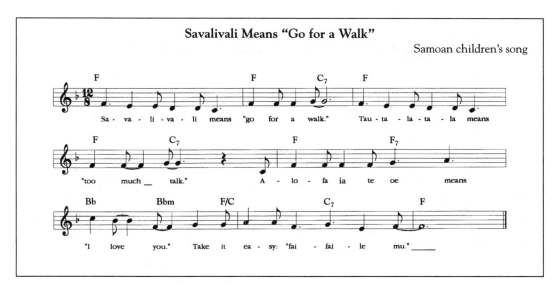

Figure 7. "Savalivali Means 'Go for a Walk'"

this song are pronounced as follows:

Savalivali	SUH-VUH-lee-VUH-lee	
Tautalatala	TOW*-TUH-luh-TUH-luh	(*"tow" rhymes with "cow")
Alofa ia te oe	uh-LOH-fuh YUH tay OY*	(*"oy" rhymes with "toy")
Faifailemu	FYE-FYE-leh-MOO	

Although the letter K does not officially exist in the Samoan alphabet, the sound of the English K is freely interchangeable with T. *Tautalatala*, therefore, is sometimes pronounced *kaukalakala* (COW-KUH-luh-KUH-luh). T is generally used in more formal speech and consistently in church services.

Take note of duplicated syllables—*valivali, talatala, faifai*—in the above words. In Samoan, as in other Polynesian languages, duplication is used to indicate intensity. *Tautala*, for example, means "to talk." *Tautalatala* means "to talk quite a bit," or as the song says, "too much."

All children who grow up in Samoa are bilingual. Most often, they learn Samoan first and then English, particularly as they approach school age. This song (see figure 7) helps them connect some of the Samoan words they have been hearing with their English equivalents. Notice that the Samoan phrase is usually given first in this song.

3. After students have learned the song, they may create their own motions for each phrase ("go for a walk," "too much talk," "I love you," and "take it easy"). This is typical of an approach Samoans would take, as movement is at least as important as singing is to performance or music. The exact movements for a song like this are not extremely important, as they tend to vary from village to village anyway. Chances are very good that the hand motions or marching motions your students think up might be the same as some of those used by Samoan students.

4. If students are familiar with guitar and/or Autoharp, they can incorporate the chords indicated on the music.

Figure 8. "Ata, Ata Mai Pe'ā E Fiafia"

L E S S O N   4

■ Objectives

Students will:
1. Discuss the importance of the Samoan language to the Samoan people.
2. Learn a song sung entirely in Samoan with an understanding of key vocabulary used.
3. Associate Samoan vocabulary with actions rather than with English equivalents.
4. Accompany the song on guitar and/or Autoharp with F, C_7, and B♭ chords.

■ Materials

1. "Ata, Ata Mai Pe'ā E Fiafia"
2. Guitar and/or Autoharp

■ Procedures

1. Most Samoan songs are sung completely in the Samoan language and are not translated into English (because all Samoans speak both languages). In fact, many American songs have been translated into Samoan because Samoans so strongly prefer their own language.
2. "Ata Ata Mai Pe'ā E Fiafia" (see figure 8) is sung by children and adults alike. It is often used in schools, large community gatherings, and churches as a means to get people acquainted with each other. To learn this song, one must know the meaning of the tag, "pe'ā fiafia" (pay-UH FEE-uh FEE-uh), which is "if you're happy." To be able to sing the remainder of each verse, you simply need to know the first word:

Ata ata mai	UH-tuh UH-tuh MY	Smile
Oso oso mai	OH-so OH-so MY	Jump
Patipati mai	PUH-tee PUH-tee MY	Clap
Siva siva mai	SEE-vuh SEE-vuh MY	Dance
Fa-atalofa mai	FUH-uh-tuh-LOH-fuh MY	Shake hands*
		*(literally: "greet")

"Mai" at the end of each phrase means "in my direction."

3. Encourage students to improvise movements associated with the initial word of each verse. This will reinforce the meanings of these Samoan words.
4. This song is generally sung with a country-music feel and is limited to three chords in the accompaniment. Guitar, ukulele, Autoharp, and even piano are commonly used.

L E S S O N   5

■ Objectives

Students will:
1. Understand the importance of the farewell song in Polynesian cultures.

2. Learn the song "Haere Ra" with an understanding of the Maori text.
3. Discuss the context in which Polynesian farewell songs are generally sung and perform the song in that manner.

■ Materials
1. "Haere Ra" (see figure 9)
2. Guitar, Autoharp, and/or ukulele

■ Procedures
1. Possibly the most familiar song in Polynesia is "Aloha 'Oe," composed by Hawaii's Queen Lili'uokalani. Samoans are all familiar with "Tōfā Mai Feleni" ("Goodbye, My Friend), another prominent farewell song from the Pacific. The Maori song, "Haere Ra" (see figure 9), is known to many outside the Pacific as "Now Is the Hour." The melody of this song has also been borrowed and used in a number of Christian hymns. Polynesians use considerable and elaborate protocol for greeting people and sending them off. This song is a longstanding example of that practice.
2. The pronunciation and literal translation of the text follows. A singing English translation, provided in the song, follows the literal translation fairly closely but does not quite convey the depth of emotion indicated in the literal translation.

   Verse 1:   *Te iwi, te iwi, e te iwi e*
   TEH EE-wee, TEE EE-wee, AYE TEH EE-wee AYE.
   The Maori race, the Maori race, the Maori race

           Ta huri mai ra, Te ngakau e,
   TUH HOO-ree MY RUH, TEH nguh-KUH-oo AYE
   You turn to me with emotion.

           Ki nga kapu, O te nogo pai
   KEE NGUH kuh-POO, OH teh ROH-ngo PYE
   I hear you walking away

           Hei oranga o te iwi e
   HEY oh-RUH-nga oh teh EE-vee eh
   With the comfort of the Maori people.

   Verse 2:   *Haere ra, te manu tangi pai*
   HUH-EH-ray RUH, tay MUH-noo TUH-ngi PYE.
   Leaving, among our tears

           E haere ana, Koe ki pamamao
   AYE HYE-ray UH-nuh, KOY kee PUH-muh-MUH-oh
   You will leave toward the distant lands

           Kite tau, E tangi atu nei.
   KEE-tay* TOW, aye TUH-ngee UH-too NAY. (*"tow" rhymes with "cow")
   Know that we are here, crying as you depart.

3. The standard context of singing Polynesian farewell songs in contemporary settings has perhaps been influenced by the commercial Polynesian shows found throughout the Pacific. All those in attendance generally form a circle around the perimeter of the room and join hands. As the song is sung, the entire circle sways in the same direction.

Figure 9. "Haere Ra"

BIBLIOGRAPHY

Armstrong, Alan. *Maori Games and Hakas*. Wellington, New Zealand: A. H. and A. W. Reed, 1974. This book contains instruction, words, and actions for dance movements for Maori songs.

Armstrong, Alan. *Games and Dances of the Maori People*. Wellington, New Zealand: Viking Seven Seas, 1986. Maori games and *hakas* are explained in English with song texts in Maori.

Armstrong, Alan, and Reupena Ngata. *Maori Action Songs*. Wellington, New Zealand: A. H. and A. W. Reed, 1960. This book contains words, music, actions, and instructions.

Buck, Elizabeth Bentzel. *Paradise Remade: The Politics of Culture and History in Hawaii*. Philadelphia: Temple University Press, 1993.

Brunke, Keala, ed. *Traditional Chants and Hulas*. Honolulu: Beamer Hawaiiana, 1982. Thirteen Hawaiian chants with hula instructions, translations, and music notation are in this book.

Canterbury Education Centre. *Samoa: Resource Pack for Secondary Schools*. Christchurch, New Zealand. This resource pack contains thirty-three sheets in portfolio form and includes maps, a cassette on Samoan legends, and notes for the film, *We Call Samoa Home*, designed for secondary school social studies classes.

Elbert, Samuel H., and Noelani Mahoe. *Na Mele o Hawaii Nei*. Honolulu: University of Hawaii Press, 1970. This book contains 101 song texts with translations, but with no score.

Freedman, Sam. *Maori Songs of New Zealand*. Wellington, New Zealand: Seven Seas Publishing, Ltd., n.d. This book contains information on Maori people, Maori love legends, the story of Maori music, and 104 Maori songs with piano accompaniment.

Freedman, Sam. *Solid Gold Maori Songs*. Wellington, New Zealand: Seven Seas Publishing, Ltd., 1973. This is a compilation of twelve best sellers: traditional and contemporary Maori music arranged for piano.

Henry, Fred. *History of Samoa*. Apia, Western Samoa: Commercial Printers, 1992. This is an outline of Samoan history from 1250 to the present.

Hopkins, Jerry. *The Hula*. Hong Kong: Apa Productions, 1982. This book contains historical information, a bibliography, a discography, and a filmography.

Kaeppler, Adrienne. *Polynesian Music and Dance*. In *Musics of Many Cultures*, E. May, ed. Berkeley, CA: University of California Press, 1980.

Ladd, Dennis. *Pese Samoa: Samoan Songs for Children*. Honolulu: The Hawaii Bilingual/Bicultural Education Project, 1970. This book contains children's songs in Samoan and English.

Mahoe, Noelani Kanoho. *E Himeni Hawaii Kakou: Let's Sing Hawaiian Songs*. Honolulu: Governor's Committee on Hawaiian Text Materials, 1973. This is a compilation of forty-nine popular songs with accompanying tape recordings.

Punana, Leo. *Pai Ka Leo: A Collection of Original Hawaiian Songs for Children*. Honolulu: Bess Press, 1989. This book contains fifteen songs composed in Hawaiian with a score, chord symbols, and English translations.

Smith, Barbara B., ed. *Pacific Islands: Samoa*. In *The New Grove Dictionary of Music and Musicians*. London: Macmillan, 1980.

Smith, Barbara B. "Musics of Hawaii and Samoa: Exemplar of Annotated Resources," *Music Educators Journal* 69, no. 9 (1983): 62–65.

Trippert, Alan R. *People Movements in Southern Polynesia*. Chicago: Moody Press, 1971.

DISCOGRAPHY

American Samoa Spectacular. Viking, New Zealand. This is a recording of several traditional Samoan songs sung by the American Samoa Arts Council Choir at the South Pacific Festival of the Arts in Suva, Fiji, 1972.

Maori Magic. Island Viking, Honolulu. This cassette tape features traditional Maori songs with a solo singer and instrumental accompaniment.

Meet the Samoan. Viking, New Zealand. This recording contains several traditional Samoan songs sung by various groups with instrumental accompaniment.

The Music of Samoa. Hibiscus, New Zealand, 55. This recording contains several traditional Samoan songs, drum beats, and chants recorded by anthropologist Richard Moyle in Western Samoa between 1966–69.

Na Mele Hawaii o ke Keiki. Hula Records, Honolulu. This is a recording of fourteen songs composed for children and sung in Hawaiian with instrumental accompaniment by the Maile Serenaders.

Samoan Song and Rhythm. Musical Heritage Society MHS 3326. A Hibiscus, New Zealand, recording. This recording contains several traditional songs in Samoan (with English liner notes), recorded by the Western Samoa Teacher Training College.

Songs and Dances of Samoa. Viking, New Zealand. This recording contains traditional Samoan chants and popular songs performed by both girls and boys choirs.

Twenty-two Golden Maori Songs of New Zealand. Viking, New Zealand. The songs on this recording are performed by the Turakina Maori Girls College Choir.

Editor's Note. These recordings may be ordered from: House of Music, Ala Moana Center, Honolulu, HI 96814.

FILMOGRAPHY

Children of the Long Canoes: A Unique History of Hawaii. 55-minute videotape, color. 1991. Produced by the Albert and Trudy Kallis Foundation. This video depicts Hawaiian history through the historical paintings of Herb Kawainui Kane. Topics include the early Polynesian voyages of discovery, life in precontact Hawaii, the bloody warfare between island chiefs, and the story of the *Hokulea* canoe.

Everything You Wanted to Know about Hawaiian Hula. 80-minute videotape, color. 1990. Produced by Shamani Enterprises, Ft. Myers, FL. This video provides instruction on the various steps and movements of the hula and covers the history of the dance, Hawaiian language terms, costuming, and implements.

Hawaiians and the Sea. *Hawaiian Language: Hope for the Future*. *Hawaiian History: A Hawaiian Perspective*. *Hawaiian Health: Cause and Cure*. 30-minute videotape, color. 1986. Produced by Juniroa Productions, Honolulu. This videotape contains four short programs in a *Sixty Minutes* format that detail the Hawaiian tradition of approaching the sea, communities on the Big Island in which Hawaiian is the exclusive language, the Hawaiian resistance movement, and health problems of contemporary Hawaiians.

Ka Hula Auwana: Modern Hawaiian Dance. 20-minute videotape, color. 1986. Produced by the Hawaii State Department of Education. The beauty of this art form, its significance to Hawaiian culture, and the importance of the *halau* hula (hula schools) are discussed.

Ka Hula Kahiko: Traditional Hawaiian Dance. 20-minute videotape, color. 1986. Produced by the Hawaii State Department of Education. The significance of the ancient hula to the Hawaiian culture is examined in this program.

Hula Pai: Hula Beat. 15-minute videotape, color. 1989. Produced by LPIM, Ft. Collins, CO. This videotape gives hula instruction, including descriptions and uses of Hawaiian dance implements, and choreography for five songs: "Green Rose Hula," "Hawaiian War Chant," "Haleakala," "Na ka Pueo," and "O Kona Hema."

The Kamaka Ukulele. *Olelo Hawaii*. *The Saltmakers*. *Keiki Hula*. 30-minute videotape, color. 1987. Produced by Juniroa Productions, Honolulu. This videotape contains four short programs in a *Sixty Minutes* format that detail how ukuleles are made, how the Hawaiian language is taught in immersion schools, how salt is farmed in salt flats, and how young children are first taught the hula.

Keiki Hula. 45-minute videotape, color. 1989. Produced by LPIM in Fort Collins, CO. This video gives beginning hula instruction for adults and/or children, including the history of the hula, costuming, Hawaiian language terms, and choreography for three songs: "Kahana Kamalii,"

"Kaleponi Hula," and "That's the Hawaiian in Me."

Language Is the Root. 29-minute videotape, color. 1984. Produced by Hawaii Public Television, Honolulu. This videotape explores the importance of chant in Hawaii's precontact oral culture. Chants were used to record and pass on Hawaii's history, genealogies, philosophy, and legends. The hula and chant were Hawaii's pictorial art, along with petroglyphs.

Na Mea Hookani: Instruments of the Hula. 20-minute video, color. 1987. Produced by the Hawaii State Department of Education. The traditional instruments that accompany hula kahiko (traditional hula) are discussed in this program.

Pele. Dante Carpenter, Mayor of Hawaii. Puuhonua-o-Honaunau. Moki's Music. 30-minute videotape, 1986. Produced by Juniroa Productions, Honolulu. This videotape contains four short programs in a *Sixty Minutes* format that detail the legends of Pele across the Pacific, an overview of the Big Island, the story of the City of Refuge, and a performance of a Hawaiian song.

Queen Liliuokalani (1838–1917), the Last Ruling Hawaiian Monarch. 13-minute videotape, color. 1992. Produced by the Northeast Metro Minnesota Branch, American Association of University Women, Shoreview, MN. Follows the life of Queen Liliuokalani through songs.

Secret Blossoms: Na Pua Hana. 24-minute videotape, color. 1993. Produced by Green Glass Productions. This is an introduction to the traditional Hawaiian culture by Native Hawaiian practitioners. The video covers *heiau* (temples), *mana* (spiritual power), hula (dance), *pohaku* (sacred stones), *aumakua* (ancestral gods), *lua* (martial arts), *laau lapaau* (herbal medicine), *pua* (flower leis), and *hooponopono* (conflict resolution).

We Call Samoa Home. 23-minute videotape, 1989. Produced by the Christian World Service, Christchurch, New Zealand. This videotape contains an overview of Samoan traditions with emphasis on the church, Samoan history since independence, the country's economic problems, and the conditions and lives of overseas Samoans living in New Zealand.

You Can Do the Hula. 37-minute videotape, 1986. Produced by Rainforest Publishing, Honolulu. Printed diagrams of hula hand and foot movements and lyrics of the song, "Lehua," accompany this videotape. The video also includes warm-up and breathing exercises and a history of the hula.

Editor's Note. These films can be ordered from the Wong Audio-Visual Center, Sinclair Undergraduate Library, University of Hawaii at Manoa, Honolulu, HI 96822.

GLOSSARY

acculturation: culture change that results from contact and interaction between two cultural traditions; an equivalent term is transculturation

aerophone: the category of instruments in which the sound is produced by activating a moving, vibrating column of air

alap \à-làp\: the first segment of many Indian compositions; characterized by improvisation and flexible rhythm

alphorn \'alp-hōrn\: a long, wooden wind instrument used by herdsmen in the Alps for signalling and playing simple melodies

amadinda \'àm-à-'din-d\: a wooden-keyed xylophone of the Ganda people of Uganda; with twelve keys resting on rails made from banana-tree trunks and held in place by small, upright sticks

anacrusis \à-nà-'krü-sis\: upbeat

andalusian cadence: a type of ending for music that shows Spanish influence; consists of the chord progression A minor, G, F, and E (when the music is in A minor); may reflect ancient Moorish roots of Spanish music

arka \'ər-kə\: one half (the follower) of an Amayra Indian panpipe or *siku* (the *ira* half is the leader); usually has seven tubes

arullo \ə-'rrü-yü\: literally "cooing"; a song form that can be a lullaby or a song sung by women to honor a saint on a special saint's day in Colombia

atouta \ä-tō-ü-ta\: the closing song of a Japanese *tegotomono* composition

avāz \a-'va-z\: Persian vocal and instrumental improvisations

bajo \'bə-hō\: Spanish word for bass, meaning the string bass in a salsa orchestra

balafon \'bal-à-fōn\: this word is formed from *Bala* (a general name for West African xylophones) and *fōn* (to play or to sound); refers to the act of playing a xylophone as well as the instrument itself

ballad: a narrative song, usually handed down orally, that tells a story

bandurria \ban-'dü-rē-à\: Spanish lute, like a guitar but with six double courses of strings

banqian \ban-chīn\: the melo-rhythmic motivic type of vocal composition used in Peking opera and other Chinese operas

baquiné \bə-kē-nä\: a word used in Puerto Rico to refer to a funeral wake

Bayt al-Hikma \Bīt al-'Hik-ma\: the "house of wisdom," a combination library, research facility, and center for the translation of Greek, Persian, and Hindu books; founded in Baghdad by the caliph al-Ma'-mün

bear's roar: a friction drum that, when played, imitates the growl of a bear

bhupali \bhü-pà-lì\: an evening *raga*

bianqing \byan-chiŋ\: series of tuned stone chimes used in Chinese music

bianzhong \byan-zhōŋ\: series of tuned bronze bells used in Chinese music

binary structure: a two-part structure such as a verse-chorus or A-B structure

bitonic: a musical scale that has only two notes

bluegrass music: a type of country music that is performed by singers with acoustic stringed instruments including the guitar, fiddle, banjo, mandolin, Hawaiian steel guitar (Dobro), and double bass

blue notes: notes used in African-American music and derived from an altered version of the major scale; this blues scale contains third, fifth, and seventh steps lowered by an interval that approximates a quarter tone and cannot be played on the piano keyboard

blues: a type of early African-American folksong, characterized by frequent use of blue notes

bodhran \'bō-dràn\: a large Irish hand drum, played with a small, thick mallet

bo \bō\: Chinese cymbals

bols \bōls\: mnemonic syllables that facilitate the learning and playing of rhythms on Indian drums

bombo \\'bōm-bō\\: a Spanish term for the large double-headed drum of Latin America, particularly the Andes

bongos \\bōŋ-'gōs\\: the Spanish name (perhaps African in origin) for two small single-headed drums used in salsa and other forms of Caribbean music

bouzouki \\bə-'zü-kē\\: a Greek long-necked lute, popular in dance ensembles

branco \\'brə-kō\\: the Portuguese term for "white," in this case a person with white skin; or in Brazil, a person who has been socially accepted as being economically "white" regardless of skin color

branle \\'bràn-əl\\: a traditional French dance in duple meter, dating from the fifteenth century

bullroarer: a musical instrument, made from a slat of wood with holes cut into it, that is tied to a string and swung through the air to produce whistle-like sounds; used by Native Americans and other cultures

bunraku \\bün-rä-kü\\: a Japanese theater tradition

call-and-response: a musical form that features a lead singer who sings a short phrase that is answered by a chorus or small group of singers; also applies to instrumental music when one instrument is answered by several

calypso: the predominant musical form in Trinidad and Tobago; sung by a solo singer, a calypso is a song form that often makes comments on people, events, and social situations

candomble \\kàn-dōm-'blä\\: a religious form, type of music, and place of worship among the blacks and other inhabitants of Bahia, Brazil; a syncretic blend of African and Catholic religious elements

canonic technique: a compositional device in which a single melody or musical layer is repeated, starting at different times, to create a layered musical work

cante jondo \\'kən-tä 'hōn-dō\\: literally "deep song," this was the predominant vocal musical form of the Spanish gypsies and others in Andalusia, Spain; developed into the Spanish *flamenco*

Cariban: the language of the Carib Native Americans who inhabit parts of northern South America, and who were the predominant cultural group of Native Americans in the Caribbean when Columbus arrived

Carnatic system of music \\kàr-na-tic\\: the music system of South India

castanets \\kas-tə-'nets\\: a Spanish clapper instrument consisting of two wooden pieces tied together with a string that passes over the player's thumb and first finger; played by *flamenco* dancers

celtic harp \\'kel-tik harp\\: the national instrument of Ireland; smaller than the orchestral harp

ceremonial song: song to accompany certain ancient rituals of birth, adolescence, marriage, and death

charango \\chə-'rən-gō\\: a small guitar-type instrument found in the Andean highlands of Peru, Bolivia, northern Chile, and northern Argentina; many *charangos* are constructed from armadillo shells

cheng \\chəŋ\\: "inheriting": the second idea or phrase of a four-line Chinese composition

ching \\chiŋ\\: Thai finger cymbals that keep the pulse in that country's classical (and some folk) music

chiz \\chiz\\: a composed segment in a North Indian vocal composition; cast in a particular *tala*

chordophone: the category of instruments in which sound is produced by a vibrating string or strings

cimbalum \\'sim-bu-lùm\\: the hammered dulcimer of Hungary

claves \\'klə-väs\\: two hardwood dowels or sticks that are used to play rhythmic patterns (the *clave* rhythm) in *salsa*

clog: a heavy shoe that has a thick sole; clog dancing, a dance step traditionally used in the Southern Appalachians, is a flat-footed walk with embellishments

colonial rhythm: the predominant rhythm of Spanish-derived Latin America; consists of $\frac{6}{8}$ and $\frac{3}{4}$ meters, played simultaneously

concertina: a small accordion popular in Britain and France

congas \\'kōn-gəs\\: the Spanish name (perhaps African in origin, from the Bantu *Congo*) for a large single-headed, barrel-shaped drum; two are used together in *salsa* and other Caribbean musics

conjunct motion: melodic motion by step

coyote tales: Native American stories with a moral, used for entertainment and for teaching right and wrong

cueca \kü-'wā-kə\: the African-influenced national dance of Chile, featuring colonial rhythm and rapid dancing by a man and a woman; originated from the *zamacueca* of colonial Afro-Peru

currulao \kü-rrü-'laů\: a rhythmic music and dance form of the blacks of the Pacific coast of Colombia and Ecuador: features the dancing of couples to the music of a marimba, drums, and a rattle

czardas \'chȧr-dȧs\: Hungarian national dance in duple meter, performed in circles and by partners

dagu \dä-gü\: a large, skinned, Chinese drum, usually played with two sticks

daluo \dä-lō\: a large Chinese gong, usually played with a padded mallet

dan bau \dȧn baů\: a monochord; an indigenous instrument of Vietnam

dan ko \dȧn kō\: Vietnamese two-stringed fiddle

danmono \dä-n-mō-nō\: a Japanese music form; a strict set of variations

dan tranh \dȧn trȧn\: Vietnamese sixteen-stringed zither

dan ty ba \dȧn tē bə\: Vietnamese four-stringed, long-necked lute

darabukkah \da-ra-'buk-ka\: a cylindrical- and conical-shaped clay drum with a head made from the Nile fish skin

dastgāh \dast-'ga\: the Persian equivalent of the Arabic *maqām*

desafío \de-sə-'fē-yō\: the Brazilian term for a challenge song or musical duel; this term was also found in Renaissance Spain and Portugal

diatonic: not chromatic; diatonic modes use a fixed pattern (traditional in Western music) of intervals

disjunct motion: melodic movement in skips

dizi: \di-z\: a Chinese transverse flute, usually made of bamboo

drone: long sustained notes, usually in the lower-pitched parts of a composition; in Indian music, often played on the *tambura*

Dr. Watts style: a hymm-singing procedure among African Americans consisting of one individual chanting one or two lines of a tune at a time, ending on a definite pitch, and a group responding to that pattern with the same line or an elaboration of that line

dulcimer \'dul-si-mər\: a plucked zither that consists of an elongated sound box with three or four strings that sound a melody and drone; traditional in the Southern Appalachian Mountains

dumm \dům\: a low, resounding sound produced on Middle Eastern percussion instruments; represented in notation by a note with the stem up

dziro \'dzē-rō\: a term for the basic rhythm pattern of a Shona (Zimbabwe) work; it means "foundation you put in before building your house"

electrophones: the category of instruments in which the sound is produced and transmitted or modified by electric or electronic circuitry

entamivu \en-tȧ-'mē-vü\: a xylophone and drum ensemble of the Ganda people of Uganda

entenga \en-'ten-gȧ\: a set of fifteen tuned drums of the *Kabaka*, or traditional ruler of the Ganda people of Uganda

epic: a long, narrative song

erhu \ər-hü\: a two-stringed Chinese fiddle

fandango \fȧn-'dan-gō\: a Spanish dance for couples, in moderate to quick triple time, accompanied by guitar and castanets

flamenco \flȧ-'men-kō\: a southern Spanish (Andalusian) dance, with accompanying music that includes guitar and singer and uses ornamented melodies

flauta \flə-'ü-tə\: the Spanish term for flute, one of the featured solo instruments in *salsa*

flipper-dinger: a folk toy, made of a hollow reed with a cup attached at one end, that has a lightweight ball in it; when air is blown into the reed, the ball in the cup rises into the air

friction drum: a membranophone in which the sound is produced by rubbing the stretched drum with the fingers or other material or by stroking a stick or string that has been fixed to the drumhead, causing it to vibrate

gaeng \gāŋ\: a Hmong mouth organ, a free-reed bamboo instrument with several pipes, each generating a separate pitch

gagaku \gä-gä-kü, gä-ŋä-kü\: the traditional court music of Japan

gaida \'gī-də\: Bulgarian and Macedonian (Yugoslavian) bagpipes

gamelan \gȧ-me-län\ The Indonesian word for a musical ensemble

gat \gát\: a composed segment in a North Indian instrumental composition; cast in a particular tala

gauchos \gə-'ü-chōs\: the cowboys of Argentina

gazel \ga-'zel\: Turkish vocal improvisations

gee-haw-whimmy diddle: a folk toy, similar to a top, that can spin clockwise or counterclockwise

gong ageng \gong à-gung\: the largest gong used in *gamelan* music

gospel: a style of folksong originally associated with evangelistic revival meetings

griot \'grē-ō\: a generic term for musicians of professional status in West Africa who are hired to sing in praise of important persons and orally recount history

guiro \'wē-rō\: a scraper used in the Caribbean and made from either a gourd (the term originally means "gourd") or metal. It is an important instrument in *salsa* and other Caribbean musics, and is perhaps derived from a Native American instrument

guitarrón \gē-tə-'rrōn\: literally a "large guitar"; often resembles an oversized guitar in Peru; characterized by a very fat resonating body in Mexico

hambo \'màm-bō\: a dance for couples, in triple meter, from Sweden

he \hə\: "closed": the final idea or phrase of a four-line Chinese composition

heterophony: simultaneous use of slightly different versions of the same melody by two or more performers

hetou \hə-tò\: "refrain head": a musical motive that appears at the beginning of each section of a Chinese suite

hewei \hə-wā\: "refrain tail": a motive that appears at the end of each section of a Chinese suite

Hindustani system of music \hin-dü-stan-ì\: the music system of North India

hocket technique: a compositional device in which each musical layer consists of a single sound or a sound pattern that alternates with sounds or sound patterns of other layers—each layer resting while the other is sounded

holler: a type of work song, sung in a shouting style and originated by the African-American field worker

homophony: the multi-voiced music texture in which one voice acts as the principal melody and the other voices move in the same or in a similar rhythm

hora \hō-rə\: an Israeli circle dance

hornpipe: a duple-metered dance of the British Isles, consisting of two groups of four eighth notes

hosho \'hō-shō\: a Shona (Zimbabwe) term for a rattle made from a gourd; a network of string with beads or shells attached hangs around the head of the gourd

huasos \'wə-sōs\: the term for cowboys in Chile

hurdy-gurdy: a medieval stringed instrument whose strings are sounded by a rotating wheel that is operated by a crank at the lower end of the body of the instrument, producing melody and drone simultaneously

hyojo \hyō-jō\: a Japanese pentatonic scale without half steps

idiophone: the category of instruments in which the sound is produced by the vibration of the primary material from which the instrument is made (e.g., the struck key of a marimba)

interlocking parts: music that is made up of several melodic parts that alternate or interlock to form a single melody; a technique used by handbell ringers in America and *siku* players in Peru and Bolivia

īqā[c] \i-'ka\: the Arabic term for rhythm, also used for the concepts of meter, rhythmic mode, dynamics, timbre, and tempo; used especially to denote a pattern of attacks performed on a percussion instrument

ira \'ē-rə\: one half (the leader) of an Aymara Indian panpipe or *siku*; usually with six tubes

jaltarang \jàl-tà-rang\: an Indian idiophone consisting of a series of bowls that are graduated in size

jazz: a type of music, originally improvised but now also arranged, that is characterized by syncopation, rubato, heavily accented rhythms, dissonance, individualized melodic variation, and unusual tonal effects

jhaptal \jhàp-tàl\: a *tala* consisting of ten beats, divided 2–3–2–3

jig: a dance form of the British Isles, particularly Ireland, in compound duple or triple meter

jo-ha-kyu \jō–hä–kyü\: a tripartite design in traditional Japanese music. *Jo* is the introductory section; *ha* is the central section, containing the principal material; and *kyu* is the last section or drive toward the end

jodlers \'yōd-lùrz\: an Alpine song style that features frequent and rapid passing from a low chest voice to a high falsetto

joropo \hō-'rō-pō\: an important song and dance form in Venezuela, characterized by fast colonial rhythm, and often played on the harp

jota \'hō-tə\: a common song and dance form in Spain that features colonial rhythm

juju \'jü-jü\: a style of Nigerian urban popular music, of which King Sunny Ade is a well-known performer

kabuki \kä-bū-kē\: a type of Japanese music theater

kaede \kī-de\: a melodic part added in counterpoint to the principal line in *koto* music

kaen \kān\: a mouth organ, the national instrument of Laos; played soloistically and to accompany singers

kagura \kä-gü-rä, kä-ŋü-rä\: Shinto (Japanese) dance-song

kamanjah \ka-'man-ja\: the Arabic name for the violin

kanji \kä-n-jē\: the Japanese word for Chinese ideographs

kantele \'kän-tel\: a small Finnish zither, similar to the psaltery, shaped like a bird's wing and strung with twenty to thirty strings

katsima \ka-'tchē-mə\ the ancestral spirits of the Hopi or Zuni Indians of the southwestern United States; the masks or dolls made to personify or represent those spirits

kempul \kem-pül\: the vertically positioned, knobbed gongs used in *gamelan* music

kena \'kä-nə\: an Aymara Indian term for flute. It refers to the Andean instrument that has a notch in its end to function as a mouthpiece

kendang \ken-dáng\: drums used in *gamelan* music

kenong \ke-nòng\: the horizontally positioned knobbed gongs used in *gamelan* music

ketuk \ke-thuk\: the small, horizontally positioned gongs used in *gamelan* music

kong wong \kòŋ wòŋ\: a circle of knobbed gongs, one of the principal melody instruments in the Thai *pi phat* orchestra

kora \'kō-rä\: a twenty-one-stringed harp-lute of the Mandinka and Wolof people of Senegal and The Gambia in West Africa

koto \kō-tō\: a Japanese thirteen-stringed zither

kotsuzumi \kō-tsü-zü-mē\: a Japanese shoulder drum, used in *noh* and *kabuki* theater

kudaira \kü-dà-'ē-rə\: rhythm patterns that respond to the basic pattern of a Shona music example from Zimbabwe

kudairana \kü-dà-ē-'rà-nà\: responsive rhythm patterns in music of the Shona people of Zimbabwe

kushaura \kü-shàü-r\: the basic rhythm pattern in Shona music from Zimbabwe; the word can be translated, "what everyone relates to, the line that cuts through"

langeliek \'lang-e-līk\: a Norwegian plucked dulcimer

lavway \'lǝv-wä\: an early form of *calypso* in Trinidad and Tobago; uses the call-and-response form

layālī \la'ya-lē\: Arabic vocal improvisation on the words yā lēlī yā ᶜēnī

likembe \lē-'kem-be\: one of many names for the hand-held, keyed idiophone, played with the thumbs and index fingers, that is found in most areas of Sub-Saharan Africa

limberjack: a rhythm instrument native to the Southern Appalachian Mountains

luogu \lō-gü\ "gongs and drums": a Chinese percussion ensemble

maeuta \mī-ü-tä\: the opening song in a Japanese *tegotomono* composition for the *koto*

maqām \ma-'kam\: the complex modal system governing Arabic music; includes the concepts of melodic modes, motifs, cadences, tonics, and tonal centers

marimba \mà-'rēm-bà, mà-'rim-bà\: **1.** a xylophone, found in various sizes and shapes in music cultures across the upper two-thirds of Sub-Saharan Africa **2.** \mə-'rēm-bə\: derived from the African term; refers to a xylophone in Colombia, Ecuador, Guatemala, and elsewhere in Latin America

marinera \zmə-rē-'nä-r\: the national dance of Peru; a song and dance form of the coastal region that is very similar to the Chilean *cueca* named for the navy men killed in the War of the Pacific, which Chile lost to Peru that conflict

maru-bihag \mà-rü—bi-hàg\: an evening *raga*

mawlum \maù-lam\: a song style of Laos and northeast Thailand, accompanied by the *kaen*

mawwāl \maw-'wal\: an Arabic poem set to improvised music

mazhar \maz-har\: a large tambourine with a donkey- or goat-skin head and jingles

mbira \m-'bē-rä\: one of many names for the hand-held keyed idiophone, played with the thumbs and index fingers, found in most areas of Sub-Saharan Africa. *See also* likembe; sansa

membranophone: the category of instruments in which the sound is produced by the vibration of a stretched membrane which is struck, rubbed, or otherwise activated

mestizo \mä-'stē-sō\: literally "mixed," used in the Andes and Pacific coastal region of Latin America to refer to people whose racial background includes Spanish and Indian ancestors

metallophone: the category of instruments in which sound is produced by the vibration of tuned metal bars or slabs

microtonal: music that is based on a system in which the pitches are spaced more closely than the Western semitone

mode: on its most abstract level, a series of notes arranged in scalar fashion, with an idiosyncratic intervallic structure

monody: the music texture in which only one melody is sounded at a time

montuno \mōn-'tü-nō\: the improvisational section in a *salsa* composition; the singer makes up a melody and words, and the musicians often play solos

mordent: a short trill downward from the principal note

mulato \mü-'lə-tō\: in Latin America, a person of mixed black and white ancestry

muwashshah mù-'wash-sha\: Arabic classic song

narrative song: a song that tells a story, such as the ballad or epic

nāy \nay, nī\: a Middle Eastern, obliquely end-blown reed flute

nawbah \'nī-ba\: a North African suite-like form

ngano \n-'gà-nō\: a story-song about something that did not really happen; sung as part of storytelling occasions among the Shona people of Zimbabwe

ngodo \n-'gō-dō\: traditional dance suites, usually in nine to eleven movements, of the Chopi people of Mozambique; accompanied by a large ensemble including xylophones, drums, rattles, and the sound of shields striking the earth

noh \nō\: a six-hundred-year-old Japanese genre of drama; it is still an active form of theater

nohkan \nō-kä-n\: a transverse flute used in Japanese *noh* drama

noter: a narrow piece of dowel, approximately four inches long, that is placed on the melody string of a dulcimer (to the left of a selected fret) and used to change the pitch

nyaya \'nyà-yà\: a story-song about something that really happened; sung as part of storytelling occasions among the Shona people in Zimbabwe

nykelharpa \'nik-àl-harp-ə\: a keyed Scandinavian fiddle that was used for popular dance and festive music; often boat-shaped, with drone strings, one or two melody strings, and up to twelve wooden keys

ostinato: a musical phrase or pattern that is repeated many times. Its use in *salsa* is derived from African music practices

otsuzumi \ō-tsü-zü-mē\: a Japanese hip drum, used in *noh* and *kabuki* theater

oud \üd\: the Greek name for the 'ud

pampas \'pəm-pəs\: the vast grasslands of central Argentina

pelog \pe-lòg\: a seven-toned Indonesian scale or tuning system

pentatonic: any five-note scale

pi nai \bē nī\: a quadruple-reed instrument of the Thai orchestra that produces a sound similar to the oboe

pi phat \bē pàt\: the Thai classical ensemble of xylophones (*ranat*), gong circles, drums, oboe (*pi nai*) and cymbals

pipa \pi-pä\: a four-stringed, short-necked Chinese lute

play-party games: children's songs that combined music with prescribed movement; because selection of partners was the primary function of the songs, they often provided recreational and social activities for young, rural adults

polka: a Bohemian dance in a fast duple meter

polska \'pōls-ka\: a Swedish dance in triple meter, probably of Polish origin, similar to the *mazurka*

polymeter: the simultaneous performance of musical passages in two or more meters

polyphony: the music texture in which two or more rhythmically independent melodies are combined

polyrhythm: simultaneously sounded combinations of different rhythms that form a more or less complex rhythmic texture

power-gathering emblem: an object or symbol that represents or influences the political power of a ruler or ruling group

pueblo \\'püāb-lō\\: Native American housing complex built of adobe (sun-dried mud brick), for up to several hundred people

punteado \\pün-tā-'yə-dō\\: in playing guitar or guitar-type instruments, the style of performance in which the musician picks the individual notes of a melody or bass line

purvi \\pür-vì\\: a late afternoon *raga*

qānūn \\ka-'nün\\: an Arabic trapezoidal zither

qi \\chì\\ "open": the first idea or phrase of a four-line Chinese composition

qin \\chin\\: a seven-stringed Chinese board zither

rachenitsa \\rà-chen-'ēt-sà\\: the Bulgarian national dance in ⅞ meter with three beats: ♩ ♩ ♩.

raga \\rà-gà\\: a prescribed series of pitches from which an Indian musical composition is created

ragtime\\ a type of American music, largely composed, that was popular from about 1890 to 1915 and was characterized by strong syncopation in fast, even time, and the use of a regular phrase structure

ranat \\rà-nàt\\: a Thai wooden xylophone

rao \\ràu\\: the unmeasured, improvisatory introduction to traditional Vietnamese music

rap: a type of musical declamation in a strong set meter and rhythm; a kind of rhythmic and rhyming talking

rasqueado \\rəs-kā-'yə-dō\\: in playing guitar or guitar-type instruments, when the musician strums the strings to produce chords

reel: a dance form of northern Europe for lines of couples, with music in duple meter

reverse rondo form: a form akin to the rondo except that the refrain comes after the first verse: A–Refrain–B–Refrain–C–Refrain–D–Refrain

rhythm and blues: a form of popular African-American music, influenced by the blues and gospel music; characterized by a strong, frequently syncopated, beat

rhythmic density: the number of rhythmic pulses per second; often refers to music played with African-derived drumming

rhythmic feeling: in Sub-Saharan African music, the perceptual effect of a rhythmic pattern, which includes the timbres and the movements of musicians and dancers associated with it

rhythmic layering: in African and African-derived music, when several drums of different sizes and tone colors (or other percussion instruments) play individual patterns, the resultant sound consists of layers of rhythms

riqq \\rikk\\: a small Middle Eastern tambourine with a Nile fish-skin head and jingles

rommel pot \\'ròm-məl pòt\\: a friction drum of the Netherlands, played by pulling a rope through a small hole in a pot

runes \\rünz\\: a Finnish narrative song in ⁵⁄₄; a collection of them was gathered in the Finnish national epic, the *Kalevala*

rupak \\rü-pàk\\: a *tala* characterized by seven beats divided 3–2–2

sakkah \\'sak-ka\\: a percussive sound half way between the timbre of the *dumm* and that of the *takk*

salsa \\'səl-sə\\: literally "hot sauce," this is Afro-Cuban music from New York, Miami, Havana, San Juan, and other centers of Afro-Cuban population

samāᶜī \\sa-'ma-i\\: a rhythm in ¹⁰⁄₈; a prelude in reverse rondo form in ¹⁰⁄₈

sankyoku \\sän-kyō-kü\\: a Japanese chamber ensemble, usually consisting of *koto, shamisen, shakuhachi*, and voice

sansa \\'sàn-sà\\: one of many names for the hand-held, keyed idiophone, played with the thumbs and index fingers, that is found in most areas of Sub-Saharan Africa. *See also* likembe; mbira

sanxian \\sän-shan\\: a three-stringed, fretless Chinese banjo

sardana \\sàr-'dà-na\\: a Basque circle dance in duple meter; found in southern France and the Spanish Catalan region

saron barung \\sa-ròn bà-rung\\: a metallophone used in *gamelan* music

saron demung \\sa-ròn de-mùng\\: a metallophone, sounding one octave lower than the *saron barung*, that is used in *gamelan* music

scat: a way of singing in some African-American music, in which the singer improvises using meaningless syllables in imitation of the sounds of a musical instrument

schuplattler \\'shü-plàt-lər\\: an Austrian boot-slapping dance in triple meter

seguidilla \\se-gē-'dē-yà\\: a dance of southern Spain in triple meter, with a text based on four-line poems and guitar accompaniment

sesquiáltera \\sàs-kē-'əl-tā-rə\\: an alternation of ¾ and ⁶⁄₈ meters in Latin American music

shakuhachi \shä-kü-hä-chē\: an end-blown Japanese bamboo flute with five finger holes; the player blows across a notch in the upper end of the instrument

shamisen \shä-mē-se^n \: a three-stringed Japanese plucked lute

sheng \shəŋ\: a Chinese mouth organ

Shinto \shi-n-tō\: a Japanese belief system involving the veneration of ancestors

siku \'sē-kü\: an Aymara Indian term for panpipe; the instrument consists of two halves (*ira*, or leader, and *arka*, or follower) played by two musicians who interlock their parts

silk and bamboo: the Chinese phrase that designates stringed and wind instruments

sitar \si-tàr\: one of the most important plucked chordophones of India

slendro \slen-drō\: a five-tone Indonesian scale or tuning system

slentum \slen-thùm\: a *gamelan* metallophone, constructed with thin metal plates placed over resonating tubes

soca \'sō-kə\: a modern form of calypso from Trinidad and Tobago, performed on electronic instruments and featuring singers. The term is a shortened form of "soul calypso"

strophic melodic structure: a melodic structure in which the same music or melodic material is used despite changes in the text

suona \sò-nä\ a double-reed Chinese shawm or oboe

sympathetic vibrating strings: thin metal strings that lie below the main strings of many Indian chordophones and vibrate in sympathy when the main melodic strings are activated

syncopation: a displacement of the normal metric accent; the accentuation of normally unaccented beats

tabla \tà-blà\: the most important drums of North India

tahrīr \tah-rēr\: a Persian vocal trill, akin to sobbing

taiko \tī-kō\: a round floor drum used in Japanese *Noh* and *Kabuki* music

takk \takk\: a short, crisp sound produced on percussion instruments and represented in transcriptions of Middle Eastern music by a note with the stem down

tala \tà-là\: a cycle of beats in Indian music

tambur \'tàm-bùr\: a long-necked, plucked lute of the Middle East and Yugoslavia

tambura \tam-bü-rä\: a plucked chordophone that produces the drone in Indian music

tamburitza \tàm-bùr-'it-zà\: an ensemble of *tambur*s of different sizes and pitch ranges

taphon \tà-fōn\: the large, double-headed drum used in Thai ensembles

taqsīm \tak-sēm\: Arabic and Turkish instrumental improvisations, mainly unmeasured

tarantella \tà-ràn-'te- là\: Italian (Neopolitan) dance in a quick $\frac{6}{8}$ meter, named for the tarantula spider whose poisonous bite the dance was supposed to cure

tegoto \te-gō-tō\: an instrumental interlude in Japanese *tegotomono* compositions

tegotomono \te-gō-tō-mō-nō\: the Japanese genre of songs accompanied by *koto*

tetrachord: a series of four notes with an idiosyncratic interval structure; used in Middle Eastern music to construct modes

tetratonic: a four-toned scale

timbales \tēm-'bə-läs\: a Spanish term for two single-headed, shallow-bodied drums in Caribbean *salsa*. They are placed on stands and played by one musician

time-line: in African and African-derived music, the basic rhythmic line that is played by the *claves* in *salsa* and by a bell or bottle in other African-American forms of music

tintala \tin-tà-là\: a *tala* consisting of sixteen beats divided 4–4–4–4

tonal language: a language in which meaning is determined by the difference in the pitches of spoken syllables

tres \'träs\: a Caribbean guitar-type instrument that has three courses of double strings and is often used in Cuban *salsa*

tritonic: a three-toned scale

tsamiko \sà-mē-kō\: a Greek line dance in slow $\frac{6}{8}$ meter (here grouped in steps alternating slow-quick, slow-quick)

TUBS notation: a form of notation designed by James Koetting for African drumming. The term refers to "time unit box system": Individual beats of a percussion instrument are indicated by an individual box in a series of boxes

^{c}ud \üd\: **1**: an Arabic short-necked, plucked lute. **2.** a lute, brought by the Moors to Spain; ancestor of the Spanish guitar

vals \vàls\: a Scandinavian waltz, or triple-meter dance

vaquero \bə-'kä-rō\: the term for a cowboy in Venezuela and Colombia; derived from *vaca* (cow)

vina \vi-nȧ\: one of the oldest plucked chordophones of India

vocable\ syllables with extra-linguistic meaning, such as *he, ne, yo,* or *heyo,* used by Native Americans to communicate special messages in their songs

waslah \'was-la\: a suite-like form from nineteenth- and early twentieth-century Egypt

wayno \'wəy-nō\: an Andean Native American dance and song form (also spelled *huayno*)

work song: any type of song that accompanies work or that may be used to make work easier or more efficient; often using rhythms that imitate the type of work being done

xiao \siaȯ\: an end-blown Chinese bamboo flute

xiaoluo \siaȯ-lō\: a small Chinese gong, usually played with a thin, wooden mallet

zamba \'səm-bə\: a song and dance form from Argentina

zambo \'səm-bō\: Latin American, especially Peruvian, term for an individual of mixed black and native American descent

zheng \zheŋ\ a Chinese board zither with an individual, adjustable bridge for each string

zhuan \zhwän\: "turned": the third idea or phrase of a four-line Chinese composition

INDEX

Nāy, 258, 259
New Guinea. *See* Oceania
New Zealand. *See* Oceania
Nigeria. *See* Africa
Noh, 330, 332, 336
Nohkan, 330
North America
    culture of, 11, 12–14, 17, 18, 20–21,
        25, 42–43, 79
    ethnic groups of, 2–3, 77, 79, 110
    geography of, 10, 12, 40, 76, 79
    history of, 2, 11, 20, 25, 27, 30, 32,
        45, 79
    immigration to, 2, 69
    languages of, 2, 14, 17, 45
Nyckelharpa, 183, 184

Oboe, 335, 353
Oceania
    culture of, 397, 398, 399, 412
    ethnic groups of, 398
    geography of, 396, 397, 398, 408
    history of, 397, 398, 399
    languages of, 398, 408–9, 411
Olsen notation, 133, 139
Opera, 313, 315, 326, 353
Oral transmission of songs, 79, 262, 263
Orff, Carl, pedagogy of, 6
Orff instruments,146, 374. *See also*
    Melodic instruments; *names of*
    individual instruments
Organum, 183
Oriental Jewish immigrants, 262, 263
Ornamentation, 46, 183, 243, 246, 286,
    324, 352, 353
Ostinatos. *See* Melodic ostinatos; Rhythm
Otsuzumi, 330, 336

Pacific islands. *See* Oceania
Pahu, 400
Panpipe. *See Siku*
Peking, 372
Pelog, 366, 367
Pentachord, 243
Pentatonic. *See* Scales
Performing activities, 4, 6, 22, 25, 31,

47, 54, 68, 89, 94, 98, 133, 141, 148,
    152, 159, 165, 187, 189, 192, 196,
    198, 219, 247, 249, 268, 273, 290,
    295, 298, 323, 368, 374, 408. *See*
    also Dance; Instruments,
    ensembles of; Movement;
    Singing activities
Peru. *See* Latin America
Piano, 47, 82, 314
Pi nai, 353
Pipa, 314, 315
Pipe and drum, 185
Pi phat, 353, 356
Play-party games. *See* Songs, game and
    party
Plena, 161
Polkas, 186
Polska, 183
Polymeter. *See* Rhythm
Polymusicality, 5
Polynesia. *See* Oceania
Polyphony. *See* Texture, polyphonic
Polyrhythm. *See* Rhythm
Powwow, 14, 20
Program music, 316
Puppets, use of, 2, 87, 89

Qānūn, 258
Qi, 315
Qin, 313–14

Rachenitsa, 186
Ragas, 285–86
    bhairavi, 292–94
    bhupali, 285, 287, 292,
        298–301, 303
    maru-bihag, 298, 301, 302, 303
    purvi, 292–94
Ragtime, 44, 56, 57
Ranat, 353, 354
Rao, 353
Rap, 42, 44, 45, 67–68
Rattles, 7, 12, 14, 15–16, 17, 83, 84,
    185, 216, 235
Rebab, 372, 379
Recitative style, 353
Recorder, 30, 133, 137, 152, 190, 199, 222